T0330792

NEGATIVE POLITICAL ADVERTISING:
Coming of Age

COMMUNICATION

A series of volumes edited by
Dolf Zillmann and Jennings Bryant

Richards • Deceptive Advertising: Behavioral Study of a Legal Concept

Flagg • Formative Evaluation for Educational Technologies

Haslett • Communication: Strategic Action in Context

Rodda/Grove • Language, Cognition and Deafness

Narula/Pearce • Cultures, Politics, and Research Programs: An International Assessment of Practical Problems in Field Research

Kubey/Csikszentmihalyi • Television and the Quality of Life: How Viewing Shapes Everyday Experience

Kraus • Mass Communication and Political Information Processing

Dobrow • Social and Cultural Aspects of VCR Use

Barton • Ties That Blind in Canadian/American Relations: Politics of News Discourse

Bryant • Television and the American Family

Cahn • Intimates in Conflict: A Communication Perspective

Biocca • Television and Political Advertising, Volume 1: Psychological Processes

Biocca • Television and Political Advertising, Volume 2: Signs, Codes, and Images

Welch • The Contemporary Reception of Classical Rhetoric: Appropriations of Ancient Discourse

Hanson/Narula • New Communication Technologies in Developing Countries

Bryant/Zillmann • Responding to the Screen: Reception and Reaction Processes

Olasky • Central Ideas in the Development of American Journalism: A Narrative History

Semetko/Blumler/Gurevitch/Weaver • The Formation of Campaign Agendas: A Comparative Analysis of Party and Media Roles in Recent American and British Elections

Kelly • Fund Raising and Public Relations: A Critical Analysis

Brown • Television "Critical Viewing Skills" Education: Major Media Literacy Projects in the United States and Selected Countries

Johnson-Cartee/Copeland • Negative Political Advertising: Coming of Age

Donohew/Sypher/Bukoski • Persuasive Communication and Drug Abuse Prevention

NEGATIVE POLITICAL ADVERTISING:
Coming of Age

Karen S. Johnson-Cartee
Gary A. Copeland
University of Alabama

Routledge
Taylor & Francis Group
New York   London

First published by Lawrence Erlbaum Associates, Inc., Publishers
10 Industrial Avenue
Mahwah, New Jersey 07430

Transferred to digital printing 2010 by Routledge

Routledge
270 Madison Avenue
New York, NY 10016

2 Park Square, Milton Park
Abingdon, Oxon OX14 4RN, UK

Library of Congress Cataloging-in-Publication Data

Johnson-Cartee, Karen S.
    Negative political advertising : coming of age / Karen S. Johnson
 – Cartee, Gary A. Copeland.
        p.   cm. – (Communication)
    Includes bibliographical references and index.
    ISBN 0-8058-0834-5
    1. Advertising, Political. 2. Negativism. I. Copeland, Gary.
 II. Title. III. Series: Communication (Hillsdale, N.J.)
 JF2112.A4J63   1991   90-49815
 324.7′ 3 – dc20   CIP

10 9 8 7 6 5 4 3 2

To *Michael*, who shares my obsession with politics and who shares my life and love. And to my mother and father, *Betty* and *Edsel Johnson*, who gave me my strength, my belief in myself, and my capacity to love. — K. S. J. C.

To my father, *Thurman Copeland*, who still offers to pay for a shave and haircut, if I'll just get one; to my mother, *Wanda Copeland*, who offers to buy me a suit, if I'll just wear it; and to my sister, *Joyce Copeland*, who doesn't care about any of it. — G. A. C.

Contents

ix

Preface

A successful analysis of negative political advertising requires that the topic be studied from a number of different approaches. Therefore, this book is an amalgamation of political science, marketing, advertising, research methods, cognitive psychology, public relations, mass communication, political communication, speech communication, political consulting theory and research, and practical experience. Perhaps it is fitting then that the authors are an eclectic mixture of various fields. Karen Johnson-Cartee has graduate degrees in mass communication with an emphasis in journalism and political science with an emphasis in political communication. She has taught courses in a variety of areas such as broadcasting, advertising, public relations, political communication, international communication, mass communication, and American politics. Gary Copeland has graduate degrees in speech communication with emphases in mass communication effects, broadcasting aesthetics, and social psychology. He has taught courses in a variety of fields: media effects, communication theory, broadcast production, social responsibility of the mass media, nonverbal communication, and broadcast aesthetics. The authors have published in such diverse journals as: *Presidential Studies Quarterly, Journalism Quarterly, Journal of Broadcasting and Electronic Media, Critical Studies in Mass Communication, Public Relations Review, Newspaper Research Journal, Victimology, Communication Yearbook, Political Communication Yearbook*, and *Journalism Educator*, and have served on a variety of editorial review boards. Both authors are members of the American Association of Political Consultants. If the book appears rather interdisciplinary, it is, because we are.

In addition, this book offers an unusual opportunity to explore negative political advertising over a number of decades, geographical areas, and political races. As political advertising researchers, we have noticed a lack of attention to southern political advertising, which for decades has been at the forefront of negative political advertising because of its unusual political culture and history. As researchers who live in the South, we have had an unusual opportunity to explore regional variations, and we bring to this book the appreciation for those differences. As such, we hope to address this void by presenting a number of southern ads along with ads from around the country. Karen Johnson-Cartee has served as either a volunteer or paid consultant in political races for both the Democratic and Republican parties. Her work as a political communication consultant has allowed us to have an inside look at a number of federal, state, and local campaigns.

Although we discuss various channels of negative political advertising, we focus on television spots, for it is here that we believe rests the power in modern American politics. Over 1,000 polispots were reviewed for the project.

We would like to thank a number of people who helped us in this research endeavor. Jarol Manheim provided an insightful critique of the manuscript at its early stages. Jarol has been a loyal friend and a valued colleague for a number of years. His comments are always appreciated. Lynda Lee Kaid served as the reviewer of this manuscript. Lynda provided invaluable advice as to how to make this work stronger. We are indebted to her for the many hours that she spent with the manuscript. Her enthusiasm for the project buoyed our spirits and provided the needed impetus to finalizing the manuscript. We also thank her for encouraging us to write a second book on political advertising.

We were fortunate enough to have been granted either a sabbatical or research leave for the fall of 1989 from The University of Alabama. We appreciate the University's support for our research. We are grateful for the College of Communication's Research and Service Committee who provided us with seed money for this project. And we would like to recognize Ed Mullins, Loy Singleton, John Eighmey, and Arnold Barban for their encouragement and support throughout this project. Jennings Bryant and Dolf Zillmann deserve special recognition for their role in bringing this book to fruition.

Special thanks go to the Roper Opinion Research Center and *Campaigns & Elections* for their help in securing information and materials for the book. We would also like to thank Camille Elebash for allowing us access to her southern political advertising library. Jeremy Butler provided valuable insights into the field of semiotics, which proved critical in our analysis of negative political advertising messages. Special thanks to the number of advertising firms who were kind enough to share their materials. And thank you to all the political advertising researchers who have gone before us.

We were lucky enough to have a dedicated graduate student who assisted us in gathering research materials. Paige Dorman, an advertising and public relations master's student at The University of Alabama, proved to be instrumental in the completion of the project. A telecommunication and film master's student, Debbie Elliott-Taylor, spent long hours on the reference section. And Jana L. Hyde spent long hours editing the manuscript. William Nothstine provided the necessary sounding board for Gary's late night computer ravings. And to all the people we have bored with our ramblings about the book, thank you.

Special thanks go to Betty and Edsel Johnson for tireless hours of proofreading the manuscript. Karen's mother also tended to the Cartee's menagerie, ironed clothes, and served as chief cook during the duration of the project. Without her, the Cartees would not only have been very wrinkled but hungry. And special thanks to our significant others, Susan Copeland and Michael Cartee, for their support throughout the project. And to our families, we apologize for the long hours and restless nights, the upset stomachs and cranky personalities, and the constant obsessing about the book and the deadlines. And to all a good night.

Karen S. Johnson-Cartee
Gary A. Copeland

I

INTRODUCTION

*Man is the symbol-using (symbol-making, symbol-misusing) animal inventor
of the negative (or moralized by the negative) separated from his natural
condition by instruments of his own making goaded by the spirit of hierarchy
(or moved by the sense of order) and rotten with perfection.*
                                                              −K. Burke (1966, p. 16)

Today, voters no longer experience politics firsthand but rather through
the eyes and ears of the mass media system. From the mass media we
obtain symbols, which we then interpret, redefine, and alter through our
communication with other people. What we know as our political world
is not a photocopy of the objective world but rather a created world of
symbols, often mass-mediated symbols.

People use symbols without questioning or thinking about their origin. We use symbols nonchalantly without realizing the social, political, or personal ramifications for having used them. We often accept
for ourselves the symbols created by others without analyzing the merits
or appropriateness of their symbolic logic.

Politics is a symbolic world. Men and women divide the goods of
society among groups of people. The goods are mostly symbolic in nature but considered precious nevertheless. We construct our rules and
regulations based on our symbolic knowledge of the world. We know
good and bad, right and wrong, just and unjust. We deal with these polarized symbols or positive−negative dichotomies in our political negoti-

ations. We know that the opposite of wealthy is poor, the opposite of lawful is unlawful, and the opposite of good is bad. We simplify our political reality by categorizing political actors into polar opposites: white hats versus black hats, Candidate X versus Candidate Y, Democrats versus Republicans, and conservatives versus liberals.

These positive-negative dichotomies in some strange way comfort us, for we believe that the world is knowable, that our life tasks are do-able. We can make sense out of the complexities of life, and thus we can in some small way manage and control the world around us. We prioritize and order the world around us by using these dichotomies, and we establish "a definition of rulers and ruled, leaders and followers, governors and governed that corresponds to the spirit of hierarchy (status) goading us all" (Nimmo, 1978, pp. 92-93). Our world is clearly a world of positives and negatives. And because we usually associate the positives with ourselves or people like ourselves, we naturally focus our wary attention on the other or the negatives.

Yet researchers seemed befuddled by our preoccupation with both the negative and the positive. They write about bad news and negative political advertising, as if they were somehow antithetical to the natural state of humans. Rather, it should be understood as just another enigma associated with the symbol-using animal.

In this book, we also examine negative symbols in the form of negative political advertising. We do not take a pejorative stance; rather we examine and explain how negative political advertising has been used in American political history. We provide both an academic and a professional orientation toward the subject.

In Part I, we consider a wide variety of research in the areas of political science, marketing, public relations, product and political advertising, cognitive psychology, and political consulting. We offer a critical review of existing studies. Part II provides a framework from which to analyze negative political advertising: substance, style, sponsorship, and channels. Part III offers a practical guide to negative political advertising. Strategies for combating negative ads are explored and evaluated, and the legal and ethical considerations involving negative political advertising are presented. Finally, we consider the potential impact of negative political advertising on our society.

1

Negative Political Advertising: History, Research, and Analysis

THE AMERICAN TRADITION: NEGATIVE POLITICAL CAMPAIGNING

Although voters and journalists alike have lamented the rise of negative campaigning in the 1980s, it is not a new American political phenomenon. In 1952, Estes Kefauver used the first *direct attack* television ad against Eisenhower (Diamond & Bates, 1988; Wilson, 1987). And, every presidential election year since 1952 has had its share of negative television ads. What is new is the pervasiveness of this technique. Although negative political advertising has been defined in various ways, both academicians and consultants seem to agree that negative ads make up a significant portion of modern political advertising. Researchers estimate that between 30% and 50% of all political advertising produced can be described as negative (Kaid & Davidson, 1986; Sabato, 1981; Taylor, 1986). Some political observers contend that negative political advertising is the hallmark of American media politics in the late 20th century (Taylor, 1986). According to *Advertising Age*, over $450 million were spent in the 1986 House and Senate races (Colford, 1986). And over 50% of that amount was spent in negative political advertising (Taylor, 1986).

Negative political ads are now staples in federal, state, and local campaigns. But, before we examine modern negative political advertising, we must first understand the American tradition of negative campaigning.

3

The Early Years

As late 20th-century observers of the American political scene, we some-times forget that political parties and newspapers, as we know them today, did not always exist in the United States. At the time of the Constitutional Convention of 1787 there did not exist any groups that satisfy the modern-day definition of a political party, which is "any group, however loosely organized, seeking to elect governmental office-holders under a given label" (Epstein, 1967, p. 9). Instead, there were loose voting blocs, representing opposing political philosophies that have continued through the years and have led to a marked tension in our system of government. However, it is interesting to note that although the constitutional delegates were operating within voting coalitions, the constitutional fathers made no mention of political parties in the U.S. Constitution.

Bryce (1896) labeled the opposing groups the centrifugal and centripetal factions. The centrifugal group supported individual freedom as its paramount concern. The centripetal group supported a strong federal government and desired the states to be subordinate to a federal authority.

By 1791, these same factions were operating in the Congress of the United States. The centripetal faction was known as the Federalist faction, and the centrifugal faction was known as the Republican faction (Charles, 1961). These groups served as loose voting coalitions only within the houses of Congress and did not operate as a modern-day political party. Only 50% of the members of Congress belonged to either faction (Charles, 1961). It was not until 1800 that the Federalist faction held its first nominating con-gress and established itself as the first modern political party in the United States.

An analysis of early American political communication channels reveals an historical association between the growth of competing political parties and the rise of newspapers supporting them in 18th-century United States (Seymour-Ure, 1974). In 1791, the two major political factions in Congress started their own newspapers: *The Gazette of the United States* and *The National Gazette*. The Federalists operated *The Gazette of the United States*, and the Republi-cans operated *The National Gazette* (Blum et al., 1973). This period of our political-media history has become known as the party organism stage of me-dia development in the United States. During the party organism stage, "the party either owns or controls the newspaper through political cronies" (John-son, 1981, p. 133). Thus, the newspapers during this period were not the in-dependent voices that we have today, but rather the voices of the political party that controlled them. This stage lasted from 1791 until the late 19th and early 20th centuries.

It was in these early newspapers that we see the beginnings of negative po-litical campaigning. Indeed, from the earliest days of the American republic, politicians engaged in personal attacks against their opponents that, as Wood (1978) put it, were marked by their "verbal excesses and emotional extravagances" (p. 112). Wood explained: "No accusation was too coarse or too vulgar to be made—from drunkenness and gambling to impotence and adultery" (p. 109; see also Bailyn, 1967).

During the first party-contested election in 1800, the newspapers engaged in direct attacks against both opposition parties and their candidates. In 1800, *The Connecticut Courant*, a Federalist newspaper, printed the following column, which directly attacked the Republican party:

> The fate of Frenchmen will be the fate of Americans. The French boasted that they were the most civilized and humane people in the world. We can say no more of ourselves. Their Jacobins were wicked, cruel, profligate, atheistical— ours are the same. Their pretense ever was, to consult the good of the people— ours make the same. The people in that country have been robbed, enslaved, and butchered—we shall be served in the same manner, unless we arouse instantly, and rescue our government from the fangs of those who are tearing it in pieces. Look at your houses, your parents, your wives, and your children. Are you prepared to see your dwellings in flames, hoary hairs bathed in blood, female chastity violated, or children writhing on the pike and the halbred? If not, prepare for the task of protecting your Government. Look at every leading Jacobin as at a ravening wolf, preparing to enter your peaceful fold, and glut his deadly appetite on the vitals of your country. Already do their hearts leap at the prospect. Having long brooded over these scenes of death and despair, they now wake as from a trance, and in imagination seizing the dagger and the musket, prepare for the world of slaughter. GREAT GOD OF COMPASSION AND JUSTICE, SHIELD MY COUNTRY FROM DESTRUCTION. (Blum, et al., 1973, p. 154)

Similarly in that same year, a Republican, James T. Callender, printed a text entitled "The Prospect Before Us." This particular piece directly attacked the Federalist presidential candidate, John Adams:

> It is not so well known, as it should be, that this federal gem John Adams, this apostle of the parsons of Connecticut, is not only a repulsive pedant, a gross hypocrite, and an unprincipled oppressor, but that he is, in private life, one of the most egregious fools upon the continent. When some future Clarendon shall illustrate and dignify the annals of the present age, he will assuredly express his surprise at the abrupt and absurd elevation of this despicable attorney. He will enquire by what species of madness, America submitted to accept, as her president, a person without abilities, and without virtues; a being alike incapable of attracting either tenderness, or esteem. The historian will search for those occult causes that induced her to exalt an individual, who has neither that innocence of sensibility, which incites us to love, nor that omnipotence of intellect which commands us to admire. He will ask why the United States degraded them-

selves to the choice of a wretch, whose soul came blasted from the hand of nature; of a wretch, that has neither the science of a magistrate, the politeness of
a courtier, nor the courage of a man. (Blum et al., 1973, p. 154)

As Jamieson (1986) noted, "In 1800, the *Columbian Centinel* observed that
'The papers are overrunning with electioneering essays, squibs, and invectives' "
(p. 7). In addition to partisan newspapers, the political leaders of the day relied on handbills, pamphlets, banners, badges, bandannas, and kerchiefs to
bring their messages to the voters (Hart, 1956; Jamieson, 1984, 1986; Rosenberg & Rosenberg, 1962; Washburn, 1963, 1972). Political parades became
standard fare during presidential election years (Jamieson, 1984; Washburn,
1963): "Campaign banners and flags, transparencies and torches were carried
through the streets by marching enthusiasts—some professional paid marchers, some volunteers—often dressed in patriotic uniform" (Jamieson, 1986,
p. 2). The transparencies were "constructed of partially transparent cheesecloth
or cotton," which had been lettered or drawn on, and they were then "wrapped
around either wooden or steel frames and affixed to a pole" (Jamieson, 1986,
p. 3). At night, kerosene torches were placed behind the transparencies to il-
luminate the messages. The messages both supported candidates and attacked
opponents (Jamieson, 1986).

Andrew Jackson in 1828 began the tradition of campaigning with a "log
cabin and hard-cider barrel" as prominent political symbols (Hart, 1956, p.
32). But these symbols represent more than the folksy, backwoods way of life
that they are associated with in contemporary America. They were used as
political symbols in opposition to the grand palaces and fine champagnes and
wines associated with the aristocracy of the early republic (Washburn, 1963).
The log cabin and hard-cider barrel represent the early use of the implied negative political strategy.

Songs and chants became very popular during political campaigns. In 1842,
Clay supporters sang "Do you know a traitor viler, viler, viler/Than Tyler?"
(Jamieson, 1986, p. 5). Perhaps the most famous negative political chant was
the one used against Democratic candidate Grover Cleveland in 1884 by the
Republican forces supporting James G. Blaine. Cleveland had fathered a child
out of wedlock by Maria Halpin, and the Blaine forces made much use of this
dirty linen with the short chant: "Ma! Ma! Where's my Pa?" (Rosenberg &
Rosenberg, 1962, p. 4). The Reverend Mr. Ball of Buffalo joined in the Republican attacks against Cleveland and appeared in many of the nation's political
magazines. He described Cleveland in this rather colorful manner:

A champion libertine, an artful seducer, a foe to virtue, an enemy of the family,
a snare to youth and hostile to true womanhood. . . . Women now married and
anxious to cover the sins of their youth have been his victims, and are now alarmed
lest their relations with him shall be exposed. Some disgraced and broken-hearted

victims of his lust now slumber in the grave. (Rosenberg & Rosenberg, 1962, p. 8)

But Blaine had his own troubles. Before the presidential campaign had even begun, numerous charges that Blaine had used his office in the Congress for personal financial gain had surfaced. And repeatedly, personal correspondence appeared in the nation's press that supported these charges. Blaine continued to deny the accusations, but it is no wonder that the Democrats chanted: "Blaine! Blaine! Jay Gould Blaine! The Continental Liar from the state of Maine!" (Rosenberg & Rosenberg, 1962, p. 99). And, after the Democratic *Sentinel* of Indianapolis investigated his personal life, the newspaper discovered that Mrs. Blaine delivered her first child only 3 months after her wedding day. The Democratic newspaper exploited this juicy scandal to the fullest, writing that "there is hardly an intelligent man in the country who has not heard that James G. Blaine betrayed the girl whom he married, and then only married her at the muzzle of a shotgun. . . ." (Rosenberg & Rosenberg, 1962, p. 97).

After Cleveland won the election, Rosenberg and Rosenberg (1962) described the victory marchers chanting: "Ma! Ma! Where's my Pa? Gone to the White House – Ha! Ha! Ha!" (p. 100); and, "Hurrah for Maria! Hurrah for the kid! I voted for Cleveland, and I'm damned glad I did" (p. 100; see also, Will 1986).

From this albeit brief review of early American political campaigning, it is clear that "from the country's first contested election, strategists have offered voters advertising that venerated their candidate and vilified his opponents" (Jamieson, 1984, preface). Jamieson explained, "in many ways televised political advertising is the direct descendant of the advertised messages carried in song and on banners, torches, bandannas, and broadsides" during the early years of the republic (p. 448).

NEGATIVE POLITICAL ADVERTISING: RESEARCH AND ANALYSIS

Negative political advertising has certainly come of age, yet academicians are still wrestling with problems of definition, operationalization, effectiveness, and societal impact. Clear differences can be observed between the findings of early research conducted in the 1970s and that conducted in the 1980s. In addition, academicians and independent research consultants differ as to how they evaluate the effectiveness of negative political advertising. And news reports concentrating on the use of negative political advertising have done little to clear up the confusion.

The Pre-1980 Word on
Negative Political Advertising

Negative political advertising is not a new political phenomenon. Yet in 1964, Lyndon Johnson's daisy commercial attacking Goldwater's bellicose rhetoric was perceived as being a radical campaign move (Diamond & Bates, 1988). Early research supported these beliefs. In 1974, Louis Harris reported that the "public is sharply opposed to personal attacks on political opponents" (p. B-14). Stewart (1975) reported the results of a survey of registered voters in six Indiana cities. Using three open-ended questions, he explored the use of the colloquial meaning of the term *mudslinging*. Respondents identified specific candidates who they considered used mudslinging as a tactic. Stewart concluded that, "All statements that seemed to attack a political opponent—even ones referring to broken promises and voting records—were cited as mudslinging by the majority or a large minority of respondents" (p. 285). Candidates that were identified as mudslingers were "perceived to be the opposite of a highly credible candidate: to be untrustworthy, dishonest, incompetent, unqualified, unlikeable, not self-confident, and immature" (Stewart, 1975, p. 285).

Many political consultants during this time held similar views. In a series of articles in the *Potomac* section of the *The Washington Post*, Lewis Wolfson, an associate professor of communication at The American University, conducted interviews of a number of prominent Republican and Democratic political consultants. One of the areas of inquiry concerned negative ads. Robert Squier, a Democratic consultant, told Wolfson (1972a) that he did not believe that negative ads worked, because people respond "to material that shows the candidate himself has a high regard for the voter, and they respond negatively to the stuff that's low regard" (p. 18). Similarly, Republican consultant Robert Goodman maintained that there were very few effective negative advertisements, and concluded that although "it's sometimes natural for a politician to roll up his sleeves and punch the other guy in the nose. . . . the political commerical is [not] the place for it" (Wolfson, 1972b, p. 31). David Garth, an independent liberal consultant, explained to Wolfson (1972c) that: "Politics has some rabbit-punches in it. But I don't think that that is smart politics. If you throw dirt at a man in politics, what you usually end up doing is hurting him somewhat, and hurting yourself a lot, and the third guy in the race is going to win" (p. 39). Despite their continued use of negative political advertising, political consultants during the early 1970s did not evaluate the technique as being very effective.

And in fact, political consultants often told candidates who were attacked to simply ignore the accusations. They assuaged their clients' fears by telling them that negative commercials often boomeranged on the sponsor, because the public did not like negative polispots (New Campaign Techniques, 1986; Wolfson, 1972c).

THE POST-1980 WORD ON NEGATIVE
POLITICAL ADVERTISING

Academicians

Operationalization

Definitions of what constitutes a negative political advertisement have varied over the years. In 1975, Stewart called this type of political ad "a mudslinging ad" (p. 279). In 1977, Surlin and Gordon described negative political advertisements as, "the direct reference or attacking political advertisement" (p. 97). Surlin and Gordon "operationalized the genre as advertising which attacks the other candidate personally, the issues for which the other candidate stands, or the party of the other candidate" (Garramone, 1984, p. 250). Surlin and Gordon (1977) found that lower socioeconomic status (SES) respondents believed that direct reference or attack ads were "more unethical and more informative" than middle SES respondents (p. 97). Blacks found direct reference or attack ads to be more informative and more effective than did Whites. (Surlin & Gordon, 1977, p. 97). In a 1982 survey of Michigan voters, Garramone used Surlin and Gordon's operationalization of direct reference/attack ads, but simply called this type of political ad negative political advertising.

Possible Damaging Results

In 1979, the Republican Congressional Campaign Committee sponsored a study dealing with political advertising on television. The study concluded that negative political advertising was a "high-risk" approach because "it must walk the fine line between making its point and turning off the voter" (National Republican Congressional Committee, 1979, pp. 10–11). Indeed, political advertising researchers have identified three possible damaging effects as the result of using negative political advertising: the boomerang, the victim syndrome, and the double impairment effect.

The Boomerang. Garramone (1984) in a survey found evidence to support the boomerang effect for candidate-sponsored negative ads. A boomerang or backlash effect has the unintended consequence of a negative ad, which results in "more negative feelings toward the sponsor, rather than toward the target" (Garramone, 1984, p. 251; see also, Shapiro & Rieger, 1989).

   Copeland and Johnson-Cartee (1990b), in a controlled laboratory experiment, found no statistically significant evidence to support the boomerang effect for candidate-sponsored negative political advertising. Their study paralleled findings of political consultants rather than studies conducted by political advertising researchers.

Copeland and Johnson-Cartee (1990b) critiqued previous studies that either created their own commercials for use in an experimental design (e.g. Shapiro & Rieger, 1989) or utilized a single-point-in-time survey method (e.g., Garramone, 1984). Both methods have limitations. Self-created ads are rarely as sophisticated as actual political spots, and therefore, measurements of such ads' impact must be partially suspect. One-shot surveys do not provide the researcher with the necessary data to conservatively interpret that a boomerang effect exists. Copeland and Johnson-Cartee used real polispots taken from the 1986 California U.S. Senate campaign in a controlled laboratory experiment.

In addition, variations in findings may be related to the types of issue appeals used. Research has shown that the electorate finds some areas acceptable for criticism (such as the candidate's voting record or position), and they find other areas unacceptable (such as attacks on marital status or religion) (see the discussion on issue appeals later in this chapter). This area clearly needs to be explored using additional research designs. However, our study does show that the expectation for a boomerang effect as the natural and inevitable outcome of a negative political ad is overly simplistic.

The Victim Syndrome. In addition, Robinson (1981a) found evidence for yet another unintended effect in that when a negative ad is perceived as being unfair or unjustified, then the ad may in fact create a phenomenon that we call the *victim syndrome*. The unfair negative ad may "generate more positive feelings toward the target" (Garramone, 1984, p. 251; see also, Robinson, 1981a).

Copeland and Johnson-Cartee (1990b) reported no statistically significant evidence to support the victim syndrome for candidate-sponsored negative political ads. It is important to note that the only evidence that suggests a victim syndrome exists was reported from survey research conducted during one of the most vituperative negative campaigns ever presented to the public, the 1980 National Conservative Political Action Committee's (NCPAC) attacks on liberal Democratic senators (Robinson, 1981a; see chapter 5 for a discussion). Because news media coverage debunked NCPAC's ads, it is likely that such media criticism had created a unique campaign environment (see chapter 5).

The Double Impairment Effect. In 1984, Merritt also limited her analysis to direct attack ads that focused "primarily on degrading perceptions of the rival, to the advantage of the sponsor" (p. 27). Merritt's report of a telephone survey of southern California residents led her to conclude that negative political advertising "evokes a negative affect toward both the targeted opponent and the sponsor" (p. 37). And Merritt concluded that the findings raise "serious doubts about the value of negative advertising especially when used by a minority party candidate" (p. 37).

Copeland and Johnson-Cartee (1990b) reported no statistically significant evidence of the double impairment effect in their study. We are not confident that Merritt's (1984) one-time descriptive study of southern California residents serves as unqualified evidence for this effect.

Voters' Negative Political Advertising Evaluations

Garramone (1984) found that three fourths of the survey respondents expressed disapproval in their evaluation of negative political advertising. Voters reported that negative political advertising had a strong negative influence on their evaluation of the sponsor of the negative ad, and only a slight negative influence on their evaluation of the target of the negative ad.

In 1987, Johnson and Copeland reported the results of a survey ($N = 1,917$) of six southern states during the 1986 election season. They found that although 65% of survey respondents said they did not favor the use of negative ads, two thirds of the respondents were able to recall specific negative ads they had seen during the 1986 campaign season. In addition, Johnson and Copeland found that the voters' evaluation of negative political advertising was related to the nature of the negative political advertising issue appeals presented.

Copeland and Johnson-Cartee (1990b) found, in a controlled laboratory experiment, that although respondents negatively evaluated an ad as to its fairness or believability, this evaluation did not necessarily affect how persuasive or informative they judged that ad to be. These findings tend to confirm the political consultants' criticism of focus group evaluations of negative political commercials in that whereas people may say they hate negative political spots, they learn from them and are persuaded by them (Devlin, 1981; Negative Advertising Pro and Con, 1986).

Negative Issue Appeals. Johnson-Cartee and Copeland (1989b) reported that there are two types of negative advertising issue appeals: political issue appeals and personal characteristic issue appeals. The content of negative political issue appeals pertains to "political record, voting record, stands on issues, and criminal record" (p. 892); whereas the content of negative personal characteristic issue appeals pertains to "medical histories, personal life, religion, sex life, family members, and current or past marriages" (p. 892).

The term *negative issue appeals* is used because whether a negative ad uses a negative appeal directed at a traditional political issue such as stands on issues or whether it uses a personal characteristic issue such as religion, the negative appeal ultimately becomes a campaign issue—thus the name, negative issue appeals. From their analysis, Johnson-Cartee and Copeland (1989b) found that more than two thirds of the respondents said that negative political issue appeals were areas of "fair comment" (p. 893). However 44%, or nearly one half of all respondents, said that negative personal characteristic issue appeals were "unfair" (p. 892). In general, respondents viewed negative politi-cal issue appeals favorably whereas they viewed negative personal characteristic issue appeals unfavorably.

Copeland and Johnson-Cartee (1990a) found that individuals most likely to accept the use of negative political issue ads were those in higher education and income levels. These same individuals exhibited higher levels of political efficacy and political participation. Men were more likely to approve of the use of negative political issue appeals than women. Individuals who favored negative personal characteristic issue appeals were more likely to be women, poorly educated, with low incomes. In addition, they were more likely to ex-hibit lower levels of political efficacy and political participation. Both nega-tive appeal studies were conducted through a survey research design in the southeastern United States ($N = 1,917$) (Copeland & Johnson-Cartee, 1990a; Johnson-Cartee & Copeland, 1989b).

It must be noted, however, that depending on the political culture of a given area, the acceptance or rejection of negative political advertising may vary considerably. In a study of Alabama voters ($N = 404$), Johnson-Cartee and Copeland (1989a) found that there was a significant difference in the way Ala-bama voters and other voters in the Southeast perceived negative political ad-vertising. In the other southeastern states, 42% of the respondents said they "strongly disliked" the practice of negative political advertising. But in Ala-bama, only 25% of the respondents said they "strongly disliked" negative ads. However, in Alabama, respondents with high political efficacy levels are sig-nificantly more tolerant of personal attacks than in other southern states.

The general finding that negative personal characteristic issue appeals are considerably less accepted than negative political issues appeals is supported by the political consulting literature. One media consultant, John Nugent (1987), advised that personal attacks should be avoided. Nugent explained the un-popularity of negative personal issue appeals in that: "everyone has a few bones, if not a complete skeleton, in the family closet. You touch a chilling chord when your opponent seems personally vulnerable" (p. 48). Nugent cited the 1986 example of Maryland Republican Senate candidate Linda Chavez who attacked her opponent, Democratic Representative Barbara Mikulski, with charges of being a "San Francisco Democrat" who views were "clearly anti-male" (pp. 47–49; see also, Morganthau & Fineman, 1986). Chavez was heavily criticized and resoundingly defeated.

In 1988, Roddy and Garramone tested appeals and strategies used in nega-tive political advertising through a laboratory experiment. They concluded that Johnson and Copeland's (1987; see also, Johnson-Cartee & Copeland, 1989b, for a similar analysis) political issue appeals and personal characteristic issue appeals are "suggestive of political advertising issue/image distinction. Issue appeals have been defined as those concerned with specific policies . . . ; im-age appeals have been defined as those relating to personal characteristics of the candidate without advocating issue positions" (p. 417; see also, Kaid & Sanders, 1978). Roddy and Garramone found that "viewers of an [political issue appeal] issue commercial demonstrated a significantly more positive evaluation of the attacker's commercial and of the attacker's character, and a significantly lesser likelihood of voting for the target, than did viewers of an image [personal characteristic issue appeal] commercial" (p. 425).

   In a quasi-field experiment, Pfau and Burgoon (1989) found that "during the latter stages of a political campaign featuring known candidates, issue attack messages exert more change in attitudes and vote intention than character attack messages" (p. 53). Pfau and Burgoon posited that character messages are more important in the beginning of the campaign when voters are trying to come to terms with the various candidates in the race; "[h]owever, once voter judgments of candidate character take, the potential of character messages to influence voters diminishes sharply" (p. 58). And the research team concluded that issue messages exert greater influence at the middle and end of the campaign than do character messages. Pfau and Burgoon also warned that their findings may be channel determined in that they exposed their participants to print material "which may carry an inherent bias toward issue content" (p. 58). However, this seems unlikely in that channel differences in political advertising research have been found to be negligible (see chapter 5).

Negative Issue Appeals and Conflict Resolution. Every Democratic presidential candidate since 1980 has learned a simple truth about American society: We do not want to hear bad things about ourselves. We do not respond well to messages that suggest we have lost the competitive edge. We do not like being scolded for our lack of foresight, our lack of compassion, or our lack of charity for our fellow man.

   On the other hand, we do not necessarily mind hearing criticism about our leaders, as long as the candidate does not leave us on a negative note. In other words, we can face attacks, and we can face the apparent conflict of the campaign battle, but we want the problem(s) solved for us before the campaign ends. Kern (1989) suggested that each negative ad must have a resolution of conflict, or it will not be received well by the voters. The negative ad may present conflict, problems, and despair; but by the end, we must know how to solve the negative situation, that is, by voting either for the sponsoring candidate or against the candidate portrayed.

Impact of Sponsorship

Garramone and Smith (1984), in a laboratory experiment using college students, found that "an independent commercial sponsor is perceived as more trustworthy than a candidate sponsor, and consequently, the commercial itself is evaluated more positively" (p. 775). The independently sponsored ad is an ad that is not directly linked with a candidate. An organization physically separated from either a political party or a candidate's campaign organization sponsors the ad (see chapters 4 & 5). In a 1985 experiment using college students, Garramone (1985) reported that independently sponsored negative ads "resulted in greater intended effects against the targeted candidate and in reduced backlash effects against the opponent" than do candidate-sponsored negative ads (p. 157).

Independent Sponsorship and the Boomerang. Garramone (1984, 1985), Garramone and Smith (1984), and Merritt (1984) supported the pre-1980 notion that negative political advertising is perhaps a dangerous and unwise practice in that a boomerang is likely to occur with candidate-sponsored negative political advertising. However, recent evidence presented by Kaid and Boydston (1987) in their examination of independently sponsored negative political advertising found no evidence to support a boomerang or backlash effect. Using a laboratory experiment with a pretest-posttest design, Kaid and Boydston exposed members of civic groups in Oklahoma City to four print ads and one television ad. They found that negative advertising presented by an independent sponsor "reduces the image evaluation of the targeted politician. While the negative effect was greater for those in the political party opposite that of the targeted politician, respondents of the politician's own party were also affected" (p. 193). This suggests that independently sponsored negative political advertisements may be more effective than we had previously supposed in that they may do more than reinforce the already committed— they may in fact persuade the undecided or in some rare instances convert the normally hostile audience.

Political Consultants

Although academicians report a boomerang or backlash effect from negative political advertisements, political consultants have a different story (see Sabato, 1981). Based on their observations, some professional consultants suggested that "a wave of negative ads frequently reduces the attacker's poll standing a few points. But those numbers nearly always bounce back within a few days. Meanwhile, the target of the attack loses considerably more support—and that slippage lasts much longer" (New Campaign Techniques, 1986, p. 31). It is important to note that "a few points" are normally well within the margin of error associated with the normal sample size used in political campaign research. For this reason, a small drop may well not be significant. And even if it is significant, the drop for the sponsoring candidate usually disappears within a few days.

In 1988, for example, the Bush campaign was not hurt by its use of negative advertising even though one CBS News/*New York Times* poll showed that voters perceived Bush as attacking Dukakis 56% of the time, whereas Dukakis was perceived as attacking Bush 49% of the time (Devlin, 1989, p. 407). Devlin reported that the Bush campaign's media director, Janet Mullins, believed that this perception did not hurt Bush, explaining it this way: "Everybody hates negative ads; then they rate them most effective in terms of decision making. There isn't any long term effect. . . . It is kind of like birth pains. Two days later, you forget how much it hurt. The same is true for negative advertising. . . ." (p. 407).

Jill Buckley, a Democratic consultant, explained to *Congressional Quarterly*: "People say they hate negative advertising, but it works. They hate it and remember it at the same time. . . . With negative, the poll numbers will move in three or four days" (New Campaign Techniques, 1986, p. 30).

Taylor (1986) noted that, according to Democratic pollster Ed Mellman, negative political advertising is effective because: "people process negative information more deeply than positive information" (p. 47). Mellman continued, "When we ask people about negative ads, they'll say they don't like them. But that's not the point. The point is that they absorb the information" (Taylor, 1986, p. A7). Similarly, Republican consultant Roger Stone reported that: "voters will tell you in focus groups that they don't like negative ads, but they retain the information so much better than the positive ones. The point is: People like dirty laundry. Why do tabloids sell?" (Negative Advertising Pro and Con, 1986, p. 104).

NEGATIVE INFORMATION LITERATURE

This advice by political consultants of both parties is supported by research in cognitive psychology. Kellermann (1984) in *Communication Monographs* provided an excellent overview of the *negativity effect*, describing it as follows: "the tendency for negative information to be weighted more heavily than positive information when forming evaluations of social stimuli. Across widely varying events, setting, and persons, positive experiences or positive aspects of stimuli have been found to be less influential in the formation of judgments than are negative experiences or negative aspects of stimuli" (p. 37; see also, Anderson, 1965; Hamilton & Huffman, 1971; Hamilton & Zanna, 1972; Hodges, 1974; Jordan, 1965; Levin & Schmidt, 1969; Miller & Rowe, 1967; Warr & Jackson, 1976; Wyer, 1970). And, as Kellerman elaborated, "Not only is negative information weighted more heavily than positive information in the initial formation of impressions, but negative information exhibits a greater capacity to alter already existing impressions" (pp. 37–38; see also, Briscoe, Woodyard, & Shaw, 1967; Cusumano & Richey, 1970; Freedman & Steinbruner, 1964; Gray-Little, 1973; Leventhal & Singer, 1964; Mayo & Crockett, 1964). Cusumano and Richey (1970) and Richey, McClelland, and

Shimkunas (1967) found that negative first impressions are much more difficult to change than positive first impressions. Lau (1980) found that negative information obtained about presidential candidates was weighted more heavily than positive information.

Recently Shapiro and Rieger (1989) demonstrated that negative polispots are more memorable than positive polispots. A number of researchers have shown that negative information is eas:er to retrieve than positive information during information processing (Feldman, 1966; Reeves, Thorson, & Schleuder, 1986; Richey, Koenigs, Richey, & Fortin, 1975). Feldman demonstrated that negative stimuli exerted greater power in informational processing. The effect of negative information on long-term memory has been demonstrated by Richey and his associates.

Political consultants' reliance on the use of negative political advertising in recent years is strongly grounded in the evidence provided by cognitive research.

Resolving the Conflict Between Cognitive Psychology, Political Consultants, and Political Advertising Research

Operationalization

As mentioned previously, although political advertising researchers generally have not been able to empirically demonstrate the effectiveness of candidate-sponsored negative political advertising (the exception being Copeland & Johnson-Cartee, 1990b), cognitive psychologists have long been able to demonstrate the powerful influence of the negativity effect (see Kellermann, 1984). Political consultants since 1980 have also found support for the effectiveness of negative political advertising (Negative Advertising Pro and Con, 1986; New Campaign Techniques, 1986; see also Sabato, 1981). It may well be that political communication researchers, by operationalizing negative political advertising in such a way that it only referred to direct attack/direct reference ads—those ads that attack "the other candidate personally, the issues for which the other candidate stands, or the party of the other candidate" (Garramone, 1984, p. 250; see also, Garramone, 1985; Merritt, 1984; Stewart, 1975; Surlin & Gordon, 1977)—have, in effect, limited the range of possible effects.

Merritt (1984) viewed negative political advertising as a "variant" of comparative advertising (p. 27). According to Merritt:

> Both comparative and negative advertising name or identify the competitor. But while comparative advertising identifies the competitor "for the purpose of claiming superiority," negative advertising identifies a competitor for the pur-

poses of imputing inferiority. And unlike comparative advertising, negative advertising need not even mention anything about the sponsor's attributes. (p. 27)

Merritt further asserted that only ads that focus "primarily on degrading perceptions of the rival, to the advantage of the sponsor" should be classified as "negative" (p. 27). Although there is an important academic and practical distinction between comparative ads and direct attack ads (which Merritt called negative ads) and the strategies they employ, we believe it is grievous reductionism to ignore the negative strategies and resulting consequences associated with ads that directly compare candidates or that indirectly imply the candidate comparison.

Gronbeck (1985) had a similar perspective. He identified three types of negative political advertisements:

(a) the implicative ad, involving an implication or innuendo about the opponent but no direct attack. . . . (b) the comparative ad, incorporating an explicit comparison between the contenders; and (c) the assaultive ad . . . providing a direct, personal attack on the opponent's character, motives, associates, or actions, usually with little or no comparison to the originator of the advertisement. (as quoted in Hellweg, 1988, p. 13; see also, Gronbeck, 1985; Pfau & Burgoon, 1989)

In our own analysis, which we present in chapter 2, we use a typology similar to Gronbeck's (1985): direct attack ads, direct comparison ads, and implied comparison ads. Briefly stated, direct attack ads only attack. Direct comparison ads specifically compare the sponsor with the opponent, and the sponsor always has the competitive edge in the comparison. Implied comparison ads are not negative in and of themselves, but it is the public's interpretation of those ads that gives them their negative character. Implied comparison ads lure the voter into making the comparison between candidates. Some of the most famous powerful negative ads such as the "Daisy Ad" in 1964 and "The Bear Ad" in 1984 were implied comparison ads (see Jamieson, 1984; Schwartz, 1976).

It is quite conceivable that political communication researchers, by so narrowly operationalizing negative political advertising as direct attacks, have limited the range of possible effects associated with negative political advertising exposure. Neither negative information specialists nor political consultants have done so. It may be that our media-political culture dictates a negative reaction to direct attacks. Yet, the less strident ads that directly or indirectly compare candidates records, backgrounds, and so forth, may not generate such negative evaluations. In chapter 2, we examine the acceptance and effectiveness of direct attack, direct comparison, and implied comparison advertising.

A Glitch Between the Academic Research/
Professional Application of Negative
Political Advertising

An additional factor that may be separating the academicians and the consultants is the perspective of each. Political consultants are dealing with campaigns, a part of which may be the use of negative political advertising. Academic researchers usually look at negative advertising divorced from the strategy that propels it.

Research involving negative political advertising shares with all political advertising research the same fundamental problem of examining the effectiveness of various political communication messages within the context of an entire campaign. A single ad, a single press release or a single media event cannot stand alone. All campaign messages are interrelated. And to complicate the picture more, a campaign does not simply equal all of the political ads, political speeches, media events, television interviews, and events added together. There is a synergistic effect in that the totality of the political campaign is greater than the sum of the parts.

The Synergism Problem. The synergism problem becomes particularly apparent in the study of negative political advertising. As we mentioned previously, focus group research, survey research, and laboratory experimental findings tell us that people self-report they do not like negative ads. Yet, there is evidence to indicate that people remember negative political ads better than they do positive ones. And although political communication researchers and political consultants report shifts in opinions after exposure to negative political advertising, these reports do very little to clarify our understanding of how negative ads work in the real world of politics. Because the political communication messages of a given campaign are all interrelated, it is difficult to isolate the effectiveness of a single communication tool, such as a political ad, particularly when that tool is in reality the culmination of a carefully crafted persuasive message strategy that has chained-out through the media over the course of a campaign.

Textural Preconditioning. Political communication messages – ads, news accounts, speeches, and so forth – are designed to provide a rich multilayered texture to the campaign environment. Just as artists use multilayers of color to achieve the desired artistic creation, so too do political consultants use various multilayered political communication tactics to achieve campaign goals, sometimes painting with great finesse and other times painting with strokes of bold design. Although negative political advertising is an important variable in modern campaigns, the ads must be understood in the textural life of the campaign strategy. The strategy is the goal-driven force of the modern campaign. Negative ads are just one way of achieving the campaign's goals. Examining negative political ads in isolation, overlooks the highly sophisticated textural preconditioning activities that the modern political consultants undertake in order to maximize the negative ads' impact.

In other words, political consultants set the stage for the appearance of negative ads. They do this in a number of ways. Political consultants have maintained for years that if a campaign intended to use negative ads against the opponent, then the campaign first had to positively identify the candidate (see Devlin, 1981; Diamond & Bates, 1988; Hagstrom & Guskind, 1986). However, we believe that many consultants not only attempt to define their candidates in a positive light before beginning their negative attacks but also use these positive ads to position the candidates quite specifically in preparation for the planned future attack against their opponent.

For example, in the fall of 1985, Democratic consultant Bob Squier analyzed the upcoming 1986 Alabama Senate race. Squier decided that Republican Senator Jeremiah Denton was vulnerable on his social security voting record and his detached, absentee style of leadership. In January 1986, Squier began producing his first spots for Democratic challenger, Congressman Richard Shelby. Squier prepared a series of spots that positioned Shelby as an aggressive defender of social security. In addition, spots focused on a compassionate subtheme that emphasized Shelby's constituency service record, his family ties, and his record of public service. Testimonials involving his wife, constituents, and friends affirmed his caring, giving nature. Again and again, Shelby was shown in town meetings speaking with ordinary citizens, hearing their concerns, and answering their questions. A wide cross section of Alabamians appeared in the ads, but there was a decided emphasis on the elderly and the economically disadvantaged.

Other ads traced Shelby's roots as a poor-boy-who-made-good, but the ads emphasized that he had never forgotten the values his mother and father had taught him. Compassion, fairness, and equality under the law were important subthemes in the Shelby message. Shelby's sense of family pride, his pride in tradition, and his pride in Alabama were all carefully developed as themes.

In other words, Shelby's positive spots were developed with regard to the future planned attack on the incumbent. Squier deliberately positioned Richard Shelby as a candidate very different from the public's image of Denton. In effect, the Shelby package was consciously designed to stand in opposition to the Denton package. Even though Shelby did face an opponent, Jim Allen, Jr., in the Democratic primary, the positive spots associated with that party primary race were created as much, if not more, for the Denton race as they were for the Allen race. When Shelby finally did begin his negative spots against Denton, he was perceived as being highly credible on matters dealing with social security and governmental compassion. By playing on the public's doubts concerning Denton and by establishing Shelby's authority on these same issues, Squier hit the responsive chords necessary to gain credibility for the challenger.

Other examples abound in the 1986 Cranston/Zschau Senate contest in California. Cranston positioned himself as a champion of environmental concerns, while attacking Zschau on his environmental record. Zschau on the other hand positioned himself as a young, energetic, fresh-thinking conservative while portraying the aging Cranston as the embodiment of the tired, worn-out liberalism of the 1960s. When Cranston attacked Zschau on toxic waste, the attacks had the credibility generated by the early textural preconditioning spots that established Cranston as an environmental authority. On the other hand, Zschau did a series of positive spots demonstrating his youthful vitality and his wholesome traditional family values so that when he did attack Cranston for outmoded, wrong-thinking liberalism, the attacks would be more credible.

COMPARATIVE PRODUCT ADVERTISING

Comparative product advertising offers some insights into negative political advertising, and for that reason, we treat it with some detail here. Findings of comparative product advertising research offer useful discussion points for students of negative political advertising. As the reader will discover, the same operational reductionism discussed earlier also plagues the comparative product advertising literature.

Operationalization

Comparative product advertising "generally refers to the strategy of *explicitly* naming or identifying one or more competitors of the advertised brand for the purpose of claiming superiority over them either on an overall basis or in selected product attributes" (Prasad, 1976, p. 128). Although most researchers (see Boddewyn & Marton, 1978; Goodwin & Etgar, 1980; Prasad, 1976) separate those comparative ads that explicitly name the competition from the "Brand X" ads, comparison ads that euphemistically name the competition, we believe it is a false distinction (see Starch, 1926), in that by calling to mind the competition even by suggestion or inference, the competitive product is present in the mind of the receiver when evaluating the commercial. Thus we use a broader definition of comparative advertising than is generally accepted. Although we accept Prasad's definition, we interpret the identification to mean more than explicitly naming or displaying. We include the deliberate calling of the product to mind by euphemistic suggestions as a form of identification. We view comparative product advertising as having two primary forms: direct reference and Brand X ads (see Prasad, 1976; Starch, 1926).

Direct reference comparison ads specifically mention or display the competition's product that is being derogated. Brand X ads, on the other hand, "*do not explicitly name* competitors" (Prasad, 1976, p. 129), but euphemistically name the competition by using such phrases as "other leading brands" (Goodwin & Etgar, 1980, p. 188).

A Cost-Benefit Analysis of Comparative Product Advertising

In 1972, the Federal Trade Commission (FTC) encouraged advertisers to use comparative advertising for a number of reasons. First, comparative advertising is believed to encourage competition among products and/or companies, and according to traditional economic theory, that competition is healthy for both the marketplace and the consumer. Second, comparative advertising provides the consumer with more product information, so the consumer is able to make a more informed decision when it comes time to actually purchase the product (see Goodwin & Etgar, 1980; Levine, 1976; Ulanoff, 1975). Researchers estimate that comparative product ads make up between 5% and 10% of product advertising in the United States (Boddewyn & Marton, 1978).

Since 1972, however, there has been considerable debate among both practitioners and academicians concerning the effectiveness of comparative product advertising in promoting both brand and claim recall and product purchase. Some practitioners believe that comparative product advertising is very effective and some do not (see Giges, 1980; Kershaw & Tannenbaum, 1976; Levine, 1976; Rockey, 1976). Academicians have evaluated comparative product advertising research in a number of different ways. Often supportive ads that praise a particular product are compared with Brand X ads and direct reference comparative ads.

Three distinct perspectives have emerged. First, there are "those that found comparative advertising to be detrimental to the sponsoring brand" (James, 1978, p. 133; see also, Levine, 1976; McDougall, 1977; Murphy & Amundsen, 1981). Second, there are those that have found Brand X comparative ads superior to both supportive ads and direct reference comparative ads (Goodwin & Etgar, 1980). And third, there are those that have found direct reference ads as effective as supportive ads and Brand X ads (Golden, 1976; Prasad, 1976; Pride, Lamb, & Pletcher, 1977; Wilson, 1976).

All of these empirical studies had a number of shortcomings. Most significant is the single exposure treatment procedure that was used. Boddewyn and Marton (1978) concluded that comparative product advertising research evidence is scanty at best and called for additional research. We do not examine in detail the various findings of the studies categorized earlier; however, we do review Boddewyn and Marton's summary of comparative advertising directives that lend themselves to application in negative political advertising.

Comparative Product Advertising Guidelines and Recommendations for Application to Negative Political Advertising

According to Boddewyn and Marton (1978), comparative advertising should be considered when "the brand has a small market share or is a newcomer" to the market (p. 153). This concept is based on the halo effect, which posits that if a newcomer (in our case a political challenger) appears in a comparative ad with the dominant brand (the incumbent), then the prestige, credibility, and so forth of the dominant brand will in effect rub off on the newcomer or political challenger (see Boddewyn & Marton, 1978; Prasad, 1976). Thus, if a political challenger and the incumbent appear in a comparative ad together, the challenger very well may be perceived as being on the same level as the incumbent. Levine (1976) and Murphy and Amundsen (1981) had opposing viewpoints.

Boddewyn and Marton (1978) suggested that if a "brand has a built-in advantage; and the claimed superiority is meaningful, demonstrable, and verifiable by the consumer" (p. 153), then comparative advertising should or could be used effectively. In the political arena, a candidate may discover some series of actions on the part of the opponent such as voting record, public statements, political positions, and so forth that, packaged together, may represent the opponent's vulnerability and thus present a window of opportunity for the candidate. Negative ads that use charges/comparisons that are truthful, reasonable, and meaningful for the voter are most effective. Charges or claims made in the ads should be easily verifiable by either the news media or the voter. Candidates who use such an approach should present information through public relations activities (press conferences, press releases, public statements, etc.) that provide the evidence for their claims for the purpose of being reported by the news media and ultimately released to the voters. Clearly, a reinforcement posture that provides the evidence for the claims made in the ads is an important dimension of a successful negative ad strategy.

Boddewyn and Marton (1978) further suggested that the target audience should not have well-established hostile preferences, and the target market should include a "significant segment of 'undecided' consumers" (p. 153) in order to successfully use comparative advertising. Thus, candidates running in a district with no real chance of winning the race—for example, a minority party candidate running in a congressional district with 90% of the voters identifying as partisans of the majority party—should not consider direct attack negative strategies (see chapter 2). This is true for two reasons (a) There is not a significant segment of independents, and (b) attacks directed toward the majority party may only create increasingly hostile reactions to the minority party. Future inroads by the minority party in obtaining majority-party constituent support in the years ahead may be impeded by such a strategy (see Goldenberg & Traugott, 1984; Salmore & Salmore, 1985). On the other hand, candidates who have a well-defined support base and who have a realistic opportunity of winning the support of a significant segment of independents on election day may do well to consider negative advertising.

Boddewyn and Marton (1978) posited that comparative advertising should be used in situations where "one's advertising budget is much less than that of the competitor's" (p. 153), and when the competitor is the dominant brand in the marketplace. In the political arena, this suggests that challengers who are usually less well financed than incumbents should seek to crack the incumbent's candidate image through negative political advertising. As we demonstrated, negative information has higher recall, and in addition, negative advertising has been perceived as being unusual or novel by the voters. They find negative ads more interesting and therefore pay more attention to them (see Kellermann, 1984; Prasad, 1978). Clearly, challengers with smaller campaign war chests might "get more bang for the buck" by using negative ads, thus equalizing their bankroll with the incumbent's to some degree.

Boddewyn and Marton (1978) also suggested that comparative advertising is most effective when video and audio are used "with side-by-side demonstrations of the competitive products" (p. 153). In addition, when ads are directed at several competitive brands, then all the competitive brands should be shown, because "it increases the involvement potential" (p. 153). In the political arena, it might be suggested that a candidate who chooses to use negative advertising in either a multicandidate political primary or a general election campaign should consider showing his opposition in the ads.

Boddewyn and Marton (1978) went on to say that comparative advertising should not be used when the advertiser dominates the market. This supports the age-old political axiom that an incumbent who is considered to be in a "safe" seat should probably avoid negative advertising unless he or she is suddenly and unexpectedly dropping in the polls. However, there is evidence to suggest that this axiom was prematurely adopted because of faulty operationalization of negative political advertising. And indeed, popular incumbents in the 1980s have successfully used negative political advertising (Kern, 1989). As political-media culture evolves, it is likely that incumbents increasingly will use negative advertising in the future.

Boddewyn and Marton (1978) and Goodwin and Etgar (1980) suggested that comparative advertising should be used in ads that make predominantly rational claims rather than emotional claims. According to Goodwin and Etgar, there are two product types: those that satisfy task-related capacities that are able to be measured or evaluated by their physical attributes and those that satisfy the social-psychological needs of the audience. Task-related product advertising may utilize either emotional or rational appeals. But Goodwin and Etgar recommended that task-related products utilize rational claims in comparative product advertising. The use of rational appeals facilitates the voters' ability to evaluate claims and/or charges in negative ads. Researchers have observed that social-psychological products are frequently sold through emotional claims (Goodwin & Etgar, 1980). According to Goodwin and Etgar, social-psychological benefits are difficult to discuss, compare, and evaluate. Therefore, comparative ads that utilize a comparison based on these elusive benefits are judged to be less effective. On the other hand, comparative ads that demonstrate differences by discussing task-related capacities and using rational claims that can be evaluated through normal evidential procedures are judged to be more effective. Thus, a political candidate using negative political advertising should use rational claims that involve comparisons made between objective behaviors that can be clearly defined and evaluated. And, these claims should in some way satisfy the political needs of the target audience.

In addition, Boddewyn and Marton (1978) warned that comparative ads should use a limited number of comparative claims in that information overload is likely to occur if the audience is presented with too many discrepant claims (see also, Bettman, 1975; Goodwin & Etgar, 1980; Jacoby, Speller, & Kohn, 1974). Clearly then, candidates who use negative advertising should stress one or two dominant themes in their negative advertising strategies. These strategies then can be implemented with various examples that support the central themes of the campaign through a series of negative ads. Candidates should exercise care not to attack all across the board, but to selectively target attacks at vulnerable spots that have been identified and then packaged as dominant themes of the negative ad campaign. The same one or two negative central themes should be emphasized over and over for greatest effect.

Similarly, Boddewyn and Marton (1978) cautioned that comparative ads should also be sensitive to the audience's perception of "fair play," for if the "attack on the competitor is too vicious or self-serving" (p. 154), then the audience may well rally to the side of the competition. Political candidates must take care not to offend the sensibilities of the voters, and ensure that their negative claims are truthful and fair representations of the differences existing between the political candidates, parties, and so forth involved in order to avoid a backlash effect (see Johnson & Copeland, 1987). Voters do not tolerate liars.

Effectiveness of Comparative Product Advertising
Versus Negative Political Advertising

Comparative political advertising is more effective than comparative product advertising in achieving the desired communication goals of recall, image enhancement, and persuasion for a number of reasons. Viewers are three times more likely to remember political advertising than product advertising (see

Patterson & McClure, 1976b). Viewers may perceive political advertising as being more salient than product advertising, and for this reason, attend to political advertising more than they do product advertising. Prasad (1976) hypothesized that the effectiveness of comparative advertising is a "function of product involvement" (p. 135), thus suggesting that viewers have greater "product involvement" (p. 134) with political parties and candidates, for they perceive "political products" (p. 134) as having a greater impact on their lives. In addition, it may be posited that politics is a highly ego involving process that is quite unlike the evaluative process surrounding consumer product goods selection (see Prasad, 1976). In highly ego-involving situations, viewers perceive that they have more at stake and they will readily attend to communication messages that offer them situation-defining elements.

THE FUNCTIONS OF NEGATIVE POLITICAL ADVERTISING

Negative political advertising has a number of campaign functions: (a) to create awareness of political candidates and their associated issues through dramatization, (b) to assist voters in prioritizing issues on a political agenda that ultimately favors the sponsoring candidate's record, public statements, positions, and so forth, (c) to increase interest in the campaign by stimulating public talk and media coverage, (d) to increase the voters' evaluation of the sponsoring candidate while decreasing the voters' evaluation of the opposition on both key political and stylistic role dimensions, and (e) to ensure that voters' evaluations of the candidates become so polarized that their electoral choice becomes simplified (see Atkin & Heald, 1976).

THE ROLE OF NEGATIVE POLITICAL ADVERTISING IN THE POLITICAL CAMPAIGN

It must be remembered that a voter has "five principal ways to express himself in a two-party election: voting for or against either of the party nominees, or not voting at all" (Sabato, 1981, p. 324). And, as Vincent Breglio explained in 1983: "It has become vital in campaigns today that you not only present all of the reasons why people ought to vote for you but you also have an obligation to present the reasons why they should not vote for the opponent. Hence, the negative campaign, or the attack strategy becomes an essential part of any campaign operation" (as quoted in Devlin, 1986, p. 23).

A 1988 Hart poll shows that 39% of those who voted for Bush/Quayle and 34% of those who voted for Dukakis/Bentsen actually voted for them because they thought the political team was a "good choice" (Hart, 1988). In other words, the majority of people voted for a given presidential ticket because they did not want the opposition ticket in power—they voted against rather than for a given ticket.

THE EVOLUTION OF NEGATIVE POLITICAL ADVERTISING STRATEGIES

The Classic Game Plan

Diamond and Bates (1988) identified four stages of political advertising in a campaign: identification spots (which provide name identification), argument spots (which tell us what the candidate stands for or against), attack spots (which are used to suggest the opponent's inferiority and sometimes the sponsor's superiority as well), and the "I see an America" spots (which present the candidate as a political visionary and end the campaign on a positive note) (see also, Payne, Marlier, & Baukus, 1989).

Similarly, Peter Dailey, a Republican political consultant, identified three levels of a political campaign: the first, where candidates "build a base of credibility"; the second, where candidates "offer solutions to the problems that exist"; and the third, where candidates "attack your opponent" (Devlin, 1981, p. 5). In a 1986 study, Hagstrom and Guskind analyzed 375 political commercials from 14 Senate and gubernatorial races and concluded that there were three types of ads: those that "acquaint voters with the candidate's personality and background," those that "extol his or her record or plans" (p. 2619), and those that "tear apart the opponent" (p. 2619). These ad types correspond with the campaign advertising stages identified by both Diamond and Bates (1988) and Dailey.

Although these traditional phases have been identified for all campaigns, negative ads traditionally have been associated with the political challenger who is running in a competitive electoral setting (see chapter 2). Because conventionally the challenger aired more negative ads than the incumbent, negative advertising was said to be a classic challenger strategy (see Kern, 1989). Direct comparison ads were frequently used by challengers so that they would benefit from the halo effect of the challenger appearing in the same ad with the incumbent; the incumbent's prestige and credibility, in effect, wore off on the challenger (see chapter 2). And because challenger campaigns were frequently underfinanced, challengers turned to negative ads to crack the incumbents' public image. In this way, it was hoped that the positive ads would have greater impact when aired. Frequently, challengers attacked an incumbent's political record, for example, his or her voting record, public statements, and political positions, in order to gain stature as a political expert. And most significantly, negative ads were used only near the end of the campaign after the candidates had clearly identified themselves and had developed coherent issue agendas. Negative ads made up approximately 25% to 30% of the challenger's advertising portfolio. The incumbent usually used significantly fewer. Because incumbents were likely to win, they usually chose not to attack their opponent for strategic reasons. Jamieson and Campbell (1983) explained: "An attack invites reply and media coverage of the reply. This legitimizes the opponent and provides the opponent with media access. Counterattack is a legitimizing strategy that tacitly assumes comparable stature" (p. 245).

After airing negative ads, concultants advised candidates to return to a 1- to 2-week positive political ad campaign before election day (Diamond & Bates, 1988). Diamond and Bates referred to this positive, uplifting ending as a time of "resolution and reflection" (p. 344). These visionary appeals are uplifting messages designed to make the candidate appear ready to take on the mantle of power (see Johnson, 1984). However, the political times and strategies are changing.

The Campaign Battle Strategy

Kern (1989) suggested that political consultants and their candidates began to use negative political advertising differently in the 1980s. First of all, challengers are using a greater percentage of negative ads. Today, a little over half of congressional challenger ads may be characterized as negative spots (Kern, 1989). Although challengers continue to produce the majority of negative spots, vulnerable incumbents now produce negative advertising of their own. Kaid and Davidson (1986), in a study analyzing 1982 U.S. Senate races, found that only 10% of incumbent ads were negative whereas 46% of the challenger ads were negative.

In addition, negative ads no longer are aired near the end of a political race. Rather, challengers are choosing to use negative ads early in the race. Kern (1989) explained: "Early [negative] televised advertising is being used by challengers in districts in which an incumbent is potentially vulnerable for the purpose of getting news coverage that contributes to the success of fund-raising efforts and thereby helps make the race competitive" (p. 181). Kern suggested that this modern battle strategy creates what she called a "media permutation" (p. 182). The challenger moves from being a visible candidate to being a competitive candidate through his or her exposure in the news media and the subsequent ease of fund-raising activities. In other words, the media create permutations in the conventional campaign scenario by covering negative political advertising. Challengers are able to gain name recognition easier and earlier through this process, and this translates into early money for the candidate, which has been their traditionally weak area.

It is also interesting to note that incumbent California Senator Alan Cranston began his 1986 reelection campaign with negative spots, perhaps suggesting a new style of incumbent campaigning. He faced a well-financed, popular Republican Congressman Ed Zschau. In the future, challengers and incumbents may well utilize negative political advertising in order to attract media attention and gather early financial support. In addition, incumbents who are expecting to be attacked may wish to attack first in order to gain early control of the campaign agenda.

Kern ((1989) also reported that some political consultants believe that "mud" (p. 194) should come out early rather than late; if it appears late in the campaign, the voters perceive it as dirty politics or as being a low blow. One Democratic consultant advised that: "mud has to be early and consistent" (p. 194).

And most interesting, many candidates, whether incumbent or challenger, are choosing to stay negative. Gone are the "feel good" or "I see an America" spots associated with traditional campaign endings (see Diamond & Bates, 1988, p. 344). Many consultants believe it is a mistake to let up on the attack, for a change in momentum can literally happen overnight. This is particularly true in highly competitive races that go down to the wire. Challengers, in particular, in those situations are most likely to continue their attack, for they fear that, when in doubt, the voters might choose the familiar over the unfamiliar.

Negative Campaigns

In 1982, Tarrance identified a new political phenomenon: the negative campaign. According to Tarrance, the negative campaign is distinct from the more traditional campaign strategies (the classic game plan and campaign battle strategy), which use negative political advertising episodically, because the negative campaign is predominantly negative. In fact, over 60% of the political advertising during the campaign can be characterized as negative. Negative campaigns share the same characteristics of the campaign battle strategy except negative campaigns use more negative ads.

Tarrance (1982) attributed the growth of negative campaigns to the recent development and sophistication of political action committees (PAC) and their independent expenditures (see chapters 4 & 5). Such negative campaigns, according to Tarrance, have been quite "successful when used with *limited ends* in mind" (p. 11).

Tarrance (1982) stressed that for a negative campaign to be a success, it must present logical arguments with strong documentation. The arguments must have an appearance of authenticity. Logical cross-pressuring is a preferred technique (see chapter 3 for examples), which demonstrates "that the incumbent's voting record is not consistent with the shared beliefs of a particular constituency" (p. 2). Logical cross-pressuring arguments stress the campaign's research methods of roll call analysis and public opinion polling in both their advertising and public relations tactics. Although the material presented in the cross-pressuring ads may not always be full and accurate representations of the facts, the ads have a superficial believability because of their presentation style.

Since the publication of Tarrance's 1982 book, *Negative Campaigns and Negative Votes: The 1980 Elections*, candidates themselves joined with PACs in engaging in negative campaigns. A number of negative candidate campaigns may be easily identified: for example, the 1984 Helms/Hunt North Carolina Senate race, the 1986 Shelby/Denton Alabama Senate race, the 1988 Lautenberg/Dawkins New Jersey Senate race, the 1989 Florio/Courter New Jersey gubernatorial race, and the 1989 Wilder/Coleman Virginia gubernatorial contest.

Profiling the Political Campaign in
Terms of Negativity

In 1982, Tarrance developed an informal yardstick to measure individual political campaigns in terms of their negativity. What follows is a brief description of his schema and a few of our own adaptations. We call Tarrance's 10-point scale the Negativity Profile Scale (1982, p.18):

> Political campaigning in a two candidate election campaign can be viewed as existing on a pro-candidate/anti-opponent dimension. At one end are campaigns which focus exclusively on the positive attributes of the candidate and do not acknowledge or discuss his opponent. At the other end are campaigns which focus exclusively on the negative attributes and characteristics of the opponent and do not acknowledge or discuss this candidate himself. For convenience, we can create a 10-point scale, as follows:

What's Good											What's Bad About
About Me	1	2	3	4	5	6	7	8	9	10	My Opponent

According to Tarrance (1982), any campaign in which 60% or more of the political advertising can be described as negative should be considered a negative campaign. We added two other negative profile margins. A campaign that utilizes less than or equal to 30% of its political advertising in the negative form can be said to be following the classic game plan. And a campaign that can be characterized as having more than 30% but less than 60% of its advertising in the negative form is said to be following a campaign battle plan.

The Negativity Profile Scale's margin can be summarized as:

The Classic Game Plan	1%–30% Negative Ads
The Campaign Battle Strategy	31%–59% Negative Ads
The Negative Campaign	60%–100% Negative Ads

Although the margins are set arbitrarily, we believe that each of the three identified strategic models approximately represent observed real-life campaign strategies that have been used during the past 30 years.

Negative Ads: An American Political Institution

Negative political advertising has become an American institution. The negative advertising stage during a political campaign has become well established and is now recognized by both academicians and consultants alike. According to John Nugent (1987), negative political advertising is used because it works; as he stated: "Positive appeals confirm your support; negative appeals tend to convert the undecided" (p. 49). Nugent suggested that political consultants choose negative advertising over positive advertising for a number of reasons:

> A negative ad campaign is "easier to mount, often cheaper to produce, and they can undo more expensive positive campaigns. People are more apt to vote 'against' than 'for' something; it is easier to appeal to emotion than to logic. Negative ads are a form of gossip, and word-of-mouth publicity multiplies the message. A by-product of negative advertising is the free media play, decrying but repeating, an attack. (p. 49)

IN CONCLUSION

Although modern political commentators spend a great deal of time lamenting the rise of negative ads, negative campaigning is as old as the American republic. And whereas many political journalists would have us believe that 1980 signaled the beginning of negative television spots, their history stretches back into the early 1950s. Some political seasons may be viewed as being more negative than others, however the use of negative advertising remains a significant element in modern campaigns.

   Before 1980, both academicians and political consultants viewed negative political advertising as being ineffective in its attempt to hurt the opposition and warned that negative ads often create a backlash or boomerang effect against the sponsor. After 1980, the political consultants changed their tune; they came to believe that negative ads were one of the more effective political tactics.

   Academicians, on the other hand, have remained skeptical. Researchers have found that only independently sponsored negative ads have the desired effect against targeted candidates and that these ads create little if any backlash against other candidates in the race. However, it must be noted that whereas political advertising researchers usually have not been able to empirically demonstrate the effectiveness of candidate-sponsored negative political ads, cognitive psychologists have long been able to demonstrate the powerful influence of the negativity effect. Although both political consultants and cognitive psychologists have used a much broader negative spectrum in their analysis, political advertising researchers have operationalized negative political advertising in such a way that it only referred to direct attack/direct reference negative advertising. This operationalization may have lead to the obfuscation of negative political advertising effects because of the media-political culture found in the United States. A similar pervasive reductionism also exists in the comparative product advertising literature. Research is presented in chapter 2 that examines both the acceptance and effectiveness of negative direct attack, direct comparison, and implied comparison political advertising.

Research often has failed to consider the message content when analyzing the effectiveness of various negative ad appeals. We have identified two types of negative issue appeals: political issue appeals and personal characteristic issue appeals. We use the term issue appeals, because whether a negative ad mentions a traditional political issue such as a voting record or whether it mentions a personal problem such as alcoholism, both become campaign issues — thus the term, negative issue appeals. Voters accept negative political issue appeals much more readily than negative personal characteristic issue appeals. It is recommended that political actors and consultants avoid the use of negative personal characteristic issue appeals.

II

ANALYSIS OF NEGATIVE POLITICAL ADVERTISING

The National Republical Congressional Committee, which regularly conducts audience-reaction tests of political commercials, has found that no format or strategy is necessarily superior, and no style tends consistently to secure more favorable reactions. Almost always the evaluation is dependent on how appropriate *the selected style, format, and strategy is for the candidate in question, and how well the advertising seemed to fit the circumstances of a particular campaign, the personality of a particular candidate, and the electorate's preconceptions and prior prejudices about politics.*
— L. J. Sabato (1981, p. 122)

There is no magic formula for a successful negative political ad. What we have is a record of what has been used and why. Hopefully, from this record, we can learn how a negative ad is constructed, and we can begin to see the differences among the various types of negative ads. In order to facilitate an understanding of negative political ads, we have attempted to create a typology of commercials ranging from the broad to the narrow. It is hoped that this typology can be used to better integrate our knowledge of what works and how.

In Part II, we consider substance, style, origination, and channel used in negative political ads. Within these broad areas, we offer subcategories that should help explicate the general categories. Each of the areas and/or subcategories are illustrated with at least one example from a political campaign. This should allow the reader to see how each technique has been used in an actual campaign.

We believe that negative political advertising can be viewed as modern-day political short stories. It would be impossible to pinpoint the birth of the short story; it is enough to say that "much of man's literary expression in all ages can ultimately be said to have no origin more specific than the inherent creative spirit of man satisfying his desire to tell and to hear stories" (Holman, 1972, p. 495). All short stories have a beginning, a middle, and an end. They present, either explicitly or implicitly, age-old conflicts: person versus person, person versus self, person versus fate, and person versus nature. Through conflict resolution, the short story is said to ultimately reveal truth. Indeed, James Joyce called the short story an epiphany because of the revelations that emerged through its thematic conflict resolution (see Holman, 1972). A theme is the "central or dominating idea in a literary work" (Holman, 1972, p. 528). Thus, in a political ad, the theme is the underlying meaning behind the political messages presented in the ad.

As in any analysis of literary work, it is an artificial separation to discuss the substantive elements of theme away from the stylistic manner in which it is presented (i.e., plot). And in political communication analysis, we cannot separate substance and style from the message origination and the channels of communication through which the message is disseminated (see Nimmo, 1978). However, in order to understand the various types of negative advertising that have developed over the years, both in substance and style, it is necessary to consider these elements separately. For this reason, first examine substance and the thematic designs associated with negative advertising in chapters 2 and 3. We then turn in chapter 4 to the style of presentation of these thematic designs, that is, the plot or "pattern of events" that places order on the "*characters* performing actions in incidents that interrelate to comprise a 'single, whole, and complete' action. . . ." (Holman, 1972, pp. 397-398). In addition, we examine the elements of visual production that must be taken into account when analyzing political advertising content. In chapter 5, we consider the various originations of negative political advertising and the mass communication channels through which these political ads are disseminated.

2

Substance: The What in Negative Political Advertising

AN ALTERNATIVE OPERATIONALIZATION OF NEGATIVE POLITICAL ADVERTISING: THREE MODES OF ARGUMENTATION

A negative political ad, just as any short story, can be broken down into what is said, substance and its underlying themes, and how it is said, presentation style or plot. Both style and substance are important for any ad to be successful. Each of these, however, has its own individual constraints and advantages. Successful use of both style and substance make for effective political ads. The use of style and substance together provides us with a synergistic effect in that they "become related to one another and interact dynamically" (Bordwell & Thompson, 1979, p. 28), thus the total advertising package is greater than the parts.

We begin our exploration with an examination of substance, what is said. In our analysis of the substance of negative ads, we consider the argumentation mode of the negative appeal (how are arguments structured), the political symbology (are the messages manifest or latent), temporal directionality of the evidence (do the political ads deal with the past or with the future), and the thematic designs for political and personal issue appeals (what is the manifest and latent content of the substantive argument).

Argumentation

In any discussion of substance, one of the key questions is: "What arguments are presented to persuade the public?" A corollary is: "How are the arguments used in combination to provide for effective argumentation?"

Argumentation is "best defined as a method of analysis and reasoning designed to provide acceptable bases for belief and action" (McBurney & Mills, 1964, p. 1). A candidate's political advertising is a form of argument—an argument for the candidate's election and against the opponent's election. When deciding on how to structure arguments that will be effective, advertising consultants design their negative ads very carefully. According to Nimmo (1978), consultants must employ three techniques in developing their message appeals. First, the consultant "gathers intelligence about what is congenial to audience members through polling techniques. . . . Second . . . [the consultant] employs appropriate technology to disseminate a message to group members . . . , individuals . . . , or potential collaborators. . . . Finally, . . . [consultants] select appropriate linguistic devices and styles for couching their propaganda, advertising, and rhetoric" (p. 123).

The Use of Inductive and Deductive Logic

Arguments are usually constructed in one or two manners: deductively or inductively. Deductive logic moves from the general to the specific whereas induction argues from the specific to the general.

Deductive argumentation is based on the syllogism. The classic syllogism is:

All people are mortal.
Socrates is a person.
Socrates is mortal.

Reasoning from the major premise "All people are mortal," establishes something about the class "mortal." The minor or second premise, "Socrates is a person," identifies Socrates as the member of the class. Therefore, if Socrates is a member of the class, what is true for the class is true for a member. One could structure a syllogism from the arguments from the 1988 presidential election campaign as:

All liberals support tax and spend programs.
Michael Dukakis is a liberal.
Michael Dukakis supports tax and spend programs.

Although it may never have been spelled out in syllogistic form, just such an argument was made by the Republicans against Dukakis.

A special type of syllogism is the enthymeme. The enthymeme is a truncated syllogism. Part of the syllogism or reasoning is left out of the argument, and the audience is expected to complete the argument. In other words, "enthymemes are arguments that rely on the knowledge, values, attitudes, and experiences of the audience. An enthymeme is a partial or incomplete argument that prompts the audience to complete it with whatever the audience already knows, believes, or values. An argument that invites you to fill in your own experience or to draw a conclusion when no claim is made explicitly is an enthymeme" (Jamieson & Campbell, 1983, p. 168). Returning to our Dukakis example, one could say: "Michael Dukakis is a liberal. Michael Dukakis supports tax and spend programs." The major premise that all liberals support taxation and spending programs never needs to be said, because the audience can fill in the major premise for themselves.

Induction works from the specific to the general. Major premises in deductive arguments are often constructed from inductive reasoning. The conclusions of inductive reasoning are general statements.

How did we arrive at the statement that "All liberals support big spending and big tax increases"? Usually from observation. Edward Kennedy is a liberal and supports tax and spend programs. Tip O'Neil is a liberal and supports tax and spend programs. Barney Frank is a liberal and supports tax and spend programs. An inductive leap is made over all unexamined members of the class, that is, all other liberals. Therefore, all liberals support tax and spend programs.

Political advertisements usually use one of these two types of logic when structuring their arguments. They argue either from specifics leading one to a conclusion, inductive, or from the general to the specific, deductive.

The Political Ad Hominem Argument

Cragan and Cutbirth (1984) suggested that ad hominem arguments deal "directly with leadership style" (p. 229). In other words, they are arguments used to call into question a given candidate's fitness for office. Fitness for office is the crucial voter test when making the voting decision (see Nimmo & Savage, 1976; Osgood, 1957; Trent & Friedenberg, 1983). That evaluation is usually made by comparing the real candidate's images with the voter's ideal candidate's image.

Ideal Candidate. Research has shown that voters have an image of the ideal candidate (Hellweg, 1979; Nimmo & Savage, 1976). During the decision-making process known as the voting decision, voters compare their ideal candidate image with the real candidate image associated with the various contestants (see Hellweg, 1979; Nimmo & Savage, 1976). Research has indicated that voters perceive three primary dimensions of the ideal candidate: credibility, interpersonal attraction, and homophyly (Trent & Friedenberg, 1983; see also, Lashbrook, 1975; Wakshlag & Edison, 1979). Through campaign research, a candidate determines the voters' ideal candidate image, and the campaign is then focused on portraying the candidate as possessing ideal qualities while portraying the opposition as lacking in these qualities.

Ad hominem arguments are those appeals used to directly question the opposition candidate's fitness for office. Ad hominem arguments may be either true or false. Cragan and Cutbirth (1984) judged those that are truthful to be legitimate forms of argumentation. Those that are false are considered specious forms of argumentation. Cragan and Cutbirth suggested a three-part criterion for evaluating political ad hominem arguments. In order to be considered legitimate, the "argument must be: (1) logically relevant; (2) factually supportable; and (3) artistically structured" (p. 230). If the argument is not relevant to the given political situation, then the argument becomes invalid (see Cragan & Cutbirth, 1984; Woods & Walton, 1982). The argument must be valid, not in the eyes of the candidate or political consultant, but in the eyes of the voters. The arguments must be factually supportable in that the news media and the opposition are likely to take the sponsor to task for misleading the public, in which case, the sponsor making the argument calls into question his or her own fitness for public office. And finally, the argument must be artistically structured or dramatized. Appropriate political symbols must be used to reach the desired target audiences.

We identify three modes of ad hominem argumentation in negative political advertising. These negative argumentation positions are what we call argumentation modes. The three types of argumentation modes that have emerged in our study of negative political advertising are: direct attack ads, direct comparison ads, and implied comparison ads. Each of these modes generally presents its information using either an inductive or deductive means (see Table 2.1)

TABLE 2.1
Types of Negative Political Advertising

Direct Attack Ads:	Attack opposition only
Direct Comparison Ads:	Directly compare candidates on voting record, experience and so forth.
Implied Comparison Ads:	Enthymemes. Not negative in and of themselves; but, it is the public interpretation that gives them their negative character.

THREE NEGATIVE ARGUMENTATION MODES: THE DIRECT ATTACK AD, THE DIRECT COMPARISON AD, AND THE IMPLIED COMPARISON AD

The Direct Attack

The direct attack ad is probably the type of negative ad that most people think of when asked to picture a negative ad in their minds or when asked to describe a negative ad. The direct attack ad, as its name suggests, directly attacks a specific candidate or party. For our purposes, the direct attack ad only attacks;

it does not compare one candidate with another. According to Merritt (1984), a negative attack ad "focuses primarily on degrading perceptions of the rival, to the advantage of the sponsor" (p. 27). Direct attack advertising is based on the assumption that "voters mark their ballots against rather than for certain candidates" (Hellweg, 1988, p. 14).

The opponent who is attacked is either named specifically "John Doe," or euphemistically with phrases such as "my opponent," "the Republican candidate," or the "current probate judge." In some instances, the candidate who is attacked is not named but is pictured in the advertisement. Political parties may be attacked in the same way as an individual candidate, by either name, leaders associated with the party, or symbol. Direct attack ads identify the competitor "for the purpose of imputing inferiority" (Merritt, 1984, p. 27). The direct attack ad normally utilizes inductive logic in that viewers are asked to draw a conclusion from bits of specific evidence. Research has shown that such one-sided presentations are most effective in "converting the less educated" and are "generally more effective as a reinforcing device" (Weiss, 1966, p. 130).

According to Gronbeck (1985), the assaultive or direct attack spot is the riskiest of the three types of negative advertising. This conclusion is not surprising in light of studies documenting a boomerang or backlash effect (Garramone, 1984, 1985; Garramone & Smith, 1984; Merritt, 1984). Although Copeland and Johnson-Cartee (1990b) found no statistically significant evidence of a boomerang to be associated with a direct attack spot, they also warned that any analysis of the boomerang must take into account various political issue and personal characteristic issue appeals found in the ad. The nature of these issue appeals may well determine whether there is a boomerang associated with the spot. Both argumentation mode and content are important variables to consider when evaluating negative ads.

Copeland and Johnson-Cartee (1990b) found that the direct attack ad created a statistically significant decrease in the targeted candidate's evaluation scores and the targeted candidate's voting preference scores. However, the observed drop was not as great as that witnessed for the direct comparison spot.

In 1986, Ted Strickland, the Republican candidate for governor of Colorado, ran an ad called "Hats" against the Democratic candidate for governor, Roy Romer. CBS News said that "Hats" was the most effective negative ad of the 1986 election season. "Hats" is an excellent example of the direct attack spot.

The 1986 Strickland "Hats" Ad

VIDEO	AUDIO
Roy Romer in a black and white picture.	Narrator [VO]: "What is Roy Romer?"

We see Romer with various hats artificially placed on his head throughout ad.	He's a land developer who turns Colorado land into developments.
	The paid public official who opened new businesses outside of Colorado.
	The state treasurer who puts our money in banks that give him personal loans for his own businesses.
	The office holder who grows rich in public office.
	He's the politician who will raise your taxes.
	Roy Romer is not a governor for Colorado."
Still frame of head of Ted Strickland (in color).	
"For Governor Ted Strickland Kathy Arnold For Lt. Governor"	

In 1980, Democratic candidate for the U.S. House of Representatives Jim Mattox ran a "Lie Detector" ad against Tom Pauken. The ad attacks Pauken's veracity.

The 1980 Mattox "Lie Detector" Ad

VIDEO	AUDIO
A lie detector operating.	Narrator [VO]: "Testing Tom Pauken's qualifications isn't a job for the voters. It's a task for a lie detector.
	While Pauken denies he left the White House in disgrace.

	The truth is he resigned after
	his boss condemned his performance
	ıs disloyal, devious, and
	inexcusable.
Needles on lie detector	Later Pauken made a far right
speed up.	propaganda film. He claims to have
	made thousands of dollars on the
	movie. Yet he failed to list this
Needles go much faster.	money on his federal income tax
	statement. Now Pauken wants
	to be Congressman. But if a man
	won't tell you the truth before
	election, when can you believe him?"

Direct attack spots can also be directed at political parties rather than candidates. In 1988, the Democratic National Committee presented a very obnoxious Republican in their "Hey Pal" spot. According to Devlin (1989), the "Hey Pal" spot was a disaster for the Democratic party. Devlin reported that Barry Tron, a Republican National Committee advertising director, tested the spot and found that voters were so turned off by the spot that it helped the Republican numbers rather than hurting them. Adjectives like *grotesque, obscene, obnoxious*, and *offensive* have been used to describe this commercial (Devlin, 1989). This polispot provides evidence of the boomerang when advertisers offend the public's sensibilities. Johnson and Copeland (1987) warned that political advertisers must be wary of violating the public's notion of "good taste" when creating negative political ads.

The 1988 DNC "Hey Pal" Ad

VIDEO	AUDIO
Rotund man in a suit. Grinning widely. Very insincere in appearance. Looks like a stereotypical used-car salesman. Exaggerated speaking voice.	Rotund man [SOT]: "Hey Pal, how about a couple hundred billion? I'll pay you right back! (Raucous Laughter)"
"*1980* National Debt $900 Billion" (black screen with white letters)	Announcer [VO]: "This is what the Republicans call managing the economy."

Rotund man talking.

Rotund man [SOT]: "Hey Pal, half a trillion just to kind of get me over the *hump.* (Raucous Laughter)"

*"1985
National Debt
$1.8 Trillion"*

Announcer [VO]: "They should call it 'mortgaging our children's future.' "

Rotund man [SOT]: "What's another trillion between friends? (Raucous Laughter)."

*"1988
National Debt
$2.6 Trillion"*
(In much larger print)

Announcer [VO]: "They've tripled our national debt."

Rotund man [SOT]: "Hey Pal, just a few more years—*that's all I'll need.*" (underlined in regular voice)

Announcer [VO]: "Sorry, Pal."

"We can't afford the Republicans.
The Democrats
From Town Hall to the Nation."

The Direct Comparison Ad

Some negative political ads specifically compare the candidate with the opponent. Unlike the direct attack ad, the direct comparison ad features the candidate as well as the opposition. A true comparison ad actually contrasts the records, experience, or issue positions of the candidates. A direct comparison ad identifies the competitor "for the purpose of claiming superiority" (Prasad, 1976, p. 128; see also, Merritt, 1984). A direct comparison ad focuses "primarily on enhancing perceptions of the sponsor, even at the expense of the competitor" (Merritt, 1984, p. 27). According to Gronbeck (1985), the direct comparison ad "works on the assumption that voters actively compare contenders in the decision-making process" (see also Hellweg, 1988).

Some consultants (see Colford, 1986) and academicians (see Merritt, 1984) say that the direct comparison ad is not truly negative because it presents both candidates' (or parties') stands or records. However, our view is that the candidate (party or PAC) who sponsors the ad controls the content of the ad, and as such, it is virtually guaranteed that the opposition's record or policy positions will not be presented in an impartial manner. One would not run a comparison ad that touted the opposition as being superior to the candidate sponsoring the ad. Clearly, direct comparison ads do claim superiority, but by claiming superiority they are at the same time imputing the inferiority of the opposition. One cannot claim superiority in a vacuum. The concept of superiority implies a relational analysis. The question must be asked then: "Superior to whom?"; and the answer is necessarily: "to the inferior candidate, party, and so forth."

As with the direct attack ad, the direct comparison ad normally uses inductive logic, because the ad calls for the viewer to draw a conclusion based on specific bits of evidence. Using the specifics of the candidate's resume then, the direct comparison ad argues that the candidate is the best choice for the position. Comparison ads are frequently used in state and local races, but have also been used at the national level.

Many consultants believe that voters accept the comparison ad more readily than the direct attack ad in that they view the comparison ad as being fair because two sides are presented. Academic research has tended to agree with the consultants by showing that such two-sided presentations are "more effective than one-sided presentation as a device for converting the highly educated, and as a safeguard against later counter-propaganda" (Weiss, 1966, p. 130). Copeland and Johnson-Cartee (1990b) found the direct comparison spot created the greatest statistically significant decrease in the targeted candidate's evaluation scores and candidate voting preference scores. Larry Sabato, a professor of government at the University of Virginia, found that comparison ads "have a high recall and can educate the voting public" (as quoted in Colford, 1986, p. 104; see also Copeland & Johnson-Cartee, 1990b).

During the 1980 Democratic presidential primaries, Edward Kennedy's campaign adviser, David H. Sawyer, advised the Massachusetts senator to go on the offensive against incumbent Democratic President Jimmy Carter (Diamond & Bates, 1988, p. 280). The result was a series of four ads. Carter was described as misleading the American public, breaking promises, creating foreign policy blunders, and betraying Israel. Kennedy, on the other hand, was described as leading the fight for mandatory wage and price controls to stop inflation and creating innovative programs to help the poor and elderly.

In the 1986 Alabama gubernatorial race, Democratic Lieutenant Governor Bill Baxley ran a direct comparison ad against the Republican candidate, Guy Hunt. The Democratic primaries had a rather unusual ending in that the Democratic Party Executive Committee invalidated the results of the primary run-off that had left Charlie Graddick, a conservative Democrat, as victor. In an unusual turn of events, the Graddick win was thrown out. And runner-up Lieutenant Governor Bill Baxley was certified the winner. Graddick then mounted an independent protest campaign that later fizzled out. In the last days before the general election, Graddick threw his support to Guy Hunt, the Republican nominee. In a TV political advertisement, Graddick told his supporters: "To send *them* a message." In effect, Baxley was battling not only Guy Hunt and his Republican supporters but also disgruntled conservative Democrats who felt cheated by their own political party.

The 1986 Baxley "Comparison" Ad

VIDEO	AUDIO
"Governor"	Announcer [VO]: "It's now official. The race for governor is between Bill Baxley and Guy Hunt. So ask
Photos: Bill Baxley on left and Guy Hunt on right. "Guy Hunt refused to release his tax returns." (Hunt's photo gets larger)	yourself these questions. Which candidate for governor refuses to release his tax returns?
"Bill Baxley has 12 years of experience." (Baxley's photo gets larger).	Which man has 12 years of experience as attorney general and as Lt. Governor?
"Guy Hunt was forced to resign his federal job." (Hunt's photo gets larger)	Which man was forced to resign a federal position rather than face charges?
"Only Bill Baxley has a college education." (Baxley photo gets larger)	Which man has the education and training he'll need to compete with other Southern governors?
Photo of Bill Baxley, centered. Bill Baxley For Governor.	On Tuesday we're not sending a message. We're electing a governor."

This Baxley "Comparison" ad was reinforced with newspaper ads depicting famous state governors from across the United States and their educational backgrounds. In addition, Baxley and his opponent, Guy Hunt, were also pictured. All the depicted politicians had college degress except for the lone Republican candidate, Guy Hunt. These ads did not play well in Alabama, a state with decided populist leanings and a state where the great majority of citizens do not have college degrees. Indeed historically, George Wallace, the four-time governor of Alabama, frequently attacked the "pointed-headed intellectuals" or "egg-heads" in academe during his political campaigns, conveniently ignoring the fact of his own college and legal education.

In 1988, the Democratic National Committee produced a direct comparison spot that contrasted the Bush/Quayle record on the 60-day notification of plant closings with the Dukakis/Bentsen record.

The 1988 DNC "Plant Closings" Ad

VIDEO	AUDIO
Gates to factory. Chain locked. Picture gets larger.	Announcer [VO]: "The company you work for shuts down (CRASH), your job, your security gone, shouldn't there be a law to give you and your community 60-days notice?
"60 Days Notice Of Plant Closings?" with Bush's picture to left and Quayle's picture on right. A "NO" Stamp appears on frame.	George Bush says no (CRASH). And Dan Quayle led the fight in the Senate against making it a law.
Scenes of Dukakis talking with men in hard hats.	But understanding a community's needs is what Michael Dukakis is all about. That's why he passed one of the first laws in the country providing notification of plant closings. And that's one
Bentsen with Dukakis with workers. "Who care about your life? Dukakis/Bentsen"	reason he chose Lloyd Bentsen, a man who won the fight to make 60-days notification law, who cares about your life. The choice is clear."

The direct comparison ad is one that directly names or shows the opposition; it contrasts positions and records with the sponsor's candidate clearly being shown as superior.

The Implied Comparison

Implied comparison ads do not name opposition candidates either specifically or euphemistically, and in some instances may not feature the sponsoring candidate (party or PAC) until the very end (i.e., tag). These ads detail the sponsoring candidate's position, record, or some other characteristic that has become important to the campaign, but do not mention the opponent. Implied comparison ads lure the viewer into making the comparison between candidates for themselves. Implied comparison ads are not negative in and of themselves, but the public's interpretation of them that give them their negative character (see discussion, Diamond & Bates, 1988; Jamieson, 1984; Schwartz, 1976). And in this cognitive process rests their power, for they force upon the viewer a deductive analysis that stirs an internal dialogue that leaves them a learned experience residue. One advantage of the implied comparison ad is that it appears as if the sponsor-candidate is not running a negative campaign. The negative aspects are supplied by the viewer. According to one Democratic consultant, Karl Struble, the most powerful negative political ads are these "subtle ones, the ones that seduce us" (New Campaign Techniques, 1986, p. 31; see also, Schwartz, 1972). Copeland and Johnson-Cartee (1990b) found that the indirect comparison spot created statistically significant decreases in the targeted candidate's evaluation scores and targeted candidate's voting preference scores while elevating the sponsoring candidate's evaluation scores and the sponsoring candidate's voting preference scores.

Unlike direct attack ads and comparison ads, the implied comparison ad uses the deductive approach, specifically the enthymeme, in that the audience must usually supply the primary premise of who the opposition candidate is and how that candidate is being criticized. Clearly, the use of the implied comparison ad assumes that the viewer has knowledge of the candidate's various politicial positions, background, record, character, and so forth. It is this political information base that is tapped by the ad. And within that base, the comparison is made. Because of this, the successful use of implied comparison ads dictates that they not be used unt'' both candidates have been identified clearly in the campaign. Implied comparison ads are rarely used in low-involvement, low-visibility electoral contests such as state and congressional district contests, "since the voter's knowledge about the candidate is far less complete than at the presidential level" (Sabato, 1981, p. 172). However, if the race's visibility is unusually significant for the level of the election, then implied comparison ads are used.

Necessarily, implied comparison ads should be preceded by supportive or reinforcing communication messages. Previous direct attack, direct comparison ads, speeches, press releases, interviews, news media reports, and so forth should set the stage for the implied comparison ad. In this way, the viewers have the necessary political history to make the comparison on their own.

Frequently, campaign issues are constructed on the basis of determining what the opponent stands for and then determining which of these stands the candidate can capitalize on by diametrically opposing it. This involves a comparison of the voters' viewpoints with the opponent's positions. Any discrepancy is fertile ground for the development of an important campaign issue. Candidates work to point out the disparity between what their opposition stands for and how the people feel through advertising and the news media. Tarrance (1982) termed this technique "the rational cross-pressuring" (p. 2) approach. Without the appearance of a negative redundancy, this disparity may then be reinforced over and over again through an implied comparison ad.

Academicians have failed to consider the implied comparison ad as negative political advertising, because it may focus either on the candidate-sponsor or on a political theme and it does not name the opponent. It is ironic that the most famous American political ad is a negative implied comparison ad. In 1964, the Johnson campaign wanted to produce a spot that suggested if Goldwater became president the chances of nuclear war became much greater. Johnson's advertising agency, Doyle Dane Bernback, went to Democratic advertising consultant Tony Schwartz for help. The result was the "Daisy" ad.

The 1964 Johnson "Daisy" Ad

VIDEO	AUDIO
Fade up on little girl in field of flowers; She picks petals off a daisy.	Little girl [SOF]: "One, two, three, four, five, seven, six, six, eight, nine, nine—"
Girl appears startled; freeze frame on girl; Blow up into ECU of the pupil of her eye.	Man's voice, very loud as if heard over a loudspeaker at a test site [VO]: "Ten, nine, eight, seven, six, five, four, three, two, one—"
Dissolve into atom bomb explosion. CU of explosion.	Sound of explosion.
	Johnson [VO]: "These are the stakes— to make a world in which all of God's children can live, or to go into the dark. We must either love each other, or we must die."
Cut to white letters on black background: "Vote for Johnson on November 3."	Announcer [VO]: "Vote for President Johnson on November 3. The stakes are too high for you to stay home."

The "Daisy" spot is considered a classic in political advertising and deserves some close examination. This remarkable spot "ran only once, on NBC's "Monday Night at the Movies" on the night of September 7. According to Bill Moyers, the White House switchboard, 'lit up with calls protesting it, and Johnson called me and said, "Jesus Christ, what in the world happened?" and I said,

"You got your point across, that's what." He thought a minute and said, "Well, I guess we did" ' " (Diamond & Bates, 1988, p. 129). Over 50 million people saw the ad on NBC (Diamond & Bates, 1988), and all three network newscasts ran the ad in its entirety on Tuesday night (Jamieson, 1984).

Notice that Goldwater is never mentioned or shown in the advertisement. Rather, Johnson tells how he views nuclear war. And by doing so, the viewers within themselves make the comparison with Goldwater. As Schwartz (1972) explained, "The commercial *evoked* a deep feeling in many people that Goldwater might actually use nuclear weapons. This mistrust was not in the *Daisy* spot. It was in the people who viewed the commercial. The stimuli of the film and sound evoked these feelings and allowed people to express what they inherently believed" (p. 93). According to Schwartz, television is uniquely suited "for surfacing feelings voters already have, and giving these feelings a direction by providing stimuli which may evoke the desired behavior" (Schwartz, 1976 p. 351).

Much of what academicians classify as positive advertising is in reality implied negative advertising. On the surface, it may appear positive: The candidate talks about what he or she believes in or what he or she supports. But, according to Newsom, Scott, & Turk (1989), it must be remembered that "the purpose of a persuasive communication is often concealed, becoming apparent only after careful examination. The examination of the obvious content compared with its intent" (p. 176) is essential. When the political ad is constructed in such a way that it sets up a clear contrast between candidates and taps latent uncertainties within the viewer concerning the opposition, the ad should be considered a negative implied comparison ad. The classification error is made because ads are frequently analyzed outside the context of the political race. Researchers often do not have the political history/background necessary for them to perceive how the ad taps the viewer's own political imagery.

Implied Negative Tags. The tag is the optional closing line(s) that identifies the sponsor and usually directs the voter to do something; for example, "Vote for John Brown on November 7th." The tag may serve as an important element in the political commercial for a number of reasons. First of all, in many ads, it is one of the few clues that a viewer is watching a political commercial. In addition, tag lines may be more effective than commonly thought; social science research has shown that persuasion is more likely to succeed if we say directly what it is that we want the audience to do (Cutlip, Center, & Broom, 1985). Further, research has indicated that the beginning and ending of a commercial have the greatest impact on the viewers (Calder, 1978; Chestnut, 1980).

A tag is usually a directive (Searle, 1976) or "an imperative request for action" (Sanford & Roach, 1987, p. 2). But, in some instances, the tag may be more than the simple imperative request. Tags may serve as declarative statements that present an implied negative comparison by contrasting the positive attributes of the sponsor with the attacked negatives of the opponent; for example, "Richard Shelby for U.S. Senate — Leadership we *can* be proud of." Some tags are used as fear appeals that add a sense of urgency to the closing statement; for example, "On Tuesday, vote like our world is at stake" (the 1984 Mondale presidential tag), or "The stakes are too high for you to stay at home" (the 1964 Johnson presidential tag). In those two cases, the tag served as a fear appeal. And in some situations, the tag itself positions the sponsor: "Vote Democratic. The party for you — not just the few" (the 1956 Stevenson presidential campaign). In other situations, the tag makes the audience and the candidate into a team that will stand up for America; for example, "For *real* leadership in the '60s, *help* elect Senator John F. Kennedy President."

Some campaigns use more than one tag depending on the type of ad being used and its placement during the campaign season. In a 1986 U.S. Senate race in Alabama, two tags were used for the positive polispots: "Richard Shelby: A New Force For Alabama" and "Richard Shelby: A Senator For Us." In the negative ads, the Shelby team presented his opponent, incumbent Senator Jeremiah Denton, as being out of touch with Alabama. Another tag was used in the implied and direct comparison ads: "Richard Shelby — A Senator for Us." And the direct attack spots ended with the question: "Don't we deserve someone who's in touch with us?" However, by the last weeks of the campaign, the direct attack spots had changed to a tag that was also used with the positive ads: "Richard Shelby: A Senator For Us."

Although the tag may serve as an integral part of a negative political ad, it should not be analyzed as a part of the argumentation mode of the ad copy. The tag serves as a sidebar to the ad, an old appendage of the hard sell that remains with us. Frequently, the tag appears at an incongruous interruption to the negative ad story line. For this reason, tag lines should be analyzed apart from the thematic story lines that they accompany. We only comment on tag lines when they make an unusual or particularly effective sidebar to the ad.

In 1980, Robert Goodman, owner of The Robert Goodman Agency, a Republican political consultant, presented a George Bush spot that indirectly compares Bush's varied political background with the Democratic incumbent Jimmy Carter and his Republican primary opponents such as Ronald Reagan. The recurring phrase, "this time," evokes the disappointments associated with the Carter administration. The declarative tag lines act as reinforcers to the central theme of the ad: "a president we won't have to train — *This* time."

The 1980 Bush "President in Training" Spot

VIDEO	AUDIO
Bush in an enthusiastic crowd.	Announcer [VO]: "This time, Americans have seen the

opportunities of the 1980s – for the country and for the world. This time, there'll be no replays of the past. This time, there is George Bush.

A crowd gives Bush a standing ovation; Bush and his wife Barbara shaking hands with supporters.

George Bush has emerged from the field of presidential candidates because of what he is – a man who has proven that he can do the tough jobs and lead this country.

White letters against blue background: "GEORGE BUSH FOR PRESIDENT."

George Bush – a president we won't have to train. This time."

The 1984 Reagan campaign's Hal Riney developed the "Tuesday Team's Bear," which proved to be similar to the "Daisy" ad in persuasive technique (Diamond & Bates, 1985, 1988). This is an example of an indirect comparison ad using the metaphor of the bear to represent the Union of Soviet Socialist Republics.

The 1984 Reagan "Bear" Ad

VIDEO

AUDIO

A grizzly bear walks across a mountain ridge, crosses a stream, weaves through underbrush. A drum taps like a heartbeat; Oppressive music.

Announcer [VO]: "There's a bear in the woods. For some people the bear is easy to see.

The bear walks along the ridge. The bear looks up, listens. It stops suddenly and then it takes a step backward. The frame enlarges to show a man standing several yards away; The man carries a rifle. The man is silhouetted.

Others don't see it at all. Some people say the bear is tame. Others say it is vicious and dangerous. Since no one can really be sure who's right, isn't it smart to be as strong as the bear?

If there is a bear."

Graphic: "President Reagan:
Prepared for Peace."

Nowhere in the ad is Mondale's perceived weakness in foreign policy discussed; it was left to the viewer to draw such a conclusion. The Soviet Union
is not mentioned directly, though the bear is a national symbol for the Soviet
Union just as the eagle is for the United States. But, the ad evokes those feelings about the Soviet Union and Mondale in the viewers. The production cost
for this ad was about $80,000, but for that price the Republicans got an ad
that had over a 75% recall rate.

SITUATIONAL ANALYSIS AND THE SELECTION
OF NEGATIVE ARGUMENTATION MODES

Political communication professionals must take a number of factors into account when assessing the pros and cons of the three argumentation modes (a)
electoral setting, (b) the candidate status, (c) the political party status, (d) candidate style, (e) target group characteristics, and (f) negative ad repetition acceptance factors (see Table 2.2).

TABLE 2.2
Determining an Effective Negative Political Advertising Strategy

Situational Analysis	
Electoral Setting:	election level; visibility level; cultural variations
Candidate Status:	incumbent, challenger, or open seat
Political Party Status:	party affiliation; majority/minority party status
Candidate Style:	terse or prolix; effect modeling or contrasting; hot or cool; closed or open; unique style characteristics, including but not limited to the woman candidate
Target Group Characteristics:	demographics
Repetition Acceptance Indicators:	production resources evaluation

Electoral Setting

Political campaigns have different characters depending on the level of the
electoral contest. The campaign setting "determines many things about the contest itself—the amount of money spent, the campaign resources available, the
comprehensiveness of organization, and so forth" (Nimmo, 1970, p. 30). The
level of the campaign determines to some extent the degree of campaign visibility and the amount of voter involvement. Thus we can expect presidential
campaigns to be dissimilar to congressional campaigns, just as congressional
campaigns are dissimilar to district attorney races.

High/Low-Involvement Elections

Rothschild (1978) made three generalizations concerning electoral race involvement:

1. National races are more involving than local races, whereas state races have the lowest level of involvement.
2. Close races are more involving than one-sided races.
3. Volatile issues and candidates tend to make races more involving. (p. 61)

Kern (1989) argued that negative campaigns may make voters more involved and may actually increase voter turnout.

Two Cognitive Political Advertising Models

Political advertising research has developed two models to explain the cognitive processes involved in high- and low-involvement races. Ads are structured with the cognitive model appropriate to the electoral setting. High-involvement elections, in other words, those elections where voters have commitments to a given position or "concern with a specific stand on an issue" (Rothschild, 1978, p. 60), may be characterized by *AIDA*. Low-involvement elections, that is, those elections where voters have merely a "concern with the issue" (Rothschild, 1978, p. 60), may be characterized by *AIAD*.

AIDA. Involvement in a campaign is an important consideration in determining how political advertising affects the choice-making process on the part of the potential voter. Ray (1973) suggested that advertising relies on a sequence of decision-making steps on the part of the consumer. The sequence begins at awareness and progresses to final choice. The cognitive steps in this sequence have been represented by the abbreviation AIDA (Attention-Interest-Desire-Action) originally developed by Strong (1925).

The AIDA model best applies to high-involvement situations (usually operationalized as a presidential or some other national campaign) with what Robertson (1976) typified as an active audience. High-involvement audiences go through a process of a change in beliefs, then in attitudes, and then in action.

AIAD. Ray (1973) noted that the steps are different for low-involvement cases. Krugman (1965-1966) suggested that the order of the steps differed for the low-involvement group as compared to the high-involvement audience. Rather than first a change in beliefs, then in attitudes, and finally in action, Krugman deduced that the steps were beliefs, actions, and then attitudes (or Awareness-Interest-Action-Desire, AIAD). In this view, attitudes change to be consistent with behaviors.

Political Advertising Effectiveness. The effectiveness of political advertising will be strongest in low-level and local races such as primary elections, nonpartisan races, and races for state positions and campaigns for the House of Representatives (Kitchens & Stiteler, 1979; Rothschild, 1975; Wanat, 1974).

Rothschild (1975) tested the effectiveness of political advertising for high- and low-involvement races in an experimental setting and discovered that political advertising did have a greater impact for the low-involvement races (see also, Rothschild & Ray, 1974). Swinyard and Coney (1978) conducted a field experiment for high- and low-involvement races and came to the same conclusion. The evidence is convincing that political advertising is much more powerful in low-involvement races. Similar findings have been reported by a number of researchers (Grush, McKeough, & Ahlering, 1978; Hofstetter & Buss, 1980; Hofstetter, Zukin, & Buss, 1978; McClure & Patterson, 1974). Swinyard and Coney suggested the power of political advertising for influence in low-involvement races is because "voters in high-level races question, defend against, and otherwise counterargue against promotions, [and thus] they are able to protect themselves from much promotional influence" (p. 47).

Low/High-Visibility Races

The campaign setting has a great deal to do with the type of campaign that is waged. Primary elections, run-off elections, and nonparty elections are particularly influenced by political advertising because the political party does not serve as a cue to the voter. Candidates must in effect distinguish themselves from those who are generally similar to themselves. The task before them is an extraordinary positioning problem. Recently, negative campaigns have been used quite effectively in drawing distinctions and in positioning the candidates in such a way as to suggest there exists a real choice. Implied comparison ads are rarely used in primary, run-off, or nonparty elections because generally the field of candidates is larger, and the voters know less about these individual candidates than in a traditional, party-contested general election.

Low-visibility elections with low voter involvement also are influenced heavily by political advertising, because it is likely that very little news space will be devoted to these elections. These elections generally are characterized as being low in general campaign resources and financing. For this reason, some political consultants have suggested that negative political advertising is a cheap, effective means of getting out the message in these situations. Many consultants believe it is easier and more effective to say something negative about the opposition than it is to say something positive about the sponsoring candidate (see Nugent, 1987). Implied comparison ads are rarely used in low-visibility elections because there is not enough information base from which the audience can make the comparison.

In contrast, general elections for high-level, high-visibility offices can use implied comparative ads quite effectively. This is primarily true for two reasons. First, the primary/caucus season has acquainted the voters to some degree with the political candidates. And second, the news media by this time has likely covered the candidates over a number of campaign months. Thus the voter information base is much higher for these types of elections. Implied comparison ads will be naturally suited to an incumbent's campaign under these conditions (see following discussion).

Cultural Variations

In addition to the type of electoral race, professional political communicators (either political consultants or advertising specialists) must take into consideration the political culture associated with the electoral setting. There are regional, state, and local variations as to the public's expectations concerning appropriate election campaign behavior. Various political cultures exhibit greater or lesser degrees of tolerance for the introduction of negative political advertising (see Johnson-Cartee & Copeland, 1989a). Political campaigns must be sensitive to the voters' perceptions of fair play in their given constituencies (Johnson & Copeland, 1987; see also, Boddewyn & Marton, 1978).

Candidate Status

Candidate status, that is, whether the candidate is an incumbent, a challenger, or running in an open seat, has a significant impact on the campaign plan. Weaver-Lariscy and Tinkham (1987), in their survey of 1982 congressional candidates, found that "advertising media expenditure and allocation strategies vary significantly among types of campaigns: incumbent, challenger, and open-race" (p. 13). They recommended that incumbents should spend less on newspapers, radio, and outdoor advertising because "disproportionate spending in these media is negatively related to percentage of vote" (p. 20). And challengers should spend more of their dollars in the broadcast media. Weaver-Lariscy and Tinkham concluded that "not only are all campaigns not alike, but different situations call for different strategic decisions" (p. 20).

Goldenberg and Traugott, in their 1984 study of congressional elections, found three truisms associated with candidate status and campaign finance: "incumbents spend more than challengers, that candidates in open races spend even more than incumbents, and that the costs of campaigning have been increasing" (p. 78). Reid and Soley (1983) found that advertising expenditures had "a more positive effect for challengers than incumbents" (p. 49).

Trend and Friedenberg (1983) and Goldenberg and Traugott (1984) demonstrated that incumbents and challengers view their races in different ways. Incumbents are more sensitive to their attentive public, for they have been in contact with identified groups, individuals who fell into both supporting and opposing camps during their term of office. In addition, incumbents view their base of support as being much broader than challengers. Our political system is based on compromise and negotiation. And incumbents have had the experience of healing wounds and making friends in "enemy" camps during their terms of office. Thus, incumbents' party affiliations are not the only determining factor in describing candidates' coalitions of support. Incumbents view their incumbency as an advantage and they intend to use it as such. As Trent and Friedenberg explained, incumbents seek to dramatize their "incumbency status" (p. 84) by showing that they are "good enough for the office sought" (p. 84) while still possessing the office. They do this by surrounding themselves with the symbolic trappings of the office (Trent & Friedenberg, 1983), by taking advantage of the perquisites of political office (Cover, 1977), by the news media's willingness to report on incumbents (Robinson, 1981b), and by maximizing goodwill through constituency service (Fiorina, 1977). Since the 1940s, House of Representative incumbents have been reelected more than 90% of the time (Ornstein, Mann, Malbin, Schick, & Bibby, 1986). Senate incumbents have not faired as well. Return rates in the 1970s dropped to around 50%. In 1986, the return rate was 75% (see Goldenberg & Traugott, 1987).

Challengers, on the other hand, use the power of the campaign purse to nullify the advantages of incumbency (see Goldenberg & Traugott, 1984; Jacobson, 1980). And, they stress their personal characteristics and issue positions in their campaign communications (Goldenberg & Traugott, 1984). According to Trent and Friedenberg (1983), the challenger style "can be defined as a series of communication strategies designed to persuade voters that a change is needed and that the challenger is the best person to bring about the change" (p. 105) and is accomplished in a variety of ways:

1. attacking the record of opponents;
2. taking the offensive position on issues;
3. calling for a change;
4. emphasizing optimism for the future;
5. speaking to traditional values rather than calling for value changes;
6. appearing to represent the philosophical center of the political party;
7. and, delegating personal or harsh attacks in an effort to control demagogic rhetoric. (p. 106)

Clearly, the challenger style frequently will utilize negative political advertising that attacks an opponent's record and tries to establish the campaign debate agenda. Kaid and Davidson (1986) found the challengers produce the majority of negative ads in political campaigns; their study of political advertising from the 1982 U.S. Senate races revealed that 46% of challenger ads used an "opposition-negative focus" (p. 196), whereas only 10% of incumbent ads could be classified as such. Trent and Friedenberg (1983) and Kitchens and Stiteler (1979) found that challenger campaigns can be characterized by the negative attacks against the incumbent's record. We can expect challengers to take advantage of the halo effect by appearing in direct comparison ads with their opposition. Comparative advertising research has suggested that newcomers, that is challengers, benefit from appearing with the more familiar incumbent, because a "status conferral" takes place (see Boddewyn & Marton, 1978, p. 153; Prasad, 1976, p. 128; see also, chapter 1).

As we previously discussed, negative attacks should be phrased so they appear as rational claims that can be critically validated through normal evidential procedures. This is true for both challengers and incumbents. Emotional appeals should be avoided, especially against a popular incumbent, because research has shown that comparison advertising that uses emotional appeals, particularly against a popular brand, is not as successful as that based on factual, verifiable claims targeted toward the needs and concerns of the target audience (see chapter 1; see also, Boddewyn & Marton, 1978; Devlin, 1981; Goodwin & Etgar, 1980).

Although negative political advertising traditionally has been associated with political candidates who are behind in a political race (i.e., challengers or unpopular incumbents), it may be time to revise this long-held political axiom. First of all, the research has examined negative advertising only in the form of a direct attack spot. Clearly, implied negative advertising does not fit these limited definitions of negative political advertising. Incumbents have used implied negative ads in order to subtly compare themselves favorably to their opposition. In this way, the incumbent appeared above the fray of "dirty politics" and remained in a lofty, statesmanlike position while using the persuasive advantage of negative political advertising. It is likely that the incumbent's actual use of negative advertising has been underreported. Thus the old adage, that "negative ads are for the desperate and the weak at heart," may well be the result of faulty operationalization of the negative political advertising construct.

In addition, as negative political advertising has matured, we have seen an increased growth in the number of incumbents who have boldly ventured into the more obvious forms of negative ads, direct attack and direct comparison. Many voters do not perceive direct comparison ads as being negative, because they are viewed as presenting two sides of the question. Therefore, both implied comparison and direct comparison ads may well serve the incumbent's purpose of staying above politics yet remaining a master of it.

Incumbents frequently utilize increasingly sophisticated counterattacks, particularly after a heavy siege from the challenger's camp. It is in the counterattack position that we are likely to find incumbents utilizing the direct attack ad. Incumbents have learned that mud sticks if you do not get it off, fast (see chapter 6).

Political Party Status

John Kingdon (1968) found that Democratic and Republican candidates differ in their campaign strategies. Democrats address labor-oriented coalitions and tend to make liberal issue appeals. Republicans address business-oriented coalitions and tend to make conservative issue appeals (see Goldenberg & Traugott, 1984; Kingdon, 1968). Although the Republicans have had control over the White House for 17 of the past 21 years, the Democrats have maintained control over the House and Senate (except for 1980–1986 when the Republicans had a Senate majority). And obviously, there are more Democratic incumbents than Republican incumbents (see Goldenberg & Traugott, 1984). For these reasons, Republican candidates tend to use more broadly targeted appeals than do Democratic candidates (Goldenberg & Traugott, 1984). This is true even though the parties are virtually tied in terms of party identification with each party maintaining a steady 33% of the voters (see Gilligan, 1988). Republican candidates usually spend more than their Democratic counterparts in congressional elections, and they also are more likely to emphasize television advertising (Goldenberg & Traugott, 1984; Hershey, 1974).

Party-Related Negative Ad Strategies

Candidates and their advertising advisers should choose negative advertising strategies (argumentation modes) only after a careful analysis of party strengths and weaknesses. Direct attack, direct comparison, and implied comparison ads are used more effectively only after such a careful analysis.

Candidates who face an election with a significant number of independent voters who are predisposed to the candidate's political party may do well to employ direct comparison ads. Research has shown that direct comparison ads are particularly effective with ticket-splitters (Sabato, 1981). If a political candidate is of the minority party, and it is clear that the race is merely a party "showing," that is, the candidate has no chance of winning, it may do the party/candidate well to avoid the more strident direct attack ads. A party-showing election campaign should wave the flag of the party without creating increased hostility on the part of the opposition party faithful. Traditionally, secure majority party candidates are less likely to utilize negative advertising; however, it may well be that this axiom has changed in much the same way as the incumbent axiom has changed. A well-financed challenger with sophisticated political consulting and a strategically planned negative advertising campaign can spell trouble to the traditionally "safe-seated" party or incumbent (see Kitchens & Stiteler, 1979). It is dangerous for any party or candidate to ignore modern negative political advertising techniques (see chapter 6).

Candidate Style

A candidate's style is the "manner or method enacting or expressing a public character" (Combs, 1980, p. 15). According to Trent and Friedenberg (1983):

> In election campaigns, style can be seen as a blend of what candidates say in speeches, news conferences, interviews, advertisements, brochures, and so on, as well as their nonverbal political acts or behavior, such as kissing babies, wearing funny hats, shaking hands at rallies, waving at crowds from the motorcade, as well as their facial expressions and gestures while answering a question. (p. 71)

As explained by Nimmo (1978), the most general stylistic distinctions are those between "terse or prolix, effect-modeling or contrasting, and hot or cool" (p. 127). If a candidate is talkative, expressive, and verbose, the candidate is said to be prolix. Jesse Jackson is an example of such an individual. If a candidate is concise, succinct, and laconic, he or she is said to be terse. Paul Simon fits this description. Effect modeling "consists of setting an example for an audience to follow" (p. 128). Jimmy Carter gave his energy speech while sitting before a roaring fire in a fireplace and wearing a heavy winter sweater. The message was for the American people to conserve in any way possible; Carter was setting an example for the nation. Effect contrasting "occurs when a political leader distinguishes himself from followers by doing something they cannot, as when presidents bless citizens by striding through crowds shaking hands" (p. 128). A hot style is "one of high definitions" (p. 128), is emphatic, and is often perceived as strident, loud, or raucous. Again, Jesse Jackson is an example of such a style. A cool style is a "low profile" (p. 128), calm, dispassionate presentation. Bruce Babbitt's usual campaign style may be said to be cool. It should be remembered that Burgoon and King (1974) found that people react negatively to intense persuasive styles. Further, low-intensity language (a cool style) has been found to be more persuasive than high-intensity language (a hot style) (Bowers, 1963). In addition to these candidate styles, we should examine rhetorical style, which often is associated with candidate style. As Nimmo (1978) noted, candidates are perceived as being either closed or open. Closed rhetorical styles refer "to the guarded, aloof, effect-contrasting utterances" (p. 129). Richard Nixon used a closed rhetorical style, although in 1968 and 1972 his handlers attempted to soften this style. Open rhetorical styles "are more spontaneous, less programmed, sometimes revealing and even disarming" (p. 129). Jimmy Carter and Ronald Reagan both used open rhetorical styles.

Style-Related Negative Ad Strategies

Some candidates, by nature of their political style, cannot effectively use direct attack negative ads for two reasons: (a) It may violate the candidate's own personal code of conduct, and thus his or her full cooperation in the reinforcement of the negative ads (synchronization) will not be forthcoming, and (b) it may violate the public's expectations of what the candidate would or could do in public life. Some candidates simply are perceived as being too nice to effectively use negative direct attack ads. If they do use them, a violation of type may occur that will ultimately wreak havoc on the campaign (see Goffman, 1959; Johnson, 1984; Klapp, 1964). Direct comparison ads and implied comparison ads are the preferred choices in these situations.

The Special Case of the Woman Candidate. Women are increasingly becoming candidates for public office, and they are no longer the "novelty act" that Pat Schroeder once lamented (as reported in Griffiths, 1985). In the 1986 election, there were 123 women candidates for national or statewide office with 15 woman-versus-woman elections in the United States (Burrell, 1987). Hedlund, Freeman, Hamm, and Stein (1979) categorized previous thinking on the reasons that women have generally stayed out of politics as personality differences, situational factors, and sex role socialization. Ekstrand (1978) concluded from experimental evidence and Hedlund et al. (1979) from survey research that there is a growing acceptance of women as elected officials among the electorate.

The research indicates that there are special considerations to be accounted for as a candidate in women's campaigns and by men who run against them. Declercq, Benze, and Ritchie (1983) reported that, as candidates, women rely more heavily on advertising and particularly television advertising than men. Burrell (1987) found that the average amount of money raised for women was less than for men in the 1984 general election, but that the deficit can be explained by the incumbency factor. Those women running as challengers or in open races on the average raised more money than their men counterparts.

Benze and Declercq (1985) reported that consultants have three concerns about women candidates: (a) Women must appear strong but not too aggressive, (b) women must appear professional, and (c) women must not be too attractive. On this latter point, Mandel (1981) wrote that "not too plain, not too pretty-women must find the perfect in-between in constructing a public image" (p. 38).

In addition, consultants have voiced their concern about using negative political advertising against women. They have feared a backlash against such tactics. However, a number of consultants have used the "toughness" issue in their negative ads against women. And some consultants warned that women candidates had to be careful when they themselves use negative ads. Jamieson

(1988) cautioned women that they must be careful about attacking because they might be considered, "unfeminine, shrill, and nagging" (p. 86). Similarly, Trent and Friedenberg (1983) warned that women should avoid attacking opponents, because the public would perceive them as being "unfeminine, shrill, vicious, nagging, or . . . a 'superbitch' " (p. 115).

Benze and Declercq (1985) compared actual television spots for both men and women candidates. They found that the construction of spots for women were very similar and in some cases identical to spots for men. Kaid, Myers, Pipps, and Hunter (1985), using an experimental situation, reported that men and women make equally favorable impressions when their advertising is set in the same surroundings. Benze and Declercq concluded from their content analysis that men usually stress their toughness whereas women usually stress their compassion. Wadsworth et al. (1987) tested in a laboratory experiment whether female candidates would be penalized for pursuing traditionally masculine strategies. Masculine strategies were defined as those styles that exhibited aggression and ambition. Interestingly, the results shows that "an aggressive stance by a female candidate – one where she uses attacks on her opponent – is more desirable than a nonaggressive, passive stance" (Wadsworth et al., 1987, p. 91). In addition, a woman candidate exhibiting a career orientation was evaluated more highly than one who exhibits a family orientation. Clearly, these findings are contrary to traditional beliefs about women candidates and suggest that it is time to reevaluate much of the early research and thinking about women's campaigns. It is quite possible that with the rapid societal changes experienced in the late 1970s and the 1980s and the increasing number of women running for office, society's expectations concerning appropriate woman candidate behavior has changed as well (see Johnson-Cartee, Copeland, & Huttenstine, in press).

Archer and his colleagues (Archer, Kimes, & Barrios, 1978; Archer, Iritania, Kimes, & Barrios, 1983) discovered a propensity for men to be favored when their faces were featured and women when their bodies were seen in photographs and draw-a-person protocols. Adams, Copeland, Fish, and Hughes (1980) concluded from their experimental studies of photographs of candidates that, whereas this framing effect was not as simple as Archer and his colleagues (Archer et al., 1978, 1983) had suggested, registered voters did tend to prefer photographs of candidates that featured the faces of men and more exposure of the body for women. Sparks and Fehlner (1986), in a content analysis of newsmagazine coverage of the 1984 presidential election, found that for Geraldine Ferraro there was no difference between the photographic framing of her and the other presidential ticket candidates.

Target Group-Related Negative Ad Strategies

A target market is "a group of people defined by certain characteristics and focused on as the intended receivers of the advertising message" (Dunn & Barban, 1986, p. 793; see also, Patti & Frazer, 1988). In political campaigning, a target market is a group of people who are eligible to vote or who will be eligible to vote by election day and who are likely to be predisposed toward a particular candidate and/or party because of their demographic and psychographic characteristics.

As Weiss (1966) noted, research has shown that "one-sided presentations" (p. 130), that is, direct attack ads, are more effective in reinforcing the less educated. On the other hand, "two-sided presentations" (p. 130), or direct comparison ads, are more effective in converting the highly educated, and these ads will work well in safeguarding against future counterattacks. Implied comparison ads work to evoke stored information, attitudes, and so forth, within the voter. Obviously, the voter must have the stored political information from which to evoke, and therefore the targeted voter needs to be somewhat interested and somewhat educated. In practice, this means that either voters must have been exposed to sufficient campaign information before the implied comparison ad is aired, and/or the implied comparison ad must evoke fundamental political myths shared by the targeted group.

Negative Ad Repetition Acceptance Factors

According to Ray and Sawyer (1971), a great deal of attention has been directed to repetition acceptance factors in product advertising research. "The general nature of the repetition function in advertising appears to be some sort of modified negative exponential curve" (p. 22) that demonstrates at some point the law of diminishing returns. They showed that prolonged repetition of ads devoted to large ticket purchase items, for example, shopping goods (which necessarily have more ego involvement than consumer goods, e.g., foods), does not have much influence on attitudes or purchase intention measures. We believe this finding gives us some clues as to how repetition functions in political advertising, particularly negative political advertising. Specific negative political ads should have a short life span, as in ads for shopping goods. After the initial negative advertising stimulation, voters turn to other sources such as opinion leaders, newspapers, and television news to verify the claims in negative ads, just as consumers verify shopping goods product claims by talking with salespersons or opinion leaders and by reading consumer materials or product brochures. Thus, after the initial learning period of the negative ad exposure period, the ads should be replaced with other ads reinforcing the same theme but with other dramatized examples. This is particularly true for direct attack ads that may appear strident or shrill to some voters. The more often these ads are repeated, the more likely that some voters will react negatively to the ad. Therefore, campaigns with limited financial resources should consider carefully their choice of negative argumentation mode before implementing the production schedule.

In Summary

We have identified three types of negative argumentation positions that the candidate's advertising may take in relation to the candidate's opponent. These argumentation modes used in negative political advertising are called the direct attack, the direct comparison, and the implied comparison. The direct attack mode specifically attacks a political candidate or party. It does not make any comparisons between candidates. The direct comparison mode compares both candidates or parties on their record, experience, background, and so forth. In the direct comparison ad, targeted candidates are identified directly or euphemistically. The implied comparison ad does not identify targeted candidates. The ads are not negative in and of themselves, but rather, it is the public interpretation of those ads that gives them their negative character. Professional political communicators, whether they are national political consultants or local advertising firms with a political specialization, must examine the political situation before embarking on a negative ad campaign. A number of situation factors must be considered before designing the negative advertising strategy: electoral setting, candidate status, party status, candidate style, target group characteristics, and negative ad repetition acceptance factors.

MANIFEST AND LATENT SYMBOLOGY

In order to understand the political symbols used to construct negative political advertising, we must first examine manifest and latent symbology.

Political Symbols

Burke (1950) and Arnold (1972) defined rhetoric in highly similar ways. For Burke, rhetoric is "the use of the words by human agents to form attitudes or induce actions in other human agents" (p. 41). And for Arnold, rhetoric is "the process of manipulating symbolic devices for the purpose of gaining one's own or someone else's adherence" (p. 4). For our purposes, we combine the definitions. Thus rhetoric becomes the process of manipulating symbolic devices by human agents to form attitudes or induce actions in other human agents.

Perrucci and Knudsen (1983) defined symbols as the "words, actions, body movements, and visual cues that stand for ideas and objects and to which members of a culture attach similar meanings" (p. 77). Edward Sapir (1934) distinguished between two types of symbols: referential and condensational. A referential symbol indicates "particular or general categories of objects, be those objects physical, social or abstract. . . . Referential symbols have denotative meanings, meanings that link the symbol to its referent" (Nimmo, 1978, p. 68). On the other hand, a condensation symbol is "a highly condensed form of substitutive behavior for direct expression, allowing for the ready release of emotional tension in conscious or unconscious form" (Sapir, 1934, p. 493; see also, Edelman, 1964; Graber, 1976). According to Nimmo (1978), condensational symbols have more connotative meaning than denotative meaning. Political symbols are said to have a mixture of both referential and condensational qualities. Although the use of phrases such as "Ted Kennedy-Democrat" or "Liberal" do refer to a real individual or an abstract political philosophy, the significance of the use of the phrase is not in its referential or symbol-referent attachment, but rather rests with the meanings that reside within individuals that are evoked when the phrases are used. Mead (1934) called condensation symbols that are "commonly salient across individuals" (Cobb & Elder, 1972, p. 80), "significant symbols" (pp. 71-72).

The use of such highly condensed, significant symbols in negative political advertising is very important. Simply put, political advertising consultants are able to telegraph a wealth of meaning by the use of condensational symbols, which have been developed through experience over a long period of time. As McGee (1980) put it, "Human beings are 'conditioned,' not directly to belief and behavior, but to a vocabulary of concepts that function as guides, warrants, reasons, or excuses for behavior and belief" (p. 6).

Resonance Strategy

Schwartz (1972, 1976) called an advertising strategy that takes advantage of condensational symbols to evoke meaning in the voter the resonance strategy. Such a strategy selects persuasive messages that are "harmonious with the experience of the audience" (Patti & Frazer, 1988, p. 301; see also, Schwartz, 1976). Campaign messages must resonate "with information already stored within an individual and thereby induces the desired learning or behavioral effect. Resonance takes place when the stimuli put into our communication evoke *meaning* in a listener or viewer" (Schwartz, 1972, pp. 24-25). The political consultant is the one who usually works to discover the political/cultural myths that are shared by groups of voters and that can be evoked by mass-mediated messages that strike the responsive chords within voters (Combs, 1979; Schwartz, 1972, 1976; see also, Nimmo & Combs, 1980). Diamond and Bates (1988) suggested that, by striking these chords, consultants and candidates attempt to reach the "inner core" (p. 115) of the voter's psyche. Democratic political consultant, Robert Squier, called these responsive chords, "hot buttons" (Squier, 1987; see also, Diamond & Bates, 1988, p. 7). According to Squier, "once those buttons are pushed, I know I've got them. I've touched their emotions." Schwartz (1976) concluded: "Commercials which attempt to tell the listener something are inherently not as affective as those which attach to something that is already in him. We are not focused on getting things across to people as much as *out* of people" (p. 352).

Significant Symbols

Significant symbols may appear in the form of both manifest and latent content (Freud, 1952; see also, Hale & Mansfield, 1986; Nimmo & Combs, 1983; Nimmo & Felsberg, 1986). Befo· e we examine the distinction between what Freud described as manifest content (or that which is obvious, easily perceived, on the surface) and what he termed latent content (or the underlying meaning, present but not obvious, hidden), we first turn to the work of Saussure (1966). Saussure suggested that in order to understand semiology, we must understand that symbols have three-fold dimensionality: the signs, the signifiers, and the signified. The signifiers are the letters, characters, drawings, or sounds that stand for something that exists in the world. The signified on the other hand are the referents, or those physical objects, events, places, people, things, ideas, concepts, and so forth that exist in the world. The sign is the combination of both the signifier and the signified. Saussure's analysis pointed out the importance of the totality of the symbolic device. We cannot separate the signifier from the signified. We must consider the sign in its totality, the totality of the context.

According to Saussure (1966), we cannot hope to understand the meaning of symbols without analyzing the social and linguistic context in which they exist. Leymore (1975) and Nimmo and Felsberg (1986) emphasized the importance of analyzing advertising symbols in their contextual environment. With regard to product advertising, Nimmo and Felsberg wrote: "It is not sufficient, for instance, to analyze a single ad for a product or brand in isolation, either from other ads for that product or brand or in isolation from competing products or brands. All ads in the same product field must be included in the analysis" (p. 251).

When we analyze verbal behavior in politics, Graber (1976) asserted that we must use a situational context analysis; that is, we must examine the "total societal context in which communication occurred, an evaluation of each of the communicators and of their interactions, and judgments concerning the long-term and short-term objectives of the communication" (p. 101). This type of approach employs an educated "intuitive" (p. 100) strategy. By examining the thematic consistencies "displayed in concrete verbal and visual methods" (Nimmo & Felsberg, 1986, pp. 253-254) and then by considering these consistencies in their situational context, we are able to decode political advertising, that is, transform latent symbols into manifest symbols. As Breen and Corcoran (1982) explained, "The story is often made meaningful only when its manner of encoding interlocks with the perceptual process supplied by the viewer [the perceived situational context], which is itself culturally mediated" (p. 128). Cobb and Elder (1972) elaborated, "Because individual symbolic orientations are necessarily a function of an individual's socialization and life experiences, differences in symbolic orientations are likely to cluster in either an additive or an interactive way along standard demographic dimensions which provide indices of common socialization, life experiences, and patterns of signification" (p. 85).

A situational analysis of concrete signifiers found in political advertising will ultimately reveal the candidate/consultant's perception of the political symbology of various target groups. Cobb and Elder (1972), through their analysis and testing of work done by Parsons and Shils (1951) and Smelser (1963), developed a hierarchical typology of political symbols: "(1) symbols of the political community or core values; (2) regime symbols or symbols relating to political norms; (3) symbols associated with formal political roles and institutions; and (4) situational symbols to include (a) governmental authorities, (b) non-governmental personalities and groups, and (c) political issues" (p. 85; cf. Gold, 1980; Nimmo & Combs, 1980). Those symbols located "higher in the typology tend to be the most abstract and general, while those lower in the scheme tend to be more specific and concrete" (p. 86). Political scientists have long noted that there is more consensus concerning the more abstract notions of freedom, equality, and liberty than in the more specific applications of these terms, such as whether an individual would allow a Communist, a woman, or a Black to become president of the United States (see Cobb & Elder, 1972; for other examples, see Walker, Lindquist, Morey, & Walker, 1968). Whether the symbols used are abstract or specific, it is important to remember that both manifest and latent political symbols are powerful in their impact.

George Wallace, longtime governor of Alabama and frequent presidential candidate, was a master of the use of latent political symbols. Wallace frequently used the symbolic phrase "states' rights" in his public appearances, writings, and political advertising; however, "states' rights" meant more to Wallace and Wallace supporters than the political construct that states should maintain their individual sovereignty when functioning as a part of a federation of states. "States' rights" was a euphemism for segregation. Wallace and his supporters were fighting the federal court-mandated integration of schools, buses, neighborhoods, restaurants, and so on. According to Makay (1970), The Alabama governor "spoke in a kind of code" (p. 172); that is, Wallace used latent political symbols. Makay recounted a statement that was supposed to have been said by an Alabama state senator: Wallace "can use all other issues – law and order, running your own schools, protecting property rights – and never mention race. But people will know he is telling them 'a nigger's trying to move into your neighborhood' " (p. 172).

TEMPORAL DIRECTIONALITY

When examining negative political ads, it is clear that the ads deal with events that have happened in the past, the present, or may happen in the future. They look either backward or forward. This temporal directionality of negative attacks either compares contrasts, and/or implies that the opponent has either done something in the past or is doing something in the present, with plans to continue doing it in the future, with which the candidate's campaign disagrees. Thus we can characterize attacks as prospective attacks (looking to the future to something that may be done) or retrospective attacks (looking backward to things that have been done) (see Joslyn, 1986).

Prospective Attacks

A prospective attack criticizes the opposition's stated intentions if elected. In terms of direction of time, it deals with tomorrow, the future. This technique frequently is used against challengers, those who are opposing an incumbent, who are trying to position themselves by declaring future intent.

Fear Arousal

Americans have viewed their world with "remarkable stability" over the years. They continue to say, as Nimmo (1978) put it, their primary personal fears concern "their standard of living, economic well-being, and physical health" (p. 271); and their primary concerns for the nation include "peace and war," "economic stability and instability," "national unity and disunity," and "prosperity and lack of prosperity" (p. 271). Political consultants understand these personal and national fears, and they often capitalize on them by using fear-inducing techniques.

Many of the prospective ads use a fear-inducing tactic that suggests if the opponent is elected, he or she would do things that the voter would judge to be disastrous for the collectivity (i.e., nation, state, city) as well as for the voter's immediate family. Charges that a candidate would do away with social security, aid to dependent children, and so forth create this type of anxiety.

Although the academic research concerning fear-arousal communications is mixed (Burgoon & Bettinghaus, 1980; see also, Nimmo, 1978), political consultants frequently resort to this technique. Little consensus exists among academicians as to the basic effectiveness of fear appeals or as to the effectiveness of specific types or degrees of fear appeals.

Much of both product fear-appeal and political fear-appeal advertising is based on two early studies: Janis and Feshback (1953) and Colburn (1967). Janis and Feshback found that low-level fear appeals were more successful in terms of persuasion than high-level fear appeals. However, Colburn found that high-level fear appeals may be effective when communicating to groups who regard the topic at hand as being highly salient. Thus a high-level fear appeal suggesting that Candidate X supported the dismantling of social security might be particularly effective in persuading the elderly.

In 1986, Mark White, the Texas Democratic candidate for governor, ran a direct attack-prospective-fear-arousal ad against gubernatorial candidate, Bill Clements.

The 1986 White "Cuts" Ad

VIDEO	AUDIO
Black and White Screen "Paid by Governor Mark White Committee:	
Elderly man with grocery bag.	Narrator [VO]: "Bill Clements says he would cut the budget. But here's where he'd have to cut.
A black rip appears across the elderly man, tear edged in white. "117,000 cut from meal program" appears in tear.	*Our elderly*—117,000 elderly and disabled cut from meal programs.
A blue-collar worker in a hard hat. Tear goes across face. "22,000 cut in road jobs" appears in tear.	*Our workers*—22,000 jobs cut in road construction.
Little girl. Tear goes across face. "Cutbacks in education" appears.	*Our children*—Cutbacks in the new education program.
Elderly lady. Tear across face.	Medical care for the elderly—CUT.
Little girl with glasses. Tear across face.	Eyeglasses for kids and seniors—CUT.
Little boy looking said. Tear across face.	Child abuse programs—CUT.
Picture of Clements with two tears across the screen. "Doesn't He Know?" And "Doesn't He Care?"	The cuts Bill Clements would have to make. Doesn't he know? Or doesn't he care?"

Retrospective Attacks

A retrospective attack addresses what the opponent has done in the past, his or her record and accomplishments. This advertising technique is frequently used to attack incumbents or candidates who have previously held some other political office. Incumbents are particularly susceptible to these types of ads because they have a record in office that a challenger can run against. An example of this technique is an ad that was produced by the National Conservative Political Action Committee (NCPAC) and used against Jimmy Carter in 1980. Carter had appointed a series of individuals who had difficulty with the law and/or the mass media.

The 1980 NCPAC "Why Not The Best" Ad

VIDEO	AUDIO
A black and white photograph of Carter appears on a table.	Announcer [VO]: "In 1976, Jimmy Carter said, "Why not the best?" Let's look at what he gave us.
A photo of Andrew Young appears.	Andrew Young, Carter's UN Ambassador who called Iran's Ayatollah Khomeni "a saint": forced to resign after lying to the president. (Camera clicks as if moving frames.)
A photo of Bert Lance appears.	Bert Lance also forced to resign.
A photo of Peter Borne appears.	Dr. Peter Borne, the Carter drug expert: forced to resign after supplying drugs to a White House staff member.
Photos appear rapidly of: William Miller Cyrus Vance Hamilton Jordan	(Camera clicks quickly as each picture appears and follows.) Announcer: And the list goes on.
The words "Ronald Reagan for President" appear on a blue background.	If you want a president whose judgments you can trust for a change, then vote for Ronald Reagan for President." (Devlin, 1986, p. 54)

In Summary

We can identify negative political advertising is terms of the temporal Directionality used in the ads. Candidates choose either a retrospective or prospective focus. Challengers who have tried to project what they will do if elected are usually attacked with prospective arguments. Frequently, the prospective arguments will use fear-inducing tactics. Incumbents and challengers who have previously held public office are frequently attacked on their record, a retrospective focus.

IN CONCLUSION

Negative political advertising can be viewed as modern-day political short stories. They present, either explicitly or implicitly, age-old conflicts: human versus human, human versus self, human versus fate, and human versus nature. Through the conflict resolution process, the short story arrives at truth. This emergent truth or theme of the political ad is the underlying meaning behind the political messages presented in the ad.

Although we cannot actually separate the various political advertising elements of substance, style, origination, and channel from the synergistic Gestalt communication experience, for purposes of discussion we are artificially separating them in our analysis because of the conventions within the literature. Thus, it will be easier for researchers in the future to integrate our findings with those of other scholars.

In chapter 2, we have been concerned with the substance or the what of negative political ads. We first identified an operationalization controversy surrounding negative political advertising effects research. Political advertising researchers, for the most part, have operationalized negative political advertising in such a way that it only referred to direct attack/direct reference ads. It is suggested that this operationalization has in effect limited the range of possible negative political advertising effects.

As an alternative to this pervasive reductionism, we suggested a broader operationalization of negative political advertising. As Gronbeck (1985) proposed, negative political advertising comes in more than one form. We have identified three argumentation modes used in negative political ads: direct attack, direct comparison, and indirect comparison. These modes of argumentation differ as to the type of logic used (inductive or deductive). In the course of a campaign, different argumentation modes are chosen based on a number of factors: election level, candidate status, party status, and target group characteristics. Different argumentation modes require more or less preadvertising set-up before dissemination. In addition, various advertising modes must be utilized in a media buy in different ways, because repetition tolerances are likely to be different for the various argumentation modes.

Political communication professionals construct negative political ad arguments with various tactics in mind. First, the nature of the significant symbols that will be used must be considered. Significant symbols are the hot buttons or responsive chords that are able to telegraph meaning to people because they are culturally recognized symbols that have been developed over time through the process of societal interaction. Meaning is evoked within people based upon their previous conditioning experiences.

Significant symbols may be presented in manifest and latent content forms. Manifest symbols are those that are obvious and easily perceived. Latent symbols, on the other hand, are present but not as obvious; they are hidden. When using a negative ad that might prove to be offensive to a significant bloc of the audience, the political communication professional may downplay the potential controversial nature of the message by phrasing the message in latent symbols. People who agree with the communicator will pick up on the message even through the message is latent. And people who do not agree with the message will not as likely pick up on it, and if they do, it will not seem as inflammatory as the same message constructed with manifest symbols. When using a negative ad to reinforce the party faithful, a manifest message might be most appropriate.

Ad content may be directed in terms of time. Joslyn (1986) identified two forms of temporal directionality: prospective messages and retrospective messages. Challengers frequently attempt to position themselves on the political spectrum by defining what it is they stand for and what their political agenda would be if elected. This material provides a fertile ground for incumbents looking for something to attack. Incumbents use prospective messages to attack challengers on what they intend to do rather than on what they have done in the past. It must be noted that fear-arousal techniques are frequently associated with these prospective messages. Challengers use retrospective messages against incumbents who have a political track record to criticize. In some situations, retrospective messages are used against challengers who have previously held another elected office.

3

Negative Political Advertising Thematic Designs

THEMATIC DESIGNS

Through the years, a number of standardized thematic designs have emerged in the dissemination of substantive negative arguments. These standardized themes appear as both manifest and latent symbolic constructs in the political messages presented in the negative ads. The thematic design is constructed through the careful management of conflict and conflict resolution in the advertisement. Both political and personal characteristic issue appeals are used in the development of the negative political advertising themes.

In some instances, ads will utilize more than one thematic design, because the advertising consultants may be using complementary or overlapping themes in order to create a powerful persuasive message. When multiple thematic designs are used, we can characterize these ads as being multi-layered thematic ads. Five overarching thematic designs are considered: being your own worst enemy, the people against you, transfer, us against them, and disparagement humor. A variety of thematic subcategories are also explored (see Table 3.1).

Being Your Own Worst Enemy

Sometimes, it seems as if political candidates are their own worst enemies in that the opposition will use the candidates' public performances against themselves. This thematic design demonstrates that the candidates in question do

TABLE 3.1
Negative Political Advertising Thematic Designs

Being Your Own Worst Enemy

Your ad in their negative spots
Your political gaffes
Your political experience
Your political character
Your flip-flops on the issues
Your past promises and your pitiful performances
Your voting record (actual voting or whether you voted)
Your choice for Vice President
Your decision not to debate

The People Against You

The voters turn against you
The home constituency turns against you (voters or newspapers)
The party faithful reject you
Your own party primary opponents attack you

Transfer

Your comrades and supporters
Events that happened on your watch
Historical comparisons
Paid political help

Us Against Them

The Cowboys vs. the Yankees
Us against foreigners
Class warfare
The anti-Washington mentality

Disparagement Humor

---

not have the leadership attributes expected for the ideal candidate. There are a number of different approaches used in this category; we have identified nine types: your ad in their negative spots, your political gaffes, your political experience, your political character, your flip-flops on the issues, your past promises and your pitiful performances, your voting record (actual voting or whether you voted), your choice for vice president, and your decision not to debate. The being your own worst enemy thematic design had become one of the more popular formats for negative ads.

Your Ad in Their Negative Spots. Frequently, consultants will use pieces of the opposition's advertising to attack them. This type of negative ad format relies on the repetition effect for its powerful persuasive appeal. The Democrats in 1956 were the first to develop an ad of this type. Norman, Craig & Kummel was the advertising agency for the Stevenson/Kefauver ticket. The ad used clips from Eisenhower's 1952 advertising campaign that showed Eisenhower making promises to the nation. After each promise, an announcer asked: "How's that again General?" (see Diamond & Bates, 1988). The ad used a combination of "being your own worst enemy" subthemes in that it also utilized the past promises versus pitiful performances negative thematic design.

In 1972, the November Group, a temporary advertising agency created for the sole purpose of electing Richard Nixon, ran a series of short ads that reinforced the themes "you need Nixon," and "Nixon–the man of peace" (Diamond & Bates, 1988). In one of these spots, Nixon tells the story of Tanya, a Russian girl whose family was ravaged by the tides of World War II. Nixon urged America to work for a more peaceful world and called upon the voters to "think of Tanya and of the other Tanyas and their brothers and sisters everywhere. "McGovern retaliated with a radio spot that referred to Nixon's Tanya story and then turned the story against Nixon using Vietnam as the sword. He reminded America that, during Nixon's term, over 165,000 South Vietnamese civilians had been killed by American bombs, and he urged the voters to remember Tanya and all "other defenseless children of the world" (Diamond & Bates, 1988, pp. 200-201; Jamieson, 1984, pp. 316-317).

In 1982 the Missouri Democratic candidate for the Senate, Harriet Woods, attacked Republican candidate, Senator John Danforth on his voting record for social security. Woods took an excerpt from Danforth's own positive ad that positioned him as a strong supporter of social security. The ad was particularly devastating as it was constructed in such a way that viewers thought they were actually watching a Danforth ad well into Wood's spot.

The 1982 Woods "Danforth on Social Security" Ad

VIDEO	AUDIO
John Danforth is seen talking to senior citizens at a picnic.	John Danforth [SOT]: "Social Security is the most important social program that we've ever developed in the United States."
Frame of Danforth and his name. "DANFORTH"	Narrator [VO]: "Danforth. That's what Senator John Danforth says but what are the facts?
Scroll: "The Facts." "Sen. Danforth voted against minimum Social Security Benefits Six Times. 1981"	Fact: Republican John Danforth has voted time after time to cut social security and other programs.

"Sponsored Cuts in Social
Security, 1981-1982"

"Voted to Cut Medicare
and Medicaid. 1982"

"Voted against 'Meals on wheels'
Nutrition Program for the
elderly, 1978."

| Scene of Harriet Woods talking with senior citzens. Black and White: "Harriet Woods for the U.S. Senate." | The choice: Senator Harriet Woods who wrote the Nursing Home Reform Act to protect our elderly. That's the difference. Harriet Woods for the U.S. Senate." |

Your Own Political Gaffes. During the normal political career, politicians will probably suffer from "foot-in-the-mouth disease" more than once. And, when they do, someone is waiting and watching for the gaffe. A political gaffe is the misstatement, malapropism, or use of inappropriate language or show of emotions that is brought to the public's attention by the news media or the opponent's negative advertising. Frequently, political gaffes will come back to haunt the candidate in an opponent's negative ads.

In 1964, Johnson reminded eastern voters that Goldwater had told a reporter, "this country would be better off if we could just saw off the Eastern Seaboard and let it float out to sea" (Jamieson, 1984, p. 179). Humphrey, in 1968, reminded voters of Agnew's claim that "if you've seen one slum you've seen them all" (Jamieson, 1984, p. 30). And, Carter in 1980 reminded voters that Reagan "had blamed most air pollution on trees" (Jamieson, 1984, p. 30).

The Republican presidential candidate in 1964, Barry Goldwater, will probably be remembered as one of the most self-destructive politicians in American history. Goldwater was fond of the rhetorical use of hyperbole, and it frequently got him into trouble. Hyperbole is the extravagant exaggeration used as a figure of speech. Theodore White termed Goldwater's verbel excesses "frontier hyperbole," which he explained was "the genuine literary expression of the Old West" (Jamieson, 1984, p.179). Goldwater's frontier hyperbole did not play well in Peoria or in many other cities in America. Goldwater's public utterances helped his presidential campaign self-destruct before the eyes of millions of Americans.

In 1964, Goldwater's opponent, incumbent President Lyndon Johnson, used a radio ad to inform voters of a series of Goldwater hyperboles and a television ad to reinforce the conclusions drawn from the radio ad (Jamieson, 1984). Radio ads are frequently used when advertising consulants wish to take a more strident tone. Goldwater was quoted as saying about the space race: "I don't want to hit the moon. I just want to lob one into the men's room of the Kremlin (Jamieson, 1984, p. 203). And on nuclear war, Goldwater was quoted as saying: " I don't see how it can be avoided (Jamieson, 1984, p. 203). The tag used a fear appeal that warned voters: "On November 3rd vote for President Johnson. The stakes are too high for you to stay home" (Jamieson, 1984, p. 203).

In the 1980s, Republican Senator Jeremiah Denton became noted for frequent political gaffes. Democratic Congressman Richard Shelby used Denton's misguided comments against the Republican in the 1986 Alabama Senate race. Shelby had a wide range of statements to choose from. In a meeting with a Jasper, Alabama civic group, Denton was asked why he had not come back to Alabama very much since he was elected. Denton angrily replied: "I can't be down here patting babies on the butt and get [things] done in Washington" (Farney, 1986, pp. 1, 20). Congressman Shelby's media adviser, Robert Squier, was able to capture that moment on videotape, and the resulting actuality appeared in a powerful negative spot. In another episode, Denton told a Senate committee that was considering a stronger law against spousal rape that: "Dammit, when you get married, you kind of expect you're going to get a little sex" (Farney, 1986, pp. 1, 20). That too found its way into a Shelby negative spot. And in yet another episode, Denton told the Alabama League of Municipalities that if Blacks "can operate that well on a five man basketball team, they should be able to operate that well in business" (Farney, 1986, pp. 1, 20). That statement led to a rebuke from the *Birmingham Post-Herald*.

The 1986 Shelby "Wife Abuse Insensitivity" Ad

VIDEO	AUDIO
"Wife abuse" appears on screen. Articles are shown with headlines:	Narrator [VO]: "Wife abuse. It's a national tragedy. After years of silent suffering, women
"Wife Abuse: A National Tragedy" "Women Seek Help From U.S. Congress."	are seeking compassion, and Congress is trying to help. But in a recent committee hearing,
Picture of the U.S. Capitol with photo of Denton supered. The words: "Denton on Wife Abuse" in upper left hand corner. Black band comes across screen and Denton's quote appears as it is read.	Senator Jeremiah Denton had this to say about marital abuse: 'When you get married you expect you are going to get a little sex.' That's a direct quote! Imagine that kind of insensitivity from a United

Words appear: "Don't we deserve   States Senator! Don't we deserve
someone who's in touch with us?"   someone who's in touch with us?"

Your Political Experience. Traditionally, incumbents have attacked
challengers on their lack of experience. The attacks suggest that the challengers
are not competent enough to handle the job. In some situations in an open
seat, the more politically experienced candidate will also make this charge.

Perhaps the most devastating political experience ad that was used in an
open-seat race was one that ran for John F. Kennedy in 1960. Senator Kennedy questions Vice President Richard Nixon's experience in government by capturing the comments of Republican President Eisenhower during a press
conference.

The 1960 Kennedy "Ike's Comments" Ad

VIDEO   AUDIO

Richard Nixon sitting on desk.   Narrator [VO]: "Every Republican
                                        politician wants you to believe
                                        that Richard Nixon is, quote,
Barry Goldwater at a podium.   *experienced.* They even want you
                                        to believe that he has actually
                                        been making decisions in the
President Eisenhower addressing   White House. But, listen to the
a news conference.   man who should know best – the
                                        president of the United States.
                                        A reporter recently asked President
                                        Eisenhower this question about
                                        Mr. Nixon's experience:"
CU of Ike as he listens to   Reporter [SOF]: "I just wondered
a question. And he answers it.   if you could give us an example
                                        of a major idea of his that you have
                                        adopted in that role as the
                                        decider and final. . . ."

                                        Eisenhower [SOF]: "If you give me
                                        a week, I might think of one. I
                                        don't remember."

                                        SOF Background Noise: Laughter

Ike addressing press conference.   Eisenhower [SOF] as he pounds
                                        table: "No one can make a decision
                                        but me."

CU of Ike answering question.	Narrator [VO]: "And as for any major ideas from Mr. Nixon. . . ."
	Eisenhower [SOF]: "If you give me a week, I might think of one. I don't remember."
Scene of Kennedy going through crowd, shaking hands. "John F. Kennedy President" Photo of Kennedy on right.	Narrator [VO]: "President Eisenhower could not remember. But the voters *will* remember. For real leadership in the 60s, help elect Senator John F. Kennedy President."

In a 1966 California gubernatorial race, incumbent Governor Pat Brown and Ronald Reagan faced each other in a hotly tested campaign. Brown attacked Reagan for his lack of political experience by airing an ad that showed Reagan appearing in various entertainment roles.

The 1966 Brown "No Experience" Ad

VIDEO	AUDIO
A press conference. (newsreel shot of Reagan as he replied to question by reporter)	Reagan [SOF]: "Um . . . I feel that I have had ah . . . well, if I didn't feel that I'd had experience that qualifies me to seek this job, I wouldn't do it. Now, mine was not in politics."
Old Reagan movie; the actor is dressed in cowboy costume, holding rifle. A man steps forward and Reagan guns him down with a blast from the hip.	Reagan [SOF]: "You wanted law and order in this town, you've got it. I'll shoot the first man who starts for those steps."
Reagan talking in a television commercial. He holds the product as he speaks.	Reagan [SOF]: "And here's exciting new Boraxo waterless hand cleaner. Watch."
Film of old movie with Reagan pushing a mud pie into a man's face.	

Reagan in previous advertisement.	Reagan [SOF]: "New Boraxo water-less hand cleaner removes the tough-est dirt or stains. Gets hands clean and smooth fast anytime. What a convenience. That's new Boraxo waterless hand cleaner."
Reagan in an old movie. Reagan is an ex-convict, talking with a woman in a hotel room.	Reagan [SOF]: "I see beyond this joint. Right through the dirty wallpaper."
Cut to a preview trailer for old Reagan movie; Reagan is in the jungle.	Announcer [SOF]: "Ronald Reagan as the tight-lipped soldier of fortune, whose past was a mystery."
	Narrator [SOF]: "Over the years, Ronald Reagan has played many roles. This year he wants to play governor. Are you willing to pay the price of admission?" (adapted from Rose & Fuchs, 1968, pp. 254–255)

In a 1982 Illinois attorney general's race, Republican Attorney General Ty Fahner attacked his Democratic opponent Neil Hardington on his lack of ex-perience in the crime field. The ad uses a humorous approach.

The 1982 Fahner "Double Doors" Ad

VIDEO	AUDIO
The narrator is standing in front of double doors. On the left, lettering that reads "Research Division." On the right, a sign that reads "Attorney General Ty Fahner Headquarters." The narrator opens the left door.	Narrator [SOT]: "Fighting crime is one of the important jobs of the Illinois Attorney General. So here at the Ty Fahner Campaign Headquarters, we put a researcher to work finding out what experience Fahner's opponent Neil Hardington has in the crime field. What's the record show on Hardington's crime fighting credentials?"
	Off Screen Voice: "NOTHING!"
	Narrator [SOT]: "Nothing?"

Off Screen Voice: "NA-DA!"

Narrator [SOT]: "No experience?"

Off Screen Voice: "ZERO!"

Closes door. Speaks into camera.	Narrator [SOT]: "Well, there you have it. As a crime fighter, Ty Fahner has been federal prosecutor, Illinois state law enforcement director and he's doing a great job as attorney general.
Opens door.	And Hardington?"

Off Screen Voice: "GOOSE EGGS!"

"Fahner
The Crime Fighter"

Your Political Character. Closely related to political experience appeals are ads that deal with three of the most critical elements of a candidate's image: credibility, competency, and honesty. Voters ask themselves, "Can I believe this person?"; "Is this candidate able to do the job? Does the candidate have the judgment to do the work that he or she will be called upon to do?"; and "Will this candidate hold fast to the public trust? Will he or she not violate our trust?" Since the Watergate years, honesty increasingly has become an important part of how voters evaluate politicians. These questions deal with more than the political experience record we might find on a resume; they deal with a candidate's political character. For our purposes, political character can be defined in terms of the dramatization of candidate imagery, that is, the demonstration or portrayal of credibility, competency, and honesty during public life. In some ads, both political experience and political character are addressed.

In 1984, Walter Mondale called to mind questions concerning Gary Hart's political character during the presidential primaries with what has become known as the "Red Phone" ad. The "Red Phone" is a powerful condensation symbol in American political culture. It symbolizes the United States president's personal decision to deal with the Soviet Union peacefully or to deal with them aggressively and potentially start World War III. The media had concentrated on many character contradictions in Hart's persona: his jet setting lifestyle, his changed last name, his peculiar early-life recollections, and his mismanaged presidential campaign. Millions of Americans asked themselves, "Does Hart have the necessary leadership traits to be an American president?" Mondale suggested, "NO!" Notice that the tag for this ad "On Tuesday, vote like our world is at stake" is very similar to the 1964 Johnson tag "Vote for President Johnson on November 3rd, the stakes are to high for you to stay home" that was used against Goldwater. Both evoke the fear of weak political character.

The 1984 Mondale "Red Phone" Ad

VIDEO	AUDIO
Scroll: "On Tuesday you can decide between Gary Hart and Walter Mondale for President . . . the toughest job in the world . . .	The red phone rings and continues to ring.
Scene: An empty chair in the oval office. Dark, foreboding lighting. The camera pans the room.	Narrator [VO]: "A president is tested in times of crisis. He must make the right decision under pressure, without much time. It all
The emphasis is on the red phone . . . ringing.	comes down to knowledge, experience, judgment. He must answer that phone.
Hand picks up phone.	
"Mondale for President" Photo of Mondale and wife in background, centered over logo.	On Tuesday, vote like our world is at stake. Mondale for President."

In the 1986 Alabama Democratic gubernatorial primary, Charlie Graddick attacked Bill Baxley on the character issue. Baxley's Democratic primary opponents and the state's newspapers had propagated rumors concerning Baxley's personal life. The ad copy addresses the sensitivity of raising the character issue.

The 1986 Graddick "Character" Ad

VIDEO	AUDIO
Newspaper Headlines:	Sound Effects: Drum roll with each new headline. A single tap follows.

"Baxley Scandal"

"State Cars Put to
Private Use For Lt. Gov.
Baxley."

"Baxley Rebuked For Wrongful   Announcer [VO]: "There is no easy
Conduct."   way to raise the character issue in
                                    the governor's race. But it is an
                                    issue, and it must be raised."

"Oklahoma DA Investigating
Baxley"

"A Hot Player in Las Vegas: Sound Effects: Drum Rolls and,
Blackjack Bill's $31,000 Sweep"   a single tap with each headline.

"Baxley's drinking is no
secret"

"Baxley Denies Report He
Used State Car For Female
Reporter"

Photo of Graddick with name   Announcer [SOT]: "Charlie Graddick
under.   for Governor."

Your Flip-Flops. The flip-flop ads have become very popular in recent years. These ads demonstrate inconsistencies in a candidate's public performances during his or her political career: "For these ads, a candidate's staff scours the opponent's voting record and public statements and then presents a series of apparent inconsistencies" (Hagstrom & Guskind, 1986, p. 2521).

The age of television has made politicians particularly vulnerable to having everything they say and do on the record. Public utterances are scrutinized by both the news media and potential opponents. Consistency is a virtue, inconsistency a crime. However, well before the television age, one American archetypal hero, Abraham Lincoln, was attacked for flip-flopping. After the "House Divided Speech" in which Lincoln posits that the United States would shortly have to have one policy regarding slavery, and in which he implied that he personally supported the antislavery position, Lincoln found himself attempting to explain his words to both "negrophobes" and "abolitionists" (Hofstadter, 1973, pp. 147–148). Some confusing contradictions resulted.

Abraham Lincoln addressed a gathering of abolition-minded citizens in northern Illinois on July 10, 1858. He said: "Let us discard all this quibbling about this man and the other man, this race and that race and the other race being inferior, and therefore they must be placed in an inferior position. Let us discard all these things, and unite as one people throughout this land, until we shall once more stand up declaring that all men are created equal." (Hofstadter, 1973, p. 148) But two months later, Hofstadter noted, when Lincoln addressed citizens of southern Illinois where "settlers of Southern extraction were dominant" (p. 148), he had this to say:

> I will say, then, that I am not, nor ever have been, in favor of bringing about in any way the social and political equality of the white and black races: that I am not, nor ever have been, in favor of making voters or jurors of negroes, nor of qualifying them to hold office, nor to intermarry with white people. . . .
> And inasmuch as they cannot so live, while they do remain together there must be the position of superior and inferior, and I as much as any other man am in favor of having the superior position assigned to the white race. Charleston, Illinois, September 18, 1858. (p. 148)

Lincoln's opponent, Stephen Douglas, railed against Lincoln's inconsistencies at a Galesburg debate. According to Hofstadter (1973), Douglas addressed Lincoln on the debate platform: "I would despise myself if I thought that I was procuring your votes by concealing my opinions, and by avowing one set of principles in one part of the state, and a different set in another" (p. 149). Confronted by these conflicting passages, Lincoln responded: "I have not supposed and do not now suppose, that there is any conflict whatever between them" (p. 149).

Similarly, Richard Gephardt in 1988 received his share of news media and opponent criticism during the presidential primaries for flip-flopping. *Newsweek* ran a story with the title, "The Many Faces of Dick Gephardt," and observed that:

> Gephardt was once against abortion, the Department of Education, health-care cost controls, farm-production controls, raising the minimum wage and an oil import fee. Now he's for them. He was once for social-security cuts, tuition tax credits, the B-1 bomber and the MX missile. Now he's against them. He voted for the Reagan tax cuts in 1981, appeared to condemn them in Iowa and then boasted of his tax cutting in New Hampshire—a flip-flop-flip. (Kaus & Clift, 1988, p. 46)

The newsmagazine concluded that "the consistency of his inconsistency, if you will—does suggest the cold calculations of a man who first figures out where he wants to go and then figures out what he has to believe to get there" (Kaus & Clift, 1988, p. 46). Unlike Lincoln, Gephardt did not deny the inconsistencies. Instead, he turned them into a virtue. He told *Time:* "All great political leaders have changed their minds in response to changing circumstances. It's silly to be rigid on things when circumstances change" (Stengel, 1988a, p. 22). In the New Hampshire primary, Paul Simon ran an ad demonstrating the inconsistencies between Gephardt's House voting record and his public pronouncements in the primaries (Stengel, 1988b, p. 46). Senator Al Gore and Governor Michael Dukakis also ran ads during the presidential primaries demonstrating Gerhardt's flip-flops (see chapter 4).

The 1988 Dukakis "Gephardt's Flip-Flops" Ad

VIDEO	AUDIO
A figure (man) somersaults across a black line on screen. "The Gephardt Record" "Reaganomics" "Minimum Wage" "Social Security"	Announcer [VO]: Congressman Dick Gephardt has flip-flopped on a lot of issues. He's been both for and against Reaganomics. For and against raising the minimum wage. For and against freezing social security benefits.
Figure (man) starts air punching. "Corporate PAC Money" A hoop appears. Figure somersaults through hoop.	Congressman Gephardt acts tough toward big corporations but takes their PAC money.
Shows Dukakis talking. "Michael Dukakis Democrat for President" Figure somersaults way up in the air.	Mike Dukakis refuses PAC money, opposes Reaganomics and supports a strong minimum wage and social security. You know where Mike Dukakis stands. But Congressman Gephardt, he's still up in the air."

Modern flip-flop ads usually demonstrate the idea of being two-faced. In some instances, a candidate's profile is switched from left to right to demonstrate the inconsistencies. In others, a weathervane is used to show the candidate changing to the political winds at the time. One particularly creative ad in Alabama used a bull frog hopping back and forth.

Probably the most famous flip-flop ad is the one that Humphrey ran against Nixon in 1968. The ad showed Nixon as the figurehead on a gold weathervane. The weathervane moved through the points of the compass as the various flip-flops were discussed. And finally the weathervane spun wildly.

The 1968 Humphrey "Weathervane" Ad

VIDEO	AUDIO
Black board with white lettering: "A pre-recorded	

political announcement paid
for by citizens for Humphrey . . .
Muskie."

A Gold Weathervane with Nixon as the figurehead turns through the points of a compass.	Narrator [VO]: "Ever notice what happens to Nixon when the political winds blow?" (Winds are blowing in background)
It squeaks.	Narrator [VO]: "Last year he said, 'I oppose a federal open housing law.' This year he said, 'I support the 1968 civil rights bill with
It picks up speed and spins around and around.	open housing.' Again this year he said, 'I just supported it to get it out of sight.' Which way will he blow next?
Double "H" Graphic with "Humphrey" underneath.	On November 8th vote for Hubert Humphrey."

During the 1986 California Senate race, Democratic Senator Alan Cranston used a series of flip-flop ads to point out inconsistencies in his opponent's record. The "Toxic Waste" ad, the "Golden Oldies" ad, and the "Flip-Flop Update" ad were all aired against Republican Congressman Ed Zschau.

The 1986 Cranston "Flip-Flop Update" Ad

VIDEO	AUDIO
Zschau logo appears and then flips over. Taken from Zschau Ads. Zschau Photo "For Arab Arms Deals"	Narrator, whispers: "Zschau" (an imitation of the tag from Zschau spots) Narrator [VO]: "Flip-Flop Update. In Congress, Ed Zschau has voted repeatedly to send weapons and missiles to the Arabs.
Newspaper Headlines showing flip-flops	Then he was nominated to the Senate and told a private group he wouldn't do it again. Hours later he told a press conference he would. And two days later, an *L.A. Times* reporter

	pinned him down, and he said he
Zschau's head rotates.	opposed future arms shipments to the Arabs—Probably.
"4"	One week—four flip-flops. Zschau— he's against Arab arms deals and for them.
Scene of Alan Cranston coming down U.S. Capitol steps. Scroll of Cranston's signature: "Alan Cranston"	Alan Cranston: Commitment, courage, California in the Senate."

Past Promises and Pitiful Performances. As candidates, politicians often promise the moon, but once they are in office, they often find things a bit more complicated and a bit more difficult to solve than they had originally thought or at least publicly said. These early promises make fertile fodder for negative political advertising.

Sometimes flip-flop ads are used in combination with the past promises and pitiful performances ad theme as in the 1986 Graddick "Frog" ad, which appeared during the 1986 Democratic primary gubernatorial campaign in Alabama. The flipping bullfrog visuals also add an element of humor to the spot.

The 1986 Graddick "Frog" Ad

VIDEO	AUDIO
A large bullfrog	Announcer: "When you remind Fob James of his record as governor, he flips. He called Charlie Graddick, a liar, which is like being called ugly by a frog. Fob said he was tough on criminals, but he allowed the release of 277 convicted criminals. Fob says he created jobs, but jobs decreased. Fob says he is against raising taxes, but as
Frog hops	governor he raised taxes. No wonder the facts make Fob flip. But those are the facts, warts and all."

While Graddick was showing the hopping bullfrog against former Governor Fob James, another Democratic gubernatorial candidate, Bill Baxley, was running a combination flip-flop-past promises/pitiful performances ad against Charlie Graddick.

The 1986 Baxley "Hypocrisy" Ad

VIDEO	AUDIO
Graddick talking head shot.	Announcer [VO]: "Hypocrisy, Mr. Graddick, is when your words and your actions don't match.
"From $1,350,000 in 1979 to $5,920,000 in 1986" "Source: Legislative Fiscal Office" Supered over Photo.	You call yourself a conservative, but you more than quadrupled your own budget and spent more money than any attorney general in Alabama history.
The Photo Flip-Flops	
"$1,300,000 to: Campaign Finance Director Former Top Aide 2 Former Assistants" "Source: Alabama State Comptroller's Office"	You talk about changing our state's image but then give your own cronies 1.3 million taxpayer dollars in state contracts.
"260,000,000 in Utility Rate Increases" "Source: *Birmingham Post-Herald* Aug. 29, 1981, Oct. 3, 1981	You accuse others of having ties to special interests, but you recommended more than $260 million in rate increases for the utilities who contributed to your campaign.
"Two illegal pay raises"	You ask for the voters to trust you after giving yourself two illegal $20,000 pay raises.
"Graddick Guts Environmental Division" "Source: *Montgomery Advertiser* March 18, 1983"	You brag about protecting the environment, but you eliminated the environmental division of the attorney general's office.
"Graddick's Press Conference Is Political Grandstanding" "Source: *Montgomery Advertiser* March 17, 1985	You talk tough about crime, but then do nothing but hold a press conference when prisoners riot and hold guards hostage. Hypocrisy,

| | Mr. Graddick, is when your words |
| CU of Graddick | and your actions don't match." |

"Paid for by Friends of Bill
Baxley" Small Photo of Baxley
at end of statement.

In 1988, Republican presidential candidate George Bush attacked Democratic candidate Michael Dukakis' promises and performances as governor of Massachusetts.

The 1988 Bush "Promises" Ad

VIDEO	AUDIO
"Boston, Massachusetts" A "Dukakis for Governor" Banner hanging over a door. Janitor comes through doors. Begins sweeping up the litter left from a Dukakis victory party. "He raises taxes." Dukakis poster on floor. "He lost jobs." "He increased spending."	Announcer [VO]: "Michael Dukakis promised not to raise taxes. But as governor, he imposed the largest tax increases in Massachusetts' history. He promised jobs, but since 1984, Massachusetts lost 90,000 blue-collar jobs. He promised less spending, but spent at a greater rate per capita than any other governor in America. And now he wants to do for America what he's done for Massachusetts. America can't afford that risk."

Your Own Voting Record. Frequently, politicians are directly attacked on their voting record. Voting records are very easy to attack for several reasons. First, the voting record is a matter of public record, and therefore the charge has a greater element of authenticity about it. Second, the very nature of politics means that some votes—some choices—will alienate some voters. Smart politicians know that their decisions will make some people angry, but they strive not to alienate all the voters all of the time. And third, voting records are easy to manipulate in such a way that they mislead the public as to the actual record of a candidate.

Many people do not understand or they may not even be aware of how a bill becomes a law, and for this reason, PACs and some candidates have often slanted the facts for their own political gain. Ads that attack a politician's voting record may be very misleading, in that frequently unrelated riders are attached to popular bills so they can sneak into law through the back door. A congressman or senator may feel forced to vote against a bill that he or she might ordinarily support because of the unsatisfactory rider. In other situations, the original bill may be so important to the individual congressman or senator's constituency that he or she feels forced to support the bill while disagreeing with the rider. Frequently, these riders are not minor pieces of legislation, but are significant, not only in scope but also in cost and effect. In other situations, congressmen and senators may vote for a general funding bill that gives monies to various agencies for distribution. Often, decisions about how these monies are actually spent are made on the state or local level. A number of misleading ads have been used to suggest that a congressman or senator voted "Nay" or "Yea" on a very specific controversial program, when in fact, the political leader may have voted for a very general bill that is later translated into specific policy by others much farther down the ladder of command. The congressman or senator is then blamed for how the money was distributed when election time rolls around. As George Will (1989) so aptly put it: "they use something technically true . . . in a fundamentally dishonest way" (p. 92). The Republican senator from Alabama, Jeremiah Denton, ran such an ad in 1986 against Democratic Congressman Richard Shelby.

The 1986 Denton "Bad Votes" Ad

VIDEO	AUDIO
Scroll of Audio as it is read.	Narrator [VO]: "Do you think we should use federal funds to promote the legalization of homosexuality? On June 18th, 1981, Richard Shelby voted yes. Do you think birth control devices should be given to youngsters without the consent of their parents? On June 18th, 1985, Richard Shelby voted yes. You know, we never really knew much about Richard Shelby, but now we do."
Super: 'Richard Shelby voted yes."	
Photo of Shelby on screen then fades into the background.	
Denton photo with Jeremiah Denton in signature form under photo.	

In preparing a possible rebuttal, the Shelby campaign had trouble identifying the bills that Denton was alluding to in the ad. They never discovered any bill that appropriated funds later used toward the legalization of homosexuality. However, they had more luck with the birth-control devices charge. Shelby had voted for funding for public health-care clinics. These public health-care clinics do supply indigent women with birth-control devices, if they are requested. And depending on state law, it is possible that sexually active teenagers could request them. By most evaluations, the ad was stretching the facts.

Besides attacking an incumbents's actual votes, challenger ads often attack a candidate's past attendance record on the floor of whatever legislative body of which the candidate is a member. Hagstrom and Guskind (1986) called these spots "not-on-the-job" ads (p. 2621). In 1984, Kentucky Republican Mitch McConnell attacked then Senator Walter D. Huddleston's "missed votes" by showing a hound dog rushing around Washington trying to find the "missing "Senator" (see Hagstrom & Guskind, 1986, pp. 2621, 2626). This ad has become a classic of American political advertising.

The 1984 McConnell "Hound Dog" Ad

VIDEO	AUDIO
Man with plaid shirt and a camouflage cap holding up a Huddleston T-shirt so that the bloodhounds could smell the Huddleston scent.	Tracker [VO]: "My job was to find Dee Huddleston and get him back to work. Huddleston was missing big votes on social security, the budget, defense, and even agriculture.
Tracking with dogs in front of U.S. Capitol building. Tracking with dogs through city streets. Tracking with dogs through woods.	Huddleston was skipping votes but making an extra 50,000 dollars giving speeches.
Man and dogs stop between opposite pointing road signs. Man and dogs stop beside a pool and talk to a man.	I just missed him . . . when Dee Huddleston skipped votes for his 1,000 dollar Los Angeles speech.
Tracking with dogs on a Puerto Rico Beach. Stops to talk.	I was close . . . at Dee's 2,000 dollar speech in Puerto Rico. Have you seen Dee Huddleston (to beach person)? Thank you very
"Switch to Mitch" with a photo of Mitch McConnell in upper right.	much. We can't find Dee. Maybe we ought to let him make speeches. And switch to Mitch for Senator."
	Dogs Bark: Woof, Woof!!!

The ad was so successful that the McConnell campaign ran a second "Hound Dog" spot.

The 1984 McConnell "Huddleston Treed" Ad

VIDEO   AUDIO

Dogs are gnawing at a document
called the "Huddleston Record."

The tracker and the dogs start   Tracker [VO]: "Ever since this
chasing a Huddleston look-alike   race began, Dee Huddleston has
(with a suit) through the woods   been running away from his record.
and pastures.
                                        But now Kentucky is closing in.
The Huddleston look-alike scales   Giving away school prayer; giving
a rock wall to get away from the   away our Panama Canal.
dogs.   GET HIM!!!
Chasing him through city streets.   Dee runs; Dee hides, but we're
Chasing him through a diner   going to catch him.
waving the Huddleston Record.   It's time you face your record. . . .
Chasing him through corn fields.   No wonder he's running from his
                                        record. But he can't run forever.
The dogs finally tree the
look-alike. Huddleston in the
tree, hanging on. Then the   We've got you now, Dee
tracker and dogs look up from   Huddleston!
the ground.

"Switch to Mitch McConnell for   Switch to Mitch McConnell for U.S.
U.S. Senate."   Senate.

It is important to note that McConnell was taking liberties with Huddleston's actual Senate voting record. Huddelston's attendance record had averaged 94% for several years preceding the election (Alter, 1984). However, that was not the impression one received from viewing the spots. Huddleston's 20-point lead quickly became history, and McConnell was victorious on election day (Alter, 1984).

Your Choice of Vice President. This category obviously is used only in presidential campaigns. The choice of a vice presidential running mate is one of the more critical decisions that a presidential nominee must make. Frequently, the opposition challenges the vice presidential selection by creating ads that attack the presidential nominee's judgment in selecting such a poor choice. If the news media also appear to question the vice presidential selection, then the presidential nominee may have a difficult time in dealing with attacks made against both that vice presidential choice and his or her own political acumen.

In 1956, the Democrats needed a way to indirectly attack Eisenhower's age and ill health without being vulnerable to charges of being insensitive and gauche (Diamond & Bates, 1988; Jamieson, 1984). The result was a series of ads. According to Jamieson, some were never run, and some were only produced and aired regionally. One ad asked the questions: "Nervous about Nixon? *President* Nixon?" (p. 104).

In 1968, Tony Schwartz produced a series of spots attacking Nixon's running mate, Spiro T. Agnew. Schwartz said in 1968, "If Muskie is Humphrey's secret weapon, Agnew is Nixon's Achilles' heel" (Jamieson, 1984, p. 237). Schwartz decided to aim his barbs at Nixon's heel. Schwartz asked the voters: "Who is your choice to be a heartbeat away from the presidency?" In another Schwartz ad, devastating laughter sent chills up Republican's backs. "**Agnew** for Vice-President?" appeared on the television screen. Raucous laughter followed. A slide closed the ad with the words: "This would be funny if it wasn't so series," Tony Schwartz produced a similar spot for the 1976 Carter campaign. The resulting spot was called "*Mondole*" and compared Walter Mondale and Robert Dole. Again the heartbeat question was asked: "When you know that four of the last six vice-presidents wound up being president, who would you like to see a heartbeat away from the presidency?" (Diamond & Bates, 1988, pp. 248-249; Jamieson, 1984, pp. 367-368). In 1988, Republican vice presidential nominee Dan Quayle received a great deal of criticism from not only his Democratic opposition but also the news media. In September 1988, a *Times Mirror* poll, which was conducted by the Gallup organization, shows that only one third (34%) of the voters thought Quayle was qualified to serve as president if called upon to do so (Kellerman, 1988). In two spots, the Dukakis/Bentsen campaign attacked Bush's decision to name Quayle as his running mate. In the first ad, the Democratic team uses the familiar heartbeat theme.

The 1988 Dukakis "Heartbeat" Ad

VIDEO	AUDIO
The Oval Office	Sound [VO]: Heartbeat, continues sound under.
Newspaper photo of Truman taking oath of office.	Announcer [VO]: "The most powerful man in the world is also mortal. We know this all too well in America.

Johnson taking oath of office.	One in five American vice presidents has had to rise to the duties of commander-in-chief. One in five has had to take on the responsibilities of the most powerful office in the world. For this job, after five months of reflection, George Bush made his personal choice, J. Danforth Quayle.
Newspaper Headlines of Ford's swearing in. Oval Office.	
"Hopefully, we will never know how great a lapse of judgment that really was" Superimposed over Oval Office's presidential chair.	Hopefully, we will never know how great a lapse of judgment that really was."

Your Decision Not to Debate. The choice of whether to debate is a complex one. But one thing a candidate can count on if he or she decides not to debate: The opponent will take advantage of that decision and will get political mileage out of it.

In the 1978 Alabama Democratic primary, gubernatorial candidate and Attorney General Bill Baxley attacked his millionaire opponent, Fob James, with the "Open Chair" ad.

The 1978 Baxley "Open Chair" Ad

VIDEO	AUDIO
Baxley speaking directly into camera. MCU	Baxley [SOT]: "After the slick TV Ads go off, the billboards come down, and the last jingle is played, the new governor is going to have to get down to the tough job of trying to change things in Montgomery by changing the legislature and solving our problems.
	Now being Governor is not like running a factory. Being Governor has got its own problems. It's not enough just to know what the problems in the state are. You've got to have solutions to them. And then know how to make them work.

	Now you've been hearing from me all along about what my solutions to the problems we facing [sic] in this state. You deserve to hear from both me and my millionaire opponent. And know how we stand on the issues.
Camera draws back to reveal Baxley seated in a chair with an empty chair beside him.	I've agreed to face these issues, side-by-side, with my opponent at his convenience. So far, I'm still waiting. So are you."
CU of Bill Baxley	Sound Effects: Drum Roll.
"Bill Baxley For Governor" with X in a voting box.	Announcer [VO]: "Paid for by friends of Bill Baxley."

In 1982 a Republican senatorial candidate, Ray Shamie of Massachusetts, used a negative ad to shame Democratic Senator Edward Kennedy into debating him. Shamie posted a $10,000 reward " 'to any person or nonpartisan organization, not related to Edward M. Kennedy or his staff, who was able to get the senator to schedule a one-on-one debate . . . for a statewide prime-time audience.' This ploy . . . was complemented by airplanes carrying banners throughout Massachusetts which read, '$10,000 Reward—Get Ted Kennedy to Debate Ray Shamie' " (Martel, 1983, pp. 97, 160). Teddy Kennedy debated Ray Shamie. Ultimately, Shamie won the debate war but lost the election. A similar campaign-wanted poster was used by Congressman Richard Shelby in this efforts to get Senator Jeremiah Denton to debate him during the Alabama 1986 Senate race. Denton continued to refuse to debate unlike Kennedy. But again, unlike Kennedy, Denton lost.

In a 1986 Louisiana Senate race, John Breaux ran the equivalent of the "Empty Chair" ad by using an unused lectern in its place to attack Henson Moore for his failure to debate the issues.

The 1986 Breaux "Unused Lectern" Ad

VIDEO	AUDIO
Camera on an unused lectern; cobwebs cover the stand. A "Moore" sign is printed on the lectern.	Narrator [VO]: "John Breaux has been waiting and waiting to debate the real issues of our economy.

Then camera turns to show two lecterns. The left: the empty "Moore" lectern; The right: The Breaux lectern with John Breaux behind it. Breaux taps on lectern as if he is tired of waiting.

Tell Henson Moore, it's time to come out of hiding."

The People Against You

From the earliest days of television advertising, consultants have used real voters or paid professional actors to say negative things about their candidate's opponent. Whether the "people" are voters, actors, constituencies, newspaper editorials in your home state, coworkers, fellow party members, or party primary opponents, their negative comments about a presidential candidate make for a powerful message. The theme of these spots is quite simple: "If you come to know Candidate X, as we do, you won't like Candidate X!"

The Voters Turn Against You. Dissatisfied voters make powerful enemies come election time. In a 1978 judicial race in Kentucky, the Republican candidate Mitch McConnell attacked the incumbent Judge Hollenback with the observations of a horse farmer. The ad is both humorous and effective.

The 1978 McConnell "Horse Farmer" Ad

VIDEO	AUDIO
Farmer standing in doorway of barn with a horse, Nell. Farmer talks directly to camera.	Farmer [SOT]: "Maybe I ain't that smart. But when Judge Hollenback tells me he's cut my taxes, he don't credit me with as much horse sense as Nell has."
	Background Noise: Horse Neighs!!
	Farmer [SOT]: "Since he's been judge, the taxes on my house are nearly 50 percent higher. Who's he think he's kidding?"
	Background Noise: Laughter soundtrack.

| Farmer beings to shovel horse manure. | Farmer [SOT]: "Maybe Judge Hollenback should have my job. Because in my business, I deal with that kind of stuff everyday." |

"For County Judge
Mcconnell's For Me"

Your Constituencies Turn Against You. From the first television presidential campaign year in 1952, the political parties have made extensive and rather clever use of these so-called "hometown enemies." The persuasive strategy behind these ads is a powerful argument in that the ads show people who know you the best, but who like you the least. In 1952, Ike faced a series of negative ads in the nation's newspapers. "Ex-GI's for Adlai," "Open letters from Ike's fellow veterans," and "Columbia University faculty for Adlai" attacked what they suggested was his close-minded, military-like personality (Jamieson, 1984, pp. 50-51).

In 1988, the Bush presidential campaign attacked Michael Dukakis by capturing voters from around the state of Massachusetts voicing their complaints and doubts about Dukakis's record and leadership abilities. The people pictured in the ads represent a wide range of constituencies.

The 1988 Bush "His Mistakes" Ad

VIDEO	AUDIO
White letters on black screen, "How Good a Governor Is Michael Dukakis?"	
Man "Wellesley, Massachusetts"	Man One [SOT]: "I don't think that Michael Dukakis has lived up to his promises."
Woman "Quincy, Massachusetts"	Woman One [SOT]: "He has raised taxes. And he's raised taxes."
Man "Taunta, Massachusetts"	Man Two [SOT]: "He's taking money from the retirement funds that the people have put in there. You know to balance out the mistakes that he has made."
Man "Brighton, Massachusetts"	Man Three [SOT]: "Michael Dukakis should be called Michael *Taxkakis*."

Woman   Woman Two [SOT]: "Dukakis has
"Hyde Park, Massachusetts"   made *one mess* out of
                                   Massachusetts."

Woman   Woman One [SOT]: "I'm a
"Quincy, Massachusetts"   Democrat, and I've never voted
                                   Republican before, but this time I'm
                                   voting for George Bush."
"George Bush
Experienced Leadership for
America's Future."

The Party Faithful Reject You. In 1972, then Democratic national
figure, John Connally, helped spearhead the Democrats for Nixon organization. The basic idea was to get conservative Democrats to reject the liberal
views of George McGovern and cast a conservative vote for Richard Nixon.
This type of appeal is very persuasive. If other party leaders reject a candidate, then why should the rank and file support the candidate?

The 1972 "Democrats for Nixon" Ad

VIDEO   AUDIO

Camera up on CU of Connally,   Connally [SOF]: "Good evening.
addressing camera.   I'm a Democrat, who along with
                                   many of my fellow Democrats, has
                                   become convinced that it is in
                                   the best interest of this country
                                   to reelect President Richard
                                   Nixon. . . . Senator McGovern has
                                   made proposals to cut an
                                   unprecedented thirty-two billion
                                   dollars' worth of men and
                                   weapons out of the United States
                                   defense budget. . . . The McGovern
                                   defense budget is the most
                                   dangerous document ever seriously
                                   put forth by a presidential
                                   candidate in this century. It
                                   would end the United
                                   States' military leadership in the
                                   world; it would make us inferior
                                   in conventional and strategic

weapons to the Soviets. The total
United States Armed Forces level
would be cut to a point lower
than at the time of Pearl
Harbor. Dean Rusk, Secretary of
State in the Administration of
John F. Kennedy and Lyndon
Johnson, has termed the McGovern
defense, and I quote him,
'insane'. . . ." (Diamond & Bates,
1988, pp. 204-205)

In 1972, an organization called "Democrats of West Virginia" produced
an ad for then Republican Governor Archie Moore. Moore was running against
Jay Rockefeller IV who had moved to West Virginia only a few years before.
Moore and his Democratic supporters were anxious to brand Rockefeller as
a carpetbagger (Political TV Classics, 1984). The ad producers traveled to
New York City where they asked people on the city streets how they would
like having a West Virginian for governor of New York. The ad made its point.

The 1972 Democrats of West Virginia "Carpetbagger" Ad

VIDEO	AUDIO
New York City Streets . . .	Narrator [VO]: "Excuse me, uh, what do you think about a West Virginian running for governor of New York?"
Man with a cigar and wearing a suit.	First Man [SOT]: "That might be a better question or is that a statement? That don't make no sense neither way."
Man with beard and suit.	Second Man [SOT]: "I think its preposterous. I think its ridiculous."
Blue collar worker with hard hat. Male.	Third Man [SOT]: Crazy, just crazy, I mean really . . . I mean I. . . .
Man with suit, laughing.	Fourth Man [SOT]: Laughs, Laughs. "You've got to be kidding!"
Woman with scarf.	Narrator [VO]: "West Virginian as

governor of New York — how about it?"

First Woman [SOT]: "That makes about as much sense to me as having the next governor of West Virginia be a New Yorker."

"Re-elect Arch Moore"   Narrator [VO]: "Democrats have paid for this message to re-elect a good governor."

Similar in persuasive style to the Democrats for Nixon ads are the "decision-making confessional" ads that show a citizen struggling with his or her voting decision. In 1964, a Republican actor presented a 5-minute stream-of-conscience that centered on his decision to vote for the Democratic candidate, Lyndon Johnson, and not his own party's candidate, Barry Goldwater. The ad was known as a "Confession of a Republican." In this rambling confession, the man expresses his concern over Goldwater's advisers, his policy contradictions, his nuclear war positions, his ultra-conservative backers, and the "weird groups" supporting Goldwater. He ends by saying: "I think my party made a bad mistake in San Francisco, and I'm going to have to vote against that mistake. . . ."

Your Own Party Primary Opponents. As Jamieson (1984) stated, "Under a principle comparable to 'my enemy's enemy is my friend,' opponents mine the intra-party rhetoric from their opponent's primary battles" (p. 52). Opponents scour over the primary ads, primary speeches, and primary news interviews for juicy negative tidbits to use in their own ads. Again, the resulting message is simple: "If your political comrades don't think much of you, then why should I vote for you?"

In 1964 and 1980, we find a rich crop of devastating party primary opponent(s) ads. During the general election, Goldwater said in an allusion to this advertising practice that he was "the victim of fratricide" (Jamieson, 1984, p. 177). And one Johnson media executive said, "We are humbly grateful to the Senator's Republican colleagues for giving us the two big campaign issues — the bomb and Social Security. . . . There is no weapon so effective as the words of one's friends. . . ." (Jamieson, 1984, p. 177). Johnson's ad team of Doyle Dane Bernbach produced powerful ad copy. Governor Rockefeller was quoted as saying that Goldwater's policies "spell disaster for the party and for the country." Governor Romney was quoted as saying Goldwater's nomination was the "suicidal destruction of the Republican Party." And Governor Scranton was quoted as describing Goldwater's positions as "absurd" and "dangerous."

Perhaps one of the most famous party primary opponent ads was the one that Carter ran against Ronald Reagan in 1980. George Bush was the party primary opponent and his description of Reagan's economic policy as "voodoo economics" was the subject. This ad was particularly effective in that, oddly enough, George Bush was now the Republican vice presidential nominee.

The 1980 Carter "Empty Oval Office" Ad

VIDEO	AUDIO
Camera up on an empty Oval office. Camera slowly moves in. Then crawl begins, in small white capital letters superimposed over picture.	Announcer [VO]: "When you come right down to it, what kind of person should occupy the Oval Office?"
"SHOULD IT BE A PERSON WHO, LIKE RONALD REAGAN, HAS PROPOSED THE MAGICAL KEMP/ROTH ECONOMIC PLAN, A PLAN THAT *BUSINESS WEEK* CALLED 'COMPLETELY IRRESPONSIBLE,' A PLAN THAT REAGAN'S OWN RUNNING MATE CALLED 'VOODOO ECONOMICS'?"	(Announcer reads copy as it crawls over the screen.)
Fade to photo of Carter and Mondale, alongside white letters on black background: "PRESIDENT CARTER."	Announcer [VO]: "Or should there be in the Oval Office an experienced man who is working to solve America's economic problems and isn't kidding anybody about them? Figure it out for yourself." (Diamond & Bates, 1988, pp. 288-289)

During the 1980 campaign, the Republicans used the same persuasive tactics. In the states where Edward Kennedy had placed the strongest in the Democratic primaries, the Republicans aired spots with Kennedy attacking Carter. One ad showed Kennedy yelling, "I say it's time to say no more hostages.

No more high interest rates, no more high inflation and no more Jimmy Carter" (Jamieson, 1984, p. 389).

Transfer Ads

Transfer, long a propagandistic technique, is the process of inferring either positive or negative evaluations of individuals by their association with well-known positive or negative public figures, movements, or causes (see Wilcox, Ault, & Agee, 1989). Thus, in negative political ads, individuals are judged guilty by the target audience because of their association with unpopular political symbols. The transfer may be achieved in a number of different ways. We have identified four transfer techniques (a) your comrades (members of your own party and those who share your political ideology) or supporters (constituents, powerbrokers, members of your party), (b) the events that happened on your watch, (c) historical comparisons, and (d) paid political help. The theme of transfer ads is quite simple: Your political associations (as implied by the ad, real or imaginary) make you an unacceptable candidate.

Your Comrades and Supporters. During the late 1970s and early 1980s, Republicans frequently used the terms "Ted Kennedy-Democrat" or "Tip O'Neil-Democrat" to transfer negative connotations to their opponents. In the 1988 presidential election, George Bush successfully linked Michael Dukakis with the deadly *L*-word, "liberal." By associating unpopular political leaders or philosophies with Democratic candidates, conservatives were able to short-circuit traditional discussion through what we call transfer.

In the 1986 California Senate race, Republican Congressman Ed Zschau depicted Democratic Senator Alan Cranston as an aging liberal that was out of touch with Californians. Zschau traced Cranston's voting record on the death penalty, and he also negatively associated Cranston with a liberal Supreme Court justice, Rose Bird. Bird was running for reelection, and she was widely regarded as being politically vulnerable because of her unpopular stand against capital punishment.

The 1986 Zschau "Soft on Crime" Ad

VIDEO	AUDIO
	Military cadence sound under.
A Vote Record Book appears on screen.	Narrator [VO]: "According to official voting records of the U.S. Senate, Alan Cranston believes that

TV news excerpts of same with attention to innocent victims. Newspaper Headlines.

More TV news excerpts. Black with white letters. "Maybe that's why Alan Cranston doesn't oppose Rose Bird."

if a terrorist kills an American citizen in a hijacking, if someone commits murder, treason, or kidnapping, if innocent victims die in a bombing, the killer should not get the death penalty. Alan Cranston consistently opposes the death penalty for the most vicious crimes. Maybe that's why he doesn't oppose Rose Bird."

According to Jamieson (1984), "attacking a candidate on the basis of his supporters is as old as politics; the coming of the polispot only helps dramatize this form" (p. 21). Because incumbents see their base of support as being much broader than challengers, incumbents are less likely to use negative ads that attack the opposition supporters. In some situations, candidates will praise themselves by who does not support them. Both types of supporter negative transfers send a powerful message.

Events That Happened on Your Watch

Politicians frequently get the blame for political events that happened during their tenure in office. And in some instances, they are blamed for things that happened when their party was in power. For years, all Republican candidates carried the scourge of the Great Depression, just as Democratic candidates carried the baggage of the turbulent 1960s. In 1968, the Republicans aired a television ad that showed "scenes depicting the ravages of war and the discord in the streets of Chicago" which were "juxtaposed with a picture of a smiling Hubert Humphrey" accepting the Democratic nomination (Jamieson, 1984, p. 245). According to Jamieson (1984), "the juxtaposition of highly evocative images invites the audience to impute causality" (p. 450).

Political leaders who have held executive positions such as the presidency, or a governor's or mayor's office, are particularly vulnerable to these attacks, because they ultimately are responsible for things that happen on their watch (at least in the eyes of the voters). In 1988, the Bush presidential campaign attacked Massachusetts Governor Michael Dukakis with several devastating ads of this type. Two of the most famous Bush ads are considered.

The 1988 Bush "Boston Harbor" Ad

VIDEO	AUDIO
Buoy in Boston Harbor.	Announcer [VO]: "As a candidate, Michael Dukakis called Boston

The Harbor.

Broken down pier.
Sludge.
Polluted Water.
Dead Bird.

Sign: "Danger Radiation
Hazard No Swimming"
Garbage.
Dead fish.
Garbage.

Harbor an open sewer. As governor
he had the opportunity to do something about it. But chose not to. The
Environmental Protection Agency
called his lack of action 'the most
expensive public policy mistake in
the history of New England.' Now
Boston Harbor—the dirtiest harbor
in America—will cost residents
6 billion dollars to clean. And
Michael Dukakis promises to do for
America what he's done for
Massachusetts."

The next spot is known as the "Revolving Door" spot. The door graphically demonstrated a prison furlough program in Massachusetts. Prisoners go
in and out of the revolving door at a prison. Goldman and Matthews (1989)
described the production scene:

> The revolving door was custom-made at what had once been Donny and Marie
> Osmond's studio in Provo, and was trucked in for the shoot. A cast of seventy
> was assembled, some scrubbed-up Mormon youths from Republican headquart-
> ers, some homeless men rousted out of the parks in town; they were dressed
> in prison fatigues and taped in deathly silence, filing in and out through the built-
> to-order revolving door. (p. 364)

The 1988 Bush "Revolving Door" Ad

VIDEO	AUDIO
"The Dukakis Furlough Program" Guard climbs up Prison Watch Tower. Prison Guard walking. Prison-revolving gate. Men file through revolving door.	Sound [VO]: Doomsday Music. Announcer [VO]: "As governor, Michael Dukakis vetoes mandatory sentences for drug dealers. He vetoed the death penalty. His revolving-door prison policy gave weekend furloughs to first-degree murderers not eligible for parole.
"268 Escaped" Superimposed.	While out, many committed other crimes like kidnapping and rape.
"Many are still at large" Superimposed.	And, many are still at large. Now Michael Dukakis says he wants to do for America what he's done for

Prison guard on roof.

Massachusetts. America can't
afford that risk."

According to Goldman and Matthews (1989), the "Revolving Door" ad stretched the truth quite a bit. They wrote that: "The ad did not find it necessary to explain that the 268 'escapes' had occurred over ten years; that just three of the AWOLs were still at large, as against one-third to one-half who merely had come in late on the day they were due—and that only four of the escapees over that period had in fact been murderers doing life with no parole" (p. 364). However, it is doubtful that even if Dukakis had pointed out these "stretches" it would have helped his case. Americans do not want murderers doing life without parole out on the weekends in their neighborhoods.

Historical Comparisons. In 1952, both political parties used traumatic memories associated with Hitler's Germany to make their points. The Democrats had been in power for 20 years, so the Republicans ran an ad in *The New York Times* that asked readers to "Remember—ONE PARTY RULE MADE SLAVES OUT OF THE GERMAN PEOPLE UNTIL HITLER WAS CONQUERED BY IKE" (Jamieson, 1984, p. 50). And the Democrats printed an ad that reminded voters that " 'General Hindenberg, the professional soldier and national hero, also ignorant of domestic and political affairs,' and 'cajoled from the role of soldier to that of statesman. . . . He too had advisors. The net result was his appointment of Adolf Hitler as Chancellor and then World War II' " (Jamieson, 1984, p. 50). These attempts at transfer seem way out of line by today's standards, but contemporary observers must remember that different times have different standards of conduct.

Paid Political Help. Candidates will sometimes attack their opposition's paid political help: staff, advertising agency, consultants, and so forth. In the 1986 Maryland Senate race, the Republican candidate, Linda Chavez, attacked Democratic Representative Barbara Mikulski by suggesting that she was a "San Francisco-Democrat" whose views were "clearly anti-male" (Nugent, 1987, pp. 47–49). This attempt at transfer was using the negative connotations associated with the San Francisco Democratic Convention as well as the connotations associated with the city of San Francisco being stereotypically portrayed as the city of gay and lesbian Americans.

The 1986 Chavez "Radical Feminism" Ad

VIDEO   AUDIO

White on Black Screen.

"The Truth
The Whole Truth."

"Mikulski hired a radical feminist as an official Congressional aide– –"
The Baltimore Evening Sun, May 22, 1981

Narrator [VO]: "In 1981, Barbara Mikulski hired a militant, radical feminist.

"a philosophy described as 'fascist feminism,' 'Marxist,' and 'anti-male.' "

The aide embraced a philosophy described as a 'fascist feminism,' 'Marxist,' and 'anti-male.'

"Mikulski said, 'Her philosophy has become a blueprint for my congressional work.' "

"Mikulski said, 'Her philosophy has become a blueprint for my congressional work.' "

Foreboding Music with bells.

Narrator [VO]: "And ordered the staff to implement that philosophy. Within five weeks, eight staff members *quit*."

"Within five weeks, eight staff members *quit*."

Black background with white lettering: "Linda Chavez U.S. Senate." Photo of Mikulski in upper right.

Now Mikulski wants to be our U.S. Senator. That's kind of scary. But you can do something about it."

In the 1986 Senate race in South Dakota, Republican Senator James Abdnor ran spots that linked Democratic Congressman Thomas Daschle with actress Jane Fonda who had testified before the House Agriculture Committee by Daschle's invitation. The basic idea of the spot was that if you believe that Fonda is a radical liberal then Daschle is a radical liberal by association. The Daschle campaign responded by producing a "Political Consultant" spot that showed a group of actors pretending to be political consultants in a heated discussion.

The 1986 Daschle "Consultants" Ad

VIDEO

AUDIO

"Jim Abnor's Campaign" on Door. A "Do Not Enter" sign. Consultants seated around a table. Talking.

Consultant One [SOT]: "This Daschle is good."

Consultant Two [SOT]: "So what?
We can make anyone look bad."

Consultant Three [SOT]: "That's
what you pay us for."

Consultant Four [SOT]: "We'll
say that Daschle's done nothing
for farmers."

ECU of Consultant Five.   Consultant Five [SOT]: That's
not the truth!"

Consultant Six [SOT]: "But who
cares? People will believe anything
if you say it enough."

Consultant Seven [SOT]: "We'll
distort that Florida thing. Confuse
them with Fonda. All that usual
liberal stuff."

Consultant Four [SOT]: "When
we're finished, Daschle's mother
won't vote for him."

Sound [SOT]: Laughter.

Announcer [VO]: "Don't let them
have the last laugh—Vote Daschle
for a change."

Consultant Two [SOT]: "Let's go
tell Jim."

In 1988, the Democratic National Committee (DNC) borrowed the Daschle
ad's concept and created about a dozen "Bush Package" spots (see McCabe,
1988). The spots showed Republican consultants discussing campaign tactics.
Each spot started with the visual headline "The Packaging of George Bush"
and a date and time. These spots were the most widely criticized of the Dukakis
spots. One journalist called the ads "the most harshly criticized spots in the
history of political advertising" (Battaglio, 1988, p. 23). The criticism was
not because the spots were particularly nasty, but because they were not very

effective advertising. Unlike the 1986-Daschle spot, which provided a clear visual cue as to the nature of the reenactment, the DNC spot used an ambiguous cue, "The Packaging of George Bush." Stan Bernard (1989) of NBC News reported that "voters complained they didn't know who they were for or against" (see also, Devlin, 1989). Similarly, even a Dukakis insider, ad man Ed McCabe (1988), wrote that "A lot of people thought they were commercials *for* Bush" (Emphasis in original; p. 48). Devlin (1989) reported that Dan Payne, a Dukakis media producer, told him that the packaging ads "may have only been 6% of the budget, but they accounted for 100% of the campaign's credibility. . . . People looked at them and decided Dukakis' media was incompetent (p. 401):

The 1988 DNC "Consultants/Flag" Ad

VIDEO   AUDIO

The Packaging of George Bush"

"Tuesday 10:13 A.M." Consultants talking.	Consultant One [SOT]: "In the debate, Dukakis said 37 million Americans don't have health insurance. That's not true is it?"
	Consultant Two [SOT]: "Afraid so. And Dukakis came out with that Health Insurance Plan for working people."
	Consultant Three: [SOT]: "That's gonna play real well with the middle class. We get enough problems with the middle class."
	Consultant One [SOT]: "So what does Bush do?"
	Consultant Four [SOT]: "Wraps himself up in the American Flag."
	Consultant One [SOT]: "That again?"
	Consultant Two [SOT]: "Would you rather talk about Dukakis' health insurance plan?"

Sound [SOT]: Laughter.

Consultant Two [SOT]: "Get out the flag boys."

"They'd like to sell you a   Announcer [VO]: "They'd like to
package. Wouldn't you rather   sell you a package. Wouldn't you
choose a President?"   rather choose a President?"

Dukakis photograph.

Us Against Them

The "us against them" theme appears in American politics again and again. This theme has four manifestations: the Cowboys versus the Yankees, us against the foreigners, class warfare, and the anti-Washington mentality. All four manifestations share one certain common denominator: that your group, whether the group is a region of the country, a particular political party, and so forth, is in a war with the "bad" guys. The theme here utilizes a variety of political myths from city-on-the-hill to ethnocentrism. But, the message remains clear: We're the good guys, they're the bad guys, and you and I have to fight together to hold off the bad guys.

The Cowboys Versus the Yankees

As Barrett (1988) stated, "The clash between those who represent entrenched power and those who resent it has rivaled the tension between liberalism and conservatism in defining American campaign showdowns" (p. 16). Since Andrew Jackson attacked the "Monster Bank" of the New England establishment, populism has played an important role in American political campaigns (Barrett, 1988; Washburn, 1963).

Kirkpatrick Sale (1975b) in *Power Shift* brilliantly described the populist power struggle that has dominated the spirit of American politics in the last half of the 20th century. It is not a power struggle based simply on party, but rather it is a struggle that pits different social, political, and economic cultures against one another. It is the Yankees against the Cowboys. According to Sale (1975a), the Yankees, or the eastern establishment, have long been associated with "the world of New York and Boston and Newport and Grosse Pointe and Winnetka, the world of great wealth, high culture, nurtured traditions, industrial power, and political aristocracies, the world of 'the soft heads' and 'the media,' and the 'liberal elite'. . . ." (p. 555). Literally, this takes in "the fourteen states of New England and the Great Lakes: Maine, New Hampshire, Vermont, Massachusetts, Rhode Island, Connecticut, New York, New Jersey, Pennsylvania, Ohio, Michigan, Indiana, Wisconsin, and Illinois" (Sale, 1975a, p. 559).

Between 1869 and 1945, the Yankees dominated American politics, and, as Sale (1975a) explained, it was not until an economic revolution "that created the giant new postwar industries of defense, aerospace, technology, electronics, and agribusiness, and oil-and-gas extraction" (p. 556) that the Southern Rim began to offer a challenge to the traditional powerbrokers of the North. The Southern Rim and its Cowboys reside in the "broad band of America that stretches from Southern California through the Southwest and Texas into the Deep South and down to Florida" (Sale, 1975a, p. 556). Literally, Sale's Southern Rim means the 36 remaining states outside of 14 states in the Northeast.

Sale (1975a) elaborated, "Taken loosely, this is meant to suggest the traditional, staid, oldtime, button-down, Ivy-League, tight-lipped, patrician, New England-rooted WASP culture on the one hand, and the aggressive, flamboyant, restless, swaggering, newfangled, open-collar, can-do Southern-rooted Baptist culture of the Southern Rim on the other. . ." (p. 559). Sale labeled David Rockefeller, Edmund Muskie, John Lindsey, Bill Buckley, John Kennedy, and a host of others as Yankees, and Richard Nixon, Bebe Robozo, John Wayne, Strom Thurmond, George Wallace, and others as the newly arrived Cowboys.

This seemingly light-hearted analysis reveals a deep division in the political consciousness of America. Cowboys are just different. No matter how many times they break bread with Yankees, travel north for business, and pay visits to the Liberty Bell, Cowboys are still going to be different. Many come from a world torn by the Civil War, a world that has neither forgiven nor forgotten the ravages of the war years and the humiliation of Reconstruction. And, although many of the states included in the Southern Rim do not share the same war heritage as the deep South, they do share a newness, an almost wildness of spirit, that believes everything is possible and that all people should benefit from the fruit of the land. A fierce populist streak and a strong dislike for anything remotely linked with the establishment overrides the normal party divisions that characterize American politics.

The past decade has provided us with rather unusual Cowboy-Yankee scenarios. In 1980, we had two Cowboys face off against each other. Ironically, Ronald Reagan was able to defeat Cowboy Jimmy Carter who, during his 1976 campaign, had been compared to the first populist president, Andrew Jackson (Johnson, 1984; Steele, Whitmore, Cumming, & Smith, 1976). And in 1988, we had another unique twist to the Yankee versus Cowboy tale, for we had a hybrid Cowboy meeting a rather unusual Yankee. George Bush was the son of the old Yankee establishment, but he had made his fame and fortune in the heart of the Southern Rim, the great state of Texas. And, he had ridden into the White House behind one of the greatest Cowboys of our generation (both in motion pictures and in politics), Ronald Reagan. Michael Dukakis as a Greek Orthodox married to a Jewish woman certainly did not fit the WASP stereotype of the Yankee, but the New England liberal establishment counted him as their own, nevertheless.

This Cowboys versus Yankees at high noon type of analysis is useful in describing an underlying us against them mentality that from time to time surfaces in American politics. You see it again and again in southern politics and in presidential candidates from the so-called Southern Rim. It is debatable whether the northern politicians see themselves as them or not, but it is clear after viewing political commercials from the Southern Rim that the Cowboys believe there is an us. It is not a "paranoid's invention. There is a reality to this area, a climatic, historical, and cultural cohesiveness, that serves to set this broad band off from the rest of the country in many ways" (Sale, 1975a, p. 557).

This us against them mentality is not just a crusade against the northern, New England establishment. Through the years, it has been used against a variety of power structures as remotely different as electric utilities, Korean automobile manufacturers, intellectuals, the wealthy, and those inside the Washington beltway. It seems that the citizens of the Southern Rim distrust all forms of worldly authority.

This type of negative stereotypical labeling of perceived foes is not a new American campaign device. From the battles of the log cabins and hard-cider barrels versus the grand palaces and fine champagnes and wines of the 19th century, we can see the beginnings of the Cowboy versus Yankee debate (see chapter 1.) Basic textbooks that discuss both group-think and propaganda techniques routinely cover the process of identifying and targeting civic hatred and contempt upon groups of people based on their race, religion, nationality, occupation, associations, and so forth (Moore & Kalupa, 1985; Nimmo, 1978). But, the Cowboys of the Southern Rim bring a unique flavor to a very old appeal.

George C. Wallace.   We begin our discussion of us against them negative ads with George C. Wallace of Alabama. Our discussion of Wallace is more in depth than our discussion of another southern Cowboy, Jimmy Carter, for Wallace was a master of the us against them negative campaign. George Wallace's long career as Alabama legislator, judge, governor, and presidential candidate was sprinkled with negative political advertsing campaigns. Hart (1971) called this type of political phenomenon the "torrent of negativity" (p. 253). Although he is best remembered for his anti-Black stance, Wallace had crusaded against a number of other so-called enemies of the people such as the "news media, universities, tax-exempt foundations, and all other institutions corrupted by the 'intellectual cult' " (Hogan, 1984, p. 39). Although Wallace did not attack individuals specifically, he did personify demographic groups, ideas, causes, organizations, and institutions in such a way that these "opponents" became the object of ridicule for the duration of the campaign. Wallace employed what Makay (1970) called a strategy of fear. He discovered what the people feared the most, and then he focused on those themes, riding a wave of discontent (Makay, 1970). Wallace channeled people's fears, whether they were fears concerning Blacks, economic displacement, competition, or loss of social status (see Carlson, 1981; Hogan 1984; Orum, 1972), into support for Wallace, the leader. Wallace offered no solutions. What he did offer the people was a belief in George Wallace (see Carlson, 1981; Hogan, 1984). According to *The New York Times*, Wallace's type of protest politics thrived on "turmoil, excitement, discord. He is interested in exploiting issues, not solving problems" (The Poisoned Cup, 1972, p. 36).

Wallace's political strength was primarily in the southern United States. In 1976, 46% of his supporters were from the South. The years after the Civil War had done nothing to diminish the us against them mentality that pervaded the South in the 1860s. The South and Alabama in particular perceived themselves to be the "doormat" of the nation (Carlson, 1981, p. 275). According to one political historian, Alabama felt "alienated from the nation" (Strong, 1972, p. 471). Guest (1974) demonstrated that southerners have lower levels of political efficacy than do individuals from other regions of the country.

Alienation or rather the recognition of alienation was the key to the Wallace success story. According to Carlson (1981), Wallace practiced the politics of powerlessness. Abcarian and Stanage (1965) defined powerlessness as the "feeling that one has lost personal efficacy and the ability to act influentially and significantly within his social universe" (p. 786). The bond that bound all Wallace supporters together, whether northern or southern, was their lack of political efficacy (Hogan, 1984; see also, Carlson, 1981; Orum, 1972). Hogan elaborated, "Many people felt no sense of purposeful involvement or political efficacy. Instead, they felt that they did not count or that their concerns meant nothing to mainstream politicians. George Wallace spoke to such people" (p. 27). Wallacites shared "a feeling of estrangement from politics, an attitude of intolerance towards political differences, and a view hostile to racial integration" (Orum, 1972, p. 487). In short, Wallace became the hero for the nation's politically alienated (Hogan, 1984).

Most important to understand was the commitment that Wallacites made to George Wallace. The Wallace movement was a "one-man phenomenon" (Carlson, 1981, p. 275; Hogan, 1984, p. 26). When Wallace disappeared from the political scene after the assassination attempt, the Wallace movement "disappeared as quickly as it had appeared" (Carlson, 1981, p. 275). Wallace alone was able to give voice to their discontent.

In one 15-minute advertisement during the 1968 presidential campaign, Wallace told the voters:

Yes, we fly the Confederate flag in Alabama, but no higher than the American flag . . . and you won't find a Viet Cong flag flying in Alabama. . . . The big bureaucrats in Washington never ask a good cab driver what he thinks—they only ask a pointy-headed intellectual who can't park a bicycle straight—people who write guidelines for your children. . . . The middle class is the most oppressed group of Americans, the people who fight the wars and pay their taxes; they're the ones who are ignored by the people who run the government.

Jimmy Carter. Jimmy Carter had never held national office. His political history included 4 years as a Georgia state senator and four years as governor of that same state. Gerald Rafshoon served as Carter's ad man. Rafshoon had handled both of Carter's gubernatorial campaigns in Georgia; the two men liked and trusted each other, and when Carter decided to run for the presidency, it was a Georgia ad man that was by his side (see Devlin, 1981).

In 1976, Carter waged a populist presidential campaign, portraying himself as the ultimate outsider who was against not only the Washington insiders but also the traditional liberal philosophies associated with the left wing of the Democratic party (Johnson, 1984; Witcover, 1977). Jimmy Carter knew that his presidential hopes rested in the hands of the South. And, he did not mind waving the "bloody rebel flag" to get to the White House (Diamond & Bates, 1988, p. 249). As Jamieson (1984) explained, "Carter carried not a message of tolerance but an opportunity to avenge intolerance. His message . . . was that his election symbolized Southern legitimacy and Southern power" (p. 355). Carter aired the following radio ad on White country and western stations:

The 1976 Carter "Southern" Radio Ad

AUDIO

Announcer: "On November 2nd the South is being readmitted to the Union. If that sounds strange, maybe a Southerner can understand. Only a Southerner can understand years of coarse, anti-Southern jokes and unfair comparisons. Only a Southerner can understand what it means to be a political whipping boy. But then, only a Southerner can understand what Jimmy Carter as president can mean. It's like this: November 2nd is the most important day in our region's history. Are

you going to let it pass without
having your say? Are you going
to let the Washington politicians
keep one of our own out of the
White House? Not if this man
can help it."

Carter [VO]: "We love our
country. We love our
government. We don't want
anything selfish out of
government, we just want to be
treated fairly. And we want a
right to make our own decisions."

Announcer: "The South has always
been the conscience of America—
they'll start listening to us now.
Vote for Jimmy Carter on
November 2nd."
(Diamond & Bates, 1988, pp. 249,
252)

Clearly, this radio spot pits the South against the North in no uncertain terms.
The image of the South being readmitted to the Union only after the presidential election of a southerner sets the tone of the ad. The ad conjures up the
memories of injuries and slights, imagined and real, from the Reconstruction
years to present-day America. Whether it was intended or not, the phrases
"one of our own" and "we want a right to make our own decisions" bring back
the covert and overt messages that were legendary in George Wallace's dia-
tribes against integration. In addition, the assertion that the South is the "conscience of America" suggests the moral superiority that is common of the early Wallace rhetoric. This ad clearly targeted the working class/lower-middle
class whites that still might share the us against the north-us against the Blacks
mentality that was characteristic of the Wallace presidential campaigns.

It is interesting to note that Jamieson (1984) saw this ad as a union of the
"Old" South and the "New" South, for she noted the "we shall overcome" spirit
of the ad (p. 355). According to Jamieson, this theme "honors the memory
of Martin Luther King Jr., embraces the Voting Rights Act, and condemns
the segregationist acts of Wallace and Maddox" (p. 355). But, the symbolic
language in the piece does not bear this out. The Christian religious symbology of overcoming adversity and indeed the singing of "We Shall Overcome"
is not unique to the civil rights movement; it is a song of oppressed people

everywhere, and as we mentioned earlier, this is the way in which the vast majority of southerners see themselves. And, it must repeated that this spot only aired on White country and western stations in the South (Diamond & Bates, 1988). Latent symbology is often used to mask the real intent from outsiders who might not share a given perspective.

Us Against Foreigners

Sometimes, both Cowboys and Yankees will use the us versus them technique to attack foreign countries, industry, and world leaders. It is an ethnocentric appeal that complements the populist rhetoric. Because the candidate is attacking someone outside the charmed magic circle of the United States of America, he or she is not likely to experience a backlash against the ad.

Perhaps one of the most famous us against foreigners ads was an ad created for Richard Gephardt for the 1988 presidential primary season. But before the ad ran, Gephardt had undergone what some had termed a "populist transformation." In order to understand the significance of the ad, let us first turn to this conversion process. Before the Iowa caucus season, Gephardt, a democratic congressman from Missouri, was known as "the consummate insider" (Alter & Fineman, 1988, p. 22), a man who had learned "to work within the corridors of power" (Stengel, 1988a, p. 22). But during his campaign stay in Iowa, Gephardt positioned himself as the people's candidate, nearly 180° from his former stance. Suddenly, Gephardt was "establishment-bashing" and denouncing "corporate outlaws" in order to align himself with the "culturally alienated" voters in the working- and middle-class homes of America (see Barrett, 1988, p. 16). Gephardt's message "touched a desperate fear" (Barrett, 1988, p. 16) of economic insecurity that was targeted to bring back the conservative Democrats that had voted for Reagan in 1984.

Gephardt's conversion was seen by some as a masterful stroke, in that the other presidential contenders (except for Jesse Jackson) were running on their images of being powerful Washington politicians (Kaus & Clift, 1988). But, the news media was quick to castigate "him for his politically inspired conversion from a mirky Mr. Inside to an Establishment-baiting Joe Populist" (Stengel, 1988a, p. 22). But, as *Newsweek* pointed out, "Press sniping will probably lend credence to his claim that he's fighting an 'elite' " (Kaus & Clift, 1988, pp. 46–47). The death of the Gephardt campaign is another story altogether, but for us, the importance of his campaign lies in the playing of one particular ad, which Jamieson (1984) called the "most effective ad of the early 1988 primaries" (p. xxvi). The consulting firm of Doak and Shrum produced the negative us against those foreign countries ad. Kaus and Clift (1988) elaborated, "And in what is now considered a stroke of genius, Doak and Shrum had the ad shot on film instead of cheaper videotape, producing a warm, gauzy tone" (p. 47). During the ad, the Gephardt campaign made the following claim:

"A 10,000 collar Chrysler K-car costs 48,000 dollars in Korea by the time they slap on nine separate taxes and tariffs." According to *Time*, Gephardt had told his researchers to find examples of American products that cost a great deal more in Asia. The idea was to show that American products suffer from unfair trade practices in the Far East. The researcher came back with a "Ford Taurus sedan that cost $76,000 in South Korea" (Stengel, 1988a, p. 22). The original idea had been to bash Japan, but campaign insiders decided that "everyone and their brother owns a Toyota" (Kaus & Clift, 1988, p. 47), so they decided not to pick on a popular import. The record is unclear as to why they settled on the Chrysler K-car instead of the Ford Taurus sedan, but according to *Time*, the ad is factually incorrect. The Chrysler K-car costs $28,000 in Korea, not the $48,000 specified in the advertisement (Stengel, 1988a).

One of the best political ads to come out of the 1980 presidential primaries was an ad that featured Senator Howard Baker going up against an Iranian student during a campaign speech. The ad was widely acclaimed as being a master political stroke even though the Baker campaign quickly fell into oblivion. Diamond and Bates (1988) reported that, according to his ad agency, the negative ad received "fifty times more" (p. 37) news coverage than did the actual speech. Again, it pits us against the foreigners.

The 1980 Baker "Iranian Student" Ad

VIDEO	AUDIO
Baker addressing a campaign audience.	Howard Baker [SOT]: "America must resolve that she's not going to be pushed around. That
"Howard Baker"	doesn't cause a war; that stops a war."
Baker pauses in his speech to recognize an Iranian student's question.	Iranian Student [SOT]: "When the Shah's army killed more than 60,000 Iranian people with their U.S. equipped weapons, why weren't
The student reads off a paper and waves the paper around for effect.	you raising your voice in support of international law? The United States government shipped
As this occurs, the camera goes back and forth from the student to Baker to catch the reactions of both. Baker is slow to anger.	100,000 barrels of oil for the Shah's army to kill the Iranian people. Why weren't you concerned about international law. . . ."

But, it mounts. And then Baker
explodes, interrupting the
student.

Baker points at the student with   Howard Baker [SOT]: "Cause my
finger.   friend, I'm interested in 50
                                       Americans. That's why. And
                                       when those 50 Americans are
                                       released, I'm perfectly willing
                                       to talk about that."

                                       Standing Ovation.

                                       Upbeat Music [VO]: "That old
                                       pride that we used to have, a
                                       feeling is coming back you see.
                                       What's special about America
                                       is mighty special to me."

"Baker Republican President   "That old pride that we used to
Now"   have, a feeling is coming back
                                       you see. What's special about
                                       America is mighty special to me."

Class Warfare

The us versus them song is not only heard between the Cowboys and Yankees.
It is also heard between the Democrats and the Republicans. Although traditional political science literature (see Almond & Verba, 1963) has suggested
that class differences in the United States do not exist as they do in other Western
democracies, we have seen for some time an increasing amount of attention
to class differences in our political advertising. According to the video tape
entitled *Campaigns and Elections*, the Republicans portray the Democrats as
"irresponsible spend thrifts intent on buying votes with public money," and
the Democrats portray the Republicans as "callous servants of the very rich"
(Political TV Classics, 1984).

   A great deal of political commentary since the 1980 elections has warned
that the nation is rapidly turning into two parties: the haves (Republicans) and
the have-nots (Democrats) (see Cavanagh, 1984-1985; Epstein, 1984-1985; Petrocik & Steeper, 1984-1985). Since the Reagan election in 1980, we have seen
a trend toward conservative economic policies. The New Deal, the New Frontier, and the Great Society were slowly winding down. The idea that government should do less, not more, was suddenly in vogue. This created an obvious class polarization that pitted economic arguments into such stereotypical
terms as the haves versus the have-nots. According to some analysts, this class

polarization has had a particular impact on the racial composition of each party. Several authors have noted the "white flight" from the Democratic party (Cavanagh, 1984-1985, p. 19; see also, Epstein, 1984-1985; Petrocik & Steeper, 1984-1985). Thus, these researchers noted the Republican party increasingly is becoming known as the party of Whites, and the Democratic party as the party of non-whites. According to Epstein (1984-1985), the "only region where the parties are competitive among whites is the East" (p. 3). And, Epstein has found that "the only significant demographic groups which retained their strong loyalty to the Democratic party were blacks and Jews" (p. 2). If these observations are accurate, then it is likely that we will see increased class warfare strategies utilized in our future political advertising.

Class warfare strategies are used extensively in generic party ads throughout the country. One of the most famous class warfare ads illustrates its points by the use of a tin cup and champagne flutes. The tin cup reminds us of the food lines in the Great Depression, and the champagne flutes remind us of the lifestyles of the very rich.

The 1982 Democratic "Tin Cup vs. Champagne Flutes" Ad

VIDEO	AUDIO
An arm is holding out a tin cup; the cup is catching trickles from above. The arm is dressed in a plaid work shirt.	Narrator [VO]: "The Big Republican Tax Cut — what does it mean to the average working person? About four bucks a paycheck. Not much. But it means a lot to the wealthy. It's the Republican theory called trickle down. Give to the rich, and it will eventually trickle down to everybody else. But you've got to ask yourself, just how much is trickling down to you lately?"
Suddenly champagne flute glasses appear above the tin cup. The arms are decorated with expensive diamond jewelry and watches. The champagne is poured from one champagne flute to another and finally down to the tin cup.	
Finally the plaid shirt turns the tin cup upside down. One drop falls.	Sound Effects: PLUNK!!!
	Narrator [VO]: "That's what we thought.
"It isn't Fair. It's Republican."	It isn't Fair. It's Republican."

In a 1984 Texas Senate race, Democratic candidate Lloyd Doggett ran a powerful class ad against Republican Kent Hance.

The 1984 Doggett "Butler" Ad

VIDEO	AUDIO
Scene: A beautiful parlor with plush, rich furnishings. A hidden man is in a large wing-backed chair smoking a cigar. A brandy rests on the table beside him. The arm reaches out and pulls the servant chord.	Background Music: Classical. Narrator [VO]: "As a Congressman Kent Hance has been a faithful servant of the very rich. In fact, Kent Hance wrote the new tax breaks for the wealthy, for the giant utilities, and for the huge corporations.
A book is seen. It is blue with gold lettering: "Kent Hance Tax Breaks For The Rich." A crystal chandelier is seen.	. . . tax breaks that working people must pay for.
A butler with white gloves delivers the book on a silver tray.	Kent Hance isn't a Congressman. He's a butler."
The man in chair accepts the book off the silver tray.	Man's Deep Voice [SOT]: "Very good, Hance!"

In 1984, the National Republican Congressional Committee developed a slice-of-life ad (see chapter 4) that used a subtle fear appeal to attack the Democrats' spendthrift ways.

The 1984 Republican "Grandpa" Ad

VIDEO	AUDIO
Grandpa rests in chair. Young woman enters. They talk.	Young woman [SOT]: "Grandpa, I've got to go." Grandpa [SOT]: "Thanks for the company, Susan." Young woman [SOT]: "Tomorrow

is Election Day. I'm going to vote for the first time."

Grandpa [SOT]: "Susan, did you know that the Democrats have controlled the House for the last 29 years?"

Young woman [SOT]: "Really?"

Grandpa [SOT]: "Now they're threatening to raise taxes again. Well, maybe your generation can do something about it."

Young woman [SOT]: "I hope so."

"Vote Your Future. Vote Republican."

Narrator [VO]: "Vote Republican. Keep taxes down."

The Anti-Washington Mentality

Closely aligned to the the Cowboys versus the Yankees and the class warfare advertising tactics are the anti-Washington mentality ads. The theme of the anti-Washington ads is quite simple; When political leaders go to Washington, they lose their common sense and begin legislating, appropriating, and spending money. The message is obvious: Washington is out of touch with reality. Again, it is us against them.

In a 1976 Senate campaign in Wyoming, the Republican candidate, Malcolm Wallop, attacked Washington with a portable john.

The 1976 Wallop "Potty" Ad

VIDEO	AUDIO
A cowboy is putting saddle, ropes on horse.	Narrator [VO]: "Everywhere you look these days the federal government is there, telling you what they think, telling you what they think you ought to think, telling you how you ought to do things, setting up rules you can't follow.

He straps a portable potty on a pack horse.

He rides off with pack horse and potty.

"Wallop for U.S. Senate."

I think the federal government is going too far. Now they say if you don't take the portable facility along with you on a round-up, you can't go.

We need someone to tell them about Wyoming. Malcolm Wallop will."

In a 1980 Oregon congressional race, Denny Smith graphically demonstrated that his opponent Al Almond was out of touch with Oregon.

The 1980 Smith "P.O. Box" Ad

VIDEO

AUDIO

Scene: House with Address: 3285 Balsam Dr., S.E. Salem, Oregon
Scene: Post Office Box
Scene: Two P.O. Boxes "105" & "274"

Narrator [VO]: "This is the home of Congressional candidate Denny Smith, and this is the Oregon address of Al Almond until last year. Then Al moved here—down the block so to speak.

Scene of cedar house.
Scene of beach condos.

You see, Al really lives here in Virginia except when he's here at his beach home in Maryland.

Scene: Three separate townhouses.

Or when he's collecting the rent on one of his three more homes back east.

"Denny Smith U.S. Congress" with photo on right "For Congress For Oregon For Us"

Too bad Al Almond doesn't want a home in Oregon. It would be nice to have a Congressman who likes to live here. Like Denny Smith. For Congress, for Oregon, for us."

The us against them ad, whether it manifests itself as a Cowboys versus Yankees, us against foreigners, class warfare, or anti-Washington spot, proves to be a divisive element in any campaign. The technique is dangerous because it promotes alienation and it capitalizes on the troubling divisions in American society. Barrett (1988) wrote that: "The Us-against-them formulation is often a search for easy scapegoats. It distracts from the disagreeable reality that complex problems sometimes require complex answers, and that they can be solved only at some cost to all concerned, lean cats as well as fat." (p. 16) Society's problems are not all black and white. Unfortunately, they are all gray, and this is why we call them problems, because we cannot easily distinguish the appropriate answers. For political leaders to suggest otherwise misleads the American people and serves as a great disservice to American society. We cannot hope to find solutions to our problems when we spend our time placing the blame for our problems on other people's shoulders.

DISPARAGEMENT HUMOR

Humor

Before we consider disparagement humor, it is first necessary to briefly review the literature concerning humor and persuasion. As Key (1988) stated, "Proponents of humor believe amusing advertisements are better remembered and have superior persuasion and attention-getting qualities" (p. 1; see also, Duncan, 1979; Murphy, Cunningham, & Wilcox, 1979; Sternthal & Craig, 1973). Because of this belief, between 15% and 42% of television advertising uses some form of humor (Cantor, 1976; Kelly & Solomon, 1975; Markiewicz, 1974). However, little is known concerning the impact of humor on attention, persuasion, and recall. Humorous advertising research is as inconclusive today as it was in the 1950s (see Madden & Weinberger, 1982; see also, Duncan & Nelson, 1985; Key, 1988; Sternthal & Craig, 1973).

Both psychologists and communication researchers have difficulty even defining humor (Chapman & Foote, 1976; Gruner, 1976; Zillmann, 1983). Reseachers have taken a number of different approaches in their attempts to define humor. First, humor has been defined by its stimulus properties. In other words, what types of jokes, satire, irony, and so forth were used? Second, humor has been defined in terms of an audience's observable responses. Did the audience laugh or smile? And third, humor has been defined by how various audiences perceived communication messages. Did the audience rate the communication as humorous? (Sternthal & Criag, 1973; see also, Keith-Spiegel, 1972).

Studies examining the effectiveness of humorous advertising have had mixed results. Humorous advertising messages are considered to be more interesting and, therefore, they attract greater audience attention (Duncan, 1979; Gruner, 1976; Madden & Weinberger, 1982; Markiewicz, 1974). Humorous messages may enhance source credibility (Gruner, 1976; Sternthal & Craig, 1973). And, unfortunately for advertisers, there is some evidence to indicate that humor may "detrimentally affect comprehension" (Sternthal & Craig, 1973, p. 17; see also, Brown & Bryant, 1983; Duncan, 1979; Markiewicz, 1974). Humorous advertising messages have been found to be persuasive but no more than "serious versions of the same message" (Sternthal & Craig, 1973, p. 17; see also, Duncan, 1979; Gruner, 1976). Similarly, Brooker (1981) found that although humorous advertising "was more effective than a perceived fear-arousing message, . . . it was not more effective than a straightforward message" (p. 39).

Research has indicated that when individuals are exposed to persuasive attacks, they "actively subvocalize counterarguments against the position advocated" (Miller & Burgoon, 1978–1979, p. 302; see also, Festinger & Mccoby, 1964; Osterhouse & Brock, 1970). This process is called "counterargumentation." Sternthal and Craig (1973) suggested that the persuasive power of humor rests in its ability to interfere with this counterarguing process. According to Sternthal and Craig, humor acts as a distraction that interferes with the counter-argumentation process, which then leads to increased persuasion. Other research has suggested that distraction does in fact facilitate attitude change by interfering with counterarguing (see Festinger & Maccoby, 1964; Greenwald, 1968; Miller & Burgoon, 1978–1979; Osterhouse & Brock, 1970; Rosenblatt, 1966). If, in fact, Sternthal and Craig are correct in their belief that humor acts as a distractor in persuasive message, then humor may be more persuasive than other research has indicated. However, there has not been enough scientific evaluation of this hypothesis to draw this conclusion at this time. Sternthal and Craig attributed much of the conflicting evidence concerning humor's persuasive effectiveness to the difficulties associated with humor experimentation.

Duncan and Nelson (1985) found that humor did not improve recall, product-related beliefs, or the consumer's intention to buy; however, humor did "increase attention paid to the commercial, improve liking of the commercial, reduce irritation experienced from the commercial, and increase liking of the product" (p. 38). The researchers concluded: "These results suggest that humor is more appropriate when the communication objective is to generate awareness of an advertising campaign or product. Humor seems less appropriate in achieving objectives relating to comprehension, persuasion or purchasing action" (p. 39). Thus, the effectiveness of humorous advertising remains inconclusive. However, it is utilized a great deal in both product and political advertising, and for this reason, we must seek a greater understanding of the operation of humorous political messages.

Disparagement Humor in Negative Political Advertising

For our purposes, we are concerned with the type of humor used in negative political advertising and how that type of humor is generally perceived. Negative political ads poke fun at opposition parties and candidates. A candidate's intelligence, honesty, or political record may be ridiculed. This type of humor is disparagement humor.

Disparagement humor "disparages, belittles, debases, demeans, humiliates, or otherwise victimizes" others (Zillmann, 1983, p. 85; see also, Zillmann & Cantor, 1976). Research indicates that people enjoy seeing their enemies ridiculed or debased. Wolff, Smith, and Murray (1934) suggested that we enjoy disparaging humor that is directed at *unaffiliated* objects or those things in our world not directly connected with ourselves. On the other hand, we dislike disparaging humor that is directed at *affiliated* objects or those things we normally associate as having a connection or link to ourselves. So, we might enjoy someone making disparaging comments about their own relatives, but we would not enjoy the same remarks directed at our relatives.

Zillmann and Cantor (1972, 1976) suggested a dispositional theory of humor. According to these researchers, "prediction of the enjoyment of witnessing disparagement is based on affective dispositions toward the parties involved, that is, toward the disparaging and the disparaged entities" (Zillmann, 1983, p. 90). Dispositional theory presents four postulates:

1. The more intense the negative disposition toward the disparaged agent or entity, the greater the magnitude of mirth.
2. The more intense the positive disposition toward the disparaged agent or entity, the smaller the magnitude of mirth.
3. The more intense the negative disposition toward the disparaging agent or entity, the smaller the magnitude of mirth.
4. The more intense the positive disposition toward the disparaging agent or entity, the greater the magnitude of mirth. (Zillmann, 1983, pp. 91–92)

Researchers testing these postulates have validated the explanatory usefulness of the dispositional theory (Cantor & Zillmann, 1973; Priest, 1966; Zillmann, Bryant, & Cantor, 1974; Zillmann & Cantor, 1972).

Very few studies have dealt with disparagement humor in a political setting (Priest, 1966; Zillmann et al., 1974). Zillmann et al. used disparaging 1972 political cartoons (Nixon and McGovern as the candidates) in an experimental setting. They found that "when the candidate was rejected, appreciation for the cartoon tended to decrease as the degree of brutality increased, whereas when the candidate was favored, increasing degrees of brutality tended to increase humor-appreciation ratings" (pp. 342–343). It seems that even if an individual dislikes a political figure, there is a personal limit as to how much brutality is considered fair; if the cartoon goes beyond that limit, then the cartoon is judged inordinately brutal and ceases to be as humorous as a cartoon with less brutality. In addition, even though subjects might not enjoy their favored candidate being attacked, when the attack becomes very brutal a decided change in perception occurs. This inordinate amount of brutality confirms their suspicions about the undesirability of the opposition candidate. Even though the sponsor of the cartoons was not named, respondents assumed it was the opposition who had sponsored the cartoons. So, if their favored candidate was attacked brutally, then they could enjoy this because they perceived the cartoon as being an attack of the campaign tactics of the opposition (see Zillmann et al., 1974).

In Summary. The advertising effectiveness studies indicate that viewers pay attention to humorous ads, and the source's credibility goes up as a result of the ad. And, although humorous ads are persuasive, they are not more persuasive than equivalent serious advertising messages. It has been suggested that humor may act as a distractor to the counterarguing process, which would lead to the potential for greater persuasion; however, there is as yet no experimental research conducted that has found this to be true. And, it must be noted that these advertising studies dealt with humorous product advertising, not humorous political advertising. The goals of product advertising and political advertising are different.

Negative political advertising sometimes uses disparagement humor. Disparagement humor pokes fun at opposition candidates or parties. From the psychological literature, it appears that disparaging humor is probably best used in political advertising to reinforce the faithful rather than to convert the opposition. Disparagement humor is targeted at groups of individuals who share a certain dislike for a given candidate or party. Obviously, the opposition—those who were ridiculed, debased, and so forth—would be unlikely to appreciate the humor within the political ad.

We estimate that around 15% to 20% of all negative political ads use disparagement humor. Wadsworth and Kaid (1987) found in their study of presidential advertising that between 20% and 21% of all negative ads used disparagement humor. Yet, little attention has been given to the use of humor in political advertising. Jamieson and Campbell (1983) maintained that humorous negative political ads "tend to reinforce existing attitudes rather than create positive ones" (p. 248). Jamieson (1984) suggested that the use of humor in an ad often will increase its impact on the voter, and the ad by its very nature becomes more difficult to refute. However, these hypotheses remain to be tested.

Hagstrom and Guskind (1986) said, "If you can't make them hate your opponent, the campaign motto goes, you make them laugh at him" (p. 2621). And, as Democratic pollster Mark Mellman pointed out, "once you start laughing at somebody, they don't have much of a chance" (Hagstrom & Guskind, 1986, p. 2621). In the examples that we provide (as follows and elsewhere in the book), candidates are sometimes painted as being ridiculous or disgustingly pathetic and inept. In some ads, they are depicted as cowards or compulsive liars. In others, they are shown as being absurdly insensitive to the concerns of the people. The common thematic denominator is that all the ads suggest the disparaged candidates do not deserve our respect, and thus are found not to be suitable for public office.

One of the most famous humorous ads used a unique strategy by also utilizing a flip-flop approach. Alan Cranston, the Democratic Senator from California, ran a take-off of a "Golden Oldies Ad" against the challenger, Congressman Ed Zschau. The ad pokes fun at both Ed Zschau and the "Golden Oldies Ads." The narrator imitates Wolfman Jack and calls himself "Jackman Wolf."

The 1986 Cranston "Golden Oldies Ad" Ad

VIDEO	AUDIO
Red background. Two profiles of Ed Zschau. "Greatest Hits"	Jackman Wolf [VO]: "This is Jackman Wolf with the greatest hits of the great song and dance man, Ed Zschau.
Scroll: "Caught In A Dump" "Don't Be Too Tough On Toxics" "I'd Send the Bucks To the Contras" "Caught In A Dump" "The Sanction Shuffle"	Zschau will tell you anything. You remember his classic about toxic waste. Singer I [VO]: "Caught in a Dump. I can't clean it up, because I took too much money, Baby."
"Money, Money, Money" "Who Cares About the Environment, Anyway?" "How Many Times Can A Man Change His Mind?" "Say Anything" "I Agree With Both Sides Now" "Zschau Bop Flip-Flip" "Yes, No, Maybe"	Jackman Wolf [VO]: "Or what about?" Singer II [VO]: "How many times can a man change his mind in front of twenty million people?" Singer I [VO]: "Do the Zschau Bop, Flip-Flop. Do the Zschau Bop, Flip-Flop."
"Say I Will, Say I Won't" "Never Take A Stand" "Two Face Dances" "All Over the Map" "I'll Send the Bucks To the Contras"	Jackman Wolf [VO]: "But wait, we'll give you additional Zschau Flip-Flops for free. Like they've never been released in the U.S. – International Hit . . ." Singer II [VO]: "I'll send the bucks to Nicaragua." Jackman Wolf [VO]: "Never at one

	place, at one time by one fantastic performer so many great flip-flops.
"The Incredible Shrinking Zschau"	And, it's available for a limited time only."
Block Print:	Jackman Wolf's voice changes to a normal voice. [VO]: "Because on
"On November 4th The Zschau Song & Dance Comes to an end . . .	election day, November 4th, The Zschau Song and Dance Comes to an end."

In 1986, Senator Fritz Hollings was labeled a globe-trotter by his opponent. The McMaster campaign aired a computer-generated ad that placed Hollings in various foreign settings with various foreign apparel accessories. The
result was hilarious. The ad attacks both Hollings' junkets and honoraria. As
in the "Golden Oldies" spot, the narrator imitates a famous person, Robin Leach
of "The Rich and Famous."

The 1986 McMaster "Globe-Trotter" Ad

VIDEO	AUDIO
"They may never name a battleship after him, but . . ."	Narrator (Leach Imitator) [VO]: "They may never name a battleship after Senator Hollings, but
Jet takes off.	
Photo of Hillings Head flanked by two silver wings. Looks like an Airline Logo.	But an airline in the . . . . . . Today we'll whisk you off to some of the world's most fantabulous [sic]
Scene of Italy and appropriate accessories. Scene of Greece and appropriate accessories. Scene of Bermuda and appro- priate accessories. Scene of Hong Kong and appro- priate accessories. Scene of Tahiti and appropriate accessories. Scene of Mexico and appropriate accessories.	vacation playgrounds where the rich and incompetent unwind with your tax dollars. Hong Kong, Tahiti, Mexico, France, and Egypt just to name a few. And despite a jet-setting life- style, the globe-trotting Fritz still found time to pocket more than 200,000 dollars in honoraria since 1981."

Scene of France and appropriate
accessories.
Scene of Egypt and appropriate
accessories.
Scene of England and appropriate accessories.
Scene of India and appropriate
accessories.

"$200,000 since 1981"   Sound of Cash Register.

Plane Takes off again with   Narrator (Leach Imitator) [VO]:
the Hollings Airline Emblem.   "Fritz Hollings, a world class
                                                        traveler who really knows how to
                                                        live it up on our money."

Henry McMaster for   Narrator (Regular Voice) [VO]:
U.S. Senate   "It's time for a change."

IN CONCLUSION

Political communication professionals must also consider how various political symbols chosen will be woven together to form the underlying message
or political theme of the negative ad. We have identified five overarching
thematic designs used in the dissemination of negative political and personal
characteristic issue appeals: being your own worst enemy, the people against
you, transfer, us against them, and disparagement humor. In some situations,
ads may use more than one strategy and are called multilayered thematic ads.

Many of these thematic designs have their roots in classical American political mythology. Both latent and manifest symbology are used to construct
these designs. The thematic designs have various manifestations.

4

Style: The How of
Negative Political Advertising

INTRODUCTION

Political pollster Patrick Caddell once warned Jimmy Carter that: "The old cliche about mistaking style for substance usually works in reverse in politics. Too many good people have been defeated because they tried to substitute substance for style; they forgot to give the public the kind of visible signals it needs to understand what is happening" (Sabato, 1981, p. 322).

For our purposes, style can be defined as the way in which audio, visual, and narrative techniques are used in the construction of negative political messages. Thus, style is the how of negative political advertising. Style is the way in which the story is told. Primarily, we concern ourselves with the narrative techniques that make up the plot of the negative ads. We offer our own narrative typology, and we provide a number of examples for each manifestation. (For an alternative narrative typology applied to political advertising, see Smith & Johnston, in press.)

Burnham (1983) found that "80-85 percent of the information that is retained about TV commercials is visual" (p. A6). According to Devlin (1986), "photography in spots is very important because research has shown that people remember the visual more than they retain the specifics of the audio copy" (p. 27). In fact, "the mere existence of a video image reduces recall of audio information" (Kaid & Davidson, 1986, p. 187; see also, Garramone, 1983; Warshaw, 1978).

Nonverbal cues are very important in information processing. Nimmo (1974) suggested that nonverbal cues, which he calls protolanguage, are responsible for much of America's political symbolism. Research indicates that "nonverbal channels carry more information and are more believed than the verbal band, and that visual cues generally carry more weight than vocal ones" (Burgoon, 1980, p. 184).

In this chapter, a number of various negative ad styles are identified. A warning: Researchers have used similar terms to mean widely different styles; for this reason we define the terms as we use them in this book. Our definition for a particular term may not be the same as others who have used the same term. However, the typology and terms we use are consistent within this book and should offer a means to unify the discussion of negative political advertising.

In developing our stylistic categories, we asked ourselves two sets of questions: First, "Does the candidate personally appear in the ad? If so, is the candidate speaking directly with the media audience? Or is the candidate interacting with others in the ads in some type of negative evaluation of the opposing candidate, party, and so forth?" And second, "How are the political messages organized in terms of their presentational techniques?"

We also review research findings dealing with elements of televisual style. The influence of camera perspectives, camera angle, screen asymmetry, framing, and editing on viewer's perceptions of candidates is examined. These elements comprise, in part, what Kaid and Davidson (1986) termed "videostyle."

ROLE OF CANDIDATE IN THE AD

Advertisements can be categorized as to whether or not the candidate appears in the ad. In addition, if the candidate appears, the ad can be categorized as to the role the candidate plays in delivering the negative issue appeals. Our analysis has identified three different negative political ads according to the role the candidate does or does not play within the ad: the surrogate ad, the candidate confrontation ad, and the candidate interactional ad (see Table 4.1).

Surrogate Ads

In the early days of the republic, political leaders believed that it was undignified to campaign on one's own behalf. George Washington presented a model of political behavior that suggested the office seeks the man, not the man the office. It was not until the presidential election of 1840 that this model was challenged. William Henry Harrison (Whig) faced Martin Van Buren (Democrat) in a heated electoral battle. The Democratic press had branded Harrison "a superannuated and pitiable dotard" (Jamieson, 1984, p. 13), and

TABLE 4.1
Role of Candidate in the Ad

Surrogate Ads:	Candidate does not appear in spot; sponsored or independently sponsored
Public Figure:	Widely known individuals (e.g., political leaders, interest group leaders, entertainment figures, appear in the spot)
Private Citizen:	Everyday people or paid political professional actors who are unknown to the public appear in the spot
Candidate Confrontation Ads:	Candidate appears in spot and personally delivers the negative information
Candidate Interactional Ads:	Candidate appears in spot conversing with others; the negative information is presented as an interaction between people

Harrison was forced to go on the campaign trail to refute the charges of mental and physical inadequacies. Harrison's efforts "demonstrated that a candidate could respond publicly to attack without sacrificing the presidency" (Jamieson, 1984, p. 14). However, the political model was slow to change, and it was not until the presidential election of 1912 that the modern model of an activist presidential candidate was fully accepted by both the American people and their political leaders (see Jamieson, 1984).

In the first presidential television campaign (Carroll, 1980; Diamond & Bates, 1988; Jamieson, 1984), the 1952 presidential candidates were expected to appear in their own advertising. The "Eisenhower answers America" television ads used ordinary Americans recruited from tourists visiting New York's Radio City Music Hall to question General Eisenhower on the issues of the day. However, the questions were then matched with answers that Eisenhower had previously filmed. The "Eisenhower answers America" television ads gave the illusion that Ike was answering ordinary citizens' questions. In 1956, Eisenhower appeared in a number of 5-minute ads called "Your Government and You," and his opponent, Adlai Stevenson, appeared in a number of ads that began "I'm Adlai Stevenson, and this is what I believe . . . " (see Diamond & Bates, 1988).

In 1956, the first negative political television spot that directly attacked a candidate's promises and performances was produced by the Democratic ad agency, Norman, Craig & Kummel (Diamond & Bates, 1988). In one early direct attack spot, footage from Eisenhower's previous presidential campaign's political advertising was used against him with the tag line "How's that again, General?" The promises of that earlier campaign were compared to his actual performance in office.

Incumbent presidents have been reluctant to appear in negative ads. In order to understand this reluctance, we must examine a presidential paradox: The public expects a president to be above politics yet be a master of it (see Cronin, 1977). In 1972, an advertising memo within the Nixon campaign recommended that the advertising maintain a presidential tone, which "implies a measure of dignity and a quality that is above political rhetoric. Commercials should be tasteful and thoughtful" (Jamieson, 1984, p. 301). This remains true today, for not only sitting presidents but incumbents in other offices as well.

Rarely do incumbents appear in negative advertising that directly attacks the challenger. Rather, if a direct attack ad is made, they choose to have a surrogate deliver the message. Similarly, when an incumbent is attacked by a challenger, the incumbent rarely responds to the attack personally because that would place the incumbent on the level of the challenger. So instead, a surrogate is used. A surrogate is a substitute for the incumbent. In 1972, the Nixon campaign used a series of surrogates to respond to McGovern's attacks. An internal campaign memo recommended that:

> The opposition candidates' challenges be strongly and immediately repudiated, not by the President, but by key Administration officials. If the opposition attacks the economy, the weakness of his position is pointed out by Connally. If he provides an instant solution to Vietnam, Rogers or Kissinger answers.

> The President never gets down to the level of the opposition, nor does the opposition ever get a chance in the ring on the Presidential level. (Jamieson, 1984, p. 293)

In some situations, challengers will also use surrogates in order to avoid being personally associated with negative attacks. They do this for primarily three reasons. First, they may have a public or professional image that prohibits them from making such an attack. In this situation, a candidate may have a public image of being a really nice guy or a professional image such as being a judge that prohibits the use of negative appeals, because it violates public expectations about the candidate's behavior. Second, challengers may fear a possible backlash against their candidacy or ad. Or, third, challengers simply may feel personally uncomfortable about appearing in negative advertising.

Public Figure and Private Citizen Surrogates

Public figure testimonial spots are ads in which such well known public figures as John Connally, Mary Tyler Moore, or Carroll O'Connor appear as surrogates to address the voters. It should be mentioned that surrogates do not have to be public figures. In some situations, everyday people or paid professional actors who are unknown to the general public relay the negative issue appeals. The person-in-the-street, voter editorial comment, neutral reporter, proselytizing reporter, and slice-of-life spots are examples of the use of private rather than public surrogates.

Here are two examples of candidate-sponsored surrogate advertising: a public figure surrogate spot and a private surrogate spot.

In 1980, Jimmy Carter used Jesse Jackson as a public figure surrogate in a number of radio spots that played on Black radio stations throughout the country.

A 1980 Carter "Jesse Jackson" Radio Ad

AUDIO

The Reverend Jesse Jackson: "Jobs are important. But in slavery, everybody had a job. But we had no justice, no protection under the law, no housing, no health care, no right to public education. When Reagan speaks of the good ol' days, he is serious. Reagan made 3,709 appointments in his first term as governor, nine were blacks." (Jamieson, 1984, p. 413)

Carter used Jackson because of his popularity with Black leaders and followers. The targeted appeal was used on Black radio stations only, so those outside of this minority group would not be offended.

In 1972, a McGovern private surrogate spot had an interesting ironic lead in that when a we hear the term "deep feelings," we usually associate the term with warm, loving relationships.

A 1972 McGovern "Deep Feelings" Ad

VIDEO

Camera up on black background, with orange "Nixon" filling screen. Letters change color as the people talk, from orange, to blue, to green, to yellow, to red.

AUDIO

Announcer [VO]: "People have deep feelings about President Nixon."

First woman [VO]: "He has put a ceiling on wages and has done nothing about controlling prices."

First man [VO]: "The one thing I knew his last four years was that he knew that in some way he would have to please me come this election. And what frightens me

is that if he gets in again he
doesn't have to worry about
pleasing me any more."

Second woman [VO]: "He was
caught in the act of spying and
stealing. They used to go to jail for
these things. He is the president and
should set an example."

Third woman [VO]: "There always
seem to be some big deal going on
with the Nixon people, some wheat
deal or something."

Fourth woman [VO]: "When I think
of the White House, I think of it
as a syndicate, a crime outfit, as
opposed to, you know, a
government."

Fifth woman [VO]: "All I know is
that the prices keep going up and
he is president."

Second man [VO]: "I think he's
smart, I think he's sly. He wants
to be the president of the United
States so badly he will do
anything."

Cut to black, then to slide,   Announcer [VO]: "That's exactly
white letters on black   why this is brought to you by the
background: "McGovern."   McGovern for President Committee."
                                      (Diamond & Bates, 1988, pp. 212–
                                      213)

Independently Sponsored Surrogate Ads. We have been discussing candidate-sponsored surrogate negative ads, but there is another category
of surrogate ads: the independently sponsored surrogate ad. The independently sponsored ad is an ad that is not directly linked with a candidate. An organization physically separated from either a political party or a candidate's
campaign organization sponsors the ad. In 1976, the U.S. Supreme Court ruled

in *Buckley v. Valeo* (1976) that the Federal Election Commission could not limit independent expenditures made by individuals or organizations on behalf of a candidate. An independent expenditure is when moneys are spent "without cooperation or consultation with any candidate, or any authorized committee or agent" (*Buckley v. Valeo*, 1976, pp. 20–21; for a more detailed discussion, see chapter 5). So, although individuals and groups are limited in the amount of money they can give to any one candidate, they are free to spend money on behalf of the candidate as long as they do not have any direct contact with the candidate. This ruling has significantly increased both the number of participating independent political organizations and the number of independently sponsored negative political ads in recent campaigns (see Devlin, 1986; Garramone, 1984, 1985; Jamieson, 1984; Merritt, 1984). The majority of independently sponsored ads are negative (Garramone, 1984, 1985; Jamieson, 1984; Merritt, 1984; Sabato, 1981). Thus, a candidate receives the benefit of the negative attacks against an opponent without being associated with the attacks (for a more detailed discussion concerning independently sponsored negative ads, see chapters 1 & 5). Research has shown that an independent sponsor "is perceived as more trustworthy than a candidate sponsor, and consequently, the commercial itself is evaluated more positively" (Garramone & Smith, 1984, p. 774) and that independently sponsored negative ads are effective in reducing the "image evaluation of the targeted politician" (Kaid & Boydston, 1987, p. 193).

In 1988, the Bush/Quayle presidential campaign attacked Governor Michael Dukakis on the Massachusetts furlough program. The furlough program allowed weekend passes for prisoners, some of whom were serving life without parole. Dukakis had inherited the program from a Republican predecessor (see Goldman & Matthews, 1989). Senator Al Gore had originally attacked Dukakis on his liberal furlough program during the primary debates, and Dukakis had failed to answer Gore's questions effectively. The Bush/Quayle campaign did their homework and found the case of Willie Horton. Willie Horton was a "black convict who had stabbed a white man and raped a white woman in Maryland while on furlough from a life sentence for murder in Massachusetts" (Goldman & Matthews, 1989, p. 305). The Bush/Quayle furlough ads, the revolving-door spots, never showed Horton's face or alluded to his race (see Jamieson, 1989). However "Horton's mug shot would appear in some independently produced commercials and fliers" (Goldman & Matthews, 1989, p. 307). There were those who said that these independent spots were used to play on White fears concerning Blacks and crime. Because the independent commercials were made to look like the Bush/Quayle spots, voters believed they had seen the "Willie Horton" spot much more frequently than they actually had. In addition, PAC ads began appearing that featured the relatives of Horton's victims. Bush's political speeches contained many references to Willie Horton and the Massachusetts furlough program (see Jamieson, 1989). The PAC ads, the Bush/Quayle revolving-door spots, and the campaign speeches had a synergistic effect. Dukakis and Willie Horton were linked together, and the Dukakis campaign was unable to separate the two. The National Security PAC produced one of the "Willie Horton" spots.

The 1988 NSPAC "Willie Horton" Ad

VIDEO	AUDIO
Bush photo on left. Dukakis photo on right. *"Bush and Dukakis"* "On Crime"	Announcer [SOT]: "Bush and Dukakis on crime.
Bush Photo Only "Supports Death Penalty"	Bush supports the death penalty for first degree murderers.
Dukakis Photo Only "Allowed Murderers to have Weekend Passes.	Dukakis not only opposes the death penalty, he allowed first degree murderers to have weekend passes from prison.
Willie Horton Mug Shot. "Horton received 10 weekend passes from prison." Willie Horton Mug Shot. "Kidnapping, Stabbing, and Rape."	One was Willie Horton who murdered a boy in a robbery, stabbing him 19 times. Despite a life sentence, Horton received 10 weekend passes from prison. Horton fled, kidnapped a young couple, stabbing the man and repeatedly raping his girlfriend.
Dukakis Photo. *"Weekend Prison Passes"* "Dukakis on Crime"	Weekend Passes. Dukakis on Crime.

In 1989, the Virginia gubernatorial race became one of the first statewide campaigns where the issue of abortion dominated the campaign agenda. Republican candidate Marshall Coleman was prolife, and Democratic candidate Doug Wilder was prochoice. The Virginia Society for Human Life produced a direct attack spot against Doug Wilder. The ad uses a woman's voice that alternates between business tones and a sing-song frivolous tone. The questions are given in business tones, and the refrain of "Doug Wilder does" is in the sing-song voice.

The 1989 VSHLPAC "Babies" Ad

VIDEO	AUDIO
Babies in diapers, playing	Female Announcer [VO]: "Do you

on floor with toys. Both
black and white children.

think abortion should be allowed
even in the late states of pregnancy?

"Doug Wilder Does."

Doug Wilder Does.

Do you think fathers should be
prohibited from having rights
whatsoever concerning the possible
killing of their unborn children
by abortion?

Doug Wilder Does.

Do you think abortion should be
allowed as a method of birth
control?

Doug Wilder Does.

Someone's hand plays with
a baby's hand.
"Yours or Wilder's?"

Now whose position on abortion is
extreme?
Yours or Doug Wilder's?

"Marshall Coleman."
"Vote Nov. 7"

Make the right choice Tuesday
November 7th. Vote Marshall
Coleman for Governor."

Candidate Confrontation Ads

During the 1960s to mid-1970s, some political candidates did appear in their
own negative ads, because society at the time was highly confrontational. It
fit the times; it was almost expected. One ad in the 1966 New York gubernatorial race had Rockefeller advising voters, "If you want to help keep the
crime rates high, O'Connor is your man" (Diamond & Bates, 1988, p. 327).
We call this type of ad, when the candidate personally delivers the negative
information to the media audience, a candidate confrontation ad. In a 1984
research study, Will Feltus, a Market Opinion Research consultant, found that
when a candidate appears in a negative ad and delivers the message "the credibility of the attack goes way up" (Taylor, 1986, p. A7). For this reason, we
predict that there will be an increase in candidate confrontation ads, particularly in situations where the candidate is far behind. The consultant very well
might believe that the candidate has little to lose but potentially a great deal
to gain by this advertising experiment.

In 1986, the Oregon Republican gubernatorial candidate, Norma Paulus, used a candidate confrontation, direct comparison ad against Democratic gubernatorial candidate Neil Goldschmidt. We include this as an example of when a woman candidate appears in her own negative advertising.

The 1986 Paulus "Differences" Ad

VIDEO	AUDIO
Norma Paulus talking directly into Camera in a studio setting. Name identification.	Paulus [SOT]: "People often ask me what are the differences between you and Neil Goldschmidt? I answer, *plenty.* I have eight years' statewide experience. He has none. I built my career on saving tax dollars. He built his on spending them. I've made a solemn pledge not to raise taxes. Neil? Well that answer depends on which day you ask him."
Blue background. With her signature crawled across. "Leadership *and* Experience."	Narrator [VO]: "Norma Paulus for Governor—Leadership *and* Experience."
A talking Paulus in upper left hand quarter of screen is added.	Paulus [SOT]: "I'll be a Governor you can count on."

During the 1988 Democratic presidential primaries, Senator Al Gore used footage from a Texas primary debate where he had gotten the opportunity to attack Congressman Richard Gephardt's inconsistencies. The camera captured both Gephardt's and some of the other Democratic presidential candidates' reactions. This candidate confrontation, direct attack spot was one of many Democratic primary commercials that attacked Gephardt's flip-flops.

The 1988 Gore "Flip-Flop" Ad

VIDEO	AUDIO
"Feb. 18, 1988 Dallas Texas" Senator Al Gore	Gore [SOT]: "Now let me come to the main thing, because standing up to pressure is something that the next

talking during a debate.

Congressman Gephardt smiles.

Gore talking.

Gore with Jesse Jackson listening.

Dick Gephardt (strained)

Audience members grinning. Whole floor of debating candidates over the shoulder cut of Gore. Al Gore talking.

"Gore President"

president is going to have to do, and I'm going to lay it on the line here. Dick, now look. You, you've voted against the minimum wage every time you had a chance to in the Congress. If you had your vote, it would still be $2.30 an hour. Now you say you're for it. You've voted against the Department of Education. Now you say you're for it. You voted for tuition tax credits. Now you say you're against it. You voted for Reaganomics; now you say—well where are you this week on Reaganomics? I'm not sure. And the next president of the U.S. has to be someone the American people can believe will stay with his convictions. And if pressure comes from Gorbachev, from domestic interest groups, from wherever the pressure comes, you've got to be willing to stand your ground and be consistent."

CANDIDATE INTERACTIONAL ADS

In some situations, candidates choose to appear in a television ad discussing the issues of the day with American voters. Negative issue appeals are developed through the conversational dialogue that occurs between the candidate and the voters. The conversation serves as the framework from which to develop the negative issue appeals. The candidate interactional ads may be perceived as being less strident than the candidate confrontation ads. The news interview show and cinema verité techniques are frequently used in this situation.

In 1972, George McGovern interacted with Vietnam veterans who told him about the problems they faced. McGovern was placed in opposition to the perceived uncaring, untrustworthy Richard Nixon in an implied comparison argument. The veteran's stated hope that he would like to have a "president that we can believe in" leads the voter to make the comparison between Nixon and McGovern.

The 1972 McGovern "Vietnam Veteran" Spot

VIDEO   AUDIO

Camera up on group of   Announcer [VO]: "Most of them
disabled veterans, many in   were still safe in grade school
wheelchairs. McGovern   when this man first spoke out
introduces himself, shakes   against the war, risking political
hands with them.   suicide in the hope they might be
                                  spared. For them, his early voice
                                  has now been heard too late. If
                                  the shooting stopped tomorrow,
                                  they'd still have to face their
                                  long road back, rebuilding shattered
                                  lives and broken dreams. And
                                  they're looking for all the help and
                                  understanding they can find."

Pan from McGovern to ECU   Veteran [SOF]: "There's a parking
of veteran, early twenties,   lot down here, that's especially
mustache. Camera pulls   for wheelchair people. It's got
back as he gestures to his   *ice* on the road. How far do you
wheelchair.   think you can get—we can't even
                                  put studded snow tires on these
                                  things. . . . !

Cut to CU, same veteran.   There are people that have
                                  disabilities, stuck in these
                                  things. And they don't want to
                                  be here. Some of them can't use
                                  their arms, their fingers. That
                                  doesn't make them a nonproductive
                                  individual!"

Cut to McGovern.   McGovern [SOF]: "You love the
                                  country, there's no question about
                                  that, and yet you're halfway mad at
                                  it too, aren't you?"

Cut to CU of veteran, in   Veteran [SOF]: "Believe me, when
profile.   you lose the control of your
                                  bowels, your bladder, your
                                  sterility—you'll never father a

	child—when the possibility of you ever walking again is cut off for the rest of your life, you're twenty-three years old, you don't want to be a burden on your family— you know where you go from here? To a nursing home. And you stay there till you rot . . . "
Cut to CU of McGovern. Reaction Shots.	McGovern [SOF]: " . . . I love the United States, but I love it enough so I want to see some changes made. The American people want to believe in their government, want to believe in their country. And I'd like to be one of those that provides the kind of leadership that would help restore that kind of faith. I don't say I can do it alone. Of course I can't. But the president can help set a new tone in this country. He can help raise the vision and the faith, and the hope of the American people. That's what I'd like to try to do."
Pan to same veteran.	Veteran [SOF]: "I'd like to get a president that we *can* believe in."
	McGovern [SOF]: "Well, I hope I'll be that kind of a president."
Cut to still photo of McGovern with two veterans, "McGovern" in white letters across bottom.	Announcer [VO]: "McGovern. For the people." (Diamond & Bates, 1988, pp. 191–192)

By the mid-1970s, the post-Watergate years, American society had become less directly confrontational, so candidates preferred negative surrogate ads rather than personally appearing in their own negative spots (see Diamond & Bates, 1988). These took the form of candidate-sponsored surrogate ads using public or private surrogates. And, in some instances, independently sponsored surrogate ads were produced. Although the use of surrogate ads was a general trend, it cannot be used as a universal statement. Certain regional variations did exist. In Alabama, for example, gubernatorial and attorney general candidates frequently appeared in candidate confrontation ads during the 1970s and 1980s. Recent political consulting research has shown that candidate confrontation ads are perceived as being more credible than surrogate spots. We may see more of both candidate confrontation and candidate interaction ads in the future, particularly in the campaigns of political challengers.

Candidate confrontation ads, candidate interaction ads, and surrogate ads utilize various negative dramatic narratives to frame their messages.

NEGATIVE DRAMATIC NARRATIVE TECHNIQUES

The negative dramatic narrative techniques establish the "pattern of events" that place order on the "*characters* performing actions in incidents that interrelate to comprise a 'single, whole, and complete' action . . ." (Holman, 1972, pp. 397–398). These narrative techniques have long been recognized as resembling television news. This similarity is quite purposeful.

Jamieson and Campbell (1983) observed that campaigns blur the distinctions between news and commercials in order to increase the credibility of the commercial's message. This is done in two ways: First, the actual commercial may be designed so that it resembles a news story. And second, the campaign may place their news style ads around news shows, which increases the chance that they will be perceived as a real news piece. Negative political advertising can be said to be of the news style genre.

The News Style Genre

We have identified 11 separate dramatic constructions of the news style genre: the person-in-the-street, the voter editorial comment, the public figure testimonial, the neutral reporter package, the proselytizing reporter package, the news interview show, the news show dramatization, the visual documentary, the slice-of-life, the cinema verité, and the "Saturday Night Live" news segment. All 11 dramatic constructions share certain similarities. First, the ads imitate SOT/broadcast news packages in that they contain the essential ingredients for a broadcast news story. The spots are brief and conversational. They have a beginning, a middle, and an end. There are protagonists and antagonists. There is conflict. They are fast-paced, colorful, and dramatic. They are thematic; and, they tell a story (see Garvey & Rivers, 1982). (See Table 4.2.)

The news style genre is not new. In 1934, the political consulting firm of Whitaker & Baxter produced phony newsreels to fight Sinclair Lewis, a radi-

TABLE 4.2
Negative Dramatic Narrative Techniques

The News Style Genre:	Ad resembles television news
The Person-in-the-Street Ad:	Ad resembles a street poll
Voter Editorial Comment Ad:	Voters appear in a staged setting
Public Figure Testimonial Ad:	Prominent politicians, entertainment personalities, etc., appear in the ad
Neutral Reporter Package Ad:	A neutral reporter presents "facts," and it is the public's interpretation of these facts that invites the negative judgment
Proselytizing Reporter Package Ad:	A proselytizing reporter presents emotion-laden arguments. Ad has a strong exhortative-didactic flavor
The News Interview Show Ad:	Information presented in a talk/interview show format
The News Show Dramatization Ad:	A phony news show is the format
The Visual Documentary Ad:	Negative appeals are in the interpretation of the visual messages
The Slice-of-Life Ad:	The ad is a staged enactment of life situations
The Cinema Verité Ad:	Camera captures unstaged conversation, activity. Has the appearance of a television documentary
The "Saturday Night Live" News Segment Ad:	The ad is an exaggerated news-like segment that usually uses disparagement humor appeals

cal Democratic gubernatorial candidate in California. The newsreels were aired in California movie theaters between movies. The newsreels appeared as if they were "real newsreels" that were normally aired between features (see Diamond & Bates, 1988, p. 37). In 1984, James Kelly (1984), commenting on the Reagan campaign in "Packaging the Presidency," wrote that "the managers . . . [had] done such a seamless job of presenting their candidate this year that viewers often had trouble telling the paid political announcements from the evening news" (p. 36).

As Jamieson (1984) explained, because of the very nature of the news style genre, the ads imply a "seeming neutrality" (p. 309) that appeals to the modern-day ticket-splitter. DeVries and Tarrance (1972) found that "television news and documentaries and other specials were by far the most important media influences on the split-ticket voter" (p. 78). By presenting political advertis-

ing in a news style, consultants and candidates hoped there would be a blurring of distinction, and the ads would gain credibility by their style of
presentation.

In order to reinforce the news style presentation, campaigns often buy times
within and adjacent to news programming, increasing the likelihood of the
regular news shows blurring with the news style negative political ads (see
DeVries, 1971; Diamond & Bates, 1988; Kelly, 1984; Wilson, 1987). In effect, because of where they are placed, the credibility of the news shows rubs
off on the television ads. Television news is the primary source of news for
two thirds of the American public, and the majority of Americans believe that
television news is more credible than other news forms (Sabato, 1981). Not
surprisingly, the most frequent placement spot for political ads is surrounding
news programming (Wilson, 1987; see Fig. 4.1).

Eleven Dramatic Narrative Constructions
of the News Style Genre

The Person-in-the-Street Ad.   The person-in-the-street ad uses the familiar broadcast news technique of stopping passers-by and asking their opinions. People actually are stopped and asked questions by the production crew.
In some situations, campaigns interview literally hundreds of people until they
get the right type of individuals saying the right thing. The participants are
represented as a living democratic survey because usually campaign consultants work to depict various targeted demographic groups. These ads, accord-

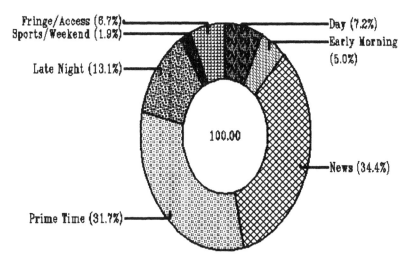

FIG. 4.1.   Advertising by time of day in 10 Democratic Senate races. (From "Presidential Advertising in 1988" by P. Wilson, 1987, *Election Politics*, *4*, p. 20. Reprinted by permission.)

ing to Jamieson (1984), "do not appear to be unfair because, first, we are taught that everyone is entitled to express his or her opinion and, second, these people are voicing opinions that the electorate presumably is disposed to share" (p. 450). These ads were used extensively in the presidential campaigns of 1976 and 1980 (see Jamieson, 1984).

Sabato (1981) reported that the person-in-the-street ad "generates the highest audience recall of all the standard formats and is helpful in communicating with targeted subgroups" (p. 123). Republican political consultant Peter Dailey claimed that person-in-the-street ads serve as excellent reinforcing tools but do not work as persuasion tools (Devlin, 1981). It seems that already committed voters identify with the participants in the ads who are perceived as being similar to themselves. The person-in-the-street ad has been found to be particularly effective with liberals (Berkman & Kitch, 1986; Sabato, 1981).

The candidate-sponsored surrogate ad discussed previously, the 1972 McGovern "Deep Feelings" ad, is an example of a negative person-in-the-street spot. In 1976, Ford's advertising agency, Bailey–Deardourff produced a negative direct comparison ad that utilized the person-in-the-street construction.

The 1976 Ford "Ford vs. Carter" Ad

VIDEO	AUDIO
Camera up on bald man, glasses.	Man [SOF]: "The thing that I like most about Mr. Ford is that he's steady. He is not erratic; we can count on him to do what's in the best interest of the country."
Cut to Black man.	Man [SOF]: "I think he offers solidarity."
Cut to woman in scarf.	Woman [SOF]: "I think he's a strong person. I think he stands up for what he thinks is right."
Cut to well-dressed young man.	Man [SOF]: "I think Ford's been very stable."
Cut to blonde woman in turtleneck.	Woman [SOF]: "He takes things very gradually, very carefully. I don't think he's going to make any big mistakes. I'm afraid that Carter's too ambiguous."

Cut to man in leisure suit.	Man [SOF]: "Carter is not quite sure which direction he goes. He changes his mind on his stand every other day or so."
Cut to man in cap.	Man [SOF]: "He contradicts himself from one day to another."
Cut to young man in T-shirt.	Man [SOF]: "He has changed his opinions from one day to the next."
Cut to middle-aged woman.	Woman [SOF]: "He is much too wishy-washy."
Cut to man with moustache.	Man [SOF]: "He's very, very wishy-washy."
Cut to heavy-set man.	Man [SOF]: "He seems to be a little wishy-washy."
Cut to earnest young man.	Man [SOF]: "If he'd stand up and say what he's for, he'd be a little easier to understand, and maybe to believe."
Cut to short-haired woman.	Woman [SOF]: "All the things we've read about Jimmy Carter, I think, are true—that he is fuzzy on a lot of the issues."
Cut to still photo of Ford at podium, smiling.	Same woman [VO], continuing: "I like President Ford—the man who will tell you just exactly where he does stand." (Diamond & Bates, 1988, p. 331)

Voter Editorial Comment Ad.   Closely akin to the person-in-the-street spots are the voter editorial comment spots. The person-in-the-street spots give the appearance that a cameraperson is stopping individuals in a public street and asking them questions about the candidates. In voter editorial comment spots, the person is usually speaking from a studio or other staged setting; the spot looks more canned than the person-in-the-street spot. They resemble the guest editorial comment spots that local television stations make available as a public service. The point remains the same: average, everyday Americans are speaking their piece about political candidates. In 1986, some spots used ordinary people going about their normal work day, talking about the candidate. In many situations, these are not average Americans but paid professional actors who are unknown to the general public.

In 1986, Judge Claude Harris used a series of voter editorial comment spots in his Alabama campaign for the U.S. House of Representatives. There were three spots using an actual steelworker, housewife, and teacher. All of these voters lived in the Seventh Congressional District. The spots emphasized a dissatisfaction with the status quo and generically attacked existing congressional officials. Harris was running for an open seat, but the theme of these spots was an underlying anti-Washington, "throw the rascals out."

The 1986 Harris "Steel Worker" Ad

VIDEO	AUDIO
White type on black screen, "Steve Adams Steel Worker"	Announcer VO: "Mr. Steve Adams, Steel Worker."
Steve Adams speaks directly to Camera for entire spot.	Steve VO: "Lots of good people lost their jobs when the steel industry went bad . . .
	. . . I just don't think the lawmakers in Washington were really in-touch with what was happening in their own state . . .
	. . . we've got to have a Congressman who really understands that unfair trade practices are stealing our jobs . . .
	. . . someone's got to put a stop to it . . .
	Yeah, I think Claude Harris understands. And I think he'll do something about it."
Type is supered over a black screen.	Announcer [VO]: "On November 4th elect Claude Harris, United States

Congress. He'll speak for the
people."

Public Figure Testimonial Ad. Instead of ads using average Americans, the public figure testimonial ads use "prominent politicians, movie stars or television personalities speaking on behalf of the candidate" (Devlin, 1986, p. 31), or in some situations speaking negatively about the opponent. The candidate may actually appear in the ad and speak directly to the media audience.

In the 1980 presidential primaries, Edward Kennedy used Carroll O'Connor, known to America as Archie Bunker, for ads targeting President Jimmy Carter.

The 1980 Kennedy "Carroll O'Connor" Ad

VIDEO	AUDIO
Carroll O'Connor sits facing the camera; he is wearing an open-collared shirt and a leisure jacket.	O'Connor [VO]: "Friends, Herbert Hoover hid out in the White House too, responding to desperate problems with patriotic pronouncements, and we got a hell of a depression. But I'm afraid Jimmy's depression is going to be worse than Herbert's. I'm supporting Senator Kennedy because he is out there facing issues; inflation, sky high prices, an almost worthless dollar, unemployment. I trust Ted Kennedy. I believe in him in every way, folks."
The words "Kennedy for President" appear on a red background with a small picture of Kennedy to the right. (Devlin, 1986, p. 52)	Announcer [VO]: "Kennedy for president. Let's fight back."

Neutral Reporter Package Ad. Neutral reporter ads were used extensively in both the 1976 and 1980 presidential campaigns (Jamieson, 1984, 1986). As Jamieson (1986) defined it, "A neutral reporter ad sets forth a series of factual statements and then invites a judgment. These are rational political ads that offer factual data, invite or stipulate a conclusion, and warrant that conclusion" (pp. 18–19).

In 1968, Richard Nixon used a neutral reporter ad to dramatize the nation's crime rate.

The 1968 Nixon "Crime" Ad

VIDEO	AUDIO
White letters over black background: "A Political Broadcast." Fade to city street, night. Reflection of shoes appears on the pavement, pan up to reveal middle-aged woman walking along empty street.	Sound of footsteps.
She has red hair, white gloves, and a blue collar beneath her coat. She holds her hand together apparently clasping her purse.	Announcer [VO]: "Crimes of violence in the United States have almost doubled in recent years. Today a violent crime is committed almost every sixty seconds. A robbery every two and a half minutes. A mugging every six minutes. A murder every forty-three minutes. And it will get worse unless we take the offensive. Freedom from fear is a basic right of every American. We must restore it."
Camera follows her as she passes several barred storefronts. Then she passes the camera; it follows her from the rear. She is completely alone throughout the sequence. No other pedestrians or vehicles. Fade to blue background, with white letters: "THIS TIME VOTE LIKE YOUR WHOLE WORLD DEPENDED ON IT."	

Cut to second super:
"NIXON." Camera zooms in
until it fills the screen.
(Diamond & Bates, 1988, pp. 167-168)

The Proselytizing Reporter Package Ad. The proselytizing reporter
is not subtle. The key to the proselytizing reporter spot is its emotion-laden
content. The ads remind the authors of the news reporting on *The 700 Club*,
where journalists who sound like television evangelists tell their flock the way
it is according to Pat Robertson. There is a strong moral undertone to the piece.
Frequently facts, manipulated facts, and emotion-laden arguments are inter-
spersed through the piece. The ads have a strong exhortative-didactic flavor.

In the 1986 Alabama Senate race, Republican incumbent Jeremiah Denton
ran a series of ads that used the proselytizing reporter style. Some of these
are reviewed in chapter 6, but one must be mentioned here.

The 1986 Denton "National Taxpayers Union" Ad

VIDEO	AUDIO
LS of a corner building.	Announcer [VO]: "For working Americans this is one of the most important addresses in the country . . .
Zoom in on nameplate of building that says, "NATIONAL TAXPAYERS UNION."	. . . the National Taxpayers Union. It's where they rate our congressmen and senators on how well . . .
Dissolve to a voting ballot.	. . . they vote to protect our tax dollars. Here in Alabama, you ought to know the latest score . . .
"Jeremiah Denton" super on screen with "71" below it.	. . . conservative Senator Jeremiah Denton, seventy-one . . .
"Richard Shelby" super on screen with "19" below it	. . . big spender Richard Shelby, nineteen . . .
Blue haze around Denton's score with Denton's photo above.	. . . now you know who really votes to save your money . . .
Red box around Shelby's name.	. . . and who votes to spend it."

The News Interview Show Ad. The news interview show ad takes its visual style from talk/interview shows such as "Meet the Press," "Donahue" or "The Oprah Winfrey Show." The ads simply look like a talk/interview show. The format has two varieties: the candidate as interviewer or the candidate as interviewee. The essential ingredient remains the same: dialogue between the candidate and the people. This style was used in early television spots in the 1952 and 1956 campaigns. In 1968, Richard Nixon created a series of ads that looked like "Meet the Press," with ordinary citizens questioning the former vice president (Jamieson & Campbell, 1983). This type of ad creates the illusion of an unstaged political environment with the candidate potentially going up against hostile critics; but, in reality, the taping environment is very controlled. These ads often seem to be more credible than other alternatives in that they resemble a news interview format. Because the candidate appears in the spots, the ads usually use an implied comparison argumentation mode.

In 1980, Reagan used a subtle implied comparison ad that suggested the Democrats were weak on defense. According to Diamond and Bates (1988), the footage easily could have been mistaken for a network news package. The Reagan campaign's media buyer, Ruth Jones, "bought Reagan time slots within or adjacent to news programs to complete the maneuver" (p. 227).

The 1980 Reagan "Defense" Ad

VIDEO	AUDIO
Camera up on Reagan at lectern.	Announcer [VO]: "An important part of Ronald Reagan's campaign are the Citizens' Press Conferences, which give the people a chance to ask the questions."
Cut to citizen in audience.	Citizen [SOF]: "As president, how would you deal with the congressional Democrats who are calling for still further cutbacks in defense spending?"
Cut to Reagan.	Reagan [SOF]: "Well, here again is where I believe a president must take his case to the people. And the people must be told the facts. The people will not make a mistake if they have the facts. But the one thing we must be sure of is,

the United States must never be
second to anyone else in the world
in military power.

Reaction shots, then cut back   [Applause] But the purpose of
to Reagan.   weapons is not to go to war;
                                       the purpose of weapons is to
                                       convince the other fellow that
                                       he better not go to war."
                                       [Applause builds]

                                       Announcer [VO]: "Reagan. He'll
                                       provide the strong new leadership
                                       America needs. Paid for by
                                       Citizens for Reagan."
                                       (Diamond & Bates, 1988, pp. 226–
                                       227)

The News Show Dramatization Ad. The news show dramatization
ad is very similar in principle to Whitaker & Baxter's 1934 phony newsreels,
but this time the ads look like a phony TV news show. The news show dramatization ad is different from the interview show ad in that there appears to be
an anchorperson in the ad. In 1986, California Representative Ed Zschau ran
a news dramatization ad against Senator Alan Cranston. In the spot, a network anchor look-alike announces a "U.S. Senate campaign update" while the
word "dramatization" appears at the beginning of the spot. Many California
television stations were very concerned that their viewers would be misled
by the Zschau spot, so they added their own disclaimer (Hagstrom & Guskind,
1986).

The 1986 Zschau "News Anchor" Ad

VIDEO   AUDIO

News Anchor behind desk.   News Anchor [VO]: "In Washington,
Chromakey of the U.S. Capitol   despite an overwhelming vote by the
in upper right. "U.S. Senate   United States Senate to impose a
Update" on same. Lower one-   death penalty for drug pushers who
third, "Dramatization Paid for by   willfully murder, California
the Ed Zschau For U.S.   Senator Alan Cranston voted NO.
Senate Committee.

Chromakey changes to picture of   The vote shouldn't come as a

Cranston.	surprise to Californians. Cranston also voted against the death penalty for terrorists and hijackers who murder.
Zschau vs. Cranston still photographs, names under photos.	However, the latest vote promises to heat up a tight Senate race against his opponent, Congressman Ed Zschau who voted for the death penalty as part of a tough anti-drug measure.
News Anchor with Capitol Chromakey again with "U.S. Senate Update."	This is a United States Senate Campaign Update."

The Visual Documentary Ad. The visual documentary is unusual in that the visual elements that appear in the ad are of primary importance. The ads appear as strings of events, places, and things that are interwoven to create a desired effect. The visual documentary uses two forms: negative visuals or positive visuals. When negative visuals are used, a neutral reporter or announcer may narrate over the video, but the primary negative ingredients rest in the visual images. In other visual documentary ads, the visuals may be quite positive; however, the narration may suggest that the scenes portrayed in the visuals will not be so positive or beautiful anymore if the opposition is elected.

In 1968, the Republicans ran a television ad against Vice President Hubert Humphrey that presented a series of negative pictures associated with the Democratic administration: the Chicago riots, the Vietnam war, and so forth. This type of presentation "invites the audience to impute causality" (Jamieson, 1984, p. 450). In other words, the Democratic party and thus Humphrey were portrayed as being guilty of having had these disastrous things occur on their watch.

In 1986, Democratic Senator Pat Leahy ran an implied negative ad against his opponent, Republican Richard Snelling, in the Vermont Senate race. The ad uses beautiful pictures of snow-topped mountains, streams, and so on. We see wildlife. We hear the wind. The film has a blue, cool feel about it. As it stands, it is a breathtaking nature film. Leahy had positioned himself as a strong environmentalist while identifying his opponent as being weak on the environment.

The 1986 Leahy "Environment" Ad

VIDEO	AUDIO
Beautiful pictures of snow covered hills, mountains.	Sound Under: Wind Blowing; Tranquil Music.

Water – blue   Narrator [VO]: "The Green Mountains
Trees. Tranquil surroundings.   can rest easy tonight. A powerful
                                       friend stopped James Watt from
                                       selling this forest land and
                                       said no to nuclear waste dumps.
Ice flows
Rushing Water   He's rated the number one
Birds   environmentalist in the U.S.
Trees   Senate.

Leahy walking away   With a mountain of seniority to
from camera through   back him up. Vermont can't afford
a path between the trees.   to start all over again.

You can help.   And Senator Pat Leahy needs you
1-800-LEAHY-6   like the Green Mountains need him.
                                       Call. It takes a long time to
                                       build a mountain."

The Slice-of-Life Ad. The slice-of-life ad is melodramatic. In the fall of 1989, the networks experimented with news shows that used news reenactments or news re-creations. This news style is very similar to the slice-of-life ad format. It "calls for paid actors in "natural" conversation during a scene from everyday life" (Sabato, 1981, p. 176; see also, Devlin, 1986). Although slice-of-life ads have been very popular in product advertising, they have had a very lukewarm reception among political consultants for a number of years because of the way in which they were written. In 1976, President Ford aired three slice-of-life ads. The ads were produced by a volunteer ad agency, Batten, Barton, Durstine and Osborne, Inc. President Ford personally approved them. One of the ads was an implied comparison ad, but the dialogue was so unbelievable that most people laughed at the spots.

First Woman: "Ellie! Are you working for President Ford?"

Second Woman: "Only about 26 hours a day. Notice anything about
                    these food prices lately?"

First Woman: "Well, they don't seem to be going up the way they
                    used to."

Second Woman: "President Ford has cut inflation in half."

First Woman: "In half! WOW!
(Devlin, 1977, p. 240).

The ads were universally ridiculed. According to Diamond (1976), one political advertising analyst concluded: They were "probably the most heavy-handed and amateurish campaign spots ever aired by a major candidate" (p. 13). It seems that the American public and modern political consultants do not like their candidates being sold like toothpaste and dishwashing liquid.

Recently, however, political consultants have chosen a more sophisticated approach to slice-of-life spots. Gone is the inane dialogue associated with product advertising, and in its place are minidramatizations that resemble contemporary movie or television exchanges.

In 1982, California Republican State Representative candidate James Peter Cost ran one of these minidramatizations against his opponent, Sam Farr. A group of multiethnic criminals were seated around a table discussing the Farr campaign.

The 1982 Cost "Criminals" Ad

VIDEO	AUDIO
Criminals seated around table. Talking.	Criminal One [SOT]: "Politics, Schmolitics [sic]. Sam Farr has always come through for us. Right?" All Criminals [SOT]: "Yeah!"
Stack of money being pushed across table.	Criminal One [SOT]: "So let's help Sam Farr out of this jam. After all, he came out against the victims' bill of rights."
	Criminal Two [SOT]: "Yeah!"
	Criminal One [SOT]: "And against tougher sentences. And we all know where Sam Farr is on the death penalty. Think of Sam Farr as a good investment."
	All Criminals [SOT]: Laughter.
Prison Guard closes doors on their prison cell.	Announcer [VO]: "Let's lock up the criminals before they lock up California. Let's keep the law working for us.
Photo of James Peter Cost "James Peter Cost"	Elect James Peter Cost for Assembly."

In the 1988 election campaign, the Democratic National Committee produced a slice-of-life spot that had two blue-collar workers going home after a day's work at the factory.

The 1988 DNC "Workers" Ad

VIDEO	AUDIO
Two workers on plant grounds walking.	Worker One [SOT]: "I voted for the Republicans but that doesn't make me a Republican. Republicans haven't been voting for me and that's for sure. They're against health care. Now my folks can't afford to get sick. They're against student loans. My kids can't afford to go to college. They're against day care. My wife can't afford to work. They're against affordable housing. Now we can't find a decent place to live. Now they want me to vote Republican. I can't afford to be a Republican.
"Let's Bring Prosperity Home."	I think it's time to check out those Democrats."

The Democratic National Committee also produced nearly a dozen ads in 1988 in which actors played Republican consultants discussing the packaging of George Bush. All of these spots were slice-of-life ads (see chapter 3).

The Cinema Verité Ad.   Cinema verité ads have the look and feel of a television documentary (Jamieson & Campbell, 1983). In the cinema verité style "the camera is looking in on unstaged conversation" (Diamond & Bates, 1988, p. 193; see also, Jamieson & Campbell, 1983) and natural lighting frequently is used. The slice-of-life ad and the cinema verité ad are very similar, but the slice-of-life is an obviously staged presentation with the use of paid professional actors. Cinema verité ads use ordinary people and give a greater sense of realism (please note that some authors use the two types of ads interchangeably, e.g., Jamieson & Campbell, 1983). As Jamieson and Campbell described them, "These commercials walk the viewer through part of the candidate's day, permitting voters to eavesdrop on exchanges with important peo-

ple, overhear warm human exchanges with constituents or would-be supporters, and see the candidate with family" (p. 237).

In 1972, McGovern hired Charles Guggenheim, a famous filmmaker, as
his advertising consultant. The ads that Guggenheim created have a distinc-
tive visual style. McGovern is seen listening and empathizing with the people
(Jamieson, 1984; see also, Agranoff, 1976a; Diamond & Bates, 1988). These
ads were used in both the primaries and the general election campaign. During the primaries, if a McGovern ad was negative, it was an attack on Nixon
and the Republicans, not on his fellow Democrats (Diamond & Bates, 1988).

The 1972 McGovern "End the War" Ad

VIDEO	AUDIO
Camera up on black letters against white background: "The following is a paid political announcement on behalf of Senator George McGovern."	Announcer [VO]: "The following is a paid political announcement on behalf of Senator George McGovern, candidate for president of the United States."
Fade to series of shots of McGovern shaking hands, talking, smiling, eating; all outdoors, with friendly voters. Camera wobbles as it moves along with candidates.	McGovern [VO]: "I think the next president of the United States has to be very, very careful to be candid and frank and honest with the American people. The 'credibility gap' is about the saddest phrase that has ever crept into the American political vocabulary, because what it means is that millions of people no longer trust even the president of the United States.
Cut to ECU of McGovern seated.	They have seen the country taken into a war that was not in the national interest, and all kinds of explanations made about how it was advancing the cause of freedom and the dignity of man.
Cut to different shot, suggesting new topic.	I think the real deterrent to a nuclear attack on this country

is not some kind of defensive, antiballistic missile system, but the certain knowledge in the mind of any attacker that if they hit the United States, they would be utterly destroyed.

Cut to different shot.

The most important and most urgent problem right now is to end the war in Southeast Asia, and beyond that, to end the assumptions behind it — the notion that somehow we have to play policeman for the world. Or the notion that you can export freedom to Asia in a B-52."

Cut to McGovern in group of people, outdoors. McGovern nods.

Yeah. Yeah. Yeah. Complete withdrawal. We've got to get out. Yeah. I'd set a date and. . . . "

Man: [SOF]: "Are you going to do it?"

McGovern [SOF]: "Absolutely.

You know, I've been advocating that for years."

Man [SOF]: inaudible

McGovern [SOF]: "I know it. But that's why I'm running against him."

Man [SOF]: "Well, you've got my vote if you can pull 'em all out."

McGovern [SOF]: "Well, you can count on it. . . . "
(Diamond & Bates, 1988, pp. 197–199).

The "Saturday Night Live" News Segment Ad. In recent years, an exaggerated news approach has been used with humorous substantive appeals. The presentations are remarkably similar to the types of stunts used during

"Saturday Night Live's" news segment. The formats run from bizarre slice-of-life segments to edited segments of spaghetti westerns. Modern, digital effects are used to mat images on and around candidates with humorous results. In some situations, the ads bring to mind such cultural icons as silent pictures and classic cartoons. Silent picture techniques reminiscent of the old Buster Keaton and Keystone Cops movies have been used: story cards, highly dramatic music compositions, and improbable settings and scenarios. Slapstick forms of comedy with actors using broadly exaggerated characterizations are common. The advertisements frequently are shot in black and white. Often, cartoons and music reminiscent of cartoon classics are used. The drama that is staged is highly exaggerated, even preposterous in its presentation. And the comedic music when used serves to accentuate the highly stylized dramas.

In 1984, Randy Patchett, a Republican congressional candidate from Illinois, ran a spot attacking his opponent, Ken Gray. The spot and the accompanying music imitated an old news reel for humorous effect.

The 1984 Patchett "News Reel" Ad

VIDEO	AUDIO
Ike's being sworn in. We see a news clip in black and white. Then we see the Marciano Fight.	Narrator [VO]: "It's 1954, Ike's in Washington. Marciano in victory.
In the next scene, several miners are standing around.	Unemployment in Southern Illinois. And Ken Gray promises us 25,000 new jobs.
Newspaper with Ken Gray photograph. "1960" supered over a rocket. The rocket takes off. A Graph is supered over the rocket. Under the graph, "Southern Illinois Unemployment"	— 1960 — The first weather satellite goes up. So does Southern Illinois unemployment.
Then we see a Jet returning. "1983" supered over scene.	— 1983 — Ken Gray returns from Florida. And promises 25,000 new jobs. And as usual delivers nothing. Old promises won't solve new
Ken Gray speaking at podium.	problems.

CU of Ken Gray standing.
CU of Ken Gray seated.

"Randy Patchett U.S. Congress" with photograph in upper right	For a newer, brighter future, elect Randy Patchett to Congress."

In 1986 Mark White, a Texas Democratic gubernatorial candidate, used footage from an old black and white western. In the ad, White attacks gubernatorial candidate Bill Clements.

The 1986 White "Cowboy" Ad

VIDEO	AUDIO
Scene from old western; cowboys standing with horses talking on a downtown street. They're getting together a posse.	First Cowboy [VO]: "You think you can find it? Second Cowboy [VO]: "If that secret plan is out there, we'll find it."
Cowboys mount up and ride off. They're seen searching, searching, searching. Back and forth. High and Low.	Group of Cowboys [VO]: "HO!! HAH!" Narrator [VO]: "They're searching and searching. Searching high and low across Texas for Bill Clements's secret plan.
More searching.	For five months, he's been talking about his secret plan to balance the state's budget without new
Cowboys looking in dresser drawers in old house.	taxes. But now he can't seem to find them.
Scenes of Cowboys, horses, and ranch life. They're still s e a r c h i n g .	Could Bill Clements just be playing old time politics? Trying to get elected anyway he can?" Cows [VO]: "MOO!!! MOO!!!"
Cowboy jumps over fence and lands on horse's back and rides off.	Narrator [VO]: "Come on, let's keep searching for Bill Clements's secret plan."

In 1986, a gubernatorial candidate in South Carolina, Carroll Campbell, used
a stereotypical, good ol' boy crook to attack his opponent. This type of ad is
used frequently in the southeastern United States. The good ol' boy crook is
usually a thinly veiled imitation of Boss Hogg on the "Dukes of Hazzard" television show. Typically, the character is overweight, chewing on a cigar, and
wearing suspenders. Such a characterization plays to the voters' stereotypes
of crooked southern politicians.

The 1986 Campbell "Good Ol' Boy" Ad

VIDEO	AUDIO
Messy desk with balding, overweight man with suspenders. Cigar in hand. Talking with a heavy Southern drawl.	"Ol' Boy" [VO]: "Oh, Hi there. I'm just tidying up a little bit before the election just in case Carroll Campbell wins. If Campbell wins, there ain't gonna be no more lawyer-legislator money-making deals, no more sky high automobile insurance rates.
	If Campbell wins, SHOOT, he'll probably spend it on education.
Holds up framed picture of opponent.	And us good ol' boys, we's gonna be gone. And so is our hero."
"Vote Campbell for Governor" Campbell Photo.	Narrator [VO]: "Campbell for Governor."

In a 1986 Texas judicial race, Bill Aleshire ran a cartoon ad against Mike
Renfro. The visual effects used in the ad were reminiscent of the fist fights in
the 1960s television show, "Batman."

The 1986 Aleshire "Cartoon" Ad

VIDEO	AUDIO
Photo of Renfro. Then crawl of VO—first paragraph.	Narrator [VO]: "During his twelve years of County Government, Mike Renfro has given management a whole new dimension."

CHAPTER 4

Cartoon Starts. POW.
UMPH. Fist going through
air. Buzzers, whistles,
bells.

Bubbles: "What me worry?"

"Close enough for government
work."
"The buck passes here."

Black and White Board:
"What did we do to deserve
this jail. Or this Judge?"

"Saturday, May 3, vote
NO on Renfro.

Background Music: Action Music

Narrator [VO]: "Mike Renfro spent
20 million dollars building a nine
million dollar jail. Renfro super-
vised a jail designed with cell
doors that open backwards. And
Renfro stuck taxpayers with a new
jail that's smaller than the old."

"Ask yourself:
What did we do to deserve this
jail. Or this Judge?

Saturday, May 3rd, vote NO
on Renfro."

In 1987, a Democratic candidate for sheriff in Jefferson Parish, Louisiana, Harry Lee, attacked the former assistant district attorney, Art Lantinni. The direct attack ad uses a form of black humor that resembles the early "Mr. Bill" shorts on "Saturday Night Live." In the place of Mr. Bill, the ad uses a Mr. Softee. Black humor displays a "*tone* of anger and bitterness as it does to the grotesque and morbid situations, which often deal with suffering, anxiety, and death" (Holman, 1972, p. 67). In the ad, a soft ice cream cone with a man's face outlined in the ice cream slowly melts and distorts the man's features.

The 1987 Lee "Mr. Softee" Ad

VIDEO

Red Neon sign saying
"Mr. Softee"

A soft ice cream cone
with a man's face outlined
in the ice cream.

The ice cream beings to melt
and it distorts the man's
features. CU.

AUDIO

Sound [VO]: Carousel music.

Announcer [SOT]: "It's Mr. Softee—
former Assistant District Attorney,
Art Lantinni. He talks tough but
has a soft heart. Especially when
prosecuting criminals. In his last
2 years as an Assistant District
Attorney, Mr. Softee tried only

"8 jury trials"	eight jury trials while plea
"135 plea bargains"	bargaining 135 others. He agreed

to reduce the charges on 135 cases including three murders and four aggravated rapes. As a crime-fighter, Mr. Art Lantinni, Mr. Softee, has made a mess." Sound [VO]: Music turns sour.

We now turn to a discussion of televisual techniques used in political advertising.

TELEVISUAL TECHNIQUES

The influence of cinematographic styles and techniques on people's attitudes toward the pictured subject has long been a given in both film and television production. The range of visual production elements easily could fill, and has, entire books. The purpose here is to acquaint the reader with some of the more important visual production elements and briefly review a sample of the political advertising research that has used some of these elements.

Camera Perspectives

The camera can adopt one of three different perspectives in relation to the photographic subject: reportorial, objective, and subjective (Burrows & Woods, 1986). The reportorial viewpoint utilizes direct eye contact between the photographic subject and the camera lens and the subject speaks directly to the audience. The reportorial viewpoint is most characteristic of the person-in-the-street ad, and the news show dramatization ad. The objective perspective oversees the action while the subject(s) ignores the presence of the camera. Almost all of entertainment television adopts the objective perspective. The objective perspective is most characteristic of the news interview show ad, the slice-of-life ad, and the cinema verité ad. The subjective perspective substitutes the camera for a person or object in the scene. The subjective angle allows the viewer to see the action through the perspective of a participant within the scene. The recent use of remote cameras in race cars or on board the United States entry in the Americas' Cup race allows the camera to participate in the event and by extension so, too, does the home viewer.

In negative political advertising, the first two perspectives (i.e., reportorial and objective) are the most common. The camera is usually addressed directly or the camera is ignored. However, some political spots may contain both reportorial and objective perspectives. Reportorial, objective, and subjective perspectives conceptualize the relationship between subjects and the camera and by extension the audience, but they do not describe how the photographic subject is framed within the screen.

Camera Angle

The use of certain camera angles may influence the viewer's perception of the power or credibility of the person viewed. The viewer is thought to adopt the relative position to the photographic subject taken by the camera. The image from the camera becomes an extension of the viewer's perception. Linden (1970) wrote about film that: "Due to the identification of his eyes with the camera viewpoint, the film viewer is subject to an experience of bi-sociation. Though he is literally in his seat, he negates that perspective and identifies with the screen perspective" (p. 26). The same is assumed to be true of television.

The relationship of the camera lens to the photographic subjects has been theorized to influence the viewer's perceptions of the framed individual. The height of the camera lens in relation to the photographic subject can be one of four types: normal camera, low camera, high camera, and canted. Our language illustrates the psychological importance of height as a metaphor for inferring inferior-superior relationships. One looks up to someone who is perceived as superior and respected or looks down on an inferior. Through production techniques, individuals may be elevated in rank, that is, placed in a superior position (Zettl, 1973).

These height metaphors also translate to camera angles. The viewer is placed into an inferior, equal, or superior height to the photographic subject depending on the positioning of the camera lens in relation to the subject's eyes. The first three camera angles that follow invoke the height metaphor to establish inferior or superior relationships between the photographic subject and the audience.

The normal camera angle has the camera lens at the same height from the ground as the subject's eyes. In the normal angle, the viewer sees the photographic subject eye to eye. This is the most unobtrusive for the viewer of the various camera angles and suggests equality in terms of power between the photographic subject and the viewer, as each is of the same height. The normal camera angle is the most often used angle in television.

The low camera angle occurs when the lens is below the eye level of the photographic subject. This is the second most commonly used angle in television. Wurtzel (1979) noted that this camera angle is frequently used in political and automobile commercials. The effect is to place the viewer in an inferior position in relation to the photographic subject. The photographic subject is above the viewer and larger than life. Such an angle helps the photographic subject take on a greater psychological importance for the viewer.

The high camera angle is the reverse of the low angle. The camera lens is placed above eye level of the photographic subject. The effect is to place the viewer in a psychologically superior role in relation to the pictured individual. The only person to our knowledge to consistently use this angle in a regularly scheduled program is Pat Robertson on his "700 Club" program.

The canted angle occurs by moving the camera through its horizontal plane. The horizon in a canted angle would no longer be perpendicular to the viewer. This type of angle is supposed to suggest a sense of unreality or fantasy to the viewer. It was frequently used when showing villains on the "Batman" TV show. It is rarely used in political commercials.

The use of angles should be consistent within the commercial. Although camera angles can add some interest, it is possible for the use of camera angles to distract. The media consultants for one candidate for U.S. Congress created a commercial using very low camera angles, so low, in fact, that the viewer appeared to be only a foot or two from the ground. The extreme angle called more attention to itself than it made the candidate appear more powerful.

Zettl (1973) made a point that these rules of thumb are contextually bound. It is possible for events surrounding a particular image or for other elements within an image to negate the general psychological meanings of these angled shots.

The camera angles and their perceived meanings reported here reflect the conventional wisdom within the television and film industries. In addition to conventional wisdom, there are social scientific studies that generally support the previous interpretation of the normal, low, and high angle shots. Studies by Tiemens (1970), Mandell and Shaw (1973), and McCain, Chilberg, and Wakshlag (1977) generally have supported the ability of camera angles to affect viewer's perceptions of the photographic subject.

Screen Asymmetry

Arnheim (1965) viewed the canvas, or in this case the television screen, as being heavier on the right. This asymmetry of the television screen affects the amount of attention given to an object based on its placement within the screen. In television, the viewer will usually give the greatest attention to the object on the right side of the screen. Zettl (1973) wrote "the right side is more conspicuous than the left side. In fact, some magazines charge more for an ad placed on the right-hand pages than on the left-hand pages" (p. 128). When constructing the screen image, that which should be focused on by the audience should be placed right of center. In a direct comparison spot, the sponsor's photograph or positions are usually presented on the right, while the opponent's is placed on the left.

Framing

The framing or field of view of the photographic subject has been shown to have differential impact on people's perceptions of the subject. Kepplinger (in press) cited evidence from Europe that people there evaluate close-ups more favorably than other shot lengths. McCain and Repensky (1972) and McCain and Divers (1973) earlier had demonstrated a similar preference for close-ups in the United States. However, McCain and Divers found a difference for men and women newscasters. Women were preferred in long shots and men in medium shots and close-ups (see also, Adams et al. 1980). In direct comparison ads, the sponsoring candidate often appears in a close-up that continues to grow more prominent, while the targeted candidate's photograph gets smaller through the course of the ad.

Editing

Editing is the process of "selection and assembly of shots" (Zettl, 1976, p. 510) to "build a screen event" (Zettl, 1973, p. 297). Editing can be used for technical reasons (continuity editing) or for aesthetic reasons (complexity editing). Penn (1971) said that rapid editing creates additional energy and excitement. However, the use of continuous, rapid cutting may distract the viewer from the subject matter and place the attention on the technique. Frequently, fast-paced editing is used in direct attack negative ads, so it appears that layers of condemning evidence are being presented against the targeted candidate.

In Summary

Thus, there is a body of research that has catalogued production techniques and their resultant effects on viewers. However, Wood (1981) correctly lamented:

> Traditionally, the theoretical justification offered in assuming that when one manipulated a technical television variable the perception of the source by the receivers would be measurably affected, has been a passing glance at Eisenstein, Schram, and the conceptualizations of communication "interference" by Barrow and Westerly. To be blunt . . . no theory for the effects of technical mediating variables of a televised speech exist. (p. 1)

Stylistic Analyses

Although many political advertising researchers discuss televisual techniques in their literature reviews, it is very rare to find these techniques coded and reported. Rose and Fuchs (1968) studied the use of visual style elements in the 1966 California gubernatorial race between Ronald Reagan and Edward G. "Pat"

Brown. Although most of the Rose and Fuchs article is a recounting of narratives, they do explicate some of Reagan's use of camera technique.

Devlin (1973, 1977) generally described the spots and how they came to be produced for the presidential elections of 1972 and 1976 with little analysis of visual techniques. He discussed the use of camera perspective within the McGovern campaign commercials, but no other style elements enumerated here play an important role in his analyses. Devlin did note that the McGovern campaign used cinema verité devices to show McGovern doing things, for example, talking to voters in informal settings.

Elebash and Rosene (1982) found that, in Alabama gubernatorial commercials, 60-second televised ads used a greater number of production techniques than did 30-second ads. Techniques coded in their content analysis included such things as the use of music, number of announcers used, and type of sets used.

Shyles (1983, 1986) has been one of the few to publish using these production techniques in the analysis of political advertising. Specifically, Shyles examined political spots for the various Republican and Democratic presidential contenders in the 1980 election. He found that candidates' images were positively related to high transition rates (editing) and that candidates oriented indirectly into the camera, as well as other variables.

In 1986, Kaid and Davidson identified two distinct candidate videostyles: the incumbent and the challenger. Videostyle can be defined as the "methods of self-portrayal" in political advertising (Kaid & Davidson, 1986, p. 185). The researchers operationalized videostyle as combining three factors: verbal content, nonverbal content, and film/video techniques. The coding choices used were cinema verité, slides with print, candidate or someone else head-on, animation/special production, and combination. They analyzed 55 political commercials from three 1982 United States Senate races. The study revealed that incumbent ads were 90% positive, whereas challenger ads were more evenly divided, with 54% positive and 46% negative. Kaid and Davidson (1986) described the incumbent and challenger videostyles as follows:

> *Incumbent videostyle.* In general, the incumbent (1) uses longer commercials; (2) uses more . . . [voter editorial comments]; (3) uses more candidate-positive focus; (4) uses more slides with print; (5) dresses more formally; (6) is represented by an announcer or other voice [neutral reporter, proselytizing reporter, visual documentary]; (7) verbally and visually stresses "competence."

> *Challenger videostyle.* In general, the challenger (1) uses more opposition-negative focus in ads; (2) uses cinema verité style; (3) uses ads where candidate appears "head-on" [public figure testimonials]; (4) uses more frequent eye contact with camera and audience; (5) dresses more casually; (6) speaks for self more frequently – is not represented by surrogates [candidate confrontation ads, candidate interaction ads]. (p. 199)

These videostyles complement the work of Trent and Friedenberg (1983), which identified incumbent and challenger campaign styles and strategies (see also, Kitchens & Stiteler, 1979; see chapter 2 for discussion concerning incumbent and challenger campaign styles).

In Summary

It should be clear from the general overview that there has been little published research dealing specifically with the production elements identified here as televisual techniques. Although many researchers acknowledge the importance of these elements, few have examined them. Perhaps the difficulty in coding or the lack of theoretical undergirding has discouraged researchers.

The question remains as to whether or not these production elements actually influence members of the electorate. One published attempt to address this issue could find no difference in recall for style versus content elements from political advertisements for a gubernatorial race (Faber & Storey, 1984).

Shyles (1986) concluded that "virtually no political media-scholar will fail to assert the importance of visual design in televised propaganda; yet compared to the ongoing research programs of other communication fields involving visual confrontations, there has been relatively little detailed analysis of the iconic meaning of televised political messages" (p. 118). Although we agree with Shyles about the scholarly interest in these elements of style, we are not sanguine that these will prove to be significant variables or predictors in the process of influencing people's vote. Elements of production techniques probably play only a minor role in the persuasion process. When used within normal professional conventions, use of the various televisual elements are invisible to the viewer. The typical television viewer neither notices nor cares about many of these visual elements.

IN CONCLUSION

We have identified three categories of ads that specify a candidate's role in the advertisement: surrogate ads, candidate confrontation ads, and candidate interaction ads. Challengers are more likely to appear in negative ads and in particular in ads that use cinema verité or public figure testimonial techniques. Incumbents rarely appear in negative ads. They are much more likely to use surrogate ads. Thus, the person-in-the-street ad, the voter editorial comment ad, the neutral reporter ad, and the proselytizing reporter ad are more likely going to be the incumbent's choice.

In addition, we have identified 11 presentational techniques that are used in negative advertising and that may be characterized as being in the news style genre. The person-in-the-street, voter editorial comment, public figure testimonial, neutral reporter, proselytizing reporter, news show dramatization, news interview show, visual documentary, slice-of-life, cinema verité spots, and "Saturday Night Live" news segments all share certain similarities that place them in that genre. These similarities include the production's sensitivity to news values such as conflict, drama, timeliness, proximity, significance, and so forth. By creating negative advertising in the news style genre, political consultants hope to blur the distinction between political news and political advertising. Because television news is considered to be the most credible and frequently used news source in the United States, negative political advertising has the look and feel of a television news package. In addition to the presentational style of the ads, the ads are routinely placed in time slots that occur during and surrounding news programming. This significantly increases the blurring of television news and political advertising.

The use of televisual production techniques as variables that may influence people's perceptions of candidates has received some attention from academic researchers despite the lack of a solid theoretical framework. Using the established professional conventions of perspective, camera angles, framing, and asymmetry of the screen, it is possible to create aesthetically astute visual political messages that will influence a positive or negative perception of the candidate. There is a need for both better cataloging of how these variables have been used, and most important, a determination of whether such variables provide any additional explanation or prediction of voters' behavior.

5

Negative Ads: Sponsor and Channel

In any discussion of political, mass-communicated messages, we must take into account not only the content of the message and the style in which it is delivered but also the sponsor of the message and the channel in which it is disseminated. Research has shown that both sponsorship and channel conditions influence the way in which individuals interpret the political message. For this reason, we consider sponsorship and communication channels as important elements to be considered when examining negative political advertising.

SPONSORSHIP

A sponsor is a person or a group that pays a mass communication channel (television, radio, newspaper, magazine) to disseminate a political advertisement. In some situations, the sponsor may not have paid for the actual production of the advertisement, but is paying for the dissemination. In our analysis, the actual producer of the spot is not as important as the person or group who pays for the dissemination of the advertising, for it is only the sponsor that is identified within the political advertising content (see Disclosure Requirement section, this chapter). And, it is only the sponsor, then, that is known to the voters who have seen the advertisement. Individuals or groups who pay for the expenses associated with a direct mail campaign, a telemarketing cam-

paign, or for the expenses associated with the distribution of campaign paraphernalia (buttons, T-shirts, yard signs, etc.) are also considered to be sponsors.
There are three primary political advertising sponsors in American politics: candidates and their campaign committees, political parties, and political
action committees. We consider each in terms of their presentation of negative political advertising. As we discussed in chapter 1, voters' evaluations
of the sponsor of a political ad affect their perceptions of the credibility of
the advertising content.

Any analysis of the sponsorship of political advertisements, whether they
are positive or negative, must include a discussion about money. Political advertising is big business, an expensive big business. According to *Advertising
Age*, over $450 million went to pay for political advertising in the 1986 House
and Senate races (Colford, 1986, pp. 3, 104). Goldenberg and Traugott (1987)
reported data that indicate House candidates spend about 58% of their campaign budgets on advertising, and Senate candidates about 66%. In the last
presidential election, the Bush campaign spent almost two thirds of its money
on television advertising alone and Dukakis only slightly more than half.

The issue of financing is becoming increasingly complex. To understand
political advertising – negative and positive – one must understand how campaigns are financed. As is shown in the section on PACs, changes in campaign financing laws have played a part in the rise of negative political
advertising.

Oversight of campaign financing is conducted by the Federal Elections Commission (FEC). Established by Congress, the FEC is mandated to serve as
the watchdog over federal elections. Federal election laws concerning campaign financing are reviewed as well as their impact on the arena of political
advertising in America. We then turn to a detailed examination of political
advertising sponsors in American politics.

Campaign Finance Laws

In the early 1970s, the Congress of the United States grappled with the problem
of rising political campaign costs and the significant ethical and legal problems
associated with campaign practices. Two major packages of legislation were
passed: the Revenue Act of 1971 and the Federal Election Campaign Act of
1971.

The Revenue Act of 1971

The Revenue Act of 1971 gave taxpayers the opportunity to voluntarily contribute $1 to a general presidential campaign fund by marking a special box
on their income tax form. Moneys collected would go into a pool that would

later serve to help fund eligible presidential and vice presidential campaigns. The Revenue Act further provided the following:

> In 1974 Congress extended the public funding provisions to presidential primary elections and national nominating conventions. Candidates who raised $5,000 [total] in individual contributions of $250 or less in 20 different states were eligible for federal matching funds. Candidates may receive individual contributions of up to $1,000, but only $250 applies toward the $5,000 total. Each candidate may spend up to $10 million, with an inflation adjustment, in primaries. No more than $200,000 (plus an inflation adjustment) may be spent in a single state. (The Campaign Finance Debate, 1988, p. 122)

However, these spending limitations only apply to candidates who take the federal matching funds.

Although only 7% of the American taxpayers chose to make a contribution to the general presidential campaign fund that first year in 1971, the percentage did improve. From 1974 to the present, roughly 22% of the American taxpayers participate each year. The fund receives approximately $35 million each year from these contributions.

The first presidential election to be partially public financed was the 1976 presidential campaign. Since that time, all major party nominees have sought and received public funding. Only one major party presidential candidate, John Connally in 1980, refused to apply for public financing in order to avoid the primary expenditure limitations (The Campaign Finance Debate, 1988).

The Federal Election Campaign Act of 1971

The Federal Election Campaign Act of 1971 (FECA) required that federal candidates (those seeking presidential or congressional offices) fully disclose both their campaign contributions and expenditures. In addition, FECA set ceilings on media expenditures for federal candidates (see Controls on Political Spending, 1986). In 1974, however, an amendment to FECA repealed the media-spending ceilings for the House and the Senate and established the Federal Election Commission (FEC) that was to serve as a watchdog over federal elections (see The Campaign Finance Debate, 1988; Controls on Political Spending, 1986). In addition, the 1974 amendment set limits on how much individuals and political committees could contribute to federal candidates. Those contribution limits were changed in 1976 and 1979 (see Fig. 5.1).

In order to understand FEC regulations, we first have to examine the commission's own political vocabulary, that is, contributions, expenditures, and political committees.

Contributions and Expenditures. According to FEC regulation, contributions are "anything of value given to influence a *Federal election*. 100.7 (a)(1)" (Campaign Guide for Political, 1985, p. 4). Contributions include such things as gifts of money, in-kind contributions (services or goods that are received either as gifts or at a discounted rate), unpaid personal loans, unpaid endorsements and loan guarantees, proceeds from sales (e.g., money paid to attend a fund-raising dinner or to buy a campaign T-shirt), or extensions of credit beyond customary business practices (Campaign Guide for Political, 1985).

Also regulated are campaign expenditures, which are generally regarded as "the utilization of contributions received" (Campaign Guide for Political, 1985, p. 3). A campaign expenditure is: "The purchase or payment made to influence a Federal election. . . . A contribution given to a *candidate committee* or other political committee is an expenditure by the donor committee. 100.8(a)(1). Contributions made, like contributions received, are subject to the Act's *contribution limits*" (italics in original; Campaign Guide for Political, 1985, p. 4). Examples of expenditures made by political committees might include: monetary contributions, in-kind contributions, or loans made to other committees (see Campaign Guide for Political, Committees, 1985; see also, Fig. 5.1).

Political Committees. Each type of political committee has a distinct set of FEC rules they must follow (see Fig. 5.1). Political committees can be categorized roughly as being either political party committees, candidate committees, or political action committees. A political party committee is any "political committee which represents a political party and is part of the official party structure at the national, state or local level. 100.5(e)(4)" (Campaign Guide for Political, 1985, p. 62). A candidate committee is "any political committee, including a principal campaign committee, authorized in writing by the candidate to receive contributions and make expenditures on his/her behalf. 100.5(f)(1)" (Campaign Guide for Political, 1985, p. 61). The FEC refers to candidate committees as authorized committees. A political action committee (PAC) is a:

Popular term for a political committee that is neither a party committee nor an authorized committee of a candidate. PACs sponsored by a corporation or labor organization are called separate segregated funds; PACs without a corporate or labor sponsor are called nonconnected PACs. (Campaign Guide for Congressional, 1988, p. 61)

The FEC categorizes all political committees as to whether they are single-candidate or multicandidate committees. Single-candidate committees make "contributions or expenditures on behalf of only one candidate" (Campaign Guide for Political, 1985, p. 63). Single-candidate committees are either authorized or unauthorized committees. An authorized committee is a committee that the candidate sanctions in writing to act on his or her behalf. An unautho-

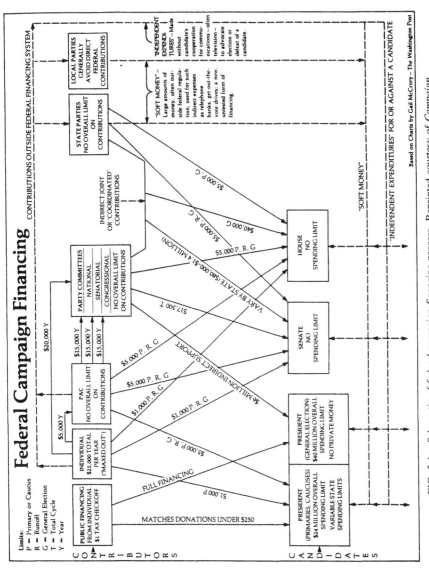

FIG. 5.1. Schematic of federal campaign financing process. Reprinted courtesy of *Campaign & Elections Magazine*, Smith (1874), p. 18).

rized committee is not sanctioned by a given candidate but does make contributions or expenditures on the candidate's behalf.

A multicandidate committee has been defined by the FEC as: "A political candidate with more than 50 contributors that has been registered for at least 6 months and, with the exception of State party committees, has made contributions to 5 or more candidates for Federal office. (110.1 (a) 110.2 (a)(1)" (Campaign Guide for Political, 1985, p. 62). We now turn to some of the more specific requirements under FECA.

Campaign Disclosure Requirements. FECA's "disclosure provisions have resulted in more campaign information than ever before being available to the public, and its compliance requirements have caused campaigns to place greater emphasis on money management and accountability" (Alexander, 1983, p. 61). However, these same compliance requirements have led to an increasing professionalization of political campaigns with accountants and lawyers who specialize in FEC guidelines becoming integral parts of the campaign process. As Alexander noted, this has had an adverse impact on the traditional "voluntaryism" (p. 62) associated with American political campaigns by increasing the number of paid professional campaign workers. Ironically, the very act that was supposed to curb some of the financial excesses associated with mass media campaigns has helped usher in the New Politics Era, which is characterized by media professionals and technocrats.

FECA's disclosure provisions provide that all contributors to a political campaign who give more than $50 must be listed by the political campaign in terms of name, address, occupation, and date and amount of expenditure, and filed with the FEC. Only minor political parties that have demonstrated that their contributors may face harassment by the government or other political actors are exempt from these contribution disclosure requirements (see *Brown v. Socialist Workers '74 Campaign Committee*, 1982; *Federal Election Commission v. Hall-Tyner Election Campaign Committee*, 1982). All campaign expenditures greater than $200 must also be filed with the FEC.

Political Advertising Disclosure Requirements. The sponsors of all political advertising that "expressly advocates the election or defeat of a clearly identified candidate, or that solicits any contribution, through any broadcasting station, newspaper, magazine, outdoor advertising facility, poster, yard sign, direct mailing, or any other form of general public political advertising" (Contribution and Expenditure Limitations and Prohibitions, 1986a) must be fully disclosed. The sponsor must be clearly identified in a conspicuous place telling "who paid for the ad and whether it is authorized by the candidate" (Middleton & Chamberlin, 1988, p. 280; see Contribution and Expenditure Limitations and Provisions, 1986b). Small campaign items such as buttons, lapel pins, or bumper stickers are excluded from this requirement because of their size (Contribution and Expenditure Limitations and Provisions, 1986b).

Political consultants have found clever ways of obfuscating the sponsor disclosure requirements for political advertising. Tony Schwartz (1976) suggested that: "The intent of the disclaimer is to frame the spot as a paid, partisan message. The problem for a media specialist is to minimize the negative effects of the label" (p. 349). Schwartz further suggested that because the name of the sponsoring committee is completely arbitrary, campaigns should choose one that works to their advantage. Compare the two examples that Schwartz gave us:

Paid for by Senator Jones Campaign Committee.

or

And that's exactly why this message was brought to you by a lot of people who want Bob Jones in the Senate. (p. 349)

Jamieson and Campbell (1983) called these "campaign friendly" tags: "no-tag tags" (pp. 143-144, 200, 239). Sometimes these no-tag tags are very simple, for example, "paid for by friends of Bill Baxley." The use of these no-tag tags increases the likelihood that political advertisements will be mistaken for other programming such as news (see Jamieson & Campbell, 1983).

Disclosure statements may occur at the beginning or the end of political ads; however, the most common position is at the end of the advertisement where they serve as disclosure tags. These tags can be either visually displayed or orally given. Frequently, they are both. In some situations, the tags are so small or appear for such a short time that they are nearly unreadable.

SPONSORS

Political Parties

A political party can be defined as "any group, however loosely organized, seeking to elect governmental office-holders under a given label" (Epstein, 1967, p. 9).

State Party Committees/Local Party Committees

As mentioned previously, state/local political parties, like other political committees, are limited in the amount of financial assistance they can give federal political candidates. A political party committee may contribute only $1,000 per candidate, per election unless it qualifies as a multicandidate committee, in which case it can contribute up to $5,000 per candidate, per election (110.1 (a) and 110.2 (a)(1); see Campaign Guide for Political, 1985). It is important to note that:

All *local party committees* of a State are presumed to be affiliates of the State committee. This means that all *contributions* made or received by the local committees count against the State committee's limitation. For example, if a State party committee is a multicandidate committee . . . then the State committee and all of its affiliated local committees may contribute a **combined total** of $5,000 to a Federal candidate, per election. 110.3(b)(2)(ii). Similarly, the State committee and its local affiliates share the same limit on contributions received: an annual limit of $5,000 for contributions from an individual, organization or non party political committee. AOs 1976-104, 1978-39, 1979-68 and 1979-77. (Campaign Guide for Political, 1985, p. 6)

It is also important to note that, whether a state/local party committee gives to several different committees or just one committee supporting a particular federal candidate, the sum of all contributions going toward the promotion of a particular candidate counts toward the contribution limit of either $1,000 for a single-candidate committee or $5,000 for a multicandidate committee (see Campaign Guide for Political, 1985).

National Political Committees

Each major political party in the United States has three main national committees. The Democrats have the Democratic National Committee (DNC), the Democratic Senatorial Campaign Committee (DSCC), and the Democratic Congressional Campaign Committee (DCCC). The Republicans have the Republican National Committee (RNC), the National Republican Senatorial Committee (NRSC), and the National Republican Congressional Committee (NRCC). The DNC and the RNC work with all federal races; the DSCC and the NRSC work solely with Senatorial races; and, the DCCC and the NRCC work solely with House of Representative races (see Political Party Campaigning, 1986).

Direct Contributions and Expenditures

The national party committees (RNC, DNC, DSCC, NRSC, DCCC, and NRCC) each may receive $20,000 per year from individuals, $20,000 per year from political committees or groups, or $15,000 per year from a multicandidate committee (see Fig. 5.1). The national committees are restricted to a $5,000 contribution to each candidate per election within a 2-year campaign cycle. The political party's Senate campaign committee and its national committee are restricted to a combined contribution of $17,500 to each Senate candidate per campaign period.

The Republican Advantage. According to *Congressional Quarterly*, the Republican national committees traditionally have had a financial advantage over the Democratic national committees (Political Party Campaigning,

1986; see also, Bonafede, 1983; Smith, 1984). However, the Democrats have been improving their financial picture in recent years. In the 1981-1982 election cycle, the Republicans spent more than Democrats, 5-to-1. But by the 1983-1984 campaign cycle, the Republicans spent more than the Democrats, only 3-to-1 (Political Party Campaigning, 1986). And by the 1987-1988 campaign cycle, the Republicans spent more than the Democrats, only 2-to-1 (see FEC Reports, 1989, p. 110).

According to *Congressional Quarterly*, the Democrats had been hampered in their contributions to political campaigns by a number of problems. First of all, the party has deep political divisions that often result in internal fighting which hinders its fund-raising efforts. Second, the Democrats struggled from 1968 to 1984 to pay off the 1968 presidential campaign debt. And third, the Democratic party has been slow to adopt the professionalization necessary in modern campaigning (Political Party Campaigning, 1986).

In-Kind Contributions

Besides direct financial contributions, the national party committees provide in-kind contributions to political campaigns. An in-kind contribution is "services, goods or property offered free or at less than the usual charge to a political committee. 100.7(a)(1)(iii)" (Campaign Guide for Political, 1985, p. 62). In-kind contributions are itemized in terms of their "cash value" as if they were cash contributions, and they are also itemized as operating expenditures (Campaign Guide for Political, 1985, p. 19). In-kind contributions might include such campaign services as media production assistance, polling information, and other technical assistance.

Campaign Services. The national Republican party was the first to provide candidates with "seminars on campaigning and fund raising; technical assistance with accounting and legal issues; use of mailing lists; shared research, including polls; and party-oriented advertising in the mass media" (Goldenberg & Traugott, 1984, p. 71; see also, Sabato, 1981). The National Republican Campaign Committee (NRCC) was the first to have its own in-house media production facility. This production facility is available to candidates desiring the facility's expertise in advertising production and media buying (see Goldenberg & Traugott, 1984; Sabato, 1981).

The Democratic National Campaign Committee (DNCC) has been slow to use modern campaign techniques (Bonafede, 1983; Goldenberg & Traugott, 1984). In particular, the DNCC was slow in providing support in the form of public opinion polls, targeting, research, and media production. In a study of the 1978 congressional elections, it was found that Republican candidates were two to five times more likely to have received media production assistance than their Democratic counterparts (Goldenberg & Traugott, 1984).

The Democrats Struggle to Compete. In 1981, Charles Manatt took over as chairman of the Democratic National Committee. Within 2 years, he had more than doubled the number of committee staff members. And as Bonefede (1983) explained, the Democrats began making some "strides down the long comeback trail" (p. 2053). He elaborated, "The well-financed, amply staffed and computerized Republican Party served as a role model, structurally and technologically, for the Democrats" (p. 2053).

Although the DNC had made some progress since the 1980 elections, it was the DCCC that by 1983 had moved to the forefront of the other Democratic national committees in terms of innovative fund-raising and campaign strategies. California Congressman Tony Coelho became chairman of the DCCC in 1981, and he quickly moved to change the course of the House's campaign committee. In just one year, Coelho nearly quadrupled the DCCC staff. Coelho fought for and got a media center that would soon rival the Republicans'. And, he worked to increase the presence of small donors on the contribution forms of the DCCC (see Political Party Campaigning, 1986).

Most significantly, Coelho turned to the business community for financing. Although business had been traditionally a Republican stronghold, Coelho sought support from independent oil producers and other conservative business interests, which pleased southern Democrats and other moderate elements in the party (Political Party Campaigning, 1986).

Coelho changed the mission of the DCCC from a committee that raised money and funneled it to House Democrats to one that raised money and targeted the money to its most efficient use (see Political Party Campaigning, 1986). Vulnerable incumbents whose candidacies were still judged as salvageable and promising Democratic challengers were the first to receive money. Other Democratic House candidates received little or no support. Although this created some dissension among his colleagues, Coelho was able to retain his chairmanship until he voluntarily resigned from Congress in 1989 when he came under public scrutiny for questionable business deals.

In 1982, the DCCC began an aggressive negative direct mail, press release campaign against Republican incumbents. They aided all Democratic challengers with analysis of Republican incumbent voting records, and they began to publish substantive analysis of legislative issues (see Political Party Campaigning, 1986). Before Coelho's initiatives, the DCCC routinely raised between $1 and $2 million per election cycle. After Coelho's efforts, in the 1981-1982 cycle the DCCC raised $5.6 million, and in 1983-1984, the DCCC raised $10.4 million (Political Party Campaigning, 1986). However, these dollar amounts should be compared with the NRCC totals: in 1981-1982, $54 million; in 1983-1984, $58 million (Political Party Campaigning, 1986).

Today, both political parties offer sophisticated services to qualified candidates for federal office. In addition, the Democratic National Committee offers help to state parties, gubernatorial campaigns, and state legislative campaigns.

The DNC offers training seminars in major American cities for interested candidates. Topics have included: campaign fund-raising, polling, direct mail, campaign management, media, voter registration, Get-Out-The-Vote (GOTV), and budgeting. The Republicans also offer training sessions designed for congressional candidates and their campaign managers. Issue and opposition research is made available to federal candidates. Although the Republican National Committee offers political services to state and local candidates through its regional field directors, the GOP concentrates its efforts on the state party organizations. By training the state organizations, the state party staff can then take the responsibility of training their own state and local candidates (personal communications with RNC and DNC, December 14, 1989).

However, it is important to note that federal candidates are supported by party committees through more than just direct or in-kind contributions. Coordinated expenditures and soft money are two very important resources in federal campaigns.

Coordinated Party Expenditures

Coordinated party expenditures, also known as joint expenditures, are expenditures made by a political party committee after consulting with a given candidate. A coordinated expenditure is not considered a contribution by the FEC in that the state and/or national party committee spends the money themselves rather than channeling it to a particular candidate for his or her discretionary use. The state or national party committee may consult with the candidate concerning the way in which the money is spent, but it is the party that spends the money, not the candidate. The party committee may make only coordinated party expenditures during general election campaigns. One of the most common forms of coordinated party expenditures is party-sponsored political advertising.

However, there are limits on coordinated party expenditures based upon a rather complicated formula involving the state's voting age population, the consumer price index, and the cost-of-living adjustment figures (COLAs) (see Campaign Guide for Political, 1985). In 1980, the national party committee could spend up to $34,720 on a House election and as much as $987,548 on a Senate race (Political Party Campaigning, 1986).

If a coordinated party expenditure, for example, a political ad, benefits more than one candidate, "the money spent must be allocated among the candidates supported. The value attributed to each candidate must be in proportion to the relative benefit each candidate receives. 104.10 and 106.1(a) and (b)" (Campaign Guide for Political, 1985, p. 11).

The Republican Advantage. The Republican national committees and their affiliated state committees have utilized coordinated expenditures to a greater degree than the Democratic national committees and their affiliated state committees (see Goldenberg & Traugott, 1984). For example, in 1982, "the Republican national committees spent more than their Democratic counterparts 4-to-1 . . . in joint [coordinated] expenditures" (Smith, 1984, p. 13). The national Republican party targets those House and Senate contests that are "open races" and/or are in competitive campaign settings (see Goldenberg & Traugott, 1984, p. 71). By the 1987-1988 campaign cycle, the Democrats had greatly increased the amounts spent in coordinated expenditures. The Democrats spent $9.4 million and the Republicans $14.4 million (see FEC Reports, 1989, p. 118).

In addition, the NRCC pioneered the use of *generic advertising*. Generic advertising is a political advertisement that promotes the political party rather than specifically supporting any political candidates. Both positive and negative generic advertising have been produced. Generic advertising is very important to both the party and its candidates – because no political candidate is specifically mentioned in the advertisement, the cost of the ad does not have to be reported to the FEC as either a coordinated party expenditure or a contribution.

Generic advertising should not be confused with *canned advertising*. Canned advertising is advertising produced by the national party committees that dramatizes a particular issue and uses a fictitious candidate as an illustration. The ads are "edited in such a way as to insert cuts of any number of candidates for whom the featured issue might be deemed appropriate" (Nimmo, 1986, pp. 77-78). Nimmo has called canned television and radio advertising, "donut ads" (p. 77). Campaign brochures are also frequently canned. But canned advertising is not a coordinated expenditure. Rather, canned advertising is a campaign contribution, because it sells a particular candidate. The party committees only help produce the ads or brochures. The candidate's campaign places the ad and pays for its dissemination.

Soft Money

According to Smith (1984), "much of the support state and local parties can provide need not be reported at all by federal candidates" such as "get-out-the-vote drives, telephone banks, coordination of volunteer programs, voter registration efforts and the purchase of campaign supplies" (p. 19). This so-called "soft money" falls "outside the scope of federal regulation" (Smith, 1984, p. 19).

Political Action Committees (PACs)

Political action committees are voluntary associations of individuals that support candidates, particular ideologies, or political parties, or that have a particular political agenda. PACs that are "sponsored by a corporation or labor organization are called separate segregated funds; PACs without a corporate or labor sponsor are called nonconnected PACs" (Campaign Guide for Congressional, 1988, p. 61). Popularly, the separate segregated funds are called sponsored PACs and the nonconnected PACs are known as independent political action committees.

The Federal Election Campaign Act of 1971 prohibits corporations and unions from making direct contributions to a candidate or from making independent expenditures on behalf of a candidate. Corporations and unions are, however, allowed to contribute money to state parties because of a 1979 amendment to the Federal Election Campaign Act. In addition, corporations and unions can also use their own money for political referenda (Middleton & Chamberlin, 1988, p. 277).

In addition to corporate and union restrictions on expenditures, these organizations may not publicly declare their support for political candidates, but they may make such statements to their internal publics: management, employees, families of employees, and shareholders (see Boyle, 1985; Middleton & Chamberlin, 1988). The courts have held that nonprofit corporations whose primary role is ideological may finance public endorsements of federal candidates (see Middleton & Chamberlin, 1988).

However, corporations and unions may sponsor political action committees, that is, the PACs known as separate segregated funds or sponsored PACs. A corporation or union may pay all costs associated with setting up a PAC, and corporate and union officers may control the decision-making processes and financial resources of the PAC. However, corporate and union PACs may solicit funding only from management, stockholders, and their families – not from the general public. And the corporation and union may not encourage their employees to contribute to the PAC through internal company communication tools (see Middleton & Chamberlin, 1988; see also, Boyle, 1985).

As we mentioned earlier, PACs can also be what the FEC calls "nonconnected" or "independent" in that they are not affiliated with any corporation or union. These PACs are "established by independent groups, partnerships, or unincorporated associations such as the California Medical Association" (Middleton & Chamberlin, 1988, p. 275). Unlike sponsored PACs, independent PACs may solicit money from the general public. However, they may not receive more than $5,000 from their parent organization for administrative and fund-raising expenses (Middleton & Chamberlin, 1988).

In 1974, there were only 608 PACs in the United States. But by July 1, 1989, there were 4,234. According to the FEC, the numbers of PACs in various committee types as of July 1, 1989 were as follows: Corporate- 1,802; Labor- 349; Trade/Membership/Health- 831; NonConnected- 1051; Cooperative- 58; and Corporation without Stock- 143. Since 1984, two PAC types have experienced the greatest growth: Trade/Membership/Health PACs (+ 133) and Corporate PACs (+ 120). Two have actually decreased in number: Labor (-45) and NonConnected (-2). Cooperative ($+6$) and Corporation without Stock ($+40$) PACs have seen some growth (personal communication with FEC, November 1, 1989).

Elliott (1980) viewed PACs as the natural replacement for precinct or neighborhood politics associated with the Old Politics Era. She suggested that during the New Politics Era, we are "not influenced by neighborhood leaders, but rather by particular occupational or socio-economic group leaders" (p. 541; see also, Nimmo & Savage, 1976). Thus, PACs "are the political manifestation of social and behavioral changes taking place in America" (p. 554).

According to Elliott (1980), PACs serve a very important function for political campaigns in America: early money. PACs provide the money that is raised early in the campaign. The old adage, it takes money to make money, is true in campaigning where you have to have raised money in order to raise more money. PACs that give early in political races provide the necessary seed money to reach the small giver through direct mail and other communication channels. And, because PACs have contributed to a campaign, individuals are much more likely to look favorably upon the candidacy because it is deemed as credible for having received the contribution.

PACs are primarily concerned with a candidate's electability (see Elliott, 1980). For this reason, a predominant amount of PAC money goes to incumbents, who traditionally have the winning edge over challengers (see Goldenberg & Traugott, 1984). In 1986, over 67% of PAC direct campaign expenditures went to incumbent senators and congressmen. During the 1987–1988 election cycle, 75% of the $147.9 million donated by PACs went to incumbents (FEC Reports, 1989). And, Democrats received a far greater share of PAC money than did Republicans. One writer explained it this way:

> Republican fund-raising woes were partly the result of a simple political equation: PAC managers wanted to maximize their influence, so they invested heavily in incumbents, most of whom were good bets to get re-elected. Because Democrats controlled both houses of Congress they got the most PAC money. (1988 Congressional Quarterly Almanac, 1989, p. 45)

In the 1987–1988 election campaign cycle, 75% of PAC contributions went to congressional incumbents; 12% went to congressional challengers; and 13% went to congressional candidates in open seats (FEC Reports, 1989). In the 1987–1988 U.S. Senate and House campaigns, Democrats received $91.6 million (62%) and the Republicans $56.3 million (38%) in direct contributions from PACs (FEC Reports, 1989).

The Controversy Over Direct Campaign Contributions

Political action committees are limited in the amount of money they may contribute to an individual candidate. PACs may contribute only $5,000 per candidate per "election"; every "primary election, caucus or convention with authority to nominate, general election, runoff election and special election" are considered to be separate elections (Campaign Guide for Congressional, 1988, p. 49). Even though the sum of money is small compared to the total campaign budget for House, Senate, and presidential races, both researchers and political observers have been concerned about PAC contributions and their potential impact on public policy.

But researchers have produced conflicting studies concerning this issue. The impact of PACs on American public policy is a hotly contested topic. Researchers and PAC critics have used both coincidental and statistical linear analysis to demonstrate a causal link between PAC money contributed to political leaders and their votes on specific issues related to the contributing PACs (Cohen, 1980; Drew, 1983; Frendreis & Waterman, 1985; Green, 1975). However, some researchers who have utilized simultaneous statistical techniques have found little evidence to support the idea that PAC contributions influence votes (Chappell, 1982; Grenzke, 1988, 1989a, 1989b). Grenzke (1988), in an examination of congressional voting records and PAC contribution records from 1973 through 1982, determined that "while members' votes influence PAC contributions, PAC contributions generally do not determine members' pro-PAC voting record" (p. 24).

Some researchers have suggested that under certain conditions, PACs do have influence. According to Frendreis and Waterman (1985), when the congressional member is faced with little constituency or party interest on a particular issue, then the individual member is likely to vote with a PAC who has established a political relationship with him or her (e.g., campaign contributions, grass-roots lobbying, or personal lobbying efforts). Sabato (1984) predicted that PACs have an impact when congressional members are dealing with: (a) low visibility issues (b) highly specialized and narrow matters, (c) matters with no organized opposition, or (d) a number of allied PACs making significant contributions.

Other researchers have also suggested that when a group-PAC-contribution situation occurs, that is, when several similar types of PACs contribute money to a campaign, the large amount of money may have an effect on voting decisions. Both Saltzman (1987) and Wilhite and Theilmann (1987) have found evidence to indicate that labor's influence is magnified when several labor organizations contribute to the same legislator. However, Grenzke (1988) was unable to document this finding when considering umbrella-PACs like COPE (the AFL-CIO's Committee on Political Education).

According to Grenzke (1988), the power of PAC money over legislative action may be greatly exaggerated. And in fact, other activities of the PACs may be much more important. First of all, PAC officials themselves see their political contributions as being only a small part of their political lobbying effort. Second, and perhaps much more important, the PAC mounts intensive grass-roots lobbying efforts for and against pending legislation. It is here that the individual congressman most frequently feels the pinch of a PAC's displeasure (see Wright, 1988). And, we must add to Grenzke's (1988) list a third reason. The potential power of independent expenditures is extreme given some PACs' media sophistication going into the 1990s.

The Controversy Over Independent Expenditures

On January 30, 1976, the U.S. Supreme Court in the *Buckley v. Valeo* (1976) decision distinguished between campaign contributions and independent expenditures. Campaign contributions are direct contributions to a candidate. An independent expenditure, on the other hand, is an expenditure made on behalf of a candidate (i.e., it can be viewed as helping or supporting a particular candidate). An independent expenditure is made "without cooperation or consultation with any candidate, or any authorized committee or agent" of a political candidate (*Buckley v. Valeo*, 1976).

The Supreme Court concluded that limits on campaign contributions cannot be construed as violations of freedom of speech, because they are not direct specific statements of support, but are indirect, general expressions. According to the Court, however, limitations on independent expenditures would be violations of freedom of speech, because they are direct statements of support for a given candidate. Limitations on independent expenditures would serve to impede the competitive flow of ideas in the political marketplace, and therefore, they were judged by the Court to be unconstitutional.

Since 1976 some PACs, particularly the independent ideological PACs, have taken full advantage of the *Buckley v. Valeo* (1976) decision to finance political advertising efforts in various federal elections (Sabato, 1984). By and large, these independent expenditures have been against a candidate, that is, they have paid for negative political advertising. As Tarrance (1982) explained, "Negative spending accounted for almost 80% of all *independent* money spent on U.S. Senate races in 1980" (p. vi). In 1982, for example, about $4.6 million of the $5.6 million spent as independent expenditures went to pay for negative political advertising (The Campaign Finance Debate, 1988). In 1984, PACs spent over $16.7 million in independent expenditures for the presidential race. Of that, 94% was spent on behalf of the incumbent, Ronald Reagan (see The Campaign Finance Debate, 1988). In 1988, PACs spent $6.9 million in independent expenditures on House and Senate races. Of that amount, 14% was spent on negative political advertising (FEC Reports, 1989). Of negative independent expenditures, 92% was spent against Democrats and 8% against Republicans (FEC Reports, 1989).

Erickson (1982) suggested that New Right political action committees began to influence elections as early as 1976. Liberal Democratic Senators Frank Moss of Utah and Gale McGee of Wyoming lost in elections where the New Right was operating. And ın 1978, "the New Right added the scalps of Senators Dick Clark of Iowa, Floyd Haskell of Colorado, Thomas McIntyre of New Hampshire, and Wendell Anderson of Minnesota" (Erickson, 1982, p. 5). But it was not until 1980 that the Democratic party and the American news media began to take notice with a very worried eye toward tides of political change in America. According to Tarrance (1982):

> The ten biggest spending political action committees that functioned as indepen-
> dent expenditure groups in 1980 were the following: The Congressional Club,
> the National Conservative Political Action Committee, Fund for a Conservative
> Majority, Americans for an Effective Presidency, Americans for Change, the
> National Rifle Association Political Victory Fund, the Christian Voice for Moral
> Government Fund, the 1980 Republican Presidential Campaign Committee, the
> American Medical Political Action Committee, and the Gun Owners of Ameri-
> ca. (p. vi)

Perhaps the most widely recognized of the New Right PACs during the 1980 election was the National Conservative Political Action Committee (NCPAC). NCPAC has extensively used the independent expenditure provision.

The FEC and the Democratic party have challenged the independent ex-penditures made by NCPAC in two court cases: *FEC v. NCPAC* (1985) and *Democratic Party of the United States and Democratic National Committee v. NCPAC* (1985). However, the Court ruled in favor of NCPAC, reiterating that independent expenditures are a matter under First Amendment protection (see Controls on Political Spending, 1986).

National Conservative Political Action Committee

Famous direct-mail king Richard Viguerie, and conservative activists Roger Stone, Terry Dolan, and Charles Black founded NCPAC in 1975 (see Sabato, 1984), and it proved to be the most successful of the New Right PACs in fund-raising. The committee raised nearly $8 million to spend in the 1980 elections (Kitchens & Powell, 1986). In 1980, NCPAC spent 79¢ to raise $1 in contri-butions (Kitchens & Powell, 1986).

According to Bannon (1982), "the term 'hit list' first became a part of our political vocabulary in 1980, when four of six incumbent [Democratic] U.S. Senators targeted for defeat by the National Conservative Political Action Com-mittee lost their re-election bids" (p. 43). Birch Bayh (Indiana), Frank Church (Idaho), John Culver (Iowa), and George McGovern (South Dakota) were defeated. Of the six targeted for defeat, only California Senator Alan Cran-ston and Missouri Senator Thomas Eagleton were returned by the voters to the U.S. Senate. According to Tarrance (1982), the 1980 "Target '80" Senate negative ads should be distinguished from other negative ads (which may ap-pear episodically in political campaigns) in that they were part of a "negative campaign" in which "the overall strategy and tactics employ rational negative or attacking forms" (p. vi). Negative campaigns operate under different game rules than other political campaigns (see chapter 1).

NCPAC began running the "Target '80" negative ads against these established Democratic incumbents well before the usual opening days of an election campaign. In some situations, negative ads went out as early as 1 1/2 years before election day (Tarrance, 1982). This caught the candidates and the Democratic party by surprise (Bannon, 1982; see also, Kitchens & Powell, 1986). The negative attacks centered on the incumbent's voting records and hammered relentlessly on such issues as national defense, abortion, and government spending. The ads were based on sophisticated political polling information. And once they began airing, tracking polls were used to provide instant feedback (Kitchens & Powell, 1986). Frequently, these polls helped develop ads directed at single-issue voters who felt very strongly about one particular issue, such as abortion (Kitchens & Powell, 1986).

According to Tarrance (1982), independent expenditures made by PACs at the early stages of a campaign may function in three political scenarios: the "lightning rod scenario," the "attention diversion scenario," and the "antecedent scenario" (p. 4). In the lightning rod scenario, the negative ads tend to reduce the positive base of the incumbent without involving the challenger who the PAC sponsor is supporting. In the attention diversion scenario, the incumbent's attention is diverted toward the PAC and away from the challenger. This gives the challenger more time to raise money and to get better organized. In the antecedent scenario, the voter is convinced that the challenger's qualities are more important to him or her personally and will vote for the challenger on this one particular occasion.

In addition to NCPAC's role in targeted U.S. Senate races, the committee also was active in the presidential campaign in 1980. According to Jamieson (1984), "NCPAC's pro-Reagan spots were concentrated in Louisiana, Mississippi and Alabama. The choice of states was skillful. Reagan won Mississippi and Alabama by less than 1% of the votes cast" (p. 422). These pro-Reagan spots were as misleading as other anticandidate ads that NCPAC used in the 1980 campaign season. Reagan's record as governor in California was aggrandized in the NCPAC ads.

In addition, NCPAC's anti-Carter ads received widespread play in the South, particularly in Alabama, Louisiana, Mississippi, and the Florida panhandle (see Jamieson, 1984). In 1980, NCPAC spent a little over $1.9 million on pro-Reagan Spots and a little over $100,000 on anti-Carter spots (Jamieson, 1984).

Although NCPAC contributed to the defeat of many prominent Democratic candidates through its negative advertising campaign, there is controversy among researchers as to the actual impact of NCPAC on the various elections in question. Some researchers such as Tarrance (1982), Boydston and Kaid (1983), and Railsback (1983) maintained that the NCPAC's political advertising proved to be very effective in defeating their targeted opponents. Tarrance

(1982) reported in an in-depth analysis of the McGovern/Abdnor race in South Dakota that the majority of survey respondents (77%) recognized the negative nature of the campaign. Voters also were able to indicate that the negative appeals were more against McGovern than Abdnor. And interestingly, two thirds of the respondents who recognized that NCPAC was operating in the elections viewed NCPAC negatively. Only 6% of respondents had a positive impression of NCPAC. South Dakota voters who reportedly disliked NCPAC said that the committee was "insensitive" (p. 24) to their interests and was too negative. Yet, Tarrance reminded us that:

"awareness and affect, however, is different than effect or impact." Advertisers have long demonstrated that consumers' attitudes toward particular advertisements are not necessarily related to the impact of these advertisements on buying behavior. Consumers may report hating a particular toilet tissue ad – and yet sales of that product may zoom in markets where the ad is heavily used. (p. 24)

Although normally "any vote in an incumbent-challenger race will be more *against* the incumbent that it is *for the* challenger because there is always more to attack about an incumbent than there is about a challenger," Tarrance suggested that in the McGovern/Abdnor race Abdnor received an unusually high anti-McGovern vote (28%) (p. 25).

But others such as Bannon (1982) and Kitchens and Powell (1986) provided mixed evaluations concerning NCPAC's political advertising effectiveness. According to Kitchens and Powell, certain conditions had to be met before a negative advertising strategy would succeed in the 1980 elections. These conditions included "a political climate which would increase the vulnerability of the incumbents, an effective fund-raising method, and efficient grassroots organizations to help run the campaign in particular areas" (p. 210). NCPAC and their affiliated organizations (Moral Majority, The Religious Roundtable, and Committee for the Survival of a Free Congress) were successful in setting up effective fund-raising and volunteer apparatuses. And because of poor economic conditions, the political climate for liberal Democrats was bleak. In addition, the committee was aided by the targeted senators reacting with a fairly typical "incumbent response" (p. 225), which centers on complaints about the "negative campaign" without directly responding to the negative attacks (see chapter 6). In addition, the negative campaigns allowed the Republican challengers to "take the high road" avoiding the "political muck" (p. 219) around them.

NCPAC also utilized in-kind contributions to the candidates they supported. Because of the 61-day clause in the Federal Election Laws, NCPAC was able to channel much-needed polling research to their candidates for a fraction of the cost. The FEC reasons that once polling data is 61 days old it is of very little value. NCPAC contributed over $112,000 to James Abdnor's campaign against George McGovern by providing old survey data, even though the legal value of the information according to the 61-day clause was well under $5,000 (Kitchens & Powell, 1986). For all these reasons, Kitchens and Powell suggested, it is impossible to separate out the effectiveness of negative ads from the rest of the negative campaign and political climate.

According to Bannon (1982), NCPAC may have received more credit for success from the mass media than they deserved (see also, Stone, 1981). First, the negative advertisements frequently contained gross inaccuracies that ultimately led to exposés in the news media. Second, public opinion polls showed that voters gave NCPAC "unfavorable ratings and indicated that they were more likely to vote for the Democratic incumbents *because* of the NCPAC attacks" (p. 44). Third, NCPAC overreported the amount of money spent in the six senatorial races by $450,000. And finally, all four defeated senators were vulnerable because of poor economic conditions in their home states and their political association with presidential incumbent Jimmy Carter, who was seen as being responsible for these conditions.

Bannon (1983) reported on survey data that indicate that although the initial wave of negative NCPAC ads had its desired effect against incumbent Democratic senators, the second wave became an issue in and of itself. The news media reports of inaccuracies in many of the ads developed voter sympathy for the attacked candidates. These inaccuracies worked to hurt NCPAC's credibility, and the political action committee became unpopular with the majority of voters. According to Bannon, "negative attacks do not have automatic credibility. To be effective, these attacks must come from a source that has some credibility with voters or from a source that, at the very least, is not unpopular" (p. 38).

Bannon (1982) suggested that NCPAC's reputation for dirty tactics significantly damaged their credibility in the 1982 campaign cycle. In addition, targeted Democratic candidates such as Senator Edward Kennedy from Massachusetts were not caught off guard as their colleagues had been in 1980. But the targeted candidates were ready early, and effectively attacked NCPAC's role as an "outsider" (p. 46) trying to manipulate state politics. Similarly, Smith (1983) suggested that NCPAC "did far more to defeat conservative candidates in 1982 than they accomplished against their targets" (p. 33).

NCPAC spent over $500,000 in each of two 1982 senatorial campaigns in an attempt to defeat Maryland's Senator Paul Sarbanes and Massachusetts's Senator Edward Kennedy. Both men won with over 60% of the vote. NCPAC's attacks against Sarbanes actually helped the incumbent, because the Sarbanes campaign was easily able to raise both money and volunteers "to fight" the invaders off (see Bannon, 1983, p. 43). Bannon concluded that "the results of the 1982 elections were a stunning blow to NCPAC's efforts to defeat liberal and moderate members of the United States Senate. Nineteen out of the 20 senators who ran for re-election and who were on NCPAC's original 'hit list' retained their seats (p. 39). The only incumbent defeated was Nevada Senator Howard Cannon, who had narrowly won his own Democratic primary and was being attacked with bribery allegations at the time of the general election. It is unlikely the NCPAC was responsible for Cannon's defeat.

The Democrats Take Notice

Whether NCPAC was significant or not in the defeat of four incumbent Democratic senators, the Democratic party took notice. After 1980, both the Democratic party and their sympathetic supporters began to utilize some of the finance and communication techniques associated with the New Right. Erickson (1982) explained their motivation: "You can take a swing at me once, twice, even three times, but by the fourth swing I'll know you're really trying to knock me out and then I'm going to be ready to fight" (p. 5).

Democrats for the 80s. Pamela Harriman, wife of elder Democratic statesman Averell Harriman, organized Democrats for the 80s, a liberal political PAC. Democrats for the 80s is known in Washington, DC as "PAMPAC" after its founder. Prominent Democratic leaders serve on its board of directors and congressional liaison committee. Although PAMPAC primarily raises money to contribute to political campaigns, the organization has taken out political advertising in its own name on occasion. During the 1982 Senate race in Maryland, PAMPAC purchased newspaper ads "identifying NCPAC as the arch villain in the 1980 campaigns" (Erickson, 1982, p. 6). PAMPAC supported Senator Paul Sarbanes in this race.

Independent Action. Arizona Democratic Congressman Mo Udall and two former veterans of Udall political campaigns, Ed Coyle and John Engber, formed the instrumental triumverate that created Independent Action, a progressive political action committee (See Sabato, 1984). Independent Action donates money primarily to liberal Democratic incumbents, but it also has given to promising Democratic liberal challengers. In 1982, Independent Action began a negative campaign against North Carolina Senator Jesse Helms, a full 2 years before election day. Primarily, the committee used negative direct mail that also served as fund-raising appeals (see Erickson, 1982). It should be noted that the Helms campaign responded with one of the earliest senatorial campaigns in our history and ultimately was successful in defining the campaign agenda and winning the election (see Kern, 1989).

Progressive Political Action Committee. The former director of the National Abortion Rights League PAC, Harriett Matthews, heads up the Progressive Political Action Committee, PROPAC (see Sabato, 1984). The Committee first used an independent expenditure attack strategy in 1982 and

1984 against conservative Republicans such as Orrin Hatch of Utah (1982) and Jesse Helms of North Carolina (1984) (see Bannon, 1982). The organization uses primarily radio and print ads in their negative campaigns (see Erickson, 1982).

Candidates and Their Campaign Committees

A candidate's campaign committee is technically called an authorized candidate committee by the FEC. An authorized candidate committee may also be the principal campaign committee that coordinates and controls the candidate's campaign. Authorized committees may receive $1,000 from an individual or other political committee or group per election. In addition, the authorized committee may receive $5,000 from multicandidate committees per election. It is important to remember that party primaries, caucuses or conventions with authority to nominate, general elections, runoff elections, and special elections are each considered a separate election (see Campaign Guide for Congressional, 1988; see Fig. 5.1).

CHANNELS

Political advertising has utilized various channels: television, newspapers, cable television, theater, magazines, radio, direct mail, billboards, poster panels, yard signs, transit advertising, airport advertising, brochures, pamphlets, buttons, lapel pins, balloons, bumper stickers, fans, pencils, pens, matches, T-shirts, emory boards, hats, keychains, calendars, airplane banners, airplane skywriting, records, and so on, ad infinitum.

Effects

Unfortunately, the relative effectiveness of channel variation for political messages has not been adequately examined by political communication researchers. There is little evidence on which to construct a comparative analysis of the various mediated channels. Research conducted in experimental settings has found no effects attributable to differences among mass communication channels (Andreoli & Worchel, 1978; Brownstein, 1971; Cohen, 1976; Garramone, 1983). These experimental results were similar to those in political science that led Arterton (1978) to conclude: "Political scientists studying the impact of listening to or reading reported news have been unable to document significant effects upon the attitudes, cognitions, or behavior of citizens. The effect may be there, but we have not been able to demonstrate it" (p. 4).

However, there is evidence that suggests the channel through which political candidates communicate is important and may affect people differently. There is also information available suggesting that people who use a particular medium may be different from one another.

Studies have shown that source variables such as trustworthiness or intensity interact with the channel of dissemination in considering channel/communication effectiveness. Cohen's (1976) research indicated that some political candidates are more effective on television and others are more effective on radio. Andreoli and Worchel (1978) found that "television is the most effective medium for a trustworthy source but the least effective medium for an untrustworthy communicator" (p. 69).

In 1934, Wilke presented evidence showing that live speeches were more persuasive than those heard on the radio or seen printed. Although there is now contrary evidence to Wilke's early work, (e.g., Frandsen, 1963; Tannenbaum & Kerrick, 1954), there seems little to contradict the finding that involvement by people increases as the sense of closeness increases, and television research has demonstrated that this medium is able to create the illusion of closeness (e.g., Weiss, 1969; Worchel, Andreoli, & Eason, 1974). Thus, television political advertising is often the medium of choice, because it is the most live of the various media (Andreoli and Worchel, 1978).

Sabato (1981) explained, "Television commercials are believed to appeal particularly to Independents, both the largely inattentive and uninformed Independent voter and the floating, highly reactive 'ticket splitter' who is unusually aware of politics" (p. 118; see also, DeVries & Tarrance, 1972). Television "is perhaps best suited for reaching a very large, undifferentiated audience with low motivational levels which can be activated by a particular symbol, catchy phrase, or stark visual display" (Strand, Dozier, Hofstetter, & Ledingham, 1983, p. 55). The theorized passivity of the general television viewer suggests that the viewer does not selectively attend to political messages based on the viewer's political orientation (Swanson, 1976).

Uses

Although some researchers have looked for the effects of mediated channels, others have studied the uses people have for the various media. In 1973, Katz, Gurevitch, and Haas examined how various mass media channels in Israel function to fulfill the satisfaction of social and psychological needs for audience members. They concluded that the 35 social and psychological needs identified from the uses and gratification literature could be classified into five categories that specify the type of need fulfilled by the communication experience: cognitive needs, affective needs, political integrative needs, social integrative needs, and escapist needs (Katz et al., 1973). Cognitive needs comprise desires for information and knowledge. Affective needs refer to desires for pleasurable emotional experiences. Political integrative needs are desires for recognition, credibility, status, and power. Social integrative needs describe desires to be liked by our families, friends, and other acquaintances. And escapist needs fulfill desires to transcend our everyday world of tension and problems. According to their findings: "Books cultivate the inner self; films and television give pleasure; and newspapers, more than any other medium, give self-confidence and stability" (p. 169). The researchers distinguished between "getting away from it all" and "killing free time — television appears to be most useful in "killing free time," but films and books provide the greatest ability to "get away from it all" (p. 169).

In the political arena, the political uses of newspapers, radio, and television border on each other and are judged to be most helpful. Political gratifications that are fulfilled by books and films are very similar to each other; those fulfilled by radio, television, and newspapers are also highly similar to one another (Katz et al., 1973). Katz et al. concluded that:

> These patterns suggest that (1) both political and personal uses of radio and television are closely allied; (2) the uses of newspapers of political needs are related to the political uses of radio and television, but the personal uses of the newspaper are rather different; (3) books and films are akin in their political uses (or nonuses), but function differently for the self. (p. 175)

Television

Historical Precursors

Political television ads had a number of electronic precursors: in radio, in film, and in televised speeches. In 1928, both political parties began producing entertainment programs for radio in order to publicize their political candidates. These entertainment programs had the nation's stars of concert and stage (Clark, 1962). Some of the early political entertainment programs incorporated listener contests into the evening's entertainment (Redding, 1958). Later, as television began, similar political entertainment programs appeared on the air (see Jamieson, 1984).

In 1934, campaign films were aired first in California theaters during a gubernatorial election. This practice became widespread and climaxed with the 1948 presidential election (Jamieson, 1984). Campaign films are still used today; however, the visual venue for their presentation is usually at national political conventions where the television networks broadcast them to people's homes.

The 1948 presidential election saw the first broadcast time purchased by presidential candidates for the purpose of delivering political messages (Jamieson, 1984). It was not until the 1952 presidential election that the political spots we know today were born.

Modern Political Television

Today in the United States, there are approximately 88 million homes of which 98% have a television. And, 96% of these homes have a color television. The average American watches over 7 hours of television a day (Dominick, Sherman, & Copeland, 1990). Clearly, television has become an integral part of our life. We turn to it for entertainment, news, and companionship.

Since 1963, television has been the primary source of national political news, and the American public has judged it to be the most credible source of news (Alexander, 1969). As Sabato (1981) elaborated, "In fact, about two-thirds of all Americans consider television their primary source of news and about half claim to rely on television whenever there are conflicting reports in the various media" (p. 117). Findings by Roper Research Reports have shown over the last 20 years where the public has gained its clearest understanding of national candidates and issues (see Table 5.1).

According to Alexander (1969), the most influential tool of the New Politics is television: "Television has changed the political campaign, changed the political candidate, and, in fact, changed the entire nature of the political discourse. Television has reordered the political campaign. Itineraries, speeches, and the nominating conventions are planned according to the dictates of prime time" (p. 260). Similarly, Tony Schwartz (1985) claimed that there are really three American political parties: ABC, NBC, and CBS.

Modern Television Political Advertising. Kaid and Davidson (1986) noted, "Television is now the dominant medium for candidate-to-voter communication in most state and national elections. . . . In fact, an estimated 50

TABLE 5.1
Sources for Information About National Candidates

	1968	1972	1976	1984	1988
Television	65	66	75	75	70
Newspapers	24	26	20	19	20
Radio	4	6	4	4	4
Magazines	5	5	5	3	3
Other people	–	5	3	3	3
Other	–	2	1	2	2

Note: Numbers in the tables represent percentages rounded to the nearest whole number. Findings of Roper Organization Surveys for the Television Information Office. Taken from a national random sample: 2,000 in-home interviews. Data provided courtesy of Roper Center for Public Opinion Research, Storrs, CT.

to 75 percent of the budget in major campaigns goes to finance the production of and to buy time for electronic advertising" (pp. 184–185; see also, Patterson, 1983). The rate of penetration for television is higher than for any other mass-mediated political message (e.g., Atkin, Bowen, Nayman, & Sheinkopf, 1973; Atkin & Heald, 1976; Hofstetter & Buss, 1980; Patterson & McClure, 1976a). Atkin (1980) reported that in two gubernatorial races, 90% of the voters could recall seeing televised political commercials for the race.

Political advertising seems to be usurping the traditional role that news has played in informing the audience about candidates and issues. Guggenheim (1986) estimated that 70% of what people know about any given political campaign comes from political advertisements, particularly television commercials (p. A31). Hofstetter and Zukin (1979) concluded their study of the 1972 presidential election by noting that "advertising may comprise, among other things, a more extreme, highly selective form of similar content than news" (p. 152). Although Patterson and McClure's (1976b) analysis of mass media effects in the 1972 presidential election suffers in light of current research findings, they were able to demonstrate early that more issue content is found in political advertising than in network news coverage of the political campaigns. Because of this, political advertising is said to have a stronger influence on an audience's issue agenda than newscasts (McClure & Patterson, 1974).

Television Watch Parties. In 1983, the Mondale presidential campaign used an innovative fund-raising event called the "America for Mondale" program. Across America, potential contributors gathered in 6,000 homes to watch a 5-minute television spot. Over $1 million was raised from small donors (Malchow & May, 1985). This was the pioneer of what Malchow and May termed "television watch parties" (p. 18). According to their research, watch parties are both excellent means of contacting "hidden contributors" and of recruiting new volunteers (Malchow & May, 1985, p. 18). In order to be successful, campaigns that use this technique must have a good organization with a broad base of support.

The television watch parties are not altogether new. For some time, internal party dinners or other fund-raising events have utilized ads in their programs. In 1978, Bailey, Deardouff & Associates produced a series of humorous negative ads for the Republican party in Michigan. The ads compared the Democrat-controlled Michigan state legislature to the Lansing, Michigan zoo. Another ad was produced for distribution at Republican party dinners and fund-raising events that used the "zoo" motif. The ad, according to Sabato (1981), served as the "video equivalent of a dirty joke, which, if properly enjoyed by participants, traditionally opens checkbooks at such affairs" (p. 158).

The 1978 Michigan Republican Party's
"The Lansing Zoo: A Painful Place"

VIDEO   AUDIO

Two large rhinoceri are mating.   "Narrator: "Do you know what is
The female appears to be an   being done to us by the
unwilling participant. The   Democratically controlled
setting is an African range.   Legislature in this state? Do you
                                   have any idea how it hurts
                                   taxpayers to have the Democrats
                                   behind things in Lansing? Why
                                   would anyone want to be in this
                                   position for ten years? Isn't it
                                   about time we get the Democrats off
                                   our back?""

The phenomenon of single-issue voting may be capitalized on by candidates through the use of single-issue negative spots distributed specifically to television watch parties. Candidates have less chance of offending those who do not share the same perspective on a particular issue, and it would serve to mobilize those who do share this perspective. In these situations, campaigns should be careful not to publicize the television watch parties to the traditional news media. If publicized, the strategy of utilizing single-issue appeals might turn off some voters.

New Electronic Media (NEM)

Writing in 1984, Paley and Moffett saw the new electronic media as changing the face of political advertising. They thought that new technologies such as teletext, interactive cable, videotext, and computerized telemarketing would be significant. Unfortunately, as with advancing technologies before, the growth of development was not as predicted. With the exception of VCRs and cable television, most of the new technologies that Paley and Moffett viewed as ushering in major changes have failed to develop.

The problem is that although the technology is available to make a new electronic media feasible, the technology fails to find an acceptable market. Dominick et al. (1990) cited the example of quadraphonic sound as a case where there was a marketed technology, but due to a number of problems it soon disappeared. For many of the new electronic media, the promise of the future is yet to arrive. One of the promises of the NEM is their ability to "personalize mass communication" (Paley & Moffett, 1984, p. 5) by differentiating audiences through a process called *narrowcasting*. Unlike its cousin, broadcasting, narrowcasting is the process of targeting specific messages to specific audiences through mass communication technology. The second promise of the NEM is their interactive components. People will be able to play a part in the media experience rather than just be passive consumers. Interactiveness can allow for a connectedness between the receiver of the messages and the sender.

Cable Television

Over 50% of American homes have cable television (see Power, 1987). As Paley and Moffett (1984) noted, "Cable is not just an entertainment medium. Its programming includes news, sports, and information narrowcast in a one-way or interactive format. It is communication on a targeted national, regional or local level" (p. 6; see also, Power, 1987) In 1980, John Anderson was a pioneer in the use of cable television in his independent presidential campaign (Jamieson, 1984).

Cable television offers two new ways to advertise: through cable networks and through purchasing time directly from the cable operator. The rise of cable penetration into homes has spawned cable networks such as ESPN, MTV, USA, and many others. These cable networks distribute programs directly to cable systems through satellite dissemination. It is possible for candidates and others to buy time on these networks just as they would on the commercial television networks.

The second way for a prospective advertiser to use cable systems is to buy time directly from the cable system operator. The cable system operator usually will sell a block of time or individual spots to a candidate's campaign. It is also possible to buy multiple cable systems through brokers or from multiple system owners, thus making the purchasing of time much easier than having to buy time from individual operators.

In 1988, both presidential and congressional cnadidates spent a larger portion of their advertising budget than ever before on cable television (Dixon, 1989). This was made possible by the publication of the Cable Advertising Bureau (CAB) Directory, which shows the cable systems' coverage by each legislative district (see Dixon, 1989). The CAB has produced the directory as another marketing tool to promote the services of local cable systems.

Cable television provides the potential for political advertisers to design specific message appeals for specific audiences within specific geographic areas and transmit these messages through the local community cable system. In some states with sizeable urban Black populations, such as Washington, DC, Mississippi, or Alabama, the use of the Black Entertainment Television Network (BET) could prove to be a very useful communication tool for targeting the Black audience. For even greater specificity in targeting of messages, access to cable audiences could be purchased on a system-by-system basis. And cable television is 30% to 50% less expensive on a cost-per-thousand basis than network broadcast television (Power, 1987).

Cable operators are eager to sell their channels to political campaigns. Because cable television usually has channels that can be made available, cable systems are much more likely to accept special advertising programs or longer commercials than broadcasters. In addition, the rapid turnover in sales of cable systems has increased the debt service that many cable owners have to meet. The chance to sell time to political campaigns is another possible profit center for the cable operator and a means to meet the debt payment.

Based upon research provided by Mediamark Research Inc., Power (1987) determined that the cable television audience tends to be "more affluent, better educated, and more likely to be registered voters and politically active individuals" (p. 55; see also, Dixon, 1989; Paley & Moffett, 1984). According to one research company, "the cable viewer is 28 times more likely to vote than the average citizen—and 50 percent more likely to work actively for a political candidate" (Dixon, 1989, p. 29).

James (1982) noted that cable viewers are more likely to be attentive in that they have purposefully sought out rather specific types of messages, for example, sports, news, and so forth. James suggested that: "Audiences motivated to seek out specialized programs on cable television are apt to have an above-average interest in their content. This higher attentiveness can be expected to extend itself to advertising within these programs" (p. Y-2).

Joe Slade White, a Democratic consultant, believed that cable may be developing into the new radio. White suggested that cable will allow political campaigns to target specific demographic groups through careful buying of cable television time (Wolff, 1989).

Interactive Cable. Interactive cable is also available in a few parts of the United States. Interactive cable systems are those that provide two-way service, from the cable operator to the home and from the home back to the cable operator. This new technology offers three types of services: monitoring services such as utility meter reading and smoke detector monitoring, interactive programming which allows viewers to actively participate through the use of pushbutton responses, and information retrieval/transactional services which use the cable for library research and home shopping (Singleton, 1989).

The most promising use of interactive cable for political campaigns is interactive programming. In this way, candidates could test the viability of political advertising, conduct public opinion polls, or conduct political referenda (see Paley & Moffett, 1984). The drawback with this system is that people generally do not wish to be bothered. Studies in Qube households with interactive cable indicated that it was the children who generally used the pushbutton boxes to register responses (Dominick et al., 1990).

In 1977, the first interactive cable system known as Qube was test marketed by Warner/Amex in Columbus, Ohio with expansion of the service into: Cincinnati, Dallas, Houston, and St. Louis. However, as Singleton (1989) noted, "Qube and other two-way systems around the country have shown the industry how two-way cable works; they just haven't demonstrated how to make it profitable" (p. 137). The interactive cable portion of Qube was eventually shut down as were most all interactive systems.

Direct Response Advertising. Cable television's narrowcasting combined with telephones and credit cards makes it possible to efficiently mount a direct response advertising drive. Direct response advertising encourages voters to call a toll-free number in order to obtain more information or make political contributions with a credit card. Because cable has a local reach, switchboards can be set up locally rather than nationally and only operate when the ads are being aired (see Paley & Moffett, 1984).

Vermont Senator Patrick Leahy used direct response advertising in his 1986 campaign. In one Leahy ad, the narrator ended by saying: "And Senator Leahy needs you like the Green Mountains need him. Call. It takes a long time to build a mountain." As the narrator read the closing message, the ad visually showed Leahy walking through the woods with the words: "You can help. 1-800-LEAHY-86."

Teletext

Teletext is "the one-way transmission of text and graphic information to TV sets using part of the normal television broadcast signal" (Singleton, 1989, p. 259). The closed captioning of television programs is a type of teletext system. Teletext systems could provide from 50 pages to 4,500 pages of text and graphics. Although teletext might be able to wed traditional print with the broadcast medium of television, it is still unclear as to whether it would be useful in getting across lengthy, complicated political presentations, such as position papers, to the voters as suggested by Paley and Moffett (1984). Teletext is also severely limited in its availability.

Videotext

Videotext is sometimes used as an umbrella term meaning any system that combines text information with television. However, it also has a more specific meaning: "Two-way home video information services in which the home TV set or terminal is linked to a computer by telephone wire or cable" (Singleton, 1989, p. 261). Videotext, unlike teletext, is not broadcast; rather, it is transmitted through cable or telephone lines and it is interactive. People may make selections and input their own information.

Teletext and videotext services have been general failures in the United States. Although they have displayed some success in foreign countries, the

United States does not seem ready to accept them. Singleton (1989) suggested that in order for these technologies to achieve market success a number of American attitudes and habits will have to be overcome: "This will require overcoming the prevailing attitude that television is watched for entertainment, not for information; the aversion of many people to reading text on a television screen more than moments at a time; and the convenience, portability and low cost of newspapers and other print media" (p. 168).

Computerized Telemarketing

Telephone computer services such as Cybertronix, Inc. of Schaumburg, Illinois are able to place over 100,000 phone calls per hour. As Boim (1984) noted, "Telemarketing is a blend of telephone technologies and marketing techniques interfaced with computers, and it is being used effectively in the private sector, bringing lower costs and increased productivity" (p. 73). A computer-generated voice or a candidate's own voice greets each recipient. Boim elaborated: "Telecomputer systems can aid in a registration campaign, recruit volunteers, seek campaign contributions, endorse a candidate, survey issues and take polls three times faster than people at one-tenth the cost" (p. 75). In 1984, completed calls cost around 50¢ a piece (Paley & Moffett, 1984). Telecomputer services are now being successfully used in fund-raising campaigns. Boim estimated that telemarketing is "three to ten times more effective than direct mail" (p. 73). It would appear to be only a matter of time before telemarketing is used in negative political advertising.

PC Networking

Personal Computer Networking is a relatively untapped resource for political campaigns at this time. But Paley and Moffett (1984) saw a large potential for PC networking in national campaigns. They called PC Networking the "ideal telecommunications tool" (p. 12). The PC Network would create an electronic bulletin board and message center. Campaign staff at different sites could then call the computer and, using passwords to safeguard the integrity of the information, check to see what the latest from the central campaign was. They would also be able to leave messages for people at either the central headquarters or other regional sites.

There are public networks like The Source and Compuserve. However, these public networks have yet to be used widely for political campaigns.

The Hopes and Failures of NEM

The new technologies offer campaigns of the future many new possibilities. However, the necessary attitudes and habits must be developed before the new technologies are greeted with much enthusiasm in the United States. As we noted in the introduction to this section, just because the technological expertise is available does not mean that people will actually buy and use it. Only time will tell how these new electronic media will fair.

Radio

For local elections, radio is one of two primary channels used by candidates, the other being television (Atkin, 1980). In 1988, radio carried more political advertising than any other medium with 1988 spending more than doubling the 1980 levels (Wolff, 1989). Radio would seem the medium to buy because research shows that radio news users know more about local political candidates than do television news users (Becker & Dunwoody, 1982). Thus, radio advertising reaches those people more interested in the election better than would television; in fact, research by Miller and Reese (1982) showed that those people who use television show the least likelihood to vote.

Because television makes negative attacks seem stronger or more strident, some political consultants have chosen to use radio for their negative advertising (*National Journal*, 1980; see also, Berkman & Kitch, 1986; Sabato, 1981). Radio has provided the venue for the attacks without the harshness sometimes associated with television attacks.

However, this use of radio may soon be declining and at a fairly rapid rate. One of the major Democratic radio consultants, Joe Slade White, has switched almost exclusively to television. His reason? – "Radio is dead, and rock and roll killed it" (Wolff, 1989, p. 33). Slade, who had previously used radio almost exclusively, said that the shift to FM and the splintering of rock and roll formats into "like-minded or micro-differentiated stations" (Wolff, 1989, p. 34) has created a station-changing audience. Previously, people had been perceived as being committed to a radio station. The type of music played on the station was a strong indicator of the demographic segment listening. One could then target demographic groups on a few stations. White said this is no longer true and is turning to television spots.

Newspapers

People who rely more heavily on newspapers than television as their primary source of information have been shown to have some differences. People who read newspapers know more about a variety of issues as compared with those people who predominately use television to gain information (Wade & Schramm, 1969). Knowledge levels of national (Robinson, 1974) and local (Becker, Sobowale, & Casey, 1979) events seem to be higher for newspaper readers than for television viewers. More specifically, people who rely principally on newspapers rather than television have a greater knowledge of what is happening in their communities (Becker et al., 1979; Becker & Whitney,

1980). Newspaper political advertising reaches "those with a higher probability of voting, especially the community activist, joiner and member of fraternal, religious, community, and service organizations—in short, the person who actively interacts with others" (Steinberg, 1976, p. 141).

Newspaper readers also know more about local political candidates than do those who rely on television for their information (Becker & Dunwoody, 1982). Miyo (1983) reported that newspaper readers have more political knowledge in general than do television viewers. This increase in knowledge for newspaper readers has been shown to allow them to differentiate among the candidates (Wagner, 1983). Roberts (1979) found that an excellent predictor of attention to other campaign media events was reading early stories about the political campaign.

Clarke and Fredin (1978) suggested that television may actually impede individuals from learning about politics whereas newspapers promote knowledge of politics. However, Becker and Whitney's (1980) evidence supported the knowledge gap construct, which suggests that the reasons for these differences may be the general education level differences between newspapers (higher) and television (lower) users.

Newspaper readers seem to make their voting choices early in a campaign and do not change their decision (Roberts, 1979). Strand et al. (1983) have shown that those people who are persuaded to change their minds or are late deciders have low levels of exposure to newspapers, contradicting Adams's (1978) earlier findings.

Newspaper political advertising as we know it today has a much shorter historical reach than many people assume. As late as 1948, some newspapers were refusing to accept political advertising from presidential candidates that the paper did not support (Redding, 1958). Newspapers, until the 20th century, were political organs that supported the cause and candidates of a particular party, not the independent agencies we think of newspapers as being today (Jamieson, 1986). Humke, Schmitt, and Grupp (1975) provided a good review of a print campaign candidate's advertising from 1933 up to, and including, 1960.

Today radio and newspaper advertising are the dominant forms of political advertising for local elections (Atkin, 1980). Newspaper advertising also is used frequently for statewide political contests (Alexander, 1969). As Israel and Williams (1988) pointed out, in areas where voters are "broadcast-isolated" (p. 18), newspapers play an important role in campaign communication in the providing of both news copy and political advertising. According to Sabato (1981), print advertising proves to be very effective in Black and ethnic newspapers and small-town weeklies, because these newspapers tend to be closely read. The utility of newspapers for building/improving a candidate's image has been suggested by O'Keefe (1980), whose study showed that newspapers were important for candidate image building.

Direct Mail

According to Craver (1985), next to a personal visit or phone call, direct mail is "the most intimate of all the media" (p. 70). Direct mail advertising has been called the poisoned pen of politics, because it is used so often in negative political appeals (see Sabato, 1981; see also, Berkman & Kitch, 1986). According to Craver (1985), direct mail, like any good action-seeking communication: "(1) establishes rapport between the writer and reader; (2) states the problem, threat or opportunity; (3) convinces the reader that there is something he/she can do about it; and (4) tells the reader in no uncertain terms what that action is" (p. 71).

However, research results are mixed concerning the utility of direct mail advertising during political campaigns (Berrigan, 1982; Heighberger & Adler, 1984; Olsen, 1984–1985; Rothenberg, 1983). Berrigan concluded that "direct mailing of brochures or pamphlets has little impact upon voter-candidate recognition, voter turnout, or voter preference" (p. 32). Strand et al. (1983) found that direct mail appears to be an effective tool in persuading those people who change their position on how to vote and for late deciders. Undecided voters "significantly increase their exposure to direct mail during the campaign" (p. 61).

Olsen (1984–1985) suggested that direct mail can be effective when messages are carefully constructed and matched to well-defined target groups, but when direct mail does not appear to work, the failure may be more the failure of the message appeals than the channel. Olsen cited successful California legislative and congressional campaigns that were direct mail-based as evidence for his conclusions. In order to be successful, direct mail must both convince readers that they can, in fact, make a difference if they respond immediately and fully describe what benefits readers will experience if action is taken now (Craver, 1985). Similarly, one study found that the degree of personalization contained in the direct mail significantly influenced whether the letter was in fact read (Campaign Insights, 1976). Sabato (1981) reported that three fourths of the individuals who receive direct political mail actually read it. In media-isolated areas, direct mail may play an important role in reaching the voters. Israel and Williams (1988) reported that over 95% of respondents in a media-isolated area recalled reading brochure material.

Sabato (1981) wrote that "direct mail combines sophisticated political judgments and psychological, emotional appeals with the most advanced computer and mailing techniques" (p. 220). Direct mail is used primarily for persuasion and fund-raising. Sabato advised that the more a candidate is perceived as being farther right or left on the political spectrum, the more likely individuals and groups can be identified who feel strongly about the candidate and, therefore, will be willing to contribute money to the cause.

Sabato (1981) explained, "The recurrent themes of direct mail are emotionalism, personalization, and gimmickry. The copy tends to be negative, sometimes vehemently so, particularly when a well-known incumbent is the target" (pp. 257–258). In one 1979 mailing of the NRSC, respondents were told to rate the Democratic incumbents on a "danger scale" (p. 238), and they were allowed to target their contributions to the defeat of one of the identified Democratic incumbents.

Billboards, Bumper Stickers, and Other Campaign Paraphernalia

Billboards, posters, yard signs, transit ads, bumper stickers, and buttons primarily are used to "show the flag" in political races (i.e., maintain a high profile) and also to increase name recognition. Volunteers enjoy the use of bumper stickers, buttons, T-shirts, and so forth, because when they display campaign paraphernalia, it gives them a sense of camaraderie, a sense of belonging to a purpose or movement greater than themselves. It builds team spirit.

Negative slogans, some using disparagement humor, are sometimes used on bumper stickers. According to Jamieson (1984), bumper stickers often offer humor that would be "inappropriate" (p. xxiii) in other mass communication channels. Because individuals make the choice to display the bumper sticker, it becomes their own personal self-expression and not that of the candidate or interest group who sponsored the production of it. In the 1964 presidential campaign, Johnson supporters paraphrased Goldwater's own tag, "In your heart, you know he's right" when they made a negative bumper sticker that warned voters: "In your heart, you know he might." In 1978, when a Republican gubernatorial candidate Lamar Alexander faced Democratic candidate Jake Butcher in Tennessee, the Alexander campaign distributed bumper stickers that read "FORSAKE JAKE IN '78." In 1984, the Republicans distributed bumper stickers that read "Honk if Mondale Promised You Anything," and the Democrats distributed one that read "Jane Wyman Was Right" (Jamieson, 1984, p. xxiii). In the 1986 Alabama gubernatorial race, the state Democratic party disqualified the winner of the Democratic primary (Charlie Graddick) and named the runner-up (Bill Baxley) the official party candidate for the general election. Graddick had 8,756 more votes than Baxley in the run-off primary. After the Democratic party decided that Republican crossover voting had given the margin of victory to Graddick, the Executive Committee of the Democratic party (five members) voted 5 to 0 to disqualify Graddick and make Baxley the party nominee. The disqualified candidate's supporters distributed a bumper sticker that read: "Graddick – 8756 Baxley – 5."

In that same election in Alabama, the Republican party took advantage of the Democratic plight by emphasizing the "backroom politics" associated with the history of the Democratic party and by reiterating Graddick's own plea to send the Democratic party a message on election day. They distributed a

bumper sticker that read "SEND 'EM A MESSAGE! VOTE *REPUBLICAN.*"
In 1988, the Alabama Democratic party, in an attempt to win back voters they
had alienated in the 1986 gubernatorial race, distributed bumper stickers with
the American flag that said: "Alabama's Democrats For the family on Main
Street. Not the big boys on Wall Street."

In the beginning of 1988, Ronald Reagan nominated conservative Republican Robert Bork to the United States Supreme Court. Democrats rallied to
fight the nomination, which was ultimately defeated. They distributed bumper stickers that said: "BLOCK BORK."

MEDIA BUYS

According to Innocenzi (1986), all too often political campaigns concentrate
only on the advertising message and not on how or when the message will
be disseminated. Because of this, precious advertising dollars are wasted because the campaign has failed to reach their targeted audiences by using inappropriate media or times.

A political campaign first must decide upon its target audiences. Second,
the campaign must design the political messages for these targeted audiences.
Finally, the campaign must turn to the task of deciding how and when to deliver
the messages (see Innocenzi, 1986). The targeting axiom, "specific messages
for specific audiences for specific results," must be followed.

Media rating services that provide estimates of effective audience media
exposure help campaign strategists make informed media buys. Examples of
such services are: Arbitron which provides local radio and television ratings,
Neilsen which provides national television ratings, the Audit Bureau of Cir-
culation which provides magazine and newspaper readership figures, and the
Traffic Audit Bureau which provides outdoor advertising figures. Research
is available that indicates demographic characteristics, cost, and lifestyle analysis for consumers of the various media (see Innocenzi, 1986). Innocenzi noted that "*light television viewers* tend to be *heavy print readers* and *radio
listeners*, especially in the 'drive times' " (p. 24). And heavy prime-time television viewers "tend to be older, less educated, and less well off" (p. 35). Bogart
(1972) found that Blacks view more non-prime-time television than Whites.
Edmonds and Roy (1984) provided a detailed analysis of computer-assisted
media buys.

Traditional descriptions of party voters have suggested that Republicans
are more "print oriented" and Democrats are more "broadcast oriented" because of the differences in their educational profiles. Recently, the majority
of political advertising, whether for Republicans or Democrats, has been concentrated on television buys. Wilson (1987) has shown that political commer-

cials appear primarily during national and local (evening and late) news and during prime-time television programming. In some situations, these time slots may not be the optimal solution for a media buy. Television is not the most efficient means of narrowcasting. Narrowcasting is difficult to do with commercial television. Like the more specialized media channels such as radio, magazines, or cable, direct mail might be more appropriate (see Berkman & Kitch, 1986; Diamond & Bates, 1988; Innocenzi, 1986).

The modern political campaign will distribute its messages through a number of mass media delivery systems. The ratio of messages in one medium versus another is called the media mix. The media mix will vary depending on the needs of the campaign and the characteristics of the media market. For a detailed analysis of the media mix in congressional campaigns, see Goldenberg and Traugott (1984).

Television Buying

Buying time on television stations and the networks requires a strategy. Sabato (1981) identified four buying schemes that campaigns have used in the past. First is the *flat buy*, the simplest of the four schemes. For the 3 weeks before an election, the campaign runs the same number of spots each week. A derivative of the flat buy is the saturation buy, which runs the candidate's spots as often as time is available on the stations. What makes this a derivation is that any fluctuations in the amount of advertising from week to week is a function of the broadcast stations' lack of available time slots.

The second scheme is the *orchestrated finish*. The number of political advertisements builds over a period of 4 weeks. Sabato (1981) broke it down: 10% 4 weeks from the election, 20% 3 weeks away; 30% 2 weeks away; and 40% during the final week before election day. Increased spending during the final week of a campaign is a frequent occurrence in presidential elections. Mullen (1963a, 1963b, 1968) has found that candidates for both president and the senate will spend the majority of their advertising budgets in the last few campaign days.

The third scheme is the *events schedule*. The airing of political spots is contingent upon important events in the campaign. These events usually are created by the candidate's campaign but may also be a response to events outside the direct control of the candidate's campaign.

The fourth is the *stop-start* scheme. This scheme is one of running ads for a period of time, stopping, and then running ads again. This strategy can be very important to nonincumbents who may begin to run political ads in order to build name recognition and credibility long before the campaign officially begins. After a period, these spots would stop and then be run again during the latter days of the campaign. This strategy could be used by a nonincumbent without a primary challenger – the nonincumbent may want to run a series of ads during the other party's primary just to maintain name recognition while the opposition is getting extended media exposure.

Since Sabato's (1981) description of political advertising buying strategies, the character of many federal campaigns has changed. As we discussed in chapters 1 and 5, campaigns are starting earlier, more money is being raised and spent on political advertising, and negative ads are appearing early as well a late in the campaign cycle (see also Kern, 1989).

IN CONCLUSION

Sponsorship, who is paying for the message, and communication channels, how the messages are getting to the audience, are important elements when examining negative political advertising. Both sponsorship of political advertising and the channel selected to send those message affect how the audience perceives political advertising.

There are three primary sponsors for political advertising: political parties, political action committees, and candidates and their campaign committees. Each of these groups must follow rather detailed guidelines set up by the FEC in terms of contributions and expenditures. The sophisticated and complicated nature of FEC guidelines and filings has helped lead to the increasing professionalization of political campaigns through the need for knowledgeable attorneys, accountants, and consultants. Ironically, it has been the Congress who has helped promote the development of the New Politics through these regulations.

Sophisticated campaign services are now the hallmark of today's national political committees. The sharing of these services by the national political campaign committees in in-kind contributions has led to the increased sophistication of political campaigns for all federal offices. Research conducted on the opposition for congressional, senatorial, and presidential candidates provides ready fuel for negative ads. And generic advertising by one party that often attacks the opposition party has served as an important coordinated expenditure in political races.

Political action committees and specifically independent political action committees have led the way in developing negative political advertising strategies. Independently sponsored negative ads have been viewed as being more credible than candidate-sponsored negative advertisements. Independent expenditures allow the PACs to maintain a powerful voice in American politics.

Channel variables have been considered in terms of how political mediated messages affect people and how people use the mediated political messages.

There is evidence to suggest that the channel or combination of channels the strategist selects is important. The media mix of channels is determined by several factors: level of the political race, financing of the political race, candidate style, and media environment of the political race.

Television is able to create the illusion of closeness, so it is often the preferred medium for political advertising. Research has shown that television is best suited to reaching large, undifferentiated audiences. However, cable television is very good at narrowcasting or reaching very specific target audiences. In addition, cable television audiences tend to be more politically active than the average citizen.

Radio and newspapers are used primarily for local and state political campaigns. In some situations, political consultants have used radio for particularly strident attacks, because audiences do not perceive radio ads as being as harsh as television ads, which also have the visuals. There is some evidence that radio is losing its appeal for political advertisers because of its extremely fragmented audiences.

Newspapers are used to reach individuals who know more about the political process and campaign issues, and are more likely to vote. Newspaper readers are early deciders in a campaign. Traditionally, late deciders have been viewed as primarily television viewers, however one study found significantly different results.

Direct mail has been called the poisoned pen of politics, because it is so often associated with negative political advertising appeals. Direct mail is particularly effective on late deciders or heavy television viewers. In media-isolated areas, direct mail has also been identified as an important campaign tool. Bumper stickers are also used to display negative advertising and are used frequently to reinforce important negative campaign themes.

Direct response advertising has been used successfully to solicit volunteers or raise money in a number of political campaigns across the United States. Direct response advertising often is used in conjunction with fear appeals that stimulate voters to act. Computerized telemarketing provides a cheap, effective means of reaching a large number of voters. Although computerized telemarketing has been used primarily for party reinforcement and GOTV appeals, it is likely to be used in the future with sophisticated targeted negative appeals.

The new electronic media are still too new and undeveloped to be of a great concern right now. It is clear that should market forces allow, the new electronic media could play an important and expanding role in campaigning. The interactive nature of many of the new media offers a number of unique opportunities.

III

NEGATIVE POLITICAL ADVERTISING AND SOCIETY

With the growth of negative political advertising in the 1980s, consultants have developed a number of combative negative political advertising strategies in order to limit the effectiveness of negative attacks against their clients. In chapter 6, we consider two combative negative political advertising strategies: proactive inoculation ads and reactive response ads.

In chapter 7, we consider both legal and ethical considerations when devising negative political advertising. And in chapter 8, we examine the possible effects of negative political advertising on American society.

6

Combating Negative Ads

INTRODUCTION

Political campaigns generally use three strategies in their political advertising:

1. *supportive messages* designed to position the candidate on the issues and increase the perceived ideal personal leadership qualities of the candidate,
2. *negative ads* designed to question the opponents suitability for office, and
3. *reactive response ads* that serve as a reply to the opposition's negative ads.

However, communication theory suggests that there is a fourth type of communication strategy that could be an effective form of political advertising: *inoculation ads*. Proactive inoculation ads are used to undermine, deflect, and reduce the power of anticipated negative attacks.

Two of these four political advertising strategies are designed to combat negative ads: proactive inoculation ads and reactive response ads. Chapter 6 is an analysis of these two strategies. Combative research techniques are an integral part of the development and application of effective proactive inoculation and reactive response ads. We explore combative research techniques as an introduction to our analysis of combative advertising strategies.

COMBATIVE CANDIDATE RESEARCH

In order for political campaigns to successfully use inoculation advertising or reactive response advertising, the campaign must be cognizant of all potential candidate vulnerabilities. This can be done only through extensive and inten-

211

sive candidate/campaign research. Only in this way can a campaign effectively anticipate negative attacks and effectively utilize damage control strategies to deal with them. Campaign research can be used to produce inoculation advertising that will successfully undermine, deflect, and reduce the power of anticipated negative attacks, or to produce reactive response advertising strategies to successfully neutralize negative attacks during the course of the campaign.

Political campaigns should conduct appropriate research so that an objective analysis of the candidate, likely opponents, and the voters' ideal candidate for the office sought is possible. This information is essential to the development of all political advertising: positive, negative, reactive response, and inoculation. This research and analysis should be conducted well before a candidate ever announces. A candidate expecting negative attacks should be particularly concerned with identifying all potential vulnerabilities in order to successfully design appropriate combative negative political advertising strategies.

Obviously, survey research provides the campaign with needed answers concerning how the voters perceive various candidates. In addition to this important survey research data, the campaign must take the proactive stance of seeking out all available information that is likely to impact on the campaign but may or may not be part of the public consciousness. Clearly, a detailed examination of the political record of all candidates should be conducted. This includes political affiliations, financial donors, voting records, past and present position statements, and the success and failures of the candidates' past performances in political offices. In addition, a close examination of the candidates' personal lives should be conducted. Are there any embarrassing personal situations associated with the candidates that if publicly aired might prove damaging to the campaigns?

In order to develop effective combative political advertising strategies, any identified candidate/campaign vulnerabilities should be identified and addressed by the campaign organization before the official opening of the campaign season. Through objective candidate/campaign research, an effective proactive or reactive advertising program or a combination thereof can be created. Appropriate combative negative advertising strategies might include a variety of proactive inoculation or reactive response advertising tactics.

A PROACTIVE DEFENSE AGAINST NEGATIVE ADVERTISING

Inoculation Theory

Inoculation theory finds its basis within the psychology and communication literature, although its underlying analogy is biological. Inoculation is a method by which a campaign may be able to prepare a candidate's supporters to withstand the attacks in the opposition's negative ads and to maintain positive attitudes toward the candidate during and after the attacks. As a defense, inoculation theory provides an additional tool in the campaign manager's arsenal.

First, we review the research to see where, how, and when inoculation is most likely to work. Second, we demonstrate how the research is suggestive of its utilization within a campaign setting.

Cooper and Jahoda (1947) observed that people prefer not to face ideas that run counter to the ones they hold. There seem to be three mechanisms through which individuals may deal with the possibility of facing contrary information: The receivers may find a way to avoid exposure to the information (selective exposure); the receivers may admit they were in error and change their minds; or, the receivers may actively defend their opinions.

Those who avoid exposure to arguments or evidence that runs counter to their own attitudes run a risk of being more open to persuasion than those who do expose themselves to challenging messages. So, in situations where avoidance is not possible for those who usually avoid contrary messages, their undefended attitudes are vulnerable to persuasion (Hovland, 1959). Papageorgis and McGuire (1961) asserted that the reason a person who actively avoids counterarguments is so vulnerable is that she or he has also avoided practicing the defense of the held attitudes. This lack of a defensive rehearsal leaves the receiver without practice defenses to deal with the counterattitudinal arguments.

McGuire and his associates (Anderson & McGuire, 1965; McGuire, 1961a, 1961b, 1962, 1964; McGuire & Papageorgis, 1961, 1962; Papageorgis & McGuire, 1961) viewed the attack of these undefended attitudes as similar to the introduction of a disease into the body of an immune-deficient patient. In order to explain how an individual's attitudes may be protected from attack, McGuire and associates formulated the inoculation theory, which was based on the familiar biological inoculation model. As McGuire (1964) wrote:

> In the biological analogy, the person is typically made resistant to some attacking virus by preexposure to a weakened dose of the virus. This mild dose stimulates his defenses so that he will be better able to overcome any massive viral attack to which he is later exposed, but it is not so strong that this pre-exposure will itself cause the disease (p. 200)

Researchers analogized that attitudes could be strengthened through the introduction of a relatively weak counterattitudinal message with the refutation to that counterattitudinal message included. The use of the defense-building counterattitudinal messages has been shown not to have a boomerang effect (McGuire & Papageorgis 1961; Papageorgis & McGuire, 1961); that is, the counterarguments used to generate the attitudinal defenses do not themselves change the receiver's attitude.

McGuire (1964) believed that for inoculation to successfully function, a person first may have sufficient knowledge to defend the preexisting attitude. Second, the individual must have the opportunity to practice the defense. And third, the individual must be motivated to use the defense. Burgoon, Cohen, Miller, and Montgomery (1978) identified three other situational factors that influence the viability of inoculation as a protective force against contrary messages. Students of inoculation should take into account the level of perceived threat to the held attitude. In addition, they should consider whether the message or the messenger violates the receiver's expectations. And finally, the context of the message should be considered.

Lumsdaine and Janis (1953) were one of the first to report that exposure to a two-sided argument—that is an argument that includes pro and con arguments—seemed to help people develop resistance to arguments that were contrary to their held attitudes. Researchers found that simply giving people more of the same supportive information, information that was consonant with the views already held, was not as likely to protect the views of people as exposing them to counterarguments. Although the exposure of people to attitude consonant material did show an increase in agreement with the attitude, it was an increase that could be easily swung around.

McGuire and Papageorgis (1961) suggested that the continued use of reinforcing support should be called the paper tiger effect. They found that although reinforcing support showed an initial strengthening of attitudes, when attitudes were subjected to a counterargument, the strengthened attitudes quickly crumbled. The superiority of defense-building counterarguments over supportive information has received strong empirical support (Anderson & McGuire, 1965; McGuire, 1961b; McGuire & Papageorgis, 1961, 1962; Tanenbaum, McCauley, & Norris, 1966).

McGuire (1961b) found that messages with additional supporting information (e.g., evidence), in addition to defense-building counterarguments, create a more effective message than one that just contained defense-building counterarguments. The combination of defense-building counterargument and supporting information was found to be the strongest for maintaining attitudes when the person was faced with a new or novel attack against a held attitude. McCroskey (1970) found that evidence serves as an "inhibitor to counterpersuasion" (p. 194).

McGuire (1962) also discovered that attitudes become more resistant to change—the inoculation increases—as the time between exposure to the defense-building counterargument and exposure to an attack increases. It was thought that as the time between inoculation and exposure to attack increased, so too did the internal practice with arguing against counterattitudes. This practice of defending against counterattitudinal ideas works to strengthen the held attitudes. The importance of practicing defenses to arguments has been shown in studies by Festinger and Maccoby (1964) and Osterhous and Brock (1970), which demonstrate that when people are distracted, unable to practice or participate in counterarguing, they are more persuadable. Similarly, McGuire and Papageorgis (1961) found that the more passive the receiver was when the inoculation material was administered the greater the resistance to change. The passive receiver is seen as being better able to understand elements of the message and practice defending attitudes as suggested by the inoculating messages.

When individuals perceive that their attitudes are being threatened, the evidence is overwhelming that this perceived threat will motivate a defense of the attitude (Burgoon et al., 1976; McGuire, 1961; McGuire & Papageorgis, 1961; Miller & Burgoon, 1978-1979; Papageorgis & McGuire, 1961; Tannenbaum, 1967). McGuire and Papageorgis (1962) have also shown that if people are warned that their ideas will be coming under attack, such a warning does work to strengthen the defenses against attack.

Burgoon et al. (1976) have shown that uncertainty as to whether or not an individual's views will be attacked creates greater inoculation effects than knowing there will be no attack or knowing for certain there will be an attack on that person's viewpoint. As Burgoon and his coauthors noted, "the presumed uncertainty associated with lack of knowledge about the likelihood of an attack would be threatening and would therefore motivate people to prepare adequate defenses (pp. 127-128).

The original topics for inoculation studies were what McGuire (1964) called cultural truisms. McGuire's work examined culturally determined mythical constructs that are generally accepted in society as fact. For example, he used topics such as: It is good to brush your teeth three times a day, or people should get a yearly medical check-up. Because of his emphasis on cultural truisms, McGuire cautioned that inoculation works only for those beliefs that have not previously been attacked.

Pryor and Steinfatt (1978) argued that inoculation applied to other attitudes besides those cultural truisms that McGuire and associates had investigated; furthermore, they contended that the attitude does not have to be attacked in exactly the same manner as suggested in the inoculating message (see also, Kiesler, Collins, & Miller, 1969). Pryor and Steinfatt were able to demonstrate that inoculation did not require attitudes that were strongly held but also worked with those that are best described as midrange. Later studies confirmed their analysis (e.g., Burgoon et al., 1976; Burgoon et al., 1978; Pryor & Steinfatt, 1978; Ullmann & Bodaken, 1975). Pryor and Steinfatt also suggested that as topic salience increases, an individual's motivation and readiness to learn defensive messages also increases.

INOCULATION DURING A POLITICAL CAMPAIGN

Pfau and Burgoon (1988) applied inoculation concepts to political communication. They determined that inoculation works in three specific manners: "[1] undermining the potential influence of the source of political attacks, [2] deflecting the specific content of political attacks, and [3] reducing the likelihood that political attacks will influence receiver voting intention" (pp. 105-106). Pfau and Burgoon (1988) also suggested that because of the volatility of political attitudes, inoculation should take place early in the campaign (see Cundy, 1986). One of the advantages of running the inoculation commercials early in the campaign is, as the evidence reviewed earlier suggests, the greater the time between the inoculation and the attack the stronger the resistance. The additional time provides more opportunities for the receiver to practice defenses.

Research that shows inoculation works best on a passive receiver is indicative that television may be the ideal place for inoculation advertising. Studies (eg., Csikszentmihalyi & Kubey, 1981; Krugman, 1965-1966) have long demonstrated the relaxing nature of television viewing and the passive state of most of its viewers. People who receive the inoculation messages from television would be in an appropriate state to practice the counterarguing defenses, which the aforementioned literature review indicates is important in the inoculation process.

Campaigns may use inoculation to prepare people leaning toward their candidate for attacks by the opposition. Cundy (1986) reported that early advertising efforts are very effective in warding off future attacks. Kern (1989) cited evidence that inoculation advertising serves as a cocoon that protects the candidate later in the race. *Congressional Quarterly* (New Campaign Techniques, 1986) reported that starting in 1986 media consultants were beginning to create inoculation spots. Political consultant Charlie Black is quoted by them as saying, "If you know what your negatives are, and you know where you're vulnerable, you can pre-empt it" (p. 31).

Although historically challengers have been associated with the use of negative ads, in recent years incumbents increasingly have been utilizing negative advertising strategies. Because challengers are usually less well known than incumbents, there had been some question as to whether inoculation techniques would protect challengers as well as incumbents. In 1979, Kitchens and Stiteler, in a case study of a local Texas election, were able to demonstrate that a challenger was successful in inoculating the voters against subsequent attacks. The inoculation advertising strategy utilized both direct mail and television advertisements. Critics might suggest that a local election is not a good testing ground for the recognition factor differences associated with challengers and incumbents, because local election candidates generally have lower recognition ratings than state or federal candidates. However, Kitchens and Stiteler (1979) presented survey data that show the candidates were not plagued with low-visibility ratings. Before the campaign began, the incumbent enjoyed a 78% recognition rating, and the challenger enjoyed a surprisingly high recognition rating of 41%.

The research indicates that inoculation ads are useful not only for the issues covered in the advertising but also for those issues that are not specifically mentioned in the inoculating material. Because the sponsor's supporters are inoculated against attacks, late campaign attacks by the opposition should meet with cognitive resistance from the sponsor's supporters.

The evidence seems to suggest that the best approach to the structure of an inoculating ad would be for the advertising to contain both refutational and supportive elements. The previous research suggests that the less committed a receiver is to the candidate the more important the supportive material will be for that person. The supportive material helps the less committed in practicing their counterarguments to forthcoming opponents' messages.

Inoculation is a proactive strategy, which may provide rich rewards for those campaigns using it. This strategy may be particularly important in those campaigns where attacks are expected from the opposition. As Republican consultant Jim Innocenzi said, "Inoculation and pre-emption are what win campaigns" (New Campaign Techniques, 1986, p. 31).

An example of an effective combative strategic plan is the 1960 presidential campaign of John Kennedy. Kennedy knew that he would have to directly address his Catholicism in the race for the American presidency. His campaign strategy to deal with the issue of his Catholicism has been characterized as "a blunt truth technique" (Diamond & Bates, 1988, p. 49). Students of American politics had suggested that it would be impossible for a Catholic to be elected as president (see Rossiter, 1960, p. 193). And Kennedy had found during the course of his presidential campaign that there was a great deal of prejudice against Catholics in the United States. His father, Ambassador Joe Kennedy, kept a political cartoon that was taken from a Baptist paper among his personal papers. Goodwin (1987) described the cartoon: "Under the title 'Big John and Little John,' the cartoon depicts Pope John XXIII on the throne with his hand on John Kennedy's head. Underneath is the caption 'Be Sure to Do What Poppa Tells You' " (p. 798). Time and time again, Kennedy was asked the religion question. In West Virginia, Kennedy told a crowd: "I am a Catholic, but the fact that I was born a Catholic, does that mean that I can't be the President of the U.S.? I'm able to serve in Congress and my brother was able to give his life, but we can't be President?" (Goodwin, 1987, p. 798; for an excellent discussion of the Catholicism issue in the 1960 election and the Kennedy campaign's handling of it, see Goodwin, 1987, pp. 794–803).

On September 12, 1960, John F. Kennedy spoke to the Greater Houston Ministerial Society. Although Kennedy spoke about issues such as a higher minimum wage and federal aid to education, he also directly addressed the issue of his Catholicism. Kennedy turned the Catholicism issue into a question of tolerance. Jamieson (1984) wrote: "A vote for Kennedy became a sign of open-mindedness, a vote against him a potential sign of bigotry" (p. 125). Kennedy evoked one of the most poignant quotes of our times. This famous quotation by Martin Niemoeller (1892-1984) addressed the dilemma of humankind during the rise of fascism in Europe:

> In Germany they came first for the Communists, and I didn't speak up because I wasn't a Communist. Then they came for the Jews, and I didn't speak up because I wasn't a Jew. Then they came for the trade unionists, and I didn't speak up because I wasn't a trade unionist. Then they came for the Catholics, and I didn't speak up because I was a Protestant. Then they came for me, and by that time no one was left to speak up. (as quoted in Bartlett, 1980, p. 824)

Kennedy told the Houston ministers: "For a while this year it may be a Catholic against whom the finger of suspicion is pointed, in other years it has been, and may someday be again, a Jew—or a Quaker—or a Unitarian—or a Baptist" (Jamieson, 1984, p. 131). He went on to say that: "It was Virginia's harassment of Baptist preachers, for example, that led to Jefferson's statute of religious freedom" (Jamieson, 1984, pp. 131-132). Kennedy had turned the tables on the Baptists in that he was identifying with them and their experience with persecution. Thus he was able to bridge the gap between Baptists and Catholics by demonstrating that they had similar histories, histories of persecution. And indirectly, Kennedy was reminding them that Nixon, too, was also a member of a nonmainstream denomination, the Society of Friends, that is, Quakers (see Costello, 1959). This worked to neutralize some of the Baptist rhetoric against Catholicism and Kennedy's candidacy.

The Kennedy campaign taped the speech and quickly made between 300 and 400 prints. The tapes were distributed by advance people before Kennedy arrived in towns and cities throughout America (see Jamieson, 1984). In this way, the Kennedy campaign helped inoculate the voters by giving them counterarguments to be used against anti-Catholic rhetoric. Kennedy used the same technique in the following television ad:

The 1960 Kennedy "Catholicism" Ad

VIDEO	AUDIO
Camera up on Kennedy holding microphone in the midst of large crowd.	Kennedy [SOF]: "The question is whether I think that if I were elected president, I would be divided between two loyalties, my church and my state. There is no article of my faith that would in any way inhibit—I think it encourages—the meeting of my oath of office. And whether you vote for me or not because of my

competence to be president, I am
sure that in this state of West
Virginia, that no one believes
I'd be a candidate for the
presidency if I didn't think I
could meet my oath of office. Now
you cannot tell me the day I was
born it was said I could never run
for president because I wouldn't
meet my oath of office. I came to
the state of West Virginia, which
has fewer numbers of my
co-religionists than any state in
the nation. I would not have come
here if I didn't feel I was going
to get complete opportunity to run
for office as a fellow American in
this state. I would not run for it
in any way if I felt that I
couldn't do the job. So I come here
today to say that I think this is
an issue. . . . "
Applause drowns out voice.
(Diamond & Bates, 1988, pp. 95-96)

In 1987, Congressman Buddy Roemer, a Democratic candidate for governor of Louisiana, ran an inoculation spot that suggested he was no ordinary politician. Roemer maintained that he often made people angry, because he was willing to tell them the truth about what they had done or what they should be doing. Roemer had been widely criticized for his frankness during his congressional years. Roemer himself appears in this inoculation spot.

The 1987 Roemer "No Ordinary Politician" Ad

VIDEO	AUDIO
Roemer talking directly into camera. "Roemer"	Roemer [SOT]: "Some insiders say I'm not a good politician, because I say things that make some people angry. They're right I do. Made some people in Washington angry when I refused to take a Congressional pay raise passed by

CU of Roemer

the politicians for the politicians. I thought the country needed to tighten its belt. I made the bureaucrats and dead-heads in Baton Rouge angry when I said I'd reduce the number of state cars and scrub the budget. I made the polluters angry when I said those who pollute the air and water should pay to clean it up. Clean it up and get out, I said. I made the education bureaucrats angry when I said I'd brick up the top three floors of the Department of Education; cut the consultants; and, pay the teachers. I noticed my opponents don't make many people angry. That doesn't surprise you does it? Politics as usual. I don't like Louisiana politics. I love Louisiana I love Louisiana enough to make some people angry.

"Roemer Governor
A Revolution for Louisiana"

A MENU OF REACTIVE RESPONSES TO NEGATIVE POLITICAL ADVERTISING

A reactive response is in essence a defensive posture in that a candidate is having to respond to an ad. Thus the candidate must adopt a defensive posture for protection. Defensive posturing is an attempt to rebuild an argument that has been attacked (McBurney & Mills, 1964). A defensive posture, being forced to make a reactive response, is not an ideal situation. It is important to remember that such a defensive situation is a difficult and potentially dangerous one, for no longer is the candidate controlling the campaign debate; rather, the candidate is reacting to another's campaign agenda.

Frequently, campaigns have failed to analyze adequately their existing environment for potential vulnerabilities or the external environment suddenly changes and creates new, unforeseen vulnerabilities. In such situations, the campaign is forced to respond in order to maintain damage control. Under such conditions, the campaign is at a clear disadvantage. In other cases, the campaign may well have known the candidate's vulnerabilities but may have chosen not to use inoculation advertising for one reason or another, then later is attacked and finds itself on the defensive. Hopefully, if the campaign was aware of the vulnerabilities, appropriate neutralizing reactive responses for the anticipated attacks had been strategized before the attacks were made. In such a situation, the campaign is still at a disadvantage, because it no longer has the controlling hand in that it is in a defensive position, but the campaign is in a far superior position to one that has failed to anticipate negative attacks entirely.

Nesbitt (1988) suggested that when reactive responses are made they be conducted via the same communication channel through which the original attack was made. In this way, the response reaches the same audience.

Eight Reactive Responses

Historically, there have been eight primary means by which a candidate hopes to weaken or destroy the effectiveness of the opposition's negative advertising: (a) silence, (b) confession/redemption, (c) sanctimonious admission, (d) denial/campaign attack, (e) counterattack, (f) refutation, (g) obfuscation, and (h) counterimaging (cf. Baukus, Payne, & Reisler, 1985). Each of these strategies has been used by various candidates at different electoral levels in our electoral history. Different problems and strengths are associated with each. In the following pages, we examine the rationale behind each of these response strategies, and we consider their effectiveness with regard to the desired goal of successfully combating negative advertising. As appropriate, we give examples of reactive response advertising. In some situations, we give both the original attack ad and the response to it. It is important to remember that some reactive response advertising strategies may utilize more than one responsive tactic at a time. For example, an attacked candidate may engage in counterattacks, denial, refutation, and counterimaging advertising (see Table 6.1).

TABLE 6.1
Combating Negative Advertising Strategies

Proactive Strategy
Inoculation Advertising
Reactive Response Strategies
Silence
Confession/Redemption
Sanctimonious admission
Denial/Campaign attack
Counterattack
Refutation
Obfuscation
Counterimaging

Silence

In the early days of negative political television advertising, candidates who were attacked were told to ignore negative ads. And they were encouraged by their advisers' belief that the ads would only boomerang in the end (New Campaign Techniques, 1986). But now, all that has changed. The 1980 elections saw "such Democratic congressional fixtures as Sens. Gaylord Nelson of Wisconsin and Herman E. Talmadge of Georgia, and Rep. Richardson Preyer of North Carolina, . . . fall victim to campaigns in which they declined to respond to challengers on the attack" (New Campaign Techniques, 1986, p. 30). In addition, most liberal Democratic senators targeted by NCPAC in 1980 also ignored the negative advertising and were defeated (see Tarrance, 1982, p. 5). Although the evidence is primarily anecdotal for both situations, consultants point to these races as evidence for a vocal strategy (see Hagstrom & Guskind, 1986; Orlik, 1990). The lesson was clear: Candidates should not ignore negative ads.

Early research and even today's news reports call negative advertising mudslinging. Perhaps that is why today's political consultants warn their clients that mud sticks if it goes unanswered. Research in political strategic silences and leadership dramatization give us clues as to why this is true.

Political Strategic Silence:
The Absence of Leadership Dramatization

Although research in the early 1970s suggested that "much political power . . . appears to be derived and . . . maintained by the manner in which silence is used" (Bruneau, 1973, p. 39; see also, Johannesen, 1974), it was not until 1980 that Brummett (1980) proposed a theory of strategic silence in politics. Brummett defined a strategic silence as "a refusal of a public figure to communicate verbally when that refusal (1) violates expectations, (2) draws public attribution of fairly predictable meanings, and (3) seems intentional and directed at an audience" (p. 289). Brummet argued that in political situations silence itself has rhetorical influence.

Brummett (1980) developed a theoretical discussion of the use of strategic silences in politics. He applied this theoretical perspective in a critical analysis of the "rose garden strategy" (p. 302) or strategic silence pursued by Jimmy Carter in July 1979, and concluded that strategic silences are not consistent with good presidential leadership. Using Brummett's critical techniques, Johnson (1984) concluded in an analysis of presidential transitions that strategic silences are not effective communication devices for president-elects in that transitions are times of great anxiety and uncertainty, and silence only serves to exacerbate this anxious situation.

Leadership is not a quality that a political leader does or does not have.

Rather it is the relationship that exists between a leader and the people. Leadership is "recognized in the response of followers to individual acts and speeches. If they respond favorably and follow, there is leadership; if they do not, there is not" (Edelman, 1964, p. 75). Thus, leadership is a constantly evolving dramatistic expression. And, the process of negotiating leadership is quite simply talk (see Brummett, 1980; Edelman, 1964; Hall, 1972). In politics, talk establishes and maintains political relationships.

By refusing to talk, political leaders or candidates leave their actions open to interpretation. The "definition of those actions has been relinquished to the speculation of press and public, speculation that will find mystery, passivity, etc., in those situations" (Brummett, 1980, p. 293). Silences create uncertainty and tension. According to Edelman (1964), "the basic condition for the displacement of political leadership is the leader's inability or lack of opportunity to convey the impression of coping with an opposition. . ." (pp. 81–82). Roper (1957) explained: "Americans are accustomed to admire men who get things done, men who radiate faith and confidence. Americans are not inclined toward doubt; they like to be all for or all against something, right away if possible" (pp. 219–220).

Silence is the temporary denial of political relationships. And according to Brummett (1980), this denial creates a situation in which "mystery, uncertainty, passivity, and relinquishment" rule the day (p. 297). Leaders who refuse to talk create an air of mystery surrounding their actions. People are not sure what to expect, which creates tension and uncertainty. And in this political talk void, the people create their own explanations for the silence. By pursuing a strategic silence, the political leader turns over the definition of the situation to others, a very dangerous political maneuver. In other words, the political leader is no longer trying to actively manage his or her political persona, rather the persona is left to the manipulation and perhaps eventual destruction by others. The leader has ceased to impression manage and to lead.

The Activism Bias. In America, successful political leaders are usually perceived as being active. According to Edelman (1964), it is important for the political leader to appear active in both word and deed: "The public official who dramatizes his competence is eagerly accepted on his own terms" (pp. 78, 82). Americans expect their leaders to both explain and educate the public about the significant matters of the day (see Hall, 1972; Kumar & Grossman, 1982; Neustadt, 1980).

Many political observers view the election campaign as a test by fire. The political leader must be an activist candidate. And some have even suggested that the manner in which a candidate handles his or her own advertising may well be an indication of the candidate's suitability to lead. In 1988, Kathleen Jamieson, a noted advertising historian, told "NBC Nightly News" that "Michael Dukakis for two-thirds of the election forfeited the opportunity to discredit

George Bush and put in place a compelling reason to vote for him—advertising ineptitude almost unparalleled. . . . Can someone who can't manage a campaign better than this, manage the government, manage the country?" (appearing in a Stan Bernard report, 1988).

Some researchers have suggested that Americans have what has been called a masculine view of leadership in that they want their leaders to be aggressive, forceful, courageous, responsible, and so forth (see Wayne, 1982a, 1982b). Cronin (1977) suggested that certain characteristics typify the great presidents: "The great Presidents have been the strong Presidents, who stretched their legal authority, who occasionally relied on the convenience of secrecy, and who dominated the other branches of government" (p. 75). Political scientists who share Cronin's view have been said to be guilty of liberal bias, for they wished the president to push the ropes of presidential power to their breaking point. These analysts have championed the vision of change. But, it is not only political scientists that often share this liberal or masculine view of leadership; it is also the presidents (and other public officials) themselves (Grossman & Kumar, 1981) and their constituents (see Nimmo & Savage, 1976).

Thus, it is of paramount importance that public officials actively dramatize their leadership role through public acts. As William Allen White once said: "A democracy cannot follow a leader unless he is dramatized. A man to be a hero must not content himself with heroic virtues and anonymous actions. He must talk and explain as he acts—drama" (as quoted in Fenno, 1975, p. 320).

Silence as a Response to a Negative Ad

Americans expect their leaders to stand up for themselves. As children, we are taught to stand up for ourselves, to fight back if necessary, for what is ours or for what we want. Perhaps this socialization analogy is too simplistic. Patterns emerge when American leadership myths are examined. We expect our leaders to stand tall and fight even when they are outnumbered or wounded. Leaders are expected to make every sacrifice, every effort to win the battle. They are expected to fight for what is right even when it is unpopular or ultimately impossible. In short, we want John Wayne and Rambo. Ed McCabe (1988), a national advertising consultant, wrote that the major problem with Michael Dukakis during the 1988 presidential campaign was that he never realized that "there's one thing the American people dislike more than someone who fights dirty. And that's someone who climbs into the ring and won't fight" (p. 48).

If a candidate ignores a negative attack, Americans give credence to the attack, because, at some level, voters believe that if the candidate does not fight back then the attack must be true. In a void, the voters fill in their own answers. Answers that are tainted with elements of guilt, cowardice, or passivity are all death knells for political candidates. In short, ignoring negative political ads will not make them go away. The ads and their consequences will return again and again to haunt the political candidate who has failed to dramatize his or her leadership abilities by dealing with the negative ads.

Confession and Redemption

Some candidates believe that if they confess their sins to the voters they will in effect be redeemed in the eyes of the voters. Although the American public dislikes silence, they often appreciate politicians who will own up to personal shortcomings and apologize for their acts. Most prominent religions in the United States teach that confessional experiences are cleansing and a route to redemption. Thus it is believed that through the visibly painful process of admitting error, the voters will forgive them. Others have called the confession/redemption ad an apolgia or an apology strategy (Berkman & Kitch, 1986; Sabato, 1981). Political consultant David Garth has frequently used confession and redemption strategies to help such incumbents as "New York Mayor John Lindsay in 1969, New Jersey Governor Brendan Byrne in 1977, and New York Governor Hugh Carey in 1978" (Berkman & Kitch, 1986, p. 160).

In 1969, John Lindsay appeared in a candidate confrontation ad that was called "Mistakes." Lindsay admitted that he had guessed wrong on a heavy snowfall during the winter that had paralyzed the city, but he went on to point out all the things he did right for New York City. After each positive point, Lindsay summed up with the phrase "and that was no mistake."

In 1978, Senator Charles Percy, a Republican from Illinois, used the confession/redemption technique in the Illinois Senate race.

The 1978 Percy "Confession" Ad

VIDEO	AUDIO
"Chuck Percy" CU of Chuck Percy	Percy [SOT]: "The polls say many of you want to send me a message. But after Tuesday, I may not be in the Senate to receive it. Believe me, I've gotten the message. And you're right, Washington has gone over board, and I'm sure I've made my share of mistakes. But in truth, your priorities are mine too—*stop* the waste—*cut* the spending—*cut* the taxes. I've worked as hard as I know how for you.

Camera opens to living room   I'm not ready to quit now, and I
with family around him.   don't want to be fired. I want to
                                   keep working for you. And, I'm
                                   asking for your vote."

Sanctimonious Admission

Some political candidates admit that they have done whatever it is their opponent has charged them with during the heat of the campaign battle; however,
they attempt to turn the tables on their opponent by making their actions appear virtuous rather than condemnatory. The candidate appears to be saying,
"Yes, I did it, and I'm damn glad I did it; and furthermore, if I had to do it
all over again, I'd do the same exact thing." Such a response attempts to place
the opposition in a negative light for even questioning the attacked candidate.
This also plays to the American public's desire to see leaders take a position
and then stand behind the position rather than caving in to the political view
of the time.
    It also should be noted that if a candidate faces a situation where the oppo-
sition has pinpointed a vulnerability, an appropriate sanctimonious admission
tactic to use might be: "Yes, I did that. I believed that I had to vote that way.
And I'd do it again. But it's important to remember that I also did this and
this, and they're more important to you." Smith and Hunt (1978) demonstrated that sources who point out both perceived weaknesses and strengths are
deemed more credible by the audience. Such a tactic saves the candidate from
asking "please forgive me," while pointing out other strengths that may be more
important to the voter than the opponent identified weakness.
    Perhaps the most famous sanctimonious admission ad is Richard Nixon's
30-minute "Checkers" ad. In 1952, The New York *Post* reported that Republican vice presidential candidate Richard Nixon was drawing on monies from
a secret fund. The headline read: "Secret Rich Men's Trust Fund Keeps Nixon
in Style Far Beyond His Salary" (Jamieson, 1984, p. 69). According to Jamieson, the Democrats quickly took advantage of the news story: "In Portland,
banner carriers wearing dark glasses and carrying tin cups hoisted signs pleading
for 'Nickels for Nixon' " (p. 70). *The Washington Post* even called upon Nixon to resign from the ticket. Strategists thought that the only way Nixon could
salvage his candidacy was to go on television and appeal directly to the American voters.
    The Republican National Committee and the Senatorial and Congressional
Campaign Committees purchased 30 minutes of network airtime so that Nixon could respond to the charges. Nixon's speech became know as the "Checkers Speech" because his dog, Checkers, was cited as the only gift that Nixon
had ever kept. Approximately 49% of the possible television viewing audience
tuned in to hear Nixon's speech.

Nixon admitted that there was a fund. But, he said he did not use the secret fund for personal use. Nixon claimed he used the fund to pay for:

Necessary political expenses of getting my message to the American people and the speeches I made, the speeches that I had printed, for the most part, concerned this one message—of exposing this Administration, the communism in it, the corruption in it—the only way I could do that was to accept the aid which people in my home state of California who contributed to my campaign and who continued to make these contributions after my election were glad to make. (Jamieson, 1984, p. 74)

Nixon went on to say:

One other thing I probably should tell you, because if I don't they will probably be saying this about me, too. We did get something, a gift, after the nomination. A man down in Texas heard Pat on the radio mention the fact that our two youngsters would like to have a dog, and believe it or not, the day before we left on this campaign trip we got a message from Union Station in Baltimore, saying they had a package for us. We went down to get it. You know what it was? It was a little cocker spaniel dog, in a crate that he had sent all the way from Texas—black and white, spotted, and our little girl Tricia, the six-year-old, named it Checkers. And you know, the kids, like all kids, loved the dog, and I just want to say this right now, that regardless of what they say about it, we are going to keep it. (Diamond & Bates, 1988, p. 72)

Diamond and Bates reported that as many as 1 million citizens sent letters or wires saying that they supported Richard Nixon.

In 1964, Republican presidential candidate Barry Goldwater was attacked as an "extremist," and he tried answering the charge by admitting: "Yes, I am an extremist but for all the right things." A campaign button had his photograph and these words: "EXTREMISM IN THE DEFENSE OF LIBERTY IS NO VICE; MODERATION IN THE PURSUIT OF JUSTICE IS NO VIRTUE. GOLDWATER IN '64" (Jamieson, 1984, pp. 182-183). But much like the 1988 Democratic presidential candidate Michael Dukakis's acceptance of and subsequent glorification of the label "liberal," it fell on deaf ears. The voters remained unconvinced.

In 1986, Ted Strickland, a Republican candidate for governor in Colorado, attacked Democratic candidate Roy Romer. The Romer campaign responded with a sanctimonious partial admission. Both the original attack ad and the reactive response ad follow.

The 1986 Strickland "Angela Davis" Ad

VIDEO	AUDIO
Still of Angela Davis	Narrator [VO]: "This communist was fired by Ronald Reagan. Who

Wanted Poster of Angela Yvonne Davis Still of Roy Romer	supported her then and now? The politician who voted against the death penalty – three times, Roy Romer.
Tape of Banks Still of Roy Romer	These banks hold your tax money. Who is the treasurer who put our money here and then got personal loans for his own businesses? Roy Romer.
Hand with fist of money. Roy Romer at a lectern, gesturing, asserting his points.	This is your money. Who says he'll take it away with higher taxes? Roy Romer. On this one, you can believe him."

For Governor
Ted Strickland
Kathy Arnold
For Lt. Governor

Although the original negative spot was a rather disjointed negative attack, the Romer campaign decided to respond with a partial admission with sanctimonious undertones.

The 1986 Romer "I love Colorado" Ad

VIDEO	AUDIO
Roy Romer walking on Wall Street, N.Y.C.	Romer [SOT]: "This is Wall Street, New York. This is where a lot of politicians said I should put all of Colorado's money. That's not the way I did it. Not on Wall
Romer on Main Street in Colorado.	Street but on Main Street . . . towns and cities like this all over Colorado. I'm Roy Romer. As State Treasurer, I made the commitment to keep our money in Colorado, to keep it safe and to keep building jobs and opportunities here. Also earning more money than ever before.
Romer Holds up a	Sorry, New York, But, I love

"I love New York" bumper	Colorado."
sticker and folds it	
in half.	

| Still of Romer | Narrator [VO]: "Roy Romer for |
| "Romer for Governor" | Governor." |

Denial and Attack of Campaign Practices

In some situations, candidates have chosen to deny the charges made against them and then turn and attack the opposition for its dirty campaigning. In other situations, the candidates attack their opposition for mudslinging and attempt to imply their denial by this dirty campaign charge. Denial ads are the most popular form of reactive response strategy (see Fig. 6.1).

Denial With Dirty Tactics Charge. Candidates choose a variety of approaches to the denial with dirty tactics charge. In some situations, the candidate appears in the ad (a candidate confrontation ad). In others, the candidate chooses a close associate such as a family member or a friend to make the response or the voters make the response for the candidate (a surrogate ad).

By using a surrogate, the candidate avoids personally going on the record to make the denial, and the candidate also avoids attacking the opponent's campaign tactics. Family surrogates are used most frequently. The family members are usually women and either the wife or mother of the candidate. The implication is clear. The wife or mother of a candidate is deemed more credible than the candidate in this situation. Kern (1989) pointed out that white-haired mothers or wives have an advantage in terms of credibility, that is, the myth that mothers and grandmothers do not lie. Also, because they are stereotypically thought to be more emotional, the message they convey may be more emotion laden. According to society's expectations, women are allowed to safely express emotions of resentment and anger more than men.

In 1980, Nancy Reagan appeared in an ad that responded to a number of negative Carter ads. She, in effect, charged the Carter campaign with dirty tactics. Mrs. Reagan (cited in Jamieson, 1984, p. 437) told the voters that she deeply resented it "as a wife, and a mother, and woman." Mrs. Reagan was portrayed as the feisty champion of her husband who had been wronged by the Carter campaign's charges.

By 1982, NCPAC's intervention into various state political races had become a hot political issue. Democratic Senator John Melcher of Montana aired a humorous reactive response ad directed at NCPAC. In the ad, Melcher both denies NCPAC's accusation that he was out of touch with Montana and attacks their city-slicker, big-money campaign tactics. Melcher's surrogates are two talking cows.

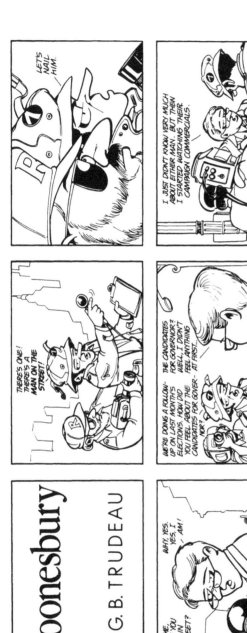
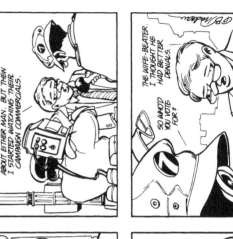

FIG. 6.1. DOONESBURY COPYRIGHT © 1989 G. B. Trudeau. Reprinted with permission of

The 1982 Melcher "NCPAC-MOOS" Ad

VIDEO	AUDIO
Airplane deplaning ramp is shown. Legs walking down the ramp in suit pants are shown. Suitcases are being carried down by the "headless" figures. On each suitcase is a NCPAC sticker. One suitcase bursts open, and money flies all over. Cows eating and mooing.	Narrator [VO]: "For over a year now, a pack of east coast politicos have been scurrying into Montana with briefcases full of money trying to convince us our Senator Melcher is out of step. Montana isn't buying it. Especially those who know bull when they hear it."
Cow speaks while chewing. A female with high voice.	First Cow [VO]: "Did you hear about those city-slickers out here, bad mouthing Doc Melcher?"
Second female cow with high voice.	Second Cow [VO]: "One of them was stepping in what they been trying to sell. He kept calling me a steer."
Calf nurses on mother. First Cow speaks.	First Cow [VO]: "That will all come as some surprise to Junior there."
Two men walking in fields together with same stride.	Narrator [VO]: "John Melcher has been solving Montana's problems most of his life. As a veterinarian, a State Legislator, a Congressman, and as our U.S. Senator. He loves this land, and he knows its people. And he works long and hard to make sure our needs are met."
First Cow	First Cow [VO]: "Now tell me does that look like a man who is out of step with Montana?"
Branding iron makes a	Narrator [VO]: "Those outsiders who say John Melcher is out of step

Montana state outline
around "Montana's
John Melcher"

with Montana just don't know
Montana.

Montana's John Melcher,
experience we can trust."

Also in 1982, Democratic Senator Lloyd Bentsen attacked NCPAC's tactics. The senator, though, tied NCPAC to his Republican opponent. The ad suggested that Republican James Collins and NCPAC were in "cahoots" in presenting all this "dirty advertising" (cited in Joslyn, 1986, p. 176). The ad paraphrased rather controversial statements by NCPAC director Terry Dolan. Without mentioning Dolan specifically, the ad told voters: "NCPAC is the same organization that said it could elect Mickey Mouse, that brags that NCPAC can lie through its teeth, and the candidate stays clean."

In 1984, Norman D'Amours attacked Republican Senator Gordon Humphrey during the New Hampshire senatorial race. The D'Amours attack centered on Humphrey's social security voting record. The Humphrey campaign used an elderly lady, Mildred Ingram, to respond to the charges. The ad has become known as the "Shame on You" spot.

The 1984 Humphrey "Shame on You" Ad

VIDEO	AUDIO
Elderly woman speaking to camera. "Mildred Ingram Acworth, NH"	Ms. Ingram [SOT]: "What do you do about a politician who tries to frighten the elderly? Well Norman D'Amours is trying to do just that.
	He claims Senator Humphrey does not believe in Social Security System. When his parents are on it? I'm on it, and many of his constituents in New Hampshire are on it. Mr. D'Amours knows this is a lie. Shame on you, Mr. D'Amours.
Photo of Humphrey "Senator Gordon Humphrey"	Senator Humphrey is a very strong supporter of Social Security."

In another 1984 Senate race in North Carolina, Jesse Helms used his wife in a surrogate response ad to say "shame on you." The Jim Hunt campaign had charged that Helms's proposed Right to Life Amendment would outlaw the birth control medication known as "the Pill." Mrs. Helms told North Carolinians that Jesse would never outlaw the Pill, saying, "Jim Hunt, you know that, and you ought to be ashamed of yourself. Some people will do *anything* for a vote" (Kern, 1989). Since 1984, the "Shame on You" spots have become quite popular as a denial response (see Kern, 1989).

In 1988, Republican Senator Pete Wilson used actor and Republican political activist, Charlton Heston, as a public surrogate in a denial/campaign attack spot against challenger Lieutenant Governor Leo T. McCarthy.

The 1988 Wilson "Charlton Heston" Ad

VIDEO	AUDIO
Charlton Heston talking directly into camera. "Charlton Heston"	Heston [SOT]: "In 1982, Leo McCarthy claimed his opponent, Carol Holnutt favored the dangerous use of pesticides. Now it wasn't true, by McCarthy won. In 1986, he insisted his opponent Mike Curb hadn't registered legally for the draft. It's also not true, but McCarthy won again. This year the *Los Angeles Daily News* calls his attack on Pete Wilson 'Leo McCarthyism.' The United States Senate is a place for integrity not Leo McCarthy."

In 1986, Alabama gubernatorial candidate Charlie Graddick claimed in a political advertisement that he sued former governor Fob James, who was also running for the nomination, for releasing criminals prematurely and had won the lawsuit. Fob James disagreed and appeared in a candidate confrontation spot making his case.

The 1986 James "Dirty Lie" Ad

VIDEO	AUDIO
Pan of jail cell bars. Fob James walks toward camera. MCU of Fob James	James [SOT]: "When I became governor, Alabama prisons were under federal control. I'm Fob James. As your governor, I built three, one-thousand inmate prisons to guarantee no hardened criminal would be turned loose to commit

When James says, "Charlie
Graddick," he points at
the camera.

another crime. On this issue an
opponent says he sued me and won.
Charlie Graddick — that's a
deliberate lie, and you know it."

Implied Denial by a Dirty Tactics Charge. The implied denial spot
simply attacks campaign tactics; however, by doing so, the denial is implicit.
As with the direct denial spots, the implied denial spots utilize both candidate
confrontation and surrogate techniques. In 1978, John Tower responded to
a series of negative ads in the Texas Senate race. Tower himself appears in
the ad.

The 1978 Tower "Handshake" Ad

VIDEO	AUDIO
John Tower sits on desk. He holds up newspaper. CU of two newspaper photos.	Tower [SOT]: "Perhaps you've seen this picture of my refusal to shake the hand of my opponent.
John Tower sits on desk with flag behind him.	I was brought up to believe that a handshake is a symbol of friendship and respect. Not a meaningless hypocritical gesture. My opponent has slurred my wife, my daughters, and falsified my record. My kind of Texan doesn't shake hands with that kind of man. Integrity is one Texas tradition you can count on me to uphold."
Signature of John Tower "He stands for Texas. Always has. Always will."	

In 1986, Alabama Democratic gubernatorial candidate, Bill Baxley, was
attacked with a number of charges relating to reported personal problems. Baxley's wife, Lucy, appeared in an advertisement protesting the attacks.

The 1986 Baxley "Lucy" Ad

VIDEO	AUDIO
MCU of Lucy Baxley	Lucy Baxley [SOT]: "I am Lucy Baxley. My home and my family

are the things I hold most dear.
Unfortunately, both have been under
attack during Bill's campaign for
Governor. I am very thankful Bill
and I share a love and commitment
strong enough to withstand such
ugly attacks. I am also thankful
that the good people of Alabama
share my disgust for such tactics.
You have given us your support,
your love, and your prayers. I ask
you to stand strong with us and
elect Bill Baxley, Governor."

In a proselytizing reporter spot in 1986, an Alabama Democratic guber-natorial candidate, Charlie Graddick, used a popular mudslinging demonstra-tion. Mudslinging demonstration ads were used across the country in the 1980s (Diamond & Bates, 1988). The format is usually the same. A campaign poster is assaulted with large globs of mud, thus the name "midslinging."

The 1986 Graddick "Mudslinging Ad"

VIDEO	AUDIO
Graddick for Governor Poster with his picture.	Sound effects: Drum beats, the "Thwack" of mud slapping up against the poster.
Mud hits poster.	Narrator [VO]: "A lot of politicians don't want for Charlie Graddick to be Governor. That's
Mud hits poster.	why they're attacking him with half-truths, untruths, and distortions. Why is Charlie Graddick the most attacked
Mud hits poster.	candidate? Because the special interest politicians and mudslingers
Mud hits poster.	know that when Graddick is in they're out for good. Enough dirty politics is enough.
Fresh Poster.	Alabama's voters deserve better. Graddick for Governor."

After the news media, pollsters, and politicians decried the negative guber-natorial race in Alabama in 1986, another Democratic gubernatorial candi-date, Bill Baxley, attempted to position himself as the positive candidate. The ad indirectly attacks the other negative candidates and their campaigns. However, it must be noted that Baxley did indeed use negative ads during the campaign.

The 1986 Baxley "Campaign Tactics" Ad

VIDEO	AUDIO
Bill Baxley talking into camera.	Baxley [SOT]: "I'm Bill Baxley. The way a person conducts himself in a campaign tells a lot about that person. I've run a positive campaign. I've talked about issues not personalities. I've presented programs to create jobs, improve education, and help our senior citizens. I've tried to *inspire* people not insult them. And I've never tried to make myself look good by making others look bad. If this is the kind of positive leadership you want, please give me your support on Tuesday. Thank you very much."
"Bill Baxley For Governor"	Narrator [VO]: "Bill Baxley Governor."

In 1988, Family Court Judge Paul Conger (Democrat) of Alabama was at-tacked in a negative voter editorial comment spot. During the spot, a teenage girl attacked Conger's rulings in a domestic matter. The spot was the only ad aired by Conger's Republican opponent, Jerry Hudson. The ad was remarkable for two reasons: First, the ad contained an extreme close-up of the teenager's face; and second, the ad content contained extremely sensitive material (in-cest, child abuse, and rape). The Conger campaign ran an implied denial by a dirty tactics charge ad that used footage from the original spot to show the teenager in a still frame over the judge's shoulder. Because the attack was so devastating, the campaign believed that Judge Conger himself had to make the response.

The 1988 Conger "Negative Advertising" Ad

VIDEO   AUDIO

Five seconds of Hudson ad.
Shrink until it freezes over
Conger's shoulder.   Conger [SOT]: "I'm Paul Conger—
                                   your family court judge.

                                   My opponent's first decision as a
                                   candidate was very telling—His
                                   decision was to attack me with
Conger pointing to still frame.   negative advertising. Negative
                                   advertising that is simply not
                                   true. And even uses a child witness
                                   to exploit the facts.
                                     On election day, ask yourself
                                   this question: 'If he would make a
                                   decision like this as a candidate,
                                   what would he do, if he was allowed
                                   to make decisions as judge?' "
                                   Narrator [VO]: "Re-elect Judge
                                   Paul Conger for responsible, fair
                                   decisions in family court."

Reactive Response to a Response. Because denial ads are so popular, some consultants have developed a ready-made reactive response to the response. In 1988, during a local Alabama probate judge race, the incumbent Hardy McCollum was attacked by challenger, Buck Burns, on a number of issues. The Burns campaign criticized McCollum on such issues as an unbalanced budget, bad roads, bad bridges, and closed-door politics. The McCollum campaign ran the traditional mudslinging, hit the campaign poster spot and a clever denial credibility spot. The Burns campaign ran a series of reactive responses to the denial ads. Both the McCollum "Credibility" spot and one of the Burns "No Mudslinging" reactive response ads are considered.

The 1988 McCollum "Credibility" Ad

VIDEO   AUDIO

"Credibility"   Narrator [VO]: "Credibility.
in white on blue   A public leader must have it. If
                                   you can't believe your elected

	officials then they have lost the right to be your leaders."
ECU of McCollum	McCollum [SOT]: "For eleven years as probate judge, I've lived by my word. I've worked hard, and I've never lied to the people of this county."
Still of Newpaper Ad A Second Newspaper Ad	Narrator [VO]: "Hardy McCollum's opponent ran this newspaper ad which contained untrue statements, implied that McCollum had lied, and ridiculed McCollum."
ECU of McCollum	McCollum [SOT]: "I've never built myself up by tearing another man down. My record is there for the public to see, and I'll stand on it."
Document: "State of Alabama Department of Examiners of Public Accounts"	Narrator [VO]: "Hardy McCollum inherited a 3.2 million dollar budget deficit eleven years ago. And according to the Report of the Examiners of Public Accounts for 8 out of the last 12 and for the last six years consecutively
"Balanced Budgets" Supered	the county has had a balanced budget.
"No New Taxes" Supered	And McCollum did this without a single new county tax."
CU McCollum	McCollum [SOT]: "We've come a long way in the last eleven years, but we still have a lot more we need to do."
An American Flag with McCollum's picture on upper left corner. "Experience Performance McCollum"	Narrator [VO]: "There are many reasons we need to keep Hardy McCollum the Probate Judge. One of them is that he tells us the truth."

The Burns campaign immediately reacted to the charges of mudslinging by denying the mudslinging.

The 1988 Burns "No Mudslinging" Ad

VIDEO	AUDIO
Buck Burns talking	Burns [SOT]: "Some of you will believe this is mud-slinging. But, in fact, it's easily verified accurate information. Our Probate Judge says that he balanced our county's budget. But documents that are public record reveal an overall deficit of 1.4 million dollars has occurred since he took office. *In fact*, we've had more years in the red than not.
	No, this isn't mud-slinging, it's simply the truth. And the truth is: it's time for new leadership."
	Narrator [VO]: "Elect Buck Burns Probate Judge."

Counterattack

Counterattack is an advertising strategy that responds to a negative ad by attacking the sponsor of the ad. The counterattack response does not refute the charges of the opponent's negative ad. Rather, the attacked candidate simply responds to a negative ad by making a negative attack of his or her own (see Baukus et al., 1985). In most instances, the original negative spot is not mentioned directly. The counterattack follows the old adage "fight fire with fire" (see Kern, 1989, p. 201).

In 1986, Republican Louisiana Senator Henson Moore charged his challenger opponent, Democratic Congressman John Breaux, with missing 1,083 crucial votes in the House of Representatives. Within 1 week, Congressman John Breaux had a reactive response ad claiming that the number 1,083 was the number of jobs lost in Louisiana each month due to Republican economic policies.

The 1986 Moore "1,083" Ad

VIDEO	AUDIO
"1083" White numbers on black.	Narrator [VO]: "The number one-thousand-eighty-three. Know what it stands for?"

Young man	Young man [SOT]: "1083."
Middle-aged woman	Middle-aged woman [SOT]: "Haven't the remotest."
Young woman	Young woman [SOT]: "Is it a tax form, something like that?"
Young black man	Young black man [SOT]: "How much money I made in the last two months."
Young white man	Young white man [SOT]: "Down payment on a car?"
Middle-aged man with hard hat	Man with hard hat [SOT]: "I don't know."
"1083" "One thousand eighty three is the number of votes Congressman John Breaux missed in Congress."	Narrator [VO]: "One thousand eighty three is the number of votes Congressman John Breaux missed in Congress. One thousand eighty three times he didn't show up for work."
The same middle-aged man with hard hat	Man with hard hat [SOT]: "Whew, wish I had a job like that!"

The Breaux Campaign turned the tables on the opposition by adopting the "1,083" as their own.

The 1986 Breaux "1,083" Ad

VIDEO	AUDIO
"1083" White numbers on black	Narrator [VO]: "The number 1,083. Know what it stands for?"
Man with cap.	Man with cap [SOT]: One thousand eighty three – 10 – 83."
Black man	Black man [SOT]: "That's the last time I think the Saints won a game."

Young woman	Young woman [SOT]: "The temperature out here right now."
Second woman	Second woman [SOT]: "I have no idea."
"1083" "One thousand eighty three is the number of jobs lost in Louisiana every few working days because of Republican policy that Henson Moore promises to continue."	Narrator [VO]: "One thousand eighty three is the number of jobs lost in Louisiana every few working days because of Republican policy that Henson Moore promises to continue.
Young woman	Young woman [SOT]: "That's incredible."
"Passage of effective legislation" "John Breaux – 18 Henson Moore – 0"	Narrator [VO]: "The numbers that count are the eighteen pieces of effective legislation John Breaux has passed and the zero for Henson Moore."

The Breaux Campaign had used portions of the Moore ad in order to make their own counterattack more credible.

In 1989 during the Republican primary season in Virginia, gubernatorial candidate Marshall Coleman counterattacked Republican Senator Paul Trible's gubernatorial campaign's negative ads.

The 1989 Coleman "A Study in Character" Ad

VIDEO	AUDIO
Photo of Trible. Photo of Trible in Senate. "Iran-Contra Hearings" ". . . responsibility . . . must rest with the President." "Paul Trible"	Announcer [VO]: "Paul Trible a study in character. He condemns his President when he thinks it is a popular thing to do. He quits the United States Senate because he's afraid to fight for his seat.
Newspaper Headline: "Trible" New Taxes May Be Needed"	He backs a plan to raise Virginia's taxes. Then blames the press for reporting it.

Newspaper Headline with CU of	He campaigns on TV with a uniform
Newspaper Photo with Trible in	he never wore in a plane he never
uniform:	flew. Today, Paul Trible is in
"A Candidate Who	trouble again. No wonder he's
Plays 'Dress Up.' "	running negative ads."
ECU of Photo	

Refutation

A refutation response ad produces hard evidence designed to logically and reasonably destroy the previous negative attack. Refutation is considered to be the optimal choice of reactive response to a negative ad (see Garramone, 1985; Salmore & Salmore, 1985). Voters tend to believe refutation responses before they will others. The presentation of what appears to be irrefutable evidence is a key ingredient in the credibility of the refutation response (see McCroskey, 1969, 1970; McGuire, 1961b).

McCroskey (1970) found that even low credibility sources were able to immediately affect attitude change when they included evidence in their messages. High credibility sources did not receive any additional credibility by the inclusion of evidence in their messages, but it is important to remember that their high credibility status already positively impacted on the degree of attitude change among the audience. And most significantly, "evidence appeared to serve as an inhibitor to counterpersuasion" (McCroskey, 1970, p. 194).

In 1986, Alabama Senator Jeremiah Denton provided evidence that he had indeed voted for social security during his term of office. The Richard Shelby campaign had charged that Denton had voted against social security a number of times, which was true. What Denton did was not to refute the times that he did vote against Social Security or to even mention them, but rather the ad showed the times that Denton had voted for Social Security. Whether evidence provided is misleading or not or truthful or not, the distinguishing characteristic of a refutation response is that it gives the appearance of producing evidence that is contrary to a negative charge.

The 1986 Denton "Social Security Votes" Ad

VIDEO	AUDIO
CU of legislative bills falling on a table.	Narrator [VO]: "Let's add it up. Jeremiah Denton has voted 38 times to save Social Security; 9 times
A horizontal scroll along the bottom of the screen gives the statistics stated.	to increase COLAs; 6 times to increase other benefits; 23 times to protect the system from cuts. . . .

Denton's name is shown on the bills.	Because of Senator Denton and his colleagues in the Senate, Social Security benefits have increased more than 40 percent in the past five years. . . .
MS of Denton speaking from a desk. Chyron of Mr. Shelby question at left, ending with "?"	Mr. Shelby, when are you going to start telling the truth? Alabama believes in their Senator, Jeremiah Denton."
CU of Denton "Denton For Alabama"	

Obfuscation

An obfuscation ad resembles a refutation response in tone; however, an obfuscation ad does not contain evidence but rather a greal deal of fast footwork and even a bit of sleight-of-hand. Only the most general platitudes are included in the obfuscation response.

In 1984, Democratic candidate Lloyd Doggett attacked Congressman Phil Gramm in the Texas Senate race. The ad attacked Gramm's record on social security and made him appear insensitive to the plight of the elderly. Gramm responded with a classic bit of razzle-dazzle obfuscation. Both ads have been included.

The 1984 Doggett "Social Security" Ad

VIDEO	AUDIO
Congressman Phil Gramm talking; Identification" "Congressman Phil Gramm"	Narrator [VO]: "When Phil Gramm was told that his Social Security cuts would hurt 80-year-olds, Gramm said:
"Phil Gramm said:" (prints quote over a newspaper)	'They're 80 years old. Most people don't have the luxury of living to be 80. So it's hard for me to feel sorry for them.' Nov. 24. 1982
Newspaper gets reduced to a small block on left side of screen. Photo of elderly couple on right.	That's what Phil Gramm actually said. Can Texas take pride in that kind of Senator? On election day cast a vote you can be proud of."

"Vote for Lloyd Doggett
The Texas Democrat"

Phil Gramm quickly responded in a candidate confrontation ad in which
he evokes the image of his mother to fight his case.

The 1984 Gramm "Momma and Social Security" Ad

VIDEO	AUDIO
CU of Gramm at desk with flag in background. "Phil Gramm" Gramm holds up Social Security check.	Gramm [SOT]: "My momma worked 39 years as a practical nurse carrying bed pans to earn this 333 dollars a month from Social Security. And I'm never gonna let anybody take this check away from my momma. If you've earned Social Security, or Federal Retirement, or Railroad Retirement, or you've earned veterans' benefits by serving our country, I'm never gonna let anybody take those away from you either. And you can take that to the bank."
Phil Gramm Photo "Phil Gramm U.S. Senate Common Sense Uncommon Courage"	Narrator [VO]: "Phil Gramm for the U.S. Senate."

Counterimaging

Counterimaging is a subtle reactive response that appears as if it is a positive
spot praising the candidate's work or stand on an issue. However, a counterimaging response ad is carefully laying out for the voter a counterproposi-
tion to the content of the opponent's negative ad. Counterimaging ads usually
are used in combination with other reactive response ads that are more direct,
such as denial, refutation, or counterattack responses.

In the 1956 presidential campaign, the issue of Stevenson's divorce came
up again and again. Stevenson's media people made the conscious decision
to show him within a family context as often as possible. His sons and daughter-
in-law appeared in advertisements with him. And Stevenson's children and sister
frequently traveled with him on campaign trips (see Jamieson, 1984). The cam-

paign knew that it needed to present a counterimage to the image of Stevenson as a failed family man. William Wilson, Stevenson's television producer, explained: "We had to find a family situation for him" (Jamieson, 1984, p. 108). Also in 1956, General Eisenhower who was 66 years old faced what many analysts called the age issue. For this reason, the campaign aired a "This is Your Life" birthday celebration for the president, showing him interacting with family and friends. In the bosom of his family, Eisenhower was the picture of health and happiness.

In 1960, the Kennedy presidential campaign feared that Kennedy's numerous health problems would weaken his chance for the presidency. Kennedy suffered from a debilitating back condition, which was caused by a war wound. He underwent several operations, and sometimes faced life-threatening infections as a result of the surgeries (see Goodwin, 1987). The infections were due to his lowered resistance brought about by Addison's disease. Kennedy and his campaign denied that he had Addison's disease, however it was well known in endocrinological circles (see Jamieson, 1984). Although Kennedy's ad team did not know personally of Kennedy's condition, Robert Kennedy, his brother and campaign manager, ensured that counterimaging spots were made. The ad team designed a series of PT 109 ads that praised both his leadership and endurance during periods of crisis. Kennedy had been a naval war hero, a fact that had been well popularized during his campaigns for the House of Representatives and the U.S. Senate. And as Jamieson (1984) put it, no one could believe that "a man who had survived the destruction of his PT boat, had towed another man in the ocean for five miles, and had survived nine days in the jungle could suffer from a supposedly serious disease" (p. 139).

In 1986, Congressman Richard Shelby attacked Senator Jeremiah Denton's voting record on social security in an Alabama Senate race. The Denton campaign responded with a number of denial, refutation, counterattack, obfuscation, and counterimaging ads. The following ad used an elderly surrogate to paint Denton as a man sensitive to the issues affecting the elderly.

The 1986 Denton "Elderly Man" Spot

VIDEO	AUDIO
LS of an elderly man sitting at a desk writing a letter. There is a slow zoom in on the man. The man is not speaking on the tape. The voice of the man reading the tape is later voiced over.	Elderly Man [VO]: "Dear Senator Denton. You know how I feel about you. How thankful I am for everything you've done. I wouldn't have a roof over my head, if you hadn't helped me. I couldn't have survived without you. When you're ninety years old and alone, you

sometimes wonder if anybody cares.
I know you do. You were the only
one who reached out when nobody
else vould. I'm happy in the
apartment you got for me. The
people here are nice. They treat me
like one of the family. I never
liked asking for help, but you
were there for me when there was no
one else to turn to, and I'll never
forget it."

Elderly Man [SOT]: "Senator

Man shifts, speaks directly   Denton, you know, there's a place in
into camera.   my heart for you!"

Photo of Senator Denton   Narrator [VO]: "Senator Jeremiah
                                     Denton."

In the 1983 Chicago mayoral race, Harold Washington, a Black candidate, was faced with a great deal of opposition from White ethnic populations in the city. The Washington campaign used a counterimaging ad that portrayed people who had been wronged and even killed as our society's heroes. Because Washington was attacked, he by inference became the hero. Those who did the attacking became the bad guys.

The 1983 Washington "Historical Moments" Ad

VIDEO   AUDIO

Stills of various shots.   Sound effects: Camera clicks with
                                     each still.

Scene of Ku Klux Klan Rally   Narrator [VO]: "There are moments
                                     in our history in which all
President Kennedy in   Americans are thoroughly and
motorcade in Dallas.   profoundly ashamed.

Presidential Car after
the bullet's are fired.

Presidential Car leaving
to get to hospital.

Scene of police dogs

turned on blacks in
Birmingham, Alabama.

American wounded in
Vietnam.

One of those moments may be
happening now, here, in Chicago.

Martin Luther King speaking
in Memphis on motel balcony.

Same scene after the shooting
of Martin Luther King.
shot.

Scene after the Kent State
Shooting. Girl kneeling in
horror.

In 1968 Democratic
Convention Riots, Chicago

Freeze Frame of Riots
in Color.
And then it rolls.
Scenes of angry white
demonstrators, screaming
insults at Harold Washington
as he marches in a Chicago
Parade.
"Vote for Harold Washington"

When you vote on Tuesday, be sure
it's a vote you can be proud of."

Reactive Response Academic Research

Reactive response research is very limited. Researchers have failed to identify the types of responses tested. It should be expected that different response
messages would have different results. A careful reading of two studies reveals that the responses tested are ones identified by our typology. We adopt
our framework when we discuss their research findings. Garramone (1985)
found in a laboratory experiment that a counterattack spot increased backlash
against the opponent, but the ad failed to improve the perceptions of the attacked candidate. In 1988, Roddy and Garramone tested four response strategies in a laboratory experiment. Both the negative-issue and the negative-image
responses where denial/campaign attacks. The positive-issue and positive-image

responses were counterimaging strategies. Roddy and Garramone found that "although viewers evaluated a negative-response commercial less favorably than a positive response commercial, the negative response was more effective in discouraging voting for the attacking candidate" (p. 415). Thus, denial/campaign attacks were more effective than counterimaging strategies.

IN CONCLUSION

Prior to announcing as a candidate, survey research should be conducted that identifies voters' evaluations of a candidate's strengths and weaknesses. This information should then be compared to the voters' evaluations of various potential opponents and their versions of the ideal candidate. In addition, the campaign should conduct a thorough analysis of the candidate's record, for example, voting record, issue positions, and political affiliations. And a candidate and the candidate's family should carefully examine their personal lives in order to pinpoint any potential vulnerabilities. Through this three-step process, a candidate is able to determine individual vulnerabilities for a given campaign. A proactive campaign will utilize inoculation techniques to neutralize the opposition's negative ads, which are likely to be based on these vulnerabilities. When the opponent's negative ads do appear, the voters have had an opportunity to develop counterarguments to them, and therefore are much less likely to be persuaded by the ads.

Not all political campaigns are sophisticated or well financed enough to engage in this costly and time-consuming soul searching. And, in some situations, it may be impossible for a campaign to identify a particular vulnerability before the actual campaign season. External influences may suddenly make a political issue a hot topic, and overnight, a seemingly insignificant vote cast years ago may become a political nightmare. In other situations, a campaign may simple choose not to pursue an inoculation advertising strategy. Under these circumstances, a campaign must utilize reactive communication tactics in order to maintain a damage control strategy. A number of communication tactics have been used as reactive responses to negative ads: silence, confession/redemption, sanctimonious admission, denial/campaign attack, counterattack, refutation, obfuscation, and counterimaging. In most situations, a campaign will utilize more than one response type.

Although denial ads are most frequently used, they are not the most effective reactive reponse form. Consultants warn that denial does not persuade anyone but loyal supporters. Refutation, on the other hand, is particularly effective in that it presents evidence that has been found to be highly persuasive in low credibility source situations. In addition, evidence works to inhibit future counterpersuasion. Silence is the least effective reactive response, because when a candidate pursues a strategic silence, the candidate has ceased to be an active manager of his or her political persona, and in essence allows others to define that candidacy, the political campaign, and so forth, for their own political purposes.

7

Law and Ethics

Congress shall make no law respecting an establishment of religion, or prohibiting the free exercise thereof; or abridging the freedom of speech, or of the press; or the right of the people peaceably to assemble, and to petition the Government for a redress of grievances.
— Constitution of the United States, Amendment 1

There are legal scholars who believe that the First Amendment to the Constitution is one of the most important tenets of our system of government. Alexander Meiklejohn (1948) suggested that all political ideas should be wielded in a free and open marketplace, no matter how egregious others may consider them to be. Meiklejohn wrote that truth:

is not our deepest need. Far more essential, if men are to be their own rulers, is the demand that whatever truth may become available shall be placed at the disposal of all the citizens of the community. The First Amendment is not, primarily, a device for the winning of new truth, though that is very important. It is a device for the sharing of whatever truth has been won. Its purpose is to give to every voting member of the body politic the fullest possible participation in the understanding of those problems with which the citizens of a self-governing society must deal. (pp. 88–89)

The late U.S. Supreme Court Justice Hugo Black believed that the First Amendment was an absolute: The U.S. government could pass no law that infringed on freedom of expression (see Middleton & Chamberlin, 1988, p. 58). Although

251

not all U.S. Supreme Court justices have shared Black's perspective, the First Amendment remains a closely guarded tenet of the American way of life.

THE TRADITIONAL PRESS AND THE BROADCASTING MEDIA

Middleton and Chamberlin (1988) noted that: "The press is the only business specifically protected by the First Amendment; indeed, it is the only business singled out for special protection in the Constitution" (p. 38). The courts have interpreted "the press" to mean other print publications such as books, magazines, and pamphlets. And it has come to mean the electronic media as well. They go on to say, however, that "the degree of constitutional protection varies with the medium" (p. 38). The print media, they explained, has "no legal obligation to be fair or evenhanded to political candidates. Publishers can ignore some or all of the candidates in an election. . . . Futhermore, they do not have to publish a paid advertisement if they do not want to" (p. 38).

Although broadcasters have First Amendment rights, they do not have the breadth of freedom of newspaper publishers. In the Radio Act of 1927, the public airwaves were considered to be a public resource which would be licensed to specific operators because there were not enough frequencies available for everyone who desired one (see Middleton & Chamberlin, 1988, p. 525). The Act created the Federal Radio Commission (FRC), which required that in order to obtain a license, broadcasters must agree to operate in the "public's interest, convenience, and necessity" (Radio Act of 1927, pp. 1162–1165, 1168). This tripartite standard serves as the fundamental means by which broadcasters' actions may be measured.

The standards of public interest, convenience, and necessity have also served as a bootstrap by which the FRC and later the Federal Communications Commission (FCC) were able to promulgate rules that might be deemed unconstitutional for the print medium. In *Red Lion Broadcasting Co. v. FCC* (1969), the U.S Supreme Court decided that broadcasters must provide the opportunity of a reply for persons who have been attacked during a discussion of a controversial issue. Yet in *Miami Herald Publishing Co. v. Tornillo* (1974), the Supreme Court said that a "government-enforced right of reply for the print media violated the First Amendment" (Middleton & Chamberlin, 1988, p. 529). Chief Justice Warren Burger said such a requirement would violate the basic premise that a newspaper can choose to publish or not to publish and that the government can not interfere with that freedom of expression.

Although the First Amendment right to free speech is fundamental in the broadcasting of political campaigns, the guarantees of a free press are not extended with the same latitude to broadcasting. Congress, the FCC, and the courts have taken the view that broadcasters are using a limited resource, and therefore, broadcasters can be regulated to serve in the public interest.

POLITICAL ADVERTISING AND THE FIRST AMENDMENT GUARANTEE OF FREE SPEECH

Broadcast political advertising has been recognized as an important element of a free society from the earliest days of radio. Section 18 of the Federal Radio Act of 1927 forbade censorship of political broadcasts. This component became Section 315 of the Communications Act of 1934 (Section 315).

Access and Equal Opportunities

Section 315 does not require that stations provide time for political candidates. But Section 312(a)(7) requires that broadcasters provide reasonable access for *federal candidates* 45 days before a primary election and 60 days before a general election. Although stations are not obligated to sell a candidate a specific time, they are required to provide time during prime time and key viewing hours (see Middleton & Chamberlin, 1988). Middleton and Chamberlin elaborated: "Although Section 312(a)(7) only applies to federal candidates, the FCC has ruled that the public interest standard requires broadcasters to devote substantial time to state and local political campaigns. However, there is no requirement that broadcast licensees provide access to every candidate" (p. 555; see Law of Political Broadcasting, 1978 (pp. 2221-2222).

Section 315 requires that broadcasters provide equal opportunities for all candidates in the same political race. If a station airs an advertisement from one political candidate, then other candidates for the same office must be given equal opportunities to purchase time. Equal opportunities has sometimes been called equal time but the requirements for equal opportunities go beyond just equal time. – "It means the right to obtain time in a period likely to attract approximately the same audience as the period in which the opposing candidate appeared" (Law of Political Broadcasting, 1978, p. 2216) for the same amount of money, that is, at the same rate. Section 315 forbids "any discrimination between candidates in rates or in any other way" (Law of Political Broadcasting, 1978, p. 2219).

The equal opportunities provisions apply only to *uses* of the broadcast stations. A *use* is any broadcast that contains the candidate's voice or picture. A use may occur even if the candidate is not talking about his of her candidacy. Showing a motion picture with Ronald Reagan performing during his election campaigns would be considered a use by the FCC. And the station would be required to provide equal opportunities to other candidates running for the same office. If a supporter of a candidate appears in the ad but the voice or picture of the candidate is not aired, then it is not considered a use. Newcasts and other news programming are not considered to be a use, and therefore, they are exempt from the equal opportunities provision.

Legally Qualified Candidate

In order to be provided equal opportunities, candidates must be legally qualified candidates. Legally qualified candidates are those individuals who meet the legal qualifications for office and who have publicly announced their candidacies. In addition, the candidate must either have qualified for a place on the ballot or have mounted a visible write-in campaign (see Law of Political Broadcasting, 1978, p. 2217).

Equal opportunities are not automatic. A candidate must request " 'equal opportunities' within seven days of his opponent's use of a station, and the station need not notify a candidate of his opponent's broadcast (Law of Political Broadcasting, 1978, pp. 2219–2220); however, that information can be obtained by examining the station's political file which is required to be open for public inspection. It is the responsibility of the candidate's campaign to monitor the political files of broadcast stations in their area.

No Censorship

Section 315 forbids broadcast stations from censoring any political messages broadcast by legally qualified candidates. This applies only to political programs or announcements (political advertising spots) that are aired because the candidate has purchased time from the station for their dissemination. And again for the no-censorship rule to apply, the program or announcement must be considered a use. In other words, "if a candidate makes any appearance in which he is identified or identifiable by voice or picture, even if it is only to identify sponsorship of the spot, the whole announcement will be considerend a use" (Law of Political Broadcasting Primer, 1984, p. 20), and the spot cannot be censored.

As the Law of Political Broadcasting and Cablecasting (1978) stated, the broadcast station:

> Cannot refuse to carry his broadcast even if it contains libelous material or is vulgar or in "bad taste." It cannot require the canidate to appear either live or on tape, or even ask to preview his script or pre-audition his tape or film, except to learn (1) whether it contains the required sponsorhip identification (if it is

paid for); (2) whether it is the agreed-upon length for the period reserved for it, or (3) whether the candidate himself will appear on the program so that it becomes a "use" and is subject to equal opportunities, the political time rate, etc. (p. 2220)

Libel and Political Advertising

The Supreme Court has said that because broadcast stations are not allowed to censor political advertising, stations are given absolute protection from libel suits as the result of the dissemination of those messages (*Farmers Educational and Cooperative Union v. WDAY, Inc.*, 1959). However, if the political advertising is sponsored by someone other than a legally qualified candidate and therefore is not a use, then "the non-censorship provision does not apply and the station is not protected against libel suits by the Supreme Court decision" (Law of Political Broadcasting, 1978, p. 2220). A station can refuse to air nonuse announcements or programs that they believe contain libelous or false statements (Law of Political Broadcasting, 1978, p. 2220). Consequently, broadcast stations in recent years have refused to air ads from political action committees that the stations have considered libelous of false.

Although broadcasters have absolute protection from possible libel suits as the result of the airing of political messages from legally qualified candidates, sponsors of political advertising may be held accountable for their political messages. They may be sued under existing libel laws or prosecuted under existing obscenity laws.

However, political candidates for public office are considered public officials by the courts, which makes winning a libel suit by a candidate very difficult. The courts have held that public officials (and later public figures — those who are "intimately involved in the resolution of important public questions or, by reason of their fame, shape events in areas of concern to society at large; see *Gertz v. Robert Welch, Inc.*, 1974) invite attention and comment upon their public lives, and for this reason, the court has made it more difficult for a public official (or public figure) to prove libel.

Political Expression. The courts have encouraged political expression as part of our First Amendment rights. The courts have found the following: (a) "There is a national commitment to principle that debate on public issues should be uninhibited, robust, and wide-open, and that it may well include vehement, caustic and sometimes unpleasantly sharp attacks on government and public officials"; (b) "The constitutional protections for speech and press do not turn upon the truth, popularity, or social utility of the ideas and beliefs which are offered. . . ."; and (c) "The constitutional protections for speech and press require a federal rule that prohibits a public official from recovering damages for a defamatory falsehood relating to his official conduct unless he proves that the statement was made with 'actual malice' that is, with knowledge that it was false or with reckless disregard of whether it was false or not" (Constitution of the United States, Amendments, 1, 14).

In *New York Times Co. v. Sullivan* (1964), the Supreme Court ruled that the constitutional guarantees of freedom of speech and of the press apply to political advertisements. The Court reiterated its ruling in the *Cantwell v. Connecticut* (1964) decision:

> In the realm of religious faith, and in that of political belief, sharp difference arise. In both fields the tenets of one man may seem the rankest error to his neighbor. To persuade others to his own point of view, the pleader, as we know, at times, resorts to exaggeration, to vilification of men who have been, or are, prominent in church or state, and even to false statement. But people of this nation have ordained in the light of history, that, in spite of the probability of excesses and abuses, these liberties are, in the long view, essential to enlightened opinion and right conduct on the part of the citizens of a democracy.

And in *New York Times Co.*, Supreme Court reaffirmed that in order for public officials to recover damages for libelous statements made about their official conduct, they must prove actual malice. Justice Brennan quoted an opinion written by Justice Burch of the Supreme Court of Kansas:

> [I]t is of the utmost consequence that the people should discuss the character and qualifications of candidates for their suffrages. The importance to the state and to society of such discussions is so vast and the advantages derived are so great that they more than counterbalance the inconvenience of private persons whose conduct may be involved, and occasional injury to the reputations of individuals must yield to the public welfare, although at times such injury may be great. The public benefit from publicity is so great and the chance of injury is to private character so small that such discussion must be privileged. *(New York Times Co. v. Sullivan, 1964)*

However, it must be noted that, whereas the *New York Times Co.* (1964) actual malice requirements only apply to defamatory comments concerning a public official's "official conduct," the Court "has interpreted official conduct broadly" (Middleton & Chamberlin, 1988, p. 107). In *Garrison v. Louisiana* (1964), the district attorney of Orleans Parish, Louisiana held a press conference in which he made disparaging comments about the Criminal District Court judges of Orleans Parish. The district attorney attributed "a large backlog of pending criminal cases to the inefficiency, laziness, and excessive vacations of the judges . . . *(Garrison v. Louisiana*, 1964) Although the lower courts have viewed these comments as pertaining to the judges' personal lives, the Supreme Court disagreed. Justice Brennan wrote that: "Anything which might touch on an official's fitness for office is relevent. Few personal attributes are more germane to fitness for office than dishonesty, malfeasance, or improper motivation, even though these characteristics may also affect the official's private character" (*Garrison v. Louisiana*, 1964).

Judicial decisions suggest that it is difficult for candidates to win libel suits against their opponents. Proving malice or reckless disregard is very difficult, and the courts, as we have seen, lean toward allowing a wide range of opinions in political settings.

Broadcast Rates

It is important to note that neither broadcasters nor print publishers are allowed to give a candidate free advertising, because it would serve as an illegal contribution (see Middleton & Chamberlin, 1988). Section 315 also controls the amount of money a station may charge a candidate during certain periods of time. As Middleton and Chamberlin explained, "The equal-opportunities provision requires that 45 days before a primary election and 60 days before a general election, broadcasters charge political candidates no more than the station's lowest advertising rates" (p. 551; see also, Section 315, 1982). The lowest unit rate for a particular length of spot and broadcast time is determined by discovering the lowest unit rate possible for a given length of spot and broadcast time for a commercial advertiser. For example, a radio station normally charges commercial advertisers $100 per 30-second spot, but if an advertiser agrees to buy a package of 10 30-second spots, then the station will reduce the cost-per-spot to $75 per spot. Thus, the lowest unit rate possible is the $75 charge. A legally qualified political candidate can then purchase the 30-second spot for $75, the lowest unit rate.

Outside of the 45- and 60-day windows, the FCC has ruled that stations may charge legally qualified candidates no higher than the station's standard commercial spots. In the aforementioned example, the radio station could charge the candidate $100 for a 30-second spot.

The lowest unit rate applies only to air time. Production time costs, the costs of creating the spot, are not regulated. It also applies only to legally qualified candidates in an election campaign. If candidates are selected by caucus or convention, the lowest unit charge does not apply except where the public participates in delegate selection (see Law of Political Broadcasting Primer, 1984).

The spots must be uses in order for the lowest unit charge to apply. And, candidates must appear either visually or orally to qualify. Spots from political action committees do not qualify. The spots also must pertain to the campaign. A candidate cannot purchase spots at the lowest unit rate to advertise a dry-cleaning business, even if the candidate did appear in the spots.

POLITICAL ADVERTISING AND
CAMPAIGN FALSITY LAWS

As of 1986, 17 states had adopted campaign falsity laws or "mud-slinging laws" (see Ryder, 1986, p. 72; Winsbro, 1987, p. 875). The states of Alaska, Colorado, Indiana, Massachusetts, Minnesota, Mississippi, Montana, Nebraska, North Carolina, North Dakota, Ohio, Oregon, Illinois, Utah, Washington, West Virginia, and Wisconsin have campaign falsity statutes. These statutes – "usually enacted as part of a state's corrupt practices act – forbid the making, publishing or circulating of false statements about a candidate for public office" (Ryder, 1986, p. 73). And some states, such as Massachusetts, Minnesota, Mississippi, and Oregon, make it also illegal for candidates to make misrepresentations about themselves (Winsbro, 1987). According to Winsbro, most of the states provide "for criminal sanctions, such as a fine or imprisonment" (pp. 875-876) for violating these campaign falsity laws, and some states even require that convicted candidates be removed from public office. Montana, North Carolina, North Dakota, Oregon, Utah, and Wisconsin allow for the removal of a convicted candidate from public office. In 1968 in *Cook v. Corbett,* the Oregon Supreme Court set aside Corbett's nomination, because the Court judged that the candidate had made misleading statements about herself during the campaign. Cook was declared the nominee because he had finished the race in the number two spot (see Winsbro, 1987; see also, *Cook v. Corbett,* 1968). Since 1900, however, there have been only two such instances where the state courts have set aside the results of an election because of violations of campaign falsity laws (Winsbro, 1987).

Although on the surface these campaign falsity acts may appear unconstitutional, state courts have applied the *New York Times* (1964) actual malice standard, thus avoiding a constitutional challenge (See Ryder, 1986). As we noted previously, the actual malice standard is a very difficult charge to prove, and therefore, few cases have been prosecuted under these statutes and fewer defendants have been convicted. A New York statute was held to be unconstitutional by a federal district court in New York in 1975. And the state of Michigan repealed such a statute in 1975.

Negative Political Advertising

It has been noted more than once that there are more regulations concerning the marketing of soap or cornflakes than there are concerning the marketing of political candidates. This observation is correct: "Because advertising is verifiable, the Court said there is less reason to tolerate false and misleading statements in commercial ads than in political debate where government attempts to prohibit falsehoods may stifle Democratic decision making" (Middleton & Chamberlin, 1988, p. 320; see also, *Virginia State Board of Pharmacy v. Virginia Citizens Consumer Council,* 1976). In addition, as we pointed out at the beginning of this chapter, one person's belief is another person's heresy.

Negative political advertising has played a large part in American political culture throughout our history. And although the political advertiser enjoys more leeway than the commercial product advertiser and even though the practice of negative political advertising has been pejoratively described as mudslinging by the news media, for the most part negative political advertising in the United States has failed to qualify as the sewage politics that Archibald (1971) described.

Sewage or dirty politics are deliberate misrepresentations, half-truths, lies, or innuendoes that smear a candidate's political record or personal qualifications for office. For the most part, negative political advertising is used to compare political records or professional qualifications either directly or indirectly. In some situations, a candidate will choose to directly attack his or her opponent's record or qualifications. Only a small percentage of negative ads fit the category of dirty politics.

This is true for a number of reasons. First and foremost is the central role of the news media and its position as the self-appointed arbiter of the political system (see Diamond & Bates, 1988; Hagstrom & Guskind, 1986). Political consultant Bradley S. O'Leary explained that: "The press regulates political broadcasts every day. If we say anything that's untrue, it's on the evening news the next day. And don't forget our candidates are also punished by the voters if we say or do something wrong" (Tucker & Heller, 1987, p. 46). Similarly, Democratic media consultant David Sawyer maintained that: "The marketplace works. You try to put an unsubstantiated ad on TV and in 48 hours the press will be all over your case" (Taylor, 1986, p. A7).

The National Association of Broadcasters have encouraged station managers to refuse to carry dirty political ads that were brought to them by some of the worst dirty politics offenders, independent political action committees (see Tucker & Heller, 1987). As we mentioned earlier, political action committees are not legally qualified candidates and therefore do not fall under the provision of Section 315. This means that the broadcast station can be held liable for any defamatory or obscene materials contained within the advertisement.

Second, a dirty political ad may give the attacked candidate an opportunity to counterattack the character and integrity of the attacking candidate. Dirty political ads leave the sponsor, whether it is a PAC or a candidate, vulnerable to counterattack (see Heller, 1987, p. 79; see chapter 6). No one likes a liar.

Three Black Eyes on Political Campaign Practices: Rare But There

Dirty Tricks

But, there are some bad apples. As we mentioned before, sewage politics or dirty politics are deliberate misrepresentations, half-truths, lies, or innuendoes that smear a candidate's political record or personal qualifications (which includes personal life) for office. Because of the potential for news media discovery and exposure, dirty tricks usually are used the last days of the campaign when the likelihood of such discovery and exposure is much less because of the time constraints (see Jamieson & Campbell, 1983). Democratic consultant Bob Squier explained: "A lot of these dirty tricks are timed for the very last minute, and the Sunday before Election Day is a black Sabbath. But usually you don't find out dirty tricks until the election is over" (Walsh & Emerson, 1986, p. 26). Dirty tricks can wreak havoc on a campaign strategy. Jamieson & Campbell explained:

> If a lie is carefully worded, the burden of establishing its falsity can divert the time and attention of the attacked candidate's top-level campaign strategists who, in the final days of a campaign, ought to be concentrating on getting out the vote. In such circumstances, a well-financed campaign with a skilled media consultant has at least the chance of placing responsive or counteractive ads on the air. A poorly financed campaign must rely on the investigative tendencies of reporters and the sympathies of columnists. (p. 246)

According to Jamieson (1984), sewage politics attacks are much more likely to appear in print publications such as newspapers, special interest magazines, and pamphlets. Rarely are dirty attacks aired on "widely viewed television channels" (p. xxiii; see also, Archibald, 1971).

Many of these so-called dirty tricks have been associated with independent political action committees such as the Christian Voice Moral Government Fund, the National Conservative Political Action Committee, and other organizations.

The Christian Voice. The Christian Voice was founded in 1979. The committee has worked to promote conservative causes and has paid for positive advertising spots for candidates such as Ronald Reagan (Political Advertising's Hitmen, 1980). In 1980, it aired spots in the southern swing states that charged incumbent Jimmy Carter with "advocating acceptance of homosexuality" (Jamieson, 1984, p. 426). Gerald Rafshoon, the Carter campaign's adman, told Kathleen Jamieson (1984) that:

> They were making people think that Jimmy Carter was not a good Christian. . . . I'm from Atlanta and I'd go down South and I would hear about these spots

run during Church time on Sunday talking about Carter meeting in the White House with homosexuals, Carter being anti-Christ. Rosalynn Carter came down and said she had this bizarre thing happen. A bunch of Church women coming up and saying "Jimmy's anti-Christ." (p. 426)

In another interview, Rafshoon told Devlin (1981) that what really hurt the Carter campaign the most were: "target spots in Mississippi and other places in the South questioning Carter's belief—hitting him as a pro-homosexual. There was some pretty vicious stuff run by the independent committees. That is the real media story of 1980. On balance they may have hurt us more than the Republican stuff" (p. 12).

But perhaps what the Christian Voice is most famous for is its Biblical Scorecard. Started in 1980, the Biblical Scorecard is a rating list of the voting records of congressmen and senators. By 1986, the organization had expanded its scope of operations by reviewing lower level races such as governor and lieutenant governor. The rating lists are published in both the *Candidates Biblical Scoreboard* magazine and in flyers entitled "Scoreboard on Traditional Values." According to *Marketing & Media Decisions,* the 1980:

> ratings . . . compare legislators' records to Christian Voice positions on issues such as support for prayer in public schools; security for Taiwan; opposition to abortion; race, sex quotas and sex education in schools; and the creation of a federal department of education. . . . the ratings . . . [are then] mailed to ministers in the legislators' home districts, with requests that clergy endorse opposition candidates. (Political Advertising's Hitmen, 1980, p. 182)

In essence, the Biblical Scorecard was the Christian Voice's way of identifying those congressmen and senators whom they wanted to be "forcibly retired" (see Political Advertising's Hitmen, 1980, p. 182).

The organization also distributed the scorecards on foot. On Sundays, volunteers would place the Biblical Scorecards on the windshields of automobiles in targeted churches' parking lots. The scorecards were distributed primarily at churches identified with the evangelical movement. This created a real problem for many congressmen and senators who were ill-prepared to respond to an organization that bore the label "Christian" and was reaching voters through church parking lots.

The tactic of publishing scorecards is not a new idea. The AFL-CIO ranks candidates and publishes their scores in their own magazine. But what is different about the Biblical Scorecard is the manner in which the Christian Voice goes about developing its ranking system. In a 1986 news broadcast, one Alabama commentator had this to say: "The Christian Voice is involved in the deliberate misrepresentation of candidates' records. No matter what your politics may be, all reasoned people must lament this public misinformation campaign."

In Alabama, the news media covered the story concerning the distribution of these scorecards. Judge Claude Harris was running for an open seat in the

U.S. House of Representatives. Operatives from the Christian Voice called the Harris campaign to poll the candidate concerning his stand on identified Christian Voice issues. Campaign manager Walter Braswell refused to answer the poll over the phone and told the caller to send him a copy of the poll, and he would see to it that Harris answered it. The organization failed to do so. Several weeks later when Harris went to his car after church services, he found a scorecard that listed him as either opposing or undecided on sensitive Christian Voice issues such as: voluntary school prayer, strong national defense, and legislation to "curtail" AIDS. Harris had never publicly addressed these issues nor had he talked with any Christian Voice spokesperson; yet he was now labeled as being "anti-traditional values." The Harris campaign immediately contacted church leaders in the community and the news media. They took an aggressive stance in order to get their word out concerning this controversy (personal communication with Walter Braswell, campaign manager, November 2, 1986).

Similarly, Alabama Democratic Senate challenger Richard Shelby was evaluated on his congressional voting record, and the scorecard listed him as opposing a balanced-budget amendment and supporting funding for the legalization of homosexuality. Shelby had cosponsored the balanced-budget amendment several times during his time in the U.S. House of Representatives, and the Shelby campaign could not identify any vote that remotely could be construed as providing funding for legalizing homosexuality. Indeed, no such bill had appeared before Congress (personal communication with Michael Cartee, campaign manager, November 2, 1986).

The Christian Voice organization had misrepresented Democratic candidates' beliefs or voting records and had labeled them as being against traditional values. Although the Christian Voice operates throughout the United States, it has its strongest supporters from the so-called Bible Belt in the South. Ironically, many of the targeted congressional southern Democrats had a more conservative voting record than many of their Republican colleagues in the House and Senate. Although it was perhaps most glaring in the South, the dirty politics of the Biblical Scorecard were apparent throughgout the nation.

National Conservative Political Action Committee. As we discussed in chapter 5, NCPAC has been recognized by both researchers and the news media for using gross inaccuracies in their negative ads (see Bannon, 1982, 1983; Smith, 1983). According to Bannon (1982), "NCPAC allowed Republican candidates the luxury of taking the 'high road.' There was no need for mud-slinging against their Democratic opponents—NCPAC did it for them" (p. 44). NCPAC director Terry Dolan told the *Washington Post:* "A group like ours could lie through its teeth and the candidate it helps stay [sic] clean (McPherson, 1980, p. F1). Dolan said that: I'm convinced that you can say almost anything. . . . you could, in fact, lie" (NCPAC's Negative Campaign, 1979).

Bannon (1982) reported that NCPAC accused Senators Dennis DeConcini of Arizona and John Melcher of Montana of voting proabortion. But both men had anit-abortion records in the U.S Senate. Similarly, NCPAC accused Melcher and North Dakota Senator Quentin Burdick of "giving away the Panama Canal" (Bannon, 1982, p. 46). Yet both men had opposed the Panama Canal Treaty. Kitchens and Powell (1986) reported that NCPAC attacked Senator Birch Bayh for voting to cut the 1979 defense budget. But Bayh had been absent from the Senate floor and had not voted.

Independent political action committees are not the only dirty politics culprits; sometimes candidates get in on the act too. In the 1976 presidential race, Lyndon LaRouche ran an ad in which he said: "It is no exaggeration to say that if Jimmy Carter were to be elected on November 2nd this nation would be committed to thermonuclear war probably no later than the summer of 1977" (Joslyn, 1986, p. 175). And in 1988, LaRouche paid CBS $250,000 to air a 30-minute program concerning the upcoming presidential election. During the program, he claimed that the AIDS virus is spread like other viruses, suggesting that the government was not telling the American people the "truth" (Jamieson, 1984, p. xxii).

In a 1986 Wisconsin senate race, "incumbent Republican Robert W. Kasten, Jr. . . . charged his Democratic challenger Edward R. Garvey, allowed $750,000 of union money to 'disappear' while Garvey headed the National Football League Players Association" (Heller, 1987, p. 79). Garvey filed a libel suit against Senator Kasten and Roger Ailes, the Kasten campaign media consultant. The parties settled out of court 8 months later. In the written settlement, Kasten acknowledged:

> The union's records on public file report for the time in question that the union funds were fully accounted for. . . . I do not suggest that Mr. Garvey engaged in anything illegal or that the union funds were spent for other than valid union purposes. There was no intent to challenge his integrity. (as quoted in Heller, 1987, p. 79)

Political Espionage or Sabotage

The stories of political espionage and sabotage in America make for important campaign legends. Although political espionage is typically associated with dirty politics in the news media, the focus here should be the unscrupulous means by which candidates and their associates obtain and distribute damaging information about their opponents.

In 1972, famed Republican campaign saboteur Donald Segretti hired a plane to fly over the Democratic party convention hall trailing a banner that read: "Peace, Pot, Promiscuity, Vote McGovern" (Agranoff, 1976b, p. 369). During the same election, Democratic prankster Dick Tuck played a number of embarrassing tricks, "such as putting on an engineer's cap and signaling a train to depart while Nixon spoke from the rear platform or getting a number of obviously pregnant women to carry signs with Nixon's campaign theme, 'Nixon's the One' " (Agranoff, 1976b, p. 370).

In 1986, *U.S. News & World Report* reported that "Electronic snooping, anonymous smear campaigns and private eyes hunting for skeletons in every closet – the stuff of Watergate legend is emerging again. . . ." (Walsh & Emerson, 1986, p. 26). The magazine further reported: "In North Dakota, packets of potentially damaging material were mailed anonymously to newspapers about Democratic Representative Byron Dorgan. Included was information about Dorgan's two divorces and his third wife's lobbying activities in Washington" (Walsh & Emerson, 1986, p. 26). And finally, "In New York, Democratic congressional challenger Michael Sullivan paid $18,000 to four female private investigators who secretly taped 14 hours of conversations with Republican Representative Raymond McGrath in a Capitol Hill bar a block from McGrath's office. . . . Their goal: Dredge up damaging details about McGrath's private life" (Walsh & Emerson, 1986, p. 26).

Bad Taste

Some ads are simply in bad taste. Ads that are in poor taste anger the viewer, although the anger is directed not toward the desired target but rather the sponsor. One consultant said that bad taste ads leave the audience with a sense of revulsion. Democratic pollster Mark Mellman suggested that bad taste spots are like bad situation comedies; "they don't last very long" (Hagstrom & Guskind, 1986, p. 2621).

In chapter 1, we demonstrated that many Americans believe attacks against a candidate's personal life are perceived as being in poor taste. In addition, some analysts suggest that not all attacks on a candidate's record are accepted by the voter. In the 1986 Missouri Senate race, Democratic candidate Harriet F. Woods aired a "Crying Farmer" spot against her opponent, former governor Christopher S. (Kit) Bond. The spot, which was produced by Democratic consultant Robert Squier, showed a farmer sobbing "as he recounted losing his family farm and an announcer linked Bond to the company that foreclosed on the farm" (Hagstrom & Guskind, 1986, p. 2624). The ad read, " 'Almost as sad as a family leaving its farm,' says the announcer in Bond's response, over a split-screen image of Bond and the sobbing farmer, 'is a politician using their pain for political advantage' " (Hagstrom & Guskind, 1986, p. 2624). According to Hagstrom and Guskind, the news media heavily criticized the original spot, calling it "sleazy and shallow" and in "poor taste" (p. 2624). Woods was reported to have dismissed Squier, a leading Democratic consultant, over the controversy.

Diamond and Bates (1988) suggested that in a 1982 Tennessee Senate race,

Republican Robin Beard stepped over the line when attacking U.S. Senator James Sasser. They called the ad a distortion and asserted that it backfired, ultimately leading to the defeat of Beard.

The 1982 Beard "Castro" Ad

VIDEO	AUDIO
Camera up to show wooden crate labeled "U.S Aid," with hands holding crowbars prying lid open. Hands grapple for stacks of dollars.	Announcer [VO]: "When it comes to spending taxpayers' money, Senator James Sasser is a master. Take foreign aid. While important programs are being cut back here at home, Sasser has voted to allow foreign aid to be sent to committed enemies of our country – Vietnam, Laos, Cambodia, Marxist Angola, and even Communist Cuba. You can bet James Sasser is making a lot more friends abroad than he is here in Tennessee."
Cut to actor dressed as Fidel Castro. Hold up a dollar bill aflame, lights this cigar.	"Castro" [SOF]: "Muchissimas gracias, Senor Sasser." (Diamond & Bates, 1988, pp. 332–333)

POLITICAL ADVERTISING REFORM MOVEMENTS

Fair Campaign Practices Committee

In 1954, a small group of citizens joined to form the Fair Campaign Practices Committee (FCPC). The FCPC's mission was to condemn "the use of campaign material of any sort which represents, distorts, or otherwise falsifies the facts regarding any candidate" (Tucker & Heller, 1987, p. 45). Clearly, the FCPC's focus was on dirty politics. According to Tucker and Heller, the FCPC:

> initially accomplished a great deal. The group acted as a clearinghouse of complaints, an investigator of wrongdoing, and an arbiter of fairness. It followed up alleged deviations from the code with an in-house investigation, discussions, and recommendations.

If it unearthed false or misleading information in an advertisement, the committee would ask the offending campaign to revise or retract the spot. Should
the campaign refuse, the committee would threaten to expose the offending campaign in the media. (p. 45)

The FCPC lasted 20 years, but their lack of steady funding brought the
group to an end. While in operation, the FCPC averaged 65 to 67 complaints
each year (Archibald, 1971; Tucker & Heller, 1987). The FCPC recorded
the number and types of complaints for each year; Archibald reported that
for the three election cycles studied (1966, 1968, 1970), the following was
the breakdown of the 201 complaints:

Falsify, misinterpret, distort	50%
Unethical practice	18%
Personal vilification	13%
Guilt by association	9%
Race	6%
Religion	3%
	100%

Roughly 44% of the complaints were made during the last 2 weeks prior to
election day, which is the traditional time period for heavy political advertising (Archibald, 1971) and dirty tricks (Walsh & Emerson, 1986). The FCPC
deemed 65% of the complaints to be valid (Archibald, 1971).

Some have suggested a replacement for the FCPC. Spero (1980) called for
the formation of a political fact bank that would monitor all political campaign
communication. The political fact bank would judge all political campaign communications by a code of political campaign ethics and citizen action, which
would be modeled after the standards used to measure false and deceptive
product advertising. It would identify violations of the code and would then
produce and air counteradvertising that would expose the untruths to the voters.

American Association of Political Consultants

In 1969, the American Association of Political Consultants (AAPC) was founded. Today the organization has 727 members (personal communication with
Ralph Murphine, AAPC, December 18, 1989). In September 1975, the AAPC
adopted a code of ethics. Sabato (1981) provided an excellent discussion of
the AAPC and the ethics code. According to Sabato, many of the clauses of
the code were taken from the "Code of Fair Campaign Practices (drawn up
by the Fair Campaign Practices Commission) and the 'Code of Ethics for Political Campaign Advertising' of the American Association for Advertising
Agencies" (p. 304).

Although the original code of ethics makes a provision in Clause 16 for an investigating mechanism embodied with punitive powers at this writing, the AAPC has never heard a complaint against a member. According to ethics committee chairman Ralph Murphine, the AAPC has never had a complaint brought against a member for advertising content infractions (personal communication, December 18, 1989).

Sabato (1981) criticized the AAPC's and the organization itself for not taking a stronger stand on ethical issues: "The professionals must only *urge*, not require, their clients to sign a Fair Campaign Practices Code (clause 6), and consultants boldly promise never to lie *intentionally* about their clients or the opposition (clause 10)" (p. 305). Sabato suggested that the organization should serve as a monitoring device similar to the now defunct Fair Campaign Practice Commission, in that the AAPC could bring to bear negative publicity against political consultants and their candidates because of code infractions.

Today, new AAPC applicants are required to sign an 8-point Code of Professional Ethics. Clearly, it is quite different from the one Sabato (1981) described. The new 8-point Code of Professional Ethics is considerably weaker than the one Sabato reviewed. After discussions with AAPC officials, including the ethics committee chairman Ralph Murphine, we conluded that current AAPC officials are not aware of an earlier 16-item version of the code (personal communications, December 18, 1989; May 11, 1990). The 8-point code is included for the reader's evaluation (see Fig. 7.1).

CONGRESSIONAL LEGISLATION

In 1985, Senators John Danforth (R-MO) and Ernest Hollings (D-SC) introduced the Clean Campaign Act of 1985 (CCA). The bill required that sponsoring candidates appear in all ads directly or indirectly attacking the opposition, that the radio or television station that aired the negative ad then provide free response time to the attacked candidate under equal opportunity conditions. In addition, the bill required any station that runs a spot either endorsing or attacking a candidate, from either a person or a political action committee, be made to give free response time to other legally qualified candidates in the race (Clean Campaign Act, 1985).

Democratic consultant Bob Squier called the CCA "the Incumbents' Preservation Act" (as quoted in Tucker & Heller, 1987, p. 43). Similarly, Ryder (1986) wrote that: "Anxious incumbents are simply trying to secure their political fiefdoms" (p. 73).

Tucker and Heller (1987) suggested that the bill has a number of negative unintended consequences:

1. It would work to promote incumbency, because challengers most often use negative advertising to attack an incumbent's record.
2. It would work to limit public information in that negative advertising often works to stimulate a "legitimate debate" (p. 43).
3. It would "enshrine broadcasters as the arbiters of fairness in election campaigns" (p. 43).
4. It would be a First Amendment abridgement.

CODE OF PROFESSIONAL ETHICS

As a member of the American Association of Political Consultants, I believe there are certain standards of practice which I must maintain. I, therefore, pledge to adhere to the following Code of Ethics:

— I shall not indulge in any activity which would corrupt or degrade the practice of political campaigning.

— I shall treat my colleagues and my clients with respect and never intentionally injure their professional or personal reputation.

— I shall respect the confidence of my client and not reveal confidential or private information obtained during our professional relationship.

— I will use no appeal to voters which is based on racism or discrimination and will condemn those who use such practices. In turn, I will work for equal voting rights and privileges for all citizens.

— I will refrain from false and misleading attacks on an opponent or member of his family and shall do everything in my power to prevent others from using such tactics.

— I will document accurately and fully any criticism for an opponent or his record.

— I shall be honest in my relationship with the press and candidly answer questions when I have the authority to do so.

— I shall not support any individual or organization which resorts to practices forbidden in this code.

_____   _____
Signature   Date

FIG. 7.1. Code of professional ethics of the AAPC. (Obtained from the American Association of Political Consultants, December, 1989.)

According to Ryder (1986), the CCA: "unquestionably raises some serious constitutional conflicts. Critics argue that it is a violation of the First Amendment guarantee of free speech, that negative campaigning is a time-honored tradition of American politics, and that attacking the incumbent's record is a proper part of the political process" (p. 72). Ailes (1985) wrote that the CCA rests on a dangerous assumption: "that it is somehow wrong for a candidate for public office to attack his opponent" (p. 59). Ailes suggested that the campaign is a natural testing ground for leadership and that the heat of battle provides for the winnowing out of unfit candidates.

However, not all political observers agree with their assessment of the CCA. In the *Journal of Law & Politics*, Clinger (1987) suggested that the CCA is constitutional in that: "1) Congress has always enjoyed broad regulatory authority over broadcasters—authority which would be considered badly unconstitutional if applied to the print media; and 2) the bill would ultimately trigger more, not less, speech by providing a free right of reply and is thus thoroughly consistent with the first amendment" (pp. 729–730). Clinger further suggested that negative political advertising and in particular negative political advertising sponsored by independent political action committees have led to the "increasing intellectual and ethical bankruptcy of modern political debate," that the "very future of democratic self-government may be threatened" in that "a government which acquiesces in the debasement of its electoral process risks the legitimacy of that government itself" (pp. 746–747).

IN CONCLUSION

Political advertising is not as regulated as product advertising, because of our First Amendment freedoms. Our constitution protects free political speech within broad boundaries, even if it is in error or is judged egregious by the general population.

If a station agrees to air political advertisements for one candidate, then other candidates for the same office must be afforded equal opportunity. The courts have found that broadcast stations can not be held responsible for political ads sponsored by legally qualified candidates, but the candidates themselves are legally responsible. Candidates may be sued under existing libel laws. However, this remains very rare because of the difficulties associated with the actual malice standard applied to defamatory statements made against public officials or public figures.

Broadcast stations are not obligated to air independent political advertising; and therefore, they may be held legally responsible for any defamatory material contained within an ad. For this reason, independent ads are strutinized carefully by station managers and attorneys, and frequently, the stations have refused to air defamatory, misleading, or false advertisements.

Negative political advertising in the United States involves the direct or indirect comparison of political records or personal qualifications for office. In some situations, ads involve a direct attack against an opponent. However, it is rare for them to contain misleading, false, or defamatory statements. When they do contain such statements, it is said to be dirty politics. In some situations, candidates have used political espionage to gather information for negative political advertising or to distribute negative political advertising. And occasionally, political consultants will cross the thin line of bad taste, and the public usually reacts negatively.

The now defunct Fair Campaigns Practices Committee used the threat of publicity to inhibit political candidates from using unfair, dirty political tactics in their advertising. It has been suggested that The American Association of Political Consultants take up where the FCPC left off. Currently, a reform movement exists in Congress that wishes to curb the tide of negative political advertising. It remains to be seen whether they are successful.

8

Effects on Society: An Unexplored Area

The controversy surrounding the use of negative political advertising is based on a set of arguments, some explicit and some implicit, that negative political advertising has an effect that is different and more harmful on the body politic than positive political advertising. These arguments may be due to the pejorative tone of the phrase "negative political advertising." Because the term includes the world "negative," there must be something bad about it. If indeed there is something bad about negative political advertising, it must be doing something bad to the individual, political institutions, and to society (QED).

Mudslinging is a popular synonym for negative political advertising. Stewart (1975) has shown that when the populous is asked to define what mudslinging tactics entail, the most popular responses were: "twists, distorts, or misleads in his charges against his opponent; attacks the personal life, or character of his opponent; presents irrelevant facts and charges against his opponent or for his own ideas" (p. 281). The populous clearly has a negative view of mudslinging. As Stewart put it, "They (the people) see mudslinging as a candidate bent on destroying his opponent with every means at his disposal, regardless of ethical considerations or simple honesty" (p. 281).

As we have shown in our research (Johnson-Cartee & Copeland, 1989b; see also, Johnson & Copeland, 1987; Pfau & Burgoon, 1989; Roddy & Garramone, 1988), it is when negative political advertising departs from the issues and becomes personal that negative political ads become the most objectionable. It is these personal areas, such as religion and family, that are identified as areas the vast majority of prospective voters believe fall outside the

271

pale of appropriate political comment. For example, despite the fact that a central issue of Ronald Reagan's two campaigns was a strengthening of traditional family values and his own family relationships were troubled, his personal problems with his children were, rightfully, never made a subject for negative political advertising.

Our research also shows that there are political issue appeals, for example, a candidate's voting record or stand on the issues, that prospective voters view as areas of fair comment in political ads. So, some ads that compare voting records of candidates are labeled negative political advertisements but should not be considered mudslinging.

Traditionally, negative political advertising has been too narrowly defined, both conceptually and operationally (see chapters 1 & 2). Negative political advertising is an umbrella term that encompasses a number of campaign advertising strategies. We might be wise to adopt the advice of one media consultant and stop using the all-inclusive term negative political advertising (Nugent, 1987.)

We also have tried in this book to move away from the typically pejorative discussion of negative political advertising. Our intent was to show both the good and bad sides of negative political advertising. The widespread belief that all negative political advertising is bad is exacerbated by the lack of differentiation between types of negative ads. Spots that truthfully compare either directly or indirectly the political records or leadership qualities of two candidates may be viewed as negative because the ads provide a relational evaluation of the opponent. However, we believe that these direct or indirect comparison ads are an appropriate part of the campaign debate. They provide the electorate with a means to compare candidates' records on the issues, define the scope of the campaign, and help individuals decide which candidate is more worthy of their vote (see chapters 1 & 2). As Nugent (1987) wrote:

> We implicitly concede to negativism each time we reuse the term. "Attack ads" sounds negative as well. Perhaps we could agree on a neutral, generic term, such as "comparative ads," "contrast ads," "hot-button ads," or opponent based ads — ads that are used in specific spots, for a limited purpose, but not intended to characterize an entire campaign. (p. 49)

The effects of negative advertising on people and institutions are not very clear. For instance, there are those who say that negative political advertising has led to voter apathy and antipathy. According to this line of thought, negative political advertising is increasing the number of politically alienated individuals in society. This chapter examines both viewpoints of negative political advertising: those who think it has positive effects and those who think not. At the end, we hope to develop some conclusions about the effects of negative political advertising.

Let us begin by noting the difference between effects and effectiveness. Nothstine and Copeland (1983) have shown that effectiveness is an evaluation concept. In product advertising the effectiveness question would be: Did the advertising produce an increase in the sales of the product advertised? Most communication research in negative political advertising has concerned itself with the effectiveness issue. Researchers have been attempting to discover whether or not negative political advertising increases the votes for a candidate and how to make the spots more effective.

Effects, on the other hand, are general in nature and are concerned more with whether or not some change or result has occurred. For example, an ad that attacked a candidate because of the candidate's religion and caused a furor among the public against the attacker would be an ad that was completely ineffective (it did not induce people to support the candidate), but it still had a strong effect.

This chapter is about the possible effects of negative political advertising, not about its effectiveness. Because researchers have neglected the political and societal effects, some of this discussion is built on informed speculation and the views of those intimately a part of the political system.

NEGATIVE POLITICAL ADVERTISING
AND VOTER TURNOUT

The highest voter activity is usually during presidential election years. Between 50% and 60% of those eligible to vote in the United States will do so during those years (Abramowitz, 1980). Compared to other industrialized democracies, these percentages are among the lowest (Why America Doesn't Vote, 1988). There has been a steady decline in voting by eligible voters since the 1960 presidential election. In 1984, only about 53% of the eligible voters took advantage of their franchise, the lowest turnout since 1948 (Diamond & Bates, 1988). The election of 1988 saw the lowest voter turnouts since Calvin Coolidge's 1924 victory (Goldman & Mathews, 1989).

Voter turnout for congressional, state, and local elections, absent a presidential race, are considerably lower (Nimmo, 1978). The 1986 elections could only muster 37% of the eligible voters to the polls (Why America Doesn't Vote, 1988).

The importance of the decline in voter participation extends beyond a failure of some to disenfranchise themselves. Crotty and Jacobson (1980) suggested that a continued decline in voting coupled with a disillusionment with political institutions (see Alienation below) threatens the stability and representativeness of U.S. governmental institutions.

This steady decline in voting has been attributed by some political observers to the increasing use of negative political advertising. Most of the evidence that is offered in either support or refutation of this issue tends to be of the post hoc ergo propter hoc variety.

The Committee for the Study of the American Electorate reviewed the 1986 campaign and suggested that " 'demagogic and distorted political advertising' was a major reason for a steep drop in voter participation" (Nugent, 1987, p. 47). Clinger (1987) found that the decline of voter participation coinciding with the Buckley v. Valeo decision, which allowed independent campaign expenditure, is more than chance. He also believed that these independently sponsored negative ads have the affect of alienating voters.

Others disagree. Nugent (1987) wrote, "To presume negative ads affected turnout is to give advertising a power it simply does not have" (p. 47). Nugent believed that voter turnout is increased in campaigns with negative ads because the ads increase voter interest in the race. Kern (1989) also argued that negative advertising is not sufficient and necessary to cause a reduction in voter participation. In her study, Kern noted that in states where heavy negative political advertising campaigns had been waged the voter turnouts were heavy. In one particular negative advertising-based campaign in North Carolina, turnout reached a 20-year high.

What seems to be missing in this debate is valid and reliable data on which to base a judgment. For political observers to say that negative political advertising does or does not decrease voter turnouts for elections, because the voting has gone up or down during a similar time frame, is basing a conclusion on weak correlational evidence at best. Without something more substantial, it is too early to lay the blame on U.S. voter apathy at the feet of negative political advertising. As Nugent (1987) said: "There are vastly more compelling reasons for voter decline, and to credit advertising alone is simplistic" (p. 47).

There are any number of factors that may have impacted on the voter participation numbers. Some political consultants believe the decline has been caused by demographic reasons. They predict that as the baby boom generation grows older, their voting will increase. Traditionally, younger people vote with less frequency than older people (Diamond & Bates, 1988). Wolfinger and Rosenstone (1980) showed that voting increases as people get older until it flattens out at age 40 and remains steady until the people reach their 70s.

NEGATIVE POLITICAL ADVERTISING AND NEGATIVE EFFECTS

In this next section, we look at some of the reasons people have argued that negative political advertising is bad for politics and the society. This is not meant to be an exhaustive list, but rather an attempt to highlight some of the major concerns that have been expressed over the use of negative political advertising in election campaigns.

Alienation

The relatively high percentage of eligible voters who do not vote in U.S. elections as compared to the numbers who do has led observers to suggest there is something wrong with the American electoral process. One of the suspected culprits, as we discussed in the previous section, is a sense of political alienation on the part of the citizenry. Many potential voters are not convinced they have any effective power to control their political destinies or that their participation can make any difference.

Alienation is a sense of powerlessness or the "feeling that one has lost personal efficacy and the ability to act influentially and significantly within his social universe" (Abcarian & Stanage, 1965, p. 786). The highest levels of alienation were during the late 1960s to the mid-1970s. During this time period, people questioned the value of their participation because government was seen as being unresponsive to the needs of the average citizen. Brody (1978) concluded that, "abstention [from voting] flows from the belief—held by an increasingly large segment of the electorate—that voting simply isn't worth the effort" (p. 306).

There are suggestions that this alienation may be decreasing, slightly. Abramson, Aldrich, and Rhode (1986) found that faith in government and political trust had increased in the mid-1980s over the previous 10 years. But alienation is still very prominent in the United States, and frequently this alienation is blamed on negative political advertising. Senator John Danforth has been quoted as saying that negative political ads create apathy and cynicism among the voting public" (Diamond & Bates, 1988, p. 385).

Research has shown that this sense of alienation is highest among the less educated and lower SES groups (cf. Almond, 1980; Almond & Verba, 1963; Ippolito, Kolson, & Walker, 1976; Wayne, 1988). Research also has shown that the politically active are generally of a higher socioeconomic status: "Higher socioeconomic status (SES) is positively associated with increased likelihood of participation in many different political acts; higher SES persons are more likely to vote, attend meetings, join a party campaign, and so forth" (Milbraith, 1965, pp. 16-17).

The people most likely to be exposed to television are those people low in SES and education—or those that are most likely to feel alienated. These are the people who would have the greatest exposure to television advertising campaigns. This may be why Clinger (1987) argued that "the evolution of campaigns into extended media events, far from piquing public interest in the process, instead has bred passive and cynical voters" (p. 733). Clinger believed that this process has caused a voting malaise.

Those people low in SES and education are most likely to need stimulation to participate in the election system, but they may be the ones who receive the least motivation. These high TV-viewing, lower educated individuals would be the ones most frequently exposed to a negative political advertising campaign, and according to this criticism, they would be the ones most likely to be alienated because of it.

Also, they would be most inclined to react as Diamond and Bates (1988) speculated: "The result may be a distancing between candidate and citizen; voting may become just one more activity being commended to us by television purveyors of goods and services. We watch the free shows but we don't necessarily get involved; we are passively entertained" (p. 386). Americans lack the will to get politically involved. It is the need to get involved that Curtis Gans, director of the Committee for the Study of the American Electorate, cited as being the key element in encouraging voter participation more than any possible legal or administrative hurdles such as voter registration. "Creating the will to participate is by far the larger enterprise," according to Gans (quoted in Why America Doesn't Vote, 1988, p. 143).

Negativity

Negative political advertising often is thought to promote alienation because it has been viewed as increasing the negativity of the political process. Political advertising in general is not the most highly regarded form of communication, and negative advertising is seen as something a bit worse. This was summed up by one respondent to a national poll, "I dislike political commercials in general, and I object to political mudslinging" (Morgan & Vadehra, 1984).

The negativity that may be engendered by negative political advertising could have significant societal effects. Wamsley and Pride (1972) and Robinson (1976) both warned that an emphasis on the negative aspects of politics and governmental process may denigrate our government. Thus, negative political advertising may be increasing our lack of trust in our political system and political leaders. Crotty and Jacobson (1980) suggested that such an alienated society is a prime breeding ground for demagoguery.

Demagoguery

Negative political advertising, as does all political advertising, often takes complex issues and reduces them to emotion-laden snippets wrapped in stirring music and patriotic symbols. Such ads could be ripe for use by a would-be demagogue by appealing to the emotions and prejudices of people, especially in order to advance his or her own political needs.

The use of production techniques to create political ads that play on the emotions rather than on logic are susceptible to demagogic manipulation. As such, this tends to reduce the debate on issues and increase the struggle over symbols. The population base their voting decisions on stereotypical symbolic constructs without evaluating these fantasies before adopting them (see chapter 2). In such situations, we can expect that political leaders will use such fantasy chaining to their own advantage. However, this is not unique to negative political advertising; rather, it is common to all political advertising.

Negative political advertising can be used by a candidate not to enlighten individuals on the issues but rather to appeal to their political responsive chords. During the summer of 1988, politicians wrapped themselves in the flag, but it did not contribute to a healthy political debate.

The use of negative political advertising has produced a situation that could be manipulated for demagogic purposes, but there are other consequences. Upon election, a candidate cannot ignore the threat of future negative political ads. This has led to a growing crisis in the management of the country.

Negative Ads and Poor Representation

Edmund Burke gave us the yardstick by which to gauge the responsibility of our elected representatives. Speaking in 1774, he said in a speech to the Electors Board: "Your representative owes you, not his industry only, but his judgment; and he betrays instead of serving you if he sacrifices it to your opinion" (Bartlett, 1980, p. 372). This ideal of representative government, that a representative is elected to use his or her good judgment to make decisions for the good of the whole, is charged with crumbling under the onslaught of negative advertising.

The former Senate majority leader, Howard Baker, provided the link between negative political advertising and failure to properly govern:

> The problem [of negative political advertising] goes beyond elections to the process of governing. Time after time when I was leader in the Senate and trying to round up votes on a controversial issue, I wold have senators say to me, "Howard, I would like to vote with you, but they would kill me with negative ads the next time I run." (quoted in Clinger, 1987, pp. 731-732)

John Danforth argued that the specter of negative advertising has not only changed the decisions but the decision-making process; he sensed "an increasing mood of defensiveness, or testiness, and a breakdown in the comity and collegiality that we need to function as a deliberative body" (as quoted in Diamond & Bates, 1988, p. 385).

This mood sometimes projects itself into what political commentator Meg Greenfield called "carefully contrived indignation" (1989, p. 78). In order to protect themselves, some politicians adopt a stance of indignation in cases where indignation seems to provide a safe haven from public opinion, even if the expressed opinion runs contrary to the representatives' held beliefs. This artful indignation can encourage the public to adopt the indignant viewpoint as reality, even though it is counter to the representatives' actual views. According to Greenfield:

> As a result, it may even, against his actual intentions, create its own uncontrollable momentum to enact the awful thing he is only pretending to be for—but, then, accidents happen and no one is perfect. This kind of cover is, of course, also a lie, but it is regarded as a higher-purpose lie, a strategic life, which is not to be condemned at all but, rather, admired for its cunning, and its ultimately beneficial effect.

The strategic lie robs the public of the wisdom and leadership of those they elected and substitutes in its place a view that the representatives think is politically expedient.

All political leaders, especially incumbents, realize that personal and political behavior is under a microscope, by not only the mass media but their potential opponents as well. Often, this can create situations where legislators know that what they are voting or supporting is wrong or even unconstitutional, but they will persevere because they fear the potential negative ads which can be used to stimulate the voters' wrath. James Broder (1982) suggested that this modern-day "gutless government" has created a situation in which "the art of survival means avoiding any controversial stands that an opponent could use in a future 'attack' ad" (p. C7).

Career politicians, people whose profession rests on their reelection, wish to avoid controversial complex issues, which a future opponent could possibly distort. Negative political advertising may be robbing the United States of the benefit of informed, deliberative decision making on the part of its representatives. They frequently betray their constituents by sacrificing their judgment for the public's opinion, which is often based on distortion, stereotypes, and fantasies.

NEGATIVE POLITICAL ADVERTISING
AND POSITIVE EFFECTS

As there are detractors of negative political advertising, so also are there supporters, people who assert that negative political advertising has positive effects for the electorate and the political process. This section looks at two arguments that can be made in favor of negative political advertising: Negative political ads increase the knowledge level of the viewer and negative political ads create a type of debate.

Increasing Information Levels

Surlin and Gordon (1977) found in their research on direct attack ads that people felt the ads were unethical, yet people also reported they were informative. Comparisons between candidates, even if tilted to one side, usually are rich with information. Even direct attack ads may provide knowledge about a candidate. Negative political advertising may well provide more information to voters than positive ads. And research has shown that people retain negative information more than positive information.

Studies indicate that there is a fundamental need for more information about politics and the political system by the American public. For example, Americans' knowledge of foreign affairs and foreign policy has been shown to be deficient (Smith, 1972), a situation which is not new. In fact, one person studying the knowledge level of Americans on foreign policy knowledge in 1949 went so far as to call this lack of knowledge on the part of the public, "dark areas of ignorance" (Kriesberg, 1949).

This lack of knowledge extends beyond the area of foreign affairs. General knowledge about domestic politics is also embarrassingly low. An examination of the distribution of general American political knowledge through the population by Glenn (1972) led him to conclude, "a large proportion of the American public can not . . . intelligently vote or participate in the democratic process" (p. 273).

The lack of knowledge leads to decision making at elections that can only be described as being based on ignorance rather than on rational choice. It may be responsible for what Clinger (1987) called irrational voting patterns on the part of the electorate.

Negative political advertising is one method that is used to provide information about the campaigns. There is ample evidence to demonstrate that political advertising affects political cognitions (Atkin et al., 1973; Atkin & Heald, 1976; Hofstetter et al., 1978; Kaid, 1976; Patterson & McClure, 1976b), attitudes (Baskin, 1976; Bowers, 1973; Meadow & Sigelman, 1982; Shaw & Bowers, 1973; Wanat, 1974; Zajonc, 1968; Zajonc & Rajecki, 1969), and behaviors (Dawson & Zinser, 1971; Grush et al., 1978; Joslyn, 1981; Kaid, 1981; Palda, 1975).

The academic research that has been done on negative political advertising does show that those exposed to these messages come away with information about the issues or the candidates, even if the information was about the candidates' images. (The interested reader may review the Results sections of the works of Garramone, 1985; Kaid & Boydston, 1987; Roddy & Garramone, 1988.) Negative political advertising has been cited as presenting greater issue clarity than positive spots (Hagstrom & Guskind, 1986), which would increase their value for people who were not as knowledgeable about the campaign or political affairs.

The charges leveled in negative ads often go beyond the 30 seconds that the spot is on the air. It is not uncommon for local or national news media to report the charges that have been made in the spots. This added exposure for the message contained in the negative ad has led many consultants to hold prescreenings of the ads for reporters, knowing that the reporters will then repeat the ad's message or even show the spot in the newscast. This is a process we call *media baiting*.

This added source of dissemination increases the coverage of the message. It is a bonus for the campaign to have the information relayed to news viewers, because they are, as a group, the people most likely to vote in the election. Not only does it provide amplification of the issues, but the charges gain credibility by being reported in the news media.

Democratic consultant Frank Greer noted that the news media may merely report the contents of the ads, or they may actually investigate the legitimacy of the claims (cited in Hagstrom & Guskind, 1986). The accuracy of the information received through negative political ads may and should be verified by the news media (see chapter 7). In a letter to its members, the American Association of Political Consultants (AAPC) reported that "The media . . . has also done a[n] excellent job of reviewing the fairness and honesty of every commercial . . . . Indeed some of these commercials receive more press review than air time." An active press should serve as one mechanism for judging truth and falsity of claims in negative political ads, providing some assurance that the viewers will receive accurate information from these negative spots.

Negative Political Advertising and Debating the Issues

As a result of the information provided by negative political advertising, a type of campaign debate ensues. Amid the charges and countercharges, the voter is asked to weigh the issues and make decisions. Negative political advertising frequently focuses on issues, as we have demonstrated in this book. It can be argued that negative political advertising actually opens up the campaign to the issues by making the candidates respond to the charges and countercharges. These negative ads are used strategically to set the terms of the campaign debate by focusing on the issues (Nugent, 1987).

Some in the consulting business view the negative political spot as a natural outgrowth of the rise of television in political campaign life. In the letter previously mentioned, the AAPC stated the issue bluntly: "Television has forced us to accept their medium as a form of debate, and these commercials are, in reality, simply a form of those debates."

Long forms of political campaign dialogue, white papers, position statements, even face-to-face debates, are rare and attention to them by the public even more so. Without these other styles of issue presentations, the campaign commercial becomes the only place in which the dialogue between candidates may take place.

Some may object to what they consider a certain stridency on the part of the candidates who use negative political advertising. One respondent in a poll for Adweek said,, "I dislike the battery back and forth between the candidates" (Morgan & Vadehra, 1984, p. 29). Yet even this verbal jousting may be good. An editorial in the Sparks *Tribune* said:

> Some would call the cross fire irresponsible mudslinging and advise the candidates to grow up. Nonsense. A little mudslinging – if that's what you call a bit of emotional exchange in a campaign – is good for any election. Fastidious candidates who take themselves too seriously and try to analyze the issues . . . are boring. (cited in Hagstrom & Guskind, 1986, p. 2621)

Even George Will (1989), no friend of negative political advertising, would like to see more "Americans . . . loosen up and welcome real verbal roughhousing from their politicians (p. 92).

Negative political advertising can play a positive role in the campaign by providing for the electorate a 30-second minidebate. This debate better prepares many potential voters in making their voting decisions.

RECOMMENDATIONS

In 1987 in an article in Campaigns and Elections entitled "Positively Negative," John Nugent made some recommendations to political consultants on how to "find positive ways to conduct 'negative' campaigns" (p. 47). Nugent suggested that the vocabulary surrounding negative advertising should be changed. We agree. Direct comparison ads, indirect comparison ads, and direct attack ads explain in their names what it is that the ad does. The generic "negative ad" label does nothing of the sort; in addition, political observers often fail to consider direct and indirect comparison ads as negative ads. The use of specific terminology would help clarify the issue.

Nugent (1987) also recommended that the quality of negative ads be improved and reminded political consultants that "advertising is a result of strategic considerations, not a substitute for them" (p. 49). Candidates should be carefully positioned and advertising designed to reflect that positioning, whether it is positive or negative.

Additional Recommendations

We would like to conclude this book by making nine other recommendations to candidates and their campaigns who are strategically assessing negative political advertising as we have defined it. They are as follows:

1. Avoid personal attacks. As we demonstrated in chapter 1, personal attack appeals have the highest negative response rate from voters.

2. Be specific in your comparison or direct attack spots. Do not generalize; generalization invites the news media to suggest that you have overstated your case. Have the evidence for the attack and be prepared to distribute the evidence to the media if the attack is disputed.

3. Be truthful and fair in your negative arguments. Americans hate liars and cheats.

4. Be relevant. Do not attack candidates on matters that the voters do not care about. If you do, you are being negative for the sake of being negative, and the voters perceive it as such.

5. Dare to be different. Dare to use innovative ads and strategies. The novelty may help you gain voter attention.

6. Dare to be strong. Do not attack and then back off. Avoid the appearance that the candidate is guilty of a hit and run. Stay with the issue until your polls tell you that you have made your point. The candidate must be comfortable with the negative arguments before airing the ad. When candidates appear in negative spots, they need to appear confident and strong. If they do not, it looks like they are lying. In a personal conversation with the author, one successful campaign manager said: "Dare to go for the jugular and have the strength of will to hang on." And as Burger and Lunde (1989) suggested: "Politics is a contact sport" (p. 64). If you can't stand the heat, stay out of the kitchen.

7. Do not get caught sleeping. Anticipate your own vulnerabilities. Be prepared for negative attacks. React quickly and efficiently. As Nugent (1987) told us: "A charge unanswered is a charge admitted" (p. 49).

8. Do not get caught short. Be prepared for dirty tricks or negative spots that occur in the last few days of the campaign. Have the money, the crew, and the consultant ready to respond.

9. When hiring political consultants, be sure to seek out those who are well versed in negative campaign strategies and tactics. Negative political advertising has come of age, and any political campaign must be prepared to both use it and deal with it.

IN CONCLUSION

Most of what we have presented in this chapter is based on speculation made by academicians, reporters, and political consultants. Currently, there is no evidence to prove that negative political advertising definitely has a positive or a negative effect on politics or people. There is a need for more research so that a definitive conclusion can be drawn.

Of the potential negative effects by negative political advertising, only its effects on representation seem most certain. There seems to be a good deal of critical evidence that negative political advertising is affecting the way in which our representatives behave and, ultimately, the quality of life in this country. The other negative aspects discussed—negativity, alienation, and demagoguery—if true, would seem to present real problems, but we do not have the information currently at hand to draw such conclusions. Rather, we offer these as warnings and areas for further study.

Some positive effects of negative political advertising have been suggested. Negative political advertising may increase voters' information levels, generate debate, and clarify issues within a campaign. We will use the oxymoron of positive negative political advertising and suggest that positive negative political advertising promotes positive effects on society.

References

Abcarian, G., & Stanage, S. M. (1965). Alienation and the radical right. *Journal of Politics, 27*, 776-96.

Abramowitz, A. (1980). The United States: Political culture under stress. In A. Almond & S. Verba (Eds.), *The civic culture revisited* (pp. 177-211). Boston: Little, Brown.

Abramson, P. R., Aldrich, J. H., & Rhode, D. W. (1986). *Change and continuity in the 1984 elections*. Washington, DC: Congressional Quarterly.

Adams, R. C. (1978, September-October). Media use patterns of decided and undecided likely voters. *Practical Politics*, pp. 12-15.

Adams, R. C., Copeland, G. A., Fish, M., & Hughes, M. (1980). The effect of framing on selection of photographs of men and women. *Journalism Quarterly, 57*, 463-467.

Agranoff, R. (1976a). Campaign consultants: Pushing sincerity in 1974. In R. Agranoff (Ed.), *The new style in election campaigns* (pp. 300-309). Boston: Holbrook.

Agranoff, R. (1976b). *The management of election campaigns*. Boston: Holbrook.

Ailes, R. (1985). Dog-gone colleague haunts Senate. *Campaigns & Elections, 6*, 57-60.

Alexander, H. E. (1969). Communications and politics: The media and the message. *Law and Contemporary Problems, 34*, 255-277.

Alexander, H. E. (1983). The regulation and funding of presidential elections. *Journal of Law & Politics*, 43-63.

Almond, G. A. (1980). The intellectual history of the civic culture concept. In G. A. Almond & S. Verba (Eds.), *The civic culture revisited* (pp. 1-36). Boston: Little, Brown.

Almond, G., & Verba S. (1963). *The civic culture*. Princeton, NJ: Princeton University Press.

Alter, J. (1984, November 5). When ads subtract. *Newsweek*, p. 71.

Alter, J., & Fineman, H. (1988, January 18). The search for the perfect sound-bite. *Newsweek*, p. 22.

Anderson, L. R., & McGuire, W. J. (1965). Prior reassurance of group consensus as a factor in producing resistance to persuasion. *Sociometry, 28*, 44-56.

Anderson, N. H. (1965). Averaging vs. adding as a stimulus-combination rule in impression formation. *Journal of Experimental Psychology, 70*, 394-400.

Andreoli, V., & Worchel, S. (1978). Effects of media, communicator and message position on attitude change. *Public Opinion Quarterly, 42*, 59-70.

Archer, D., Iritania, B., Kimes, D. D., & Barrios, M. (1983). Face-ism: Five studies of sex diff.rences in facial studies. *Journal of Personality and Social Psychology, 45*, 725-735.

Archer, D., Kimes, D. D., & Barrios, M. (1978, September). Face-ism. *Psychology Today*, pp. 65-66.

Archibald, S. J. (1971). The dynamics of clean campaigning. In S. J. Archibald (Ed.), *The pollution of politics* (pp. 8-21). Washington, DC: Public Affairs Press.

Arnheim, R. (1965). *Art and visual perception.* Berkeley: University of California Press.

Arnold, C. C. (1972, April). *Invention and pronuntiatio in a new rhetoric.* Paper presented at the Central States Speech Communication Convention, Chicago, IL.

Arterton, F. C. (1978). Campaign organizations confront the media-political environment. In J. D. Barber (Ed.), *The race for the presidency* (pp. 3-22). Englewood Cliffs, NJ: Prentice-Hall.

Atkin, C. K. (1980). Political campaigns: Mass communication and persuasion. In M. E. Roloff & G. R. Miller (Eds.), *Persuasion: New directions in theory and research* (pp. 285-308). Beverly Hills, CA: Sage.

Atkin, C. K., Bowen, L., Nayman, O. B., & Sheinkopf, K. G. (1973). Quality versus quantity in televised political ads. *Public Opinion Quarterly, 40*, 209-224.

Atkin, C. K., & Heald, G. (1976). Effects of political advertising. *Public Opinion Quarterly, 40*, 216-228.

Bailyn, B. (1967). *The ideological origins of the American Revolution.* Cambridge, MA: Belknap Press of Harvard University Press.

Bannon, B. (1982). NCPAC's role in the 1980 Senate elections. *Campaigns & Elections, 3*, 43-46.

Bannon, B. (1983). NCPAC in the 80s: Action v. reaction. *Campaigns & Elections, 3*, 36-43.

Barrett, L. (1988, February 1). Playing populist chords. *Time*, p. 16.

Bartlett, J. (1980). *Bartlett's familiar quotations* (15th ed. 125th anniversary ed.). Boston: Little, Brown.

Baskin, O. W. (1976). The effects of televised political advertisements on voter perceptions about candidates (Doctoral dissertation, University of Texas-Austin, 1975). *Dissertation Abstracts International, 36*, 6355A.

Battaglio, S. (1988, November 7). Campaign '88: Faint hearts, bloodied noses. *Adweek*, pp. 22-23.

Baukus, R. A., Payne, J. G., & Reisler, M. S. (1985). Negative polispots: Mediated arguments in the political arena. In J. R. Cox, M. O. Sillars, & G. B. Walker (Eds.), *Argument and social practice: Proceedings of the fourth SCA/AFA Conference on Argumentation* (pp. 236-252). Annandale, VA: Speech Communication Association.

Becker, L. B., & Dunwoody, S. (1982). Media use, public affairs knowledge and voting in a local election. *Journalism Quarterly, 59*, 212-218, 255.

Becker, L. B., Sobowale, I. A., & Casey, W. E. (1979). Newspaper and television dependencies: Their effects on evaluations of public officials. *Journal of Broadcasting, 23*, 465-475.

Becker, L., & Whitney, D. C. (1980). Effects of media dependencies: Audience assessment of government. *Communication Research, 7*, 95-121.

Benze, J. G., & Declercq, E. R. (1985). Content of television political spot ads for female candidates. *Journalism Quarterly, 62*, 278-283, 288.

Berkman, R., & Kitch, L. W. (1986). *Politics in the media age.* New York: McGraw-Hill.

Bernard, S. (1989, October). "NBC Nightly News" Report.

Berrigan, J. (1982). The cost-effectiveness of grass-roots campaign activities. *Campaigns & Elections, 3*, 25-33.

Bettman, J. A. (1975). Issues in designing consumer information environments. *Journal of Consumer Research, 2*, 169-177.

Blum, J., Morgan, E., Rose, A., Schlesinger, A., Jr., Stampp, K., & Woodward, C. (1973). *The national experience: Part one and part two.* New York: Harcourt Brace Jovanovich.

Boddewyn, J. J., & Marton, K. (1978). Comparison advertising: A worldwide study. In S. E. Permut (Ed.), *Proceedings of the annual conference of the American Academy of Advertising 1978: Advances in advertising, research, and management* (pp. 150-154). New Haven, CT: Yale University Printing Service.

Bogart, L. (1972). Negro and white media exposure: New evidence. *Journalism Quarterly, 49,* 15-21.

Boim, D. S. (1984). The telemarketing center: Nucleus of a modern campaign. *Campaigns & Elections, 5,* 73-78.

Bonafede, D. (1983, October 8). Democratic party takes some strides down the long comeback trail. *National Journal,* pp. 2053-2055.

Bordwell, D., & Thompson, K. (1979). *Film art.* Reading, MA: Addison-Wesley.

Bowers, J. W. (1963). Language intensity, social introversion and attitude change. *Speech Monographs, 30,* 345-352.

Bowers, T. A. (1973). Newspaper political advertising and the agenda-setting function. *Journalism Quarterly, 50,* 552-556.

Boydston, J., & Kaid, L. L. (1983, May). *An experimental study of the effectiveness of NCPAC political advertisements.* Paper presented at the International Communication Association Convention, Dallas, TX.

Boyle, L. (1985). PACs and pluralism: The dynamics of interest-group politics. *Campaigns & Elections, 6,* 6-16.

Breen, M., & Corcoran, F. (1982). Myth in the television discourse. *Communication Monographs, 49,* 127-136.

Briscoe, M. E., Woodyard, H. D., & Shaw, M. E. (1967). Personality impression change as a function of the favorableness of first impressions. *Journal of Personality, 35,* 343-357.

Broder, J. (1982, October 31). When campaigns get mean. *The Washington Post,* p. C7.

Brody, R. A. (1978). The puzzle of political participation in America. In A. King (Ed.), *The new American political system* (pp. 287-324). Washington, DC: American Enterprise Institute for Public Policy Research.

Brooker, G. (1981). A comparison of the persuasive effects of mild humor and mild fear appeals. *Journal of Advertising, 10,* 29-40.

Brown v. Socialist Workers '74 Campaign Committee, 459 U.S. 87 (1982).

Brown, D., & Bryant, J. (1983). Humor in the mass media. In P. E. McGhee & J. E. Goldstein (Eds.), *Handbook of humor research* (pp. 143-172). New York: Springer-Verlag.

Brownstein, C. N. (1971). Communication strategies and the electoral decision making process: Some results from experimentation. *Experimental Study of Politics, 1,* 37-50.

Brummett, B. (1980). Towards a theory of silence as a political strategy. *Quarterly Journal of Speech, 66,* 289-303.

Bruneau, T. (1973). Silences: Forms and functions. *Journal of Communication, 23,* 17-46.

Bryce, J. (1896). *The American commonwealth.* London: Macmillan.

Buckley v. Valeo, 424 U.S. 1 (1976).

Burger, G., Lunde, B. (1989). Yes, Mike, this campaign was about competence. *Campaigns & Elections, 9,* 64.

Burgoon, J. (1980). Nonverbal communication research in the 1970s: An overview. In D. Nimmo (Ed.), *Communication yearbook IV* (pp. 179-197). New Brunswick, NJ: Transaction.

Burgoon, M., & Bettinghaus, E. P. (1980). Persuasive message strategies. In M. E. Roloff & G. R. Miller (Eds.), *Persuasion: New directions in theory and research* (pp. 141-169). Beverly Hills, CA: Sage.

Burgoon, M., Burgoon, J. K., Riess, M., Butler, J., Montgomery, C. L., Stinnett, W. D., Miller, M., Long, M., Vaughn, D., & Caine, B. (1976). Propensity of persuasive attack and intensity of pretreatment messages as predictors of resistance to persuasion. *The Journal of Psychology, 92,* 123-129.

Burgoon, M., Cohen, M., Miller, M. D., & Montgomery, C. L. (1978). An empirical test of resistance to persuasion. *Human Communication Research, 5,* 27-39.

Burgoon, M., & King, L. B. (1974). The mediation of resistance to persuasion strategies by language variables and active-passive participation. *Human Communication Research, 1,* 30-41.

Burke, K. (1950). *A rhetoric of motives.* New York: Prentice-Hall.

Burke, K. (1966). *Language as symbolic action.* Los Angeles: University of California Press.

Burnham, D. (1983, October 27). What you see is probably what you're going to get. *Providence Evening Bulletin,* p. A6.

Burrell, B. (1987, January-February). Not a Cinderella story. *Campaigns & Elections, 287,* 32-37.

Burrows, T. D., & Woods, D. N. (1986). *Television production: Disciplines and techniques.* Dubuque, IA: Brown.

Calder, B. J. (1978). Cognitive responses, imagery, and scripts: What is the cognitive basis of attitudes? *Advances in Consumer Research, 5,* 630-634.

The campaign finance debate. (1988). In *Elections '88* (pp. 119-126). Washington, DC: Congressional Quarterly.

Campaign guide for congressional candidates and committees. (1988, July). Washington, DC: Federal Election Commission.

Campaign guide for political party committees. (1985, October). Washington, DC: Federal Election Commission.

Campaign Insights. (1976, March 1). p. 8.

Cantor, J. (1976). Humor on television. *Journal of Broadcasting, 20,* 501-510.

Cantor, J. R., & Zillmann, D. (1973). Resentment toward victimized protagonists and severity of misfortunes they suffer as factors in humor appreciation. *Journal of Experimental Research in Personality, 6,* 321-329.

Cantwell v. Connecticut, 310 U.S. 296 (1940).

Carlson, J. (1981). *George C. Wallace and the politics of powerlessness.* New Brunswick, NJ: Transaction.

Carroll, R. (1980). The 1948 Truman campaign: The threshold of the modern era. *Journal of Broadcasting, 24,* 173-188.

Cavanagh, T. E. (1984-1985). Black politics and the 1984 elections. *Election Politics, 2,* 18-20.

Chapman, A. J., & Foote, H. C. (1976). *Humor and laughter: Research, theory, and applications.* London: Wiley.

Chappell, H. (1982). Campaign contributions and congressional voting: A simultaneous probit-tobit model. *Review of Economics and Statistics, 64,* 77-83.

Charles, J. (1961). *The origins of the American system.* New York: Harper & Brothers.

Chestnut, R. W. (1980). Persuasive effects in marketing: Consumer information processing research. In M. E. Roloff & G. R. Miller (Eds.), *Persuasion: New directions in theory and research* (pp. 267-283). Beverly Hills, CA: Sage.

Clark, D. G. (1962). Radio in presidential campaigns: The early years (1924-1932). *Journal of Broadcasting, 6,* 229-238.

Clarke, P., & Fredin, E. (1978). Newspapers, television and political reasoning. *Public Opinion Quarterly, 42,* 143-160.

Clean Campaign Act of 1985, Senate Bill 1310, Sec. 2.

Clinger, J. H. (1987). The clean campaign act of 1985: A rational solution to negative campaign advertising which the one hundredth Congress should reconsider. *Journal of Law & Politics, 3,* 727-748.

Cobb, R. W., & Elder, C. D. (1972). Individual orientations in the study of political symbolism. *Social Science Quarterly, 53,* 79-90.

Cohen, A. (1976). Radio vs. TV: The effect of medium. *Journal of Communication, 26,* 29-35.

Cohen, D. (1980). PAC power: Why Common Cause fears its impact. *Campaigns & Elections, 1,* 12-17.

Colburn, C. (1967). An experimental study of the relationship between fear appeal and topic importance in persuasion. (Doctoral dissertation, University of Indiana, 1967). *Dissertation Abstracts International, 28,* 2364A-2365A.

Colford, S. (1986, November 10). Pols accentuated negative. *Advertising Age,* pp. 3, 104.

Combs, J. E. (1979). Political advertising as a popular mythmaking form. *Journal of American Culture, 2,* 231-340.

Combs, J. E. (1980). *Dimensions of political drama.* Santa Monica, CA: Goodyear.

1988 Congressional Quarterly almanac. (1989). Washington, DC: Congressional Quarterly.

Constitution of the United States, Amendment 1, U.S.C.A.

Constitution of the United States, Amendment 14, U.S.C.A.

Contribution and Expenditure Limitations and Prohibitions, 11 C.F.R. 110.11(a)(1) (1986a).

Contribution and Expenditure Limitations and Prohibitions, 11 C.F.R. 110.11(a)(2) (1986b).

Controls on political spending. (1986). In *Elections '86* (pp. 37-46). Washington, DC: Congressional Quarterly.

Cook v. Corbett, 251 Or. 263, 446 P.2d 179 (1968).

Cooper, E., & Jahoda, M. (1947). The evasion of propaganda: How prejudiced people respond to anti-prejudice propaganda. *The Journal of Psychology, 23,* 15-25.

Copeland, G. A., & Johnson-Cartee, K. S. (1990a). *The acceptance of negative political advertising in the south and political efficacy and activity levels.* Unpublished manuscript.

Copeland, G. A., & Johnson-Cartee, K. S. (1990b). *A reexamination of candidate-sponsored negative political advertising effects.* Unpublished manuscript.

Costello, W. (1959, October). A fighting Quaker's youth. *New Republic,* pp. 11-16.

Cover, A. D. (1977). One good term deserves another: the advantage of incumbency in congressional elections. *American Journal of Political Science, 21,* 523-542.

Cragan, J. F., & Cutbirth, C. W. (1984). A revisionist perspective on political ad hominem argument: A case study. *Central States Speech Journal, 35,* 228-237.

Craver, R. (1985). The direct mailbox: The tastelessness of success. *Campaigns & Elections, 6,* 70-72.

Cronin, T. (1977). The presidency and its paradoxes. In T. Cronin & T. Tugwell (Eds.), *The presidency reappraised* (2nd ed., pp. 69-85). New York: Praeger.

Crotty, W., & Jacobson, G. (1980). *American parties in decline.* Boston: Little, Brown.

Csikszentmihalyi, M., & Kubey, R. (1981). Television and the rest of life: A systematic comparison of subjective experience. *Public Opinion Quarterly, 45,* 317-328.

Cundy, D. T. (1986). Political commercials and candidate image: The effect can be substantial. In L. L. Kaid, D. Nimmo, & K. R. Sanders (Eds.), *New perspectives on political advertising* (pp. 210-234). Carbondale: Southern Illinois University Press.

Cusumano, D., & Richey, M. (1970). Negative salience in impressions of character: Effects of extremeness of salient information. *Psychonomic Science, 20,* 81-83.

Cutlip, S. M., Center, A. H., & Broom, G. M. (1985). *Effective public relations* (6th ed.). Englewood Cliffs, NJ: Prentice-Hall.

Dawson, P. A., & Zinser, J. E. (1971). Broadcast expenditures and electoral outcomes in the 1970 congressional elections. *Public Opinion Quarterly, 35,* 398-402.

Declercq, E. R., Benze, J., & Ritchie, E. (1983). *Macha women and macho men.* Paper presented at the meeting of the American Political Science Association, Chicago.

Democratic Party of the United States and Democratic National Committee v. NCPAC and Fund for a Conservative Majority (470 US 480 (1985).

Devlin, L. P. (1973). Contrasts in presidential campaign commercials of 1972. *Journal of Broadcasting, 35,* 17-26.

Devlin, L. P. (1977). Contrasts in presidential campaign commercials of 1976. *Central State Speech Journal, 28,* 238-249.

Devlin, L. P. (1981). Reagan's and Carter's ad men review the 1980 television campaigns. *Communication Quarterly, 30*, 3-12.

Devlin, L. P. (1986). An analysis of presidential television commercials, 1952-1984. In L. L. Kaid, D. Nimmo, & K. R. Sanders (Eds.), *New perspectives on political advertising* (pp. 21-54). Carbondale: Southern Illinois University Press.

Devlin, L. P. (1989). Contrasts in presidential campaign commercials of 1988. *American Behavioral Scientist, 32*, 389-414.

DeVries, W. (1971). Taking the voters' pulse. In R. Hiebert, R. Jones, E. Lotito, & J. Lorenz (Eds.), *The political image merchants: Strategies in the new politics* (pp. 62-81). Washington, DC: Acropolis.

DeVries, W., & Tarrance, V. L. (1972). *The ticket splitters: A new force in American politics.* Grand Rapids, MI: Eerdmans.

Diamond, E. (1976). The Ford and Carter commercials they didn't dare run. *More, 6*, 12-17.

Diamond, E., & Bates, S. (1985). The ads. In M. J. Robinson & R. Austin (Eds.), *The mass media in campaign '84: Articles from Public Opinion Magazine* (pp. 49-52). Washington, DC: American Enterprise Institute.

Diamond, E., & Bates, S. (1988). *The spot: The rise of political advertising on television* (rev. ed.). Cambridge, MA: MIT Press.

Dixon, K. (1989). Cable comes of age. *Campaigns & Elections, 9*, 29.

Dominick, J., Sherman, B. A., & Copeland, G. A. (1990). *Broadcasting/Cable and beyond.* New York: McGraw-Hill.

Drew, E. (1983). *Politics and money: The new road to corruption.* New York: Macmillan.

Duncan, C. P. (1979). Humor in advertising: A behavioral perspective. *Journal of the Academy of Marketing Science, 7*, 33-40.

Duncan, C. P., & Nelson, J. E. (1985). Effects of humor in a radio advertising experiment. *Journal of Advertising, 14*, 33-40.

Dunn, S. W., & Barban, A. M. (1986). *Advertising: Its role in modern marketing* (6th ed.). New York: Dryden.

Edelman, M. (1964). *The symbolic uses of politics.* Urbana: University of Illinois Press.

Edmonds, T., & Roy, S. (1984). The computer assisted media buy: A primer for campaign managers. *Campaigns and Elections, 5*, 58-67.

Ekstrand, L. (1978, May). *An experiment to determine the effect of candidate's sex on voter choice.* Paper presented at the meeting of the Midwest Political Science Association, Chicago.

Elebash, C., & Rosene, J. (1982). Issues in political advertising in a deep south gubernatorial race. *Journalism Quarterly, 59*, 420-423.

Elliott, L. A. (1980). Political action committees—precincts of the '80s. *Arizona Law Review, 22*, 539-554.

Epstein, L. (1967). *Political parties in western democracies.* New York: Praeger.

Epstein, L. K. (1984-1985). 1984-A realigning election. *Election Politics, 2*, 2-4.

Erickson, J. (1982). The Democrats: Rebuilding with support groups. *Campaigns & Elections, 3*, 4-14.

Faber, R. J., & Storey, M. C. (1984). Recall of information from political advertising. *Journal of Advertising, 13*, 39-44.

Farmers Educational and Cooperative Union v. WDAY, Inc., 360 U.S. 525 (1959).

Farney, D. (1986, September 23). Whether he likes it or not, Sen. Denton is ahead in Alabama. *The Wall Street Journal*, pp. 1, 20.

FEC reports on financial activity: 1987-1988: final report: U.S. Senate and House campaigns. (1989, September). Washington, DC: Federal Election Commission.

Federal Election Commission v. Hall-Tyner Election Campaign Committee, 678, F.2d 416 (2d. Cir. 1982).

Federal Election Commission v. National Conservative Political Action Committee, 105 S. Ct. 1459 (1985). (FEC v. NCPAC) 26 USC 9012(1).

Feldman, S. (1966). Motivational aspects of attitudinal elements and their place in cognitive interaction. In S. Feldman (Ed.), *Cognitive consistency: Motivational antecedents and behavioral consequences* (pp. 75-108). New York: Academic.

Fenno, R. (1975). The president's cabinet. In A. Wildavsky (Ed.), *Perspectives on the presidency* (pp. 318-338). Boston: Little, Brown.

Festinger, L., & Maccoby, N. (1964). On resistance to persuasive communications. *Journal of Abnormal and Social Psychology, 68*, 359-366.

Fiorina, M. (1977). *Congress: Keystone of the Washington establishment.* New Haven, CT: Yale University Press.

Frandsen, K. D., (1963). Effects of threat appeals and media transmission. *Speech Monographs, 30*, 101-104.

Freedman, J. L., & Steinbruner, J. D. (1964). Perceived choice and resistance to persuasion. *Journal of Abnormal and Social Psychology, 68*, 678-681.

Frendreis, J., & Waterman, R. (1985). PAC contributions and legislative behavior: Senate voting on trucking deregulation. *Social Science Quarterly, 66*, 401-412.

Freud, S. (1952). *On dreams.* New York: Norton.

Garramone, G. M. (1983). Issue versus image orientation and effects of political advertising. *Communication Research, 10*, 59-76.

Garramone, G. M. (1984). Voter responses to negative political ads. *Journalism Quarterly, 61*, 250-259.

Garramone, G. M. (1985). Effects of negative political advertising: The roles of sponsor and rebuttal. *Journal of Broadcasting & Electronic Media, 29*, 147-159.

Garramone, G. M., & Smith, S. J. (1984). Reactions to political advertising: Clarifying sponsor effects. *Journalism Quarterly, 61*, 771-775.

Garrison v. Louisiana, 379 U.S. 64 (1964).

Garvey, D. E., & Rivers, W. L. (1982). *Newswriting for the electronic media.* Belmont, CA: Wadsworth.

Gertz v. Robert Welch, Inc., 94 S.Ct. 2997 (1974).

Giges, N. (1980, September 22). Comparative ads; Better than . . . ? *Advertising Age*, pp. 59-62.

Gilligan, J. (Ed.). (1988). *Elections '88.* Washington, DC: Congressional Quarterly.

Glenn, N. D. (1972). The distribution of political knowledge in the United States. In D. Nimmo & D. Bonjean (Eds.), *Political attitudes and public opinion.* New York: McKay.

Goffman, E. (1959). *Presentation of self in everyday life.* New York: Doubleday.

Gold, V. (1980). Image stratagems: Pick one for the '80s. *Campaigns & Elections, 1*, 43-48.

Golden, L. (1976). Consumer reactions to comparative advertising. In B. Anderson (Ed.), *Advances in Consumer Research, 3*, 63-67.

Goldenberg, E. N., & Traugott, M. W. (1984). *Campaigning for Congress.* Washington, DC: Congressional Quarterly.

Goldenberg, E. N., & Traugott, M. W. (1987). Mass media in U.S. congressional elections. *Legislative Studies Quarterly, 12*, 317-339.

Goldman, P., & Matthews, T. (1989). *The quest for the presidency: The 1988 campaign.* New York: Simon & Schuster.

Goodwin, D. K. (1987). *The Fitzgeralds and the Kennedys: An American saga.* New York: Simon & Schuster.

Goodwin, S., & Etgar, M. (1980). An experimental investigation of comparative advertising: Impact of message appeal, information load, and utility of product class. *Journal of Marketing Research, 17*, 187-202.

Graber, D. (1976). *Verbal behavior and politics.* Urbana: University of Ilinois Press.

Gray-Little, B. (1973). The salience of negative information in impression formation among two Danish samples. *Journal of Cross-Cultural Psychology, 4*, 193-206.

Green, M. (1975). *Who runs Congress.* New York: Grossman.

Greenfield, M. (1989, July 10). Indignation on demand. *Newsweek*, p. 78.

Greenwald, A. (1968). Cognitive learning, cognitive response to persuasion, and attitude change. In A. Greenwald, T. Brock, & T. Ostrom (Eds.), *Psychological foundation of attitudes* (pp. 147-170). New York: Academic.

Grenzke, J. M. (1988). PAC money and politicians. *Election Politics, 5*, 24-27.

Grenzke, J. M. (1989a). PACs in the congressional supermarket: the currency is complex. *American Journal of Political Science, 33*, 1-24.

Grenzke, J. M. (1989b). Candidate attributes and PAC contributions. *Western Political Quarterly, 42*, 245-264.

Griffiths, M. (1985, November). "Make no heroines" may be newspapers' attitude. *Press Women*, pp. 7-9.

Gronbeck, B. E. (1985, November). *The rhetoric of negative political advertising: Thoughts on the senatorial race ads in 1984.* Paper presented at the Speech Communication Association Convention, Denver.

Grossman, M. B., & Kumar, M. J. (1981). *Portraying the president: The White House and the news media.* Baltimore: Johns Hopkins University Press.

Gruner, C. R. (1976). Wit and humor in mass communications. In A. J. Chapman & H. C. Foote (Eds.), *Humor and laughter: Theory, research and applications* (pp. 287-311). London: Wiley.

Grush, J. E., McKeough, K. L., & Ahlering, R. F. (1978). Extrapolating laboratory research to actual political elections. *Journal of Personality and Social Psychology, 36*, 257-270.

Guest, A. M. (1974). Subjective powerlessness in the United States: Some longitudinal trends. *Social Science Quarterly, 54*, 827-842.

Guggenheim, C. (1986, October 15). For accountability in political advertising. *New York Times*, p. A31.

Hagstrom, J., & Guskind, R. (1986). Selling the candidates. *National Journal, 18*, 2619-2626.

Hale, K., & Mansfield, M. (1986, March). *Politics: Tastes great or less filling?* Paper presented at the Southwestern Political Science Association Convention, San Antonio, TX.

Hall, P. (1972). A symbolic interactionist analysis of politics. *Sociological Inquiry, 42*, 35-75.

Hamilton, D. L., & Huffman, L. F. (1971). Generality of impression-formation processes for evaluative and non-evaluative judgments. *Journal of Personality and Social Psychology, 20*, 200-207.

Hamilton, D. L., & Zanna, M. P. (1972). Differential weighting of favorable and unfavorable attributes in impression formation. *Journal of Experimental Research in Personality, 6*, 204-212.

Harris, L. (1974, July 25). Poll finds hostility to personal attacks. *Lafayette* [Indiana] *Journal and Courier*, p. B-14.

Hart, J. D. (1956). They all were born in log cabins. *American Heritage, 7*, 32-33, 102-105.

Hart, P. (1988). *Chicago Tribune poll of 5 key states.* Washington, DC: Peter D. Hart Research Associates.

Hart, R. P. (1971). The rhetoric of the true believer. *Speech Monographs, 39*, 249-53.

Hedlund, R. D., Freeman, P. K., Hamm, K. E., & Stein, R. M. (1979). The electability of women candidates: the effects of sex role stereotypes. *The Journal of Politics, 41*, 513-524.

Heighberger, N. R., & Adler, R. C. (1984, October). *Use of direct mail: A campaign based field experiment.* Paper presented at the American Political Science Association Annual Meeting, Washington, DC.

Heller, D. J. (1987). In re Garvey v. Kasten: What happens when an attack ad is "wrong"? *Campaigns & Elections, 8*, 79.

Hellweg, S. (1979). An examination of voter conceptualizations of the ideal political candidate. *Southern Speech Communication Journal, 4*, 373-385.

Hellweg, S. A. (1988, May). *Political candidate campaign advertising: A selected review of the literature.* Paper presented at the International Communication Association Convention, New Orleans, LA.

Hershey, M. R. (1974). *The making of a campaign strategy.* Lexington, MA: Lexington.

Hodges, B. H. (1974). Effect of valence on relative weighting in impression formation. *Journal of Personality and Social Psychology, 30,* 378-381.

Hofstadter, R. (1973). *The American political tradition.* New York: Vintage.

Hofstetter, C. R., & Buss, T. F. (1980). Politics and last-minute political television. *Western Political Quarterly, 33,* 24-37.

Hofstetter, C. R., & Zukin, C. (1979). TV network news and advertising in the Nixon and McGovern campaigns. *Journalism Quarterly, 56,* 106-115, 152.

Hofstetter, C. R., Zukin, C., & Buss, T. F. (1978). Political imagery and information in an age of television. *Journalism Quarterly, 55,* 562-569.

Hogan, J. M. (1984). Wallace and the Wallacites: A reexamination. *The Southern Speech Communication Journal, 50,* 24-48.

Holman, C. H. (1972). *A handbook to literature* (3rd ed.). New York: Bobbs-Merrill.

Hovland, C. I. (1959). Reconciling conflicting results derived from experimental and survey studies of attitude change. *American Psychologist, 14,* 8-17.

Humke, R. G., Schmitt, R. L., & Grupp, S. E. (1975). Candidates, issues and party in newspaper political advertisements. *Journalism Quarterly, 52,* 499-504.

Innocenzi, J. (1986). Media buys & media mix. *Election Politics, 3,* 24-25.

Ippolito, D. S., Walker, T. G., & Kolson, K. L. (1976). *Public opinion and responsible democracy.* Englewood Cliffs, NJ: Prentice-Hall.

Israel, K. F., & Williams, Jr., W. (1988). Getting the message out to voters in "media isolated" districts. *Election Politics, 5,* 17-21.

Jacobson, G. (1980). *Money in congressional elections.* New Haven, CT: Yale University Press.

Jacoby, J., Speller, D. E., & Kohn, C. A. (1974). Brand choice behavior as a function of information load. *Journal of Marketing Research, 11,* 63-69.

James, J. (1982). *Television in transition.* New York: Crane.

James, W. L. (1978). Some empirical findings about comparative advertising. In S. E. Permut (Ed.), *Proceedings of the annual conference of the American Academy of Advertising 1978: Advances in advertising research and management* (pp. 133-137). New Haven, CT: Yale University Printing Service.

Jamieson, K. H. (1984). *Packaging the presidency: A history and criticism of presidential campaign advertising.* New York: Oxford University Press.

Jamieson, K. H. (1986). The evolution of political advertising in America. In L. L. Kaid, D. Nimmo, & K. R. Sanders (Eds.), *New perspectives on political advertising* (pp. 1-20). Carbondale: Southern Illinois University Press.

Jamieson, K. H. (1988). *Eloquence in an electronic age: The transformation of political speechmaking.* New York: Oxford University Press.

Jamieson, K. H. (1989). Context and the creation of meaning in the advertising of the 1988 presidential campaign. *American Behavioral Scientist, 32,* 415-424.

Jamieson, K. H., & Campbell, K. K. (1983). *The interplay of influence: Mass media and their publics in news, advertising, politics.* Belmont, CA: Wadsworth.

Janis, I. L., & Feshback, S. (1953). Effects of fear-arousing communications. *Journal of Abnormal and Social Psychology, 48,* 78-92.

Johannesen, R. (1974). The functions of silence: A plea for communication research. *Western Speech, 38,* 25-35.

Johnson, K. S. (1981). Political party and media evolutions in the United States and Great Britain: A comparative functional analysis. In J. P. McKerns (Ed.), *Fourth Annual Communications Research Symposium: A Proceedings, 4,* 122-163.

Johnson, K. S. (1984). *Impression management during the presidential transitions of Nixon, Carter, and Reagan: A quantitative content analysis and thematic analysis.* Unpublished doctoral dissertation, University of Tennessee, Knoxville, TN.

Johnson, K. S., & Copeland, G. A. (1987, May). *Setting the parameters of good taste: Negative political advertising.* Paper presented at the International Communication Association Convention, Montreal, Canada.

Johnson-Cartee, K. S., & Copeland, G. A. (1989a, May). *Alabama voters and the acceptance of negative political advertising in the 1986 elections: An historical anomaly.* Paper presented at the International Communication Association Convention, San Francisco.

Johnson-Cartee, K. S., & Copeland, G. A. (1989b). Southern voters' reaction to negative political ads in the 1986 election. *Journalism Quarterly, 66,* 888-893, 986.

Johnson-Cartee, K. S., Copeland, G. A., & Huttenstine, M. (in press). How public relations professionals view men and women expert news sources. *Public Relations Review.*

Jordan, N. (1965). The "asymmetry" of "liking" and "disliking": A phenomenon meriting further replication and research. *Public Opinion Quarterly, 29,* 315-322.

Joslyn, R. A. (1981). The impact of campaign spot advertising on voting defections. *Human Communication Research, 7,* 347-360.

Joslyn, R. A. (1986). Political advertising and the meaning of elections. In L. L. Kaid, D. Nimmo, & K. R. Sanders (Eds.), *New perspectives on political advertising* (pp. 139-184). Carbondale: Southern Illinois University Press.

Kaid, L. L. (1976). Measures of political advertising. *Journal of Advertising Research, 16,* 49-53.

Kaid, L. L. (1981). Political advertising. In D. D. Nimmo & K. R. Sanders (Eds.), *Handbook of political communication* (pp. 249-271). Beverly Hills, CA: Sage.

Kaid, L. L., & Boydston, J. (1987). An experimental study of the effectiveness of negative political advertisements. *Communication Quarterly, 35,* 193-201.

Kaid, L. L., & Davidson, D. K. (1986). Elements of videostyle: Candidate presentation through television advertising. In L. L. Kaid, D. Nimmo, & K. R. Sanders (Eds.), *New perspectives on political advertising* (pp. 184-209). Carbondale: Southern Illinois University Press.

Kaid, L. L., Myers, S. L., Pipps, V., & Hunter, J. (1985). Sex role perceptions and televised political advertising: Comparing male and female candidates. *Women & Politics, 4,* 41-53.

Kaid, L. L., & Sanders, K. R. (1978). Political television commercials: An experimental study of type and length. *Communication Research, 5,* 57-70.

Katz, E., Gurevitch, M., & Haas, H. (1973). On the use of mass media for important things. *American Sociological Review, 38,* 164-181.

Kaus, M., & Clift, E. (1988, March 7). The many faces of Dick Gephardt. *Newsweek,* pp. 46-47.

Keith-Spiegel, P. (1972). Early conceptions of humor. In J. H. Goldstein & P. E. McGhee (Eds.), *The psychology of humor.* New York: Academic.

Kellermann, D. S. (1988). *The people, the press, & politics: Pre-election typology survey.* Times Mirror/Gallup Organization Poll.

Kellermann, K. (1984). The negativity effect and its implications for initial interaction. *Communication Monographs, 51,* 37-55.

Kelly, J. (1984, November 12). Packaging the presidency. *Time,* p. 36.

Kelly, P., & Solomon, P. J. (1975). Humor in television advertising. *Journal of Advertising, 4,* 33-35.

Kepplinger, H. M. (in press). The impact of presentation techniques: theoretical aspects and empirical findings. In F. Biocca (Ed.), *Television and political advertising, Vol. 1: Psychological processes.* Hillsdale, NJ: Lawrence Erlbaum Associates.

Kern, M. (1989). *Thirty-second politics: Political advertising in the eighties.* New York: Praeger.

Kershaw, A. G., & Tannenbaum, S. I. (1976, July 5). For and against comparative advertising. *Advertising Age,* pp. 25-28.

Key, G. A. (1988). *The effects of perceived humor on perceived attention, attitude toward the brand and recall.* Unpublished master's thesis, University of Alabama, Tuscaloosa.

Kiesler, C. A., Collins, R. E., & Miller, N. (1969). *Attitude change: A critical analysis of theoretical approaches.* New York: Wiley.

Kingdon, J. (1968). *Candidates for office: Beliefs and strategies.* New York: Random House.

Kitchens, J. T., & Powell, L. (1986). A critical analysis of NCPAC's strategies in key 1980 races: A third party negative campaign. *The Southern Speech Communication Journal, 51,* 208-228.

Kitchens, J. T., & Stiteler, B. (1979). Challenge to the "rule of minimum effect": A case study of the man-out man strategy. *Southern Speech Communication Journal, 44,* 176-190.

Klapp, O. (1964). *Symbolic leaders: Public dramas and public men.* New York: Minerva Press.

Kriesberg, M. (1949). Dark areas of ignorance. In L. Markel (Ed.), *Public opinion and foreign policy* (pp. 49-64). New York: Harper and Brothers.

Krugman, H. E. (1965-1966). The impact of television advertising: Learning without involvement. *Public Opinion Quarterly, 29,* 349-356.

Kumar, M., & Grossman, M. (1982). Images of the White House in the media. In D. Graber (Ed.), *The president and the public* (pp. 85-110). Philadelphia: ISHI.

Lashbrook, V. J. (1975). Leadership emergence and source valence: Concepts in support of interaction theory and measurement. *Human Communication Research, 1,* 308-315.

Lau, R. R. (1980). *Negativity in political perceptions.* Unpublished manuscript, University of California, Department of Psychology, Los Angeles.

Law of Political Broadcasting and Cablecasting, 69 F.C.C.2d 78-523 (1978).

Law of Political Broadcasting and Cablecasting: A Political Primer, 1984 Edition. (1984). Federal Communications Commission.

Leventhal, H., & Singer, D. (1964). Cognitive complexity, impression formation, and impression change. *Journal of Personalilty, 32,* 210-226.

Levin, I. P., & Schmidt, C. F. (1969). Sequential effects in impression formation with binary intermittent responding. *Journal of Experimental Psychology, 79,* 283-287.

Levine, P. (1976). Commercials that name competing brands. *Journal of Advertising Research, 16,* 7-14.

Leymore, V. L. (1975). *Hidden myth: Structure and symbolism in advertising.* New York: Basic.

Linden, G. W. (1970). *Reflections on the screen.* Belmont, CA: Wadsworth.

Lumsdaine, A. A., & Janis, I. L. (1953). Resistance to "counter propaganda" produced by one-sided and two-sided "propaganda" presentation. *Public Opinion Quarterly, 17,* 311-318.

Madden, T. J., & Weinberger, M. G. (1982). The effects of humor on attention in magazine advertising. *Journal of Advertising, 11,* 8-14.

Makay, J. J. (1970). The rhetorical strategies of Governor George Wallace in the 1964 Maryland primary. *Southern Speech Journal, 36,* 164-175.

Malchow, H., & May, F. (1985). Television watch parties: 1984's fund-raising innovation. *Campaigns & Elections, 6,* 18-22.

Mandel, R. B. (1981). *In the running: The new woman candidate.* New Haven, CT: Ticknor & Fields.

Mandell, L. M., & Shaw, D. L. (1973). Judging people in the news unconsciously: Effect of camera angle and bodily activity. *Journal of Broadcasting, 17,* 353-362.

Markiewicz, D. (1974). The effects of humor on persuasion. *Sociometry, 37,* 407-422.

Martel, M. (1983). *Political campaign debates: Images, strategies, and tactics.* New York: Longman.

Mayo, C. W., & Crockett, W. H. (1964). Cognitive complexity and primacy-recency effects in impression formation. *Journal of Abnormal and Social Psychology, 68,* 335-338.

McBurney, J. H., & Mils, G. E. (1964). *Argumentation and debate: Techniques of a free society* (2nd ed.). New York: Macmillan.

McCabe, E. (1988, December 12). The campaign you never saw. *New York,* pp. 33-48.

McCain, T. A., Chilberg, J., & Wakshlag, J. (1977). The effect of camera angle on source credibility and attraction. *Journal of Broadcasting, 21,* 35-46.

McCain, T. A., & Divers, L. [with others]. (1973, November). *The effects of body type and camera shots on interpersonal attraction and source credibility.* Paper presented at the meeting of the Speech Communication Association, Chicago.

McCain, T. A., & Repensky, G. R. (1972, November). *The effect of camera shot on interpersonal attraction for comedy performers.* Paper presented at the meeting of the Speech Communication Association, New York.

McClure, R. D., & Paterson, T. E. (1974). Television news and political advertising: The impact on voter beliefs. *Communication research, 1,* 3-31.

McCroskey, J. (1969). A summary of experimental research on the effects of evidence in persuasive communication. *Quarterly Journal of Speech, 55,* 169-176.

McCroskey, J. (1970). The effects of evidence as an inhibitor of counter-persuasion. *Speech Monographs, 37,* 188-194.

McDougall, G. (1977). Comparative advertising: Consumer issues and attitudes. In B. A. Greenberg & D. N. Bellenger (Eds.), *Contemporary marketing thought* (pp. 286-291). Chicago: American Marketing Association.

McGee, M. (1980). The "ideograph": A link between rhetoric and ideology. *The Quarterly Journal of Speech, 66,* 1-16.

McGuire, W. J. (1961a). Resistance to persuasion conferred by active and passive prior refutation of the same and alternate counterarguments. *Journal of Abnormal and Social Psychology, 63,* 326-332.

McGuire, W. J. (1961b). The effectiveness of supportive and refutational defenses in immunizing and restoring beliefs against persuasion. *Sociometry, 24,* 184-197.

McGuire, W. J. (1962). Persistence of resistance to persuasion induced by various types of prior belief defenses. *Journal of Abnormal and Social Psychology, 64,* 241-248.

McGuire, W. J. (1964). Inducing resistance to persuasion: Some contemporary approaches. In L. Berkowitz (Ed.), *Advances in experimental social psychology* (Vol. 1, pp. 191-229). New York: Academic.

McGuire, W. J., & Papageorgis, D. (1961). The relative efficacy of various types of prior belief defense in producing immunity against persuasion. *Journal of Abnormal and Social Psychology, 62,* 327-337.

McGuire, W. J., & Papageorgis, D. (1962). Effectiveness in forewarning in developing resistance to persuasion. *Public Opinion Quarterly, 26,* 24-34.

McPherson, M. (1980, August 10). The new right brigade. *The Washington Post,* p. F1.

Mead, G. H. (1934). *Mind, self, and society.* Chicago: University of Chicago Press.

Meadow, R. G., & Sigelman, L. (1982). Some effects and noneffects of campaign commercials: An experimental study. *Political Behavior, 4,* 163-175.

Meiklejohn, A. (1948). *Free speech: And its relation to self-government.* New York: Harper & Brothers.

Merritt, S. (1984). Negative political advertising: Some empirical findings. *Journal of Advertising, 13,* 27-38.

Miami Herald Publishing Co. v. Tornillo, 418 U.S. 241 (1974).

Middleton, K. R., & Chamberlin, B. F. (1988). *The law of public communication.* White Plains, NY: Longman.

Milbraith, L. (1965). *Political participation.* Chicago: Rand McNally.

Miller, J. W., & Rowe, R. M. (1967). Influence of favorable and unfavorable information upon assessment decisions. *Journal of Applied Psychology, 51,* 432-435.

Miller, M. D., & Burgoon, M. (1978-1979). The relationship between violations of expectations and the induction of resistance to persuasion. *Human Communication Research, 5,* 301-312.

Miller, M. M., & Reese, S. D. (1982). Media dependency as interaction: Effects of exposure and reliance activity and efficacy. *Communication Research, 9,* 227-248.

Miyo, Y. (1983). The knowledge-gap hypothesis and media dependency. In R. N. Bostrom & B. H. Westley (Eds.), *Communication yearbook 7* (pp. 626-650). Beverly Hills: Sage.

Moore, H. F., & Kalupa, F. B. (1985). *Public relations: Principles, cases, and problems* (9th ed.). Homewood, IL: Irwin.

Morgan, R., & Vadehra, D. (1984, September 10). Voters already sick of mudslinging political ads. *Adweek*, p. 29.

Morganthau, T., & Fineman, H. (1986, November 3). When in doubt go negative. *Newsweek*, pp. 25-26.

Mullen, J. J. (1963a). How candidates for the Senate use newspaper advertising. *Journalism Quarterly, 40*, 532-538.

Mullen, J. J. (1963b). Newspaper advertising in the Kennedy-Nixon campaign. *Journalism Quarterly, 40*, 3-11.

Mullen, J. J. (1968). Newspaper advertising in the Johnson-Goldwater campaign. *Journalism Quarterly, 45*, 218-225.

Murphy, J. H., & Amundsen, M. S. (1981). The communications-effectiveness of comparative advertising for a new brand on users of the dominant brand. *Journal of Advertising, 10*, 14-20.

Murphy, J. H., Cunningham, I. C., & Wilcox, G. B. (1979). The impact of program environment on recall of humorous television commercials. *Journal of Advertising, 8*, 17-21.

National Journal. (1980, March 1). p. 346.

National Republican Congressional Committee. (1979). *Political advertising on television: A review*. Washington, DC: NRCC.

NCPAC's negative campaign. (1979). *Political Action Report*, p. 5.

Negative advertising pro and con. (1986, November 10). *Advertising Age*, p. 104.

Nesbitt, D. (1988). *Videostyle: In senate campaigns*. Knoxville: The University of Tennessee Press.

Neustadt, R. (1980). *Presidential power*. New York: Wiley.

New Campaign Techniques. (1986). In *Elections '86* (pp. 29-35). Washington, DC: Congressional Quarterly.

Newsom, D., Scott, A., & Turk, J. V. (1989). *This is PR: The realities of public relations* (4th ed.). Belmont CA:Wadsworth.

New York Times Co. v. Sullivan, 84 S.Ct. 710 (1964).

Nimmo, D. (1970). *The political persuaders: The techniques of modern election campaigns*. Englewood Cliffs, NJ: Prentice-Hall.

Nimmo. D. (1974). *Popular images of politics*. Englewood Cliffs, NJ: Prentice-Hall.

Nimmo, D. (1978). *Political communication and public opinion in America*. Santa Monica, CA: Goodyear.

Nimmo, D. (1986). Teleparty politics. *Campaigns & Elections, 6*, 75-78.

Nimmo, D., & Combs, J. (1980). *Subliminal politics: Myths and mythmakers in America*. Englewood Cliffs, NJ: Prentice-Hall.

Nimmo, D., & Combs, J. E. (1983). *Mediated political realities*. New York: Longman.

Nimmo, D., & Felsberg, A. J. (1986). Hidden myths in televised political advertising: An illustration. In L. L. Kaid, D. Nimmo, & K. R. Sanders (Eds.), *New perspectives on political advertising*. Carbondale: Southern Illinois University Press.

Nimmo, D., & Savage, R. (1976). *Candidates and their images: Concepts, methods, and findings*. Pacific Palisades, CA: Goodyear.

Nothstine, W., & Copeland, G. A. (1983, April). *Media criticism as argument: Conditions for defense of a judgment*. Paper presented at the meeting of the Eastern Communication Association, Ocean City, MD.

Nugent, J. H. [or F.]. (1987). Positively negative. *Campaigns & Elections, 7*, 47-49.

O'Keefe, G. J. (1980). Political malaise and reliance on media. *Journalism Quarterly, 57*, 122-128.

Olsen, H. (1984-1985). Mail box politics. *Election Politics, 2*, 25-30.

Orlik, P. (1990). Negative political commercials: A 1988 snapshot. *Feedback, 31*, 2-7.

Ornstein, N. J., Mann, T. E., Malbin, M. J., Schick, A., & Bibby, J. F. (1986). *Vital statistics in Congress: 1984-1985 edition*. Washington DC: American Enterprise Institute for Public Policy Research.

Orum, A. M. (1972). Religion and the rise of the radical white: The case of southern Wallace support in 1968. In D. Nimmo & D. Bonjean (Eds.), *Political attitudes and public opinion* (pp. 474-488). New York: McKay.

Osgood, C. E. (1957). *The measurement of meaning.* Urbana: University of Ilinois Press.

Osterhouse, R. A., & Brock, T. C. (1970). Distraction increases yielding to propaganda by inhibiting counterarguing. *Journal of Personality and Social Psychology, 15,* 344-358.

Palda, K. S. (1975). The effects of expenditure on political success. *The Journal of Law and Economics, 18,* 745-771.

Paley, W. C., & Moffett, S. (1984). The new electronic media-instant action & reaction. *Campaigns & Elections, 4,* 4-12.

Papageorgis, D., & McGuire, W. J. (1961). The generality of immunity to persuasion produced by pre-exposure to weakened counterarguments. *Journal of Abnormal and Social Psychology, 62,* 475-481.

Parsons, T., & Shils, E. (Eds.). (1951). *Toward a general theory of action.* New York: Harper & Row.

Patterson, T. E. (1983). Money rather than TV ads judged "root cause" of election costliness. *Television/Radio Age, 44,* 130-132.

Patterson, T. E., & McClure, R. D. (1976a). Television and the less interested voter: The costs of an informed electorate. *The Annals of the American Academy of Political and Social Science, 425,* 88-97.

Patterson, T. E., & McClure, R. D. (1976b). *The unseeing eye.* New York: Putnam.

Patti, C. H., & Frazer, C. F. (1988). *Advertising: A decision-making approach.* Chicago: Dryden.

Payne, J. G., Marlier, J., & Baukus, R. A. (1989). Polispots in the 1988 presidential primaries: Separating the nominees from the rest of the guys. *American Behavioral Scientist, 32,* 365-381.

Penn, R. (1971). Effects of motion and cutting-rate in motion pictures. *AV Communication Review, 19,* 29-51.

Perrucci, R., & Knudsen, D. D. (1983). *Sociology.* New York: West.

Petrocik, J., & Steeper, F. T. (1984-1985). Realignment and 1984: New coalitions and new majorities. *Election Politics, 2,* 5-9.

Pfau, M., & Burgoon, M. (1988). Inoculation in political campaign communication. *Human Communication Research, 15,* 91-111.

Pfau, M., & Burgoon, M. (1989). The efficacy of issue and character attack message strategies in political campaign communication. *Communication Reports, 2,* 52-61.

The poisoned cup. (1972, July 6). *The New York Times,* p. 36.

Political advertising's hitmen. (1980, June). *Marketing & Media Decisions,* pp. 59-61, 180-182.

Political party campaigning. (1986). In *Elections '86* (pp. 57-64). Washington, DC: Congressional Quarterly.

Political TV Classics (Producer). (1984). *Campaigns & Elections* [Videotape]. Washington, DC.

Power, J. (1987). Plug in to cable TV. *Campaigns & Elections, 8,* 54-57.

Prasad, V. K. (1976). Communications-effectiveness of comparative advertising: A laboratory analysis. *Journal of Marketing Research, 13,* 128-137.

Pride, W. M., Lamb, C. W., & Pletcher, B. A. (1977). Are comparative advertisements more informative for owners of the mentioned competing brands than for non-owners? In B. A. Greenberg & D. N. Bellenger (Eds.), *Contemporary marketing thought* (pp. 293-301). Chicago: American Marketing Association.

Priest, R. F. (1966). Election jokes: The effects of reference group membership. *Psychological Reports, 18,* 600-602.

Pryor, B., & Steinfatt, T. M. (1978). The effects of initial belief level on inoculation theory and its proposed mechanisms. *Human Communication Research, 4,* 216-230.

Radio Act of 1927, 44 Stat. 1162-1165, 1168 (1927).

Railsback, C. C. (1983, April). *The rhetoric of the New Right: Ideas and consequences.* Paper presented at the Southern Speech Communication Association Convention, Orlando.

Ray, M. L. (1973). Marketing communication and the hierarchy-of-effects. In P. Clarke (Ed.), *New models for mass communication research* (pp. 147-176). Beverly Hills, CA: Sage.

Ray, M. L., & Sawyer, A. G. (1971). Repetition in media models: A laboratory technique. *Journal of Marketing Research, 8,* 20-29.

Red Lion Broadcasting Co. v. FCC, 395 U.S. 371 (1969).

Redding, J. (1958). *Inside the Democratic party.* New York: Bobbs-Merrill.

Reeves, B., Thorson, E., & Schleuder, J. (1986). Attention to television: Psychological theories and chronometric measures. In J. Bryant & D. Zillmann (Eds.). *Perspectives on media effects* (pp. 251-279). Hillsdale, NJ: Lawrence Erlbaum Associates.

Reid, L., & Soley, L. C. (1983). Is promotional spreading in high involvement elections: An examination of the voter involvement explanation. *Journal of Advertising, 12,* 43-50.

Richey, M. H., Koenigs, R. J., Richey, H. W., & Fortin, R. (1975). Negative salience in impressions of character: Effects of unequal proportions of positive and negative information. *The Journal of Social Psychology, 97,* 233-241.

Richey, M., McClelland, L., & Shimkunas, A. (1967). Relative influence of positive and negative information in impression formation and persistence. *Journal of Personality and Social Psychology, 3,* 322-327.

Roberts, C. L. (1979). Media use and difficulty of decision in the 1976 presidential campaign. *Journalism Quarterly, 56,* 794-802.

Robertson, T. S. (1976). Low-commitment consumer behavior. *Journal of Advertising Research, 16,* 19-26.

Robinson, M. J. (1974). The impact of the televised Watergate hearings. *Journal of Communication, 24,* 17-30.

Robinson, M. J. (1976). Public affairs television and the growth of political malaise: The case of "The selling of the Pentagon." *American Political Science Review, 70,* 409-432.

Robinson, M. J. (1981a). The media in 1980: Was the message the message? In A. Ranney (Ed.), *The American elections of 1980* (pp. 171-211). Washington, DC: American Enterprise Institute for Public Policy Research.

Robinson, M. J. (1981b). Three faces of congressional media. In T. E. Mann & N. J. Ornstein (Eds.), *The new Congress* (pp. 55-96). Washington, DC: American Enterprise Institute for Public Policy.

Rockey, E. A. (1976, February 24). *Comparative advertising: Fair or unfair, effective or ineffective?* New York: ANA Television Workshop.

Roddy, B. L., & Garramone, G. M. (1988). Appeals and strategies of negative political advertising. *Journal of Broadcasting & Electronic Media, 32,* 415-427.

Roper, E. (1957). *You and your leaders.* New York: Morrow.

Roper Organization Surveys for the Television Information Office, 1968, 1972, 1976, 1984, 1988. (1989, December 13). (Information presented courtesy of Roper Opinion Research Center, Storrs, CT)

Rose, E. D., & Fuchs, D. (1968). Reagan vs. Brown: A TV image playback. *Journal of Broadcasting, 12,* 247-260.

Rosenberg, M., & Rosenberg, D. (1962). The dirtiest election. *American Heritage, 13,* 4-9, 97-100.

Rosenblatt, P. C. (1966). Persuasion as a function of varying amounts of distraction. *Psychonomic Science, 5,* 85-86.

Rossiter, C. (1960). *The American presidency.* New York: Mentor Trademark.

Rothenberg, S. (1983). *Winners & losers: Campaigns, candidates, and congressional elections.* Washington, DC: Free Congress Research & Education Foundation.

Rothschild, M. L. (1975). The effects of political advertising on the voting behavior of a low-involvement electorate. (Doctoral dissertation, Stanford University, 1974). *Dissertation Abstracts International, 35,* 7473A-7474A.

Rothschild, M. L. (1978). Political advertising: A neglected policy issue in marketing. *Journal of Marketing Research, 15,* 58-71.

Rothschild, M. L., & Ray, M. L. (1974, July). Involvement and political advertising effect: An exploratory experiment. *Communication Research*, pp. 264-285.

Ryder, J. (1986). On the docket: Mudslinging "remedies" not new. *Campaigns & Elections, 7*, 72-74.

Sabato, L. J. (1981). *The rise of political consultants: New ways of winning elections*. New York: Basic.

Sabato, L. J. (1984)' *Pac power*. New York: Norton.

Sale, K. (1975a, November 21). The cowboy challenge. *Commonweal, 12*, 555-559.

Sale, K. (1975b). *Power shift*. New York: Random House.

Salmore, S. A., & Salmore, B. g. (1985). *Candidates, parties, and campaigns: Electoral politics in America*. Washington, DC: Congressional Quarterly.

Saltzman, G. (1987). Congressional voting on labor issues: The role of PACs. *Industrial and Labor Relations Review, 40*, 163-179.

Sanford, D. L., & Roach, J. W. (1987, May). *Imperative force in request forms: The demanding vs. pleading dimensions of directives*. Paper presented at the International Communication Association Convention, Montreal, Canada.

Sapir, E. (1934). Symbolism. *Encyclopedia of the Social Sciences, 14*, 492-495.

Saussure, F. (1966). *Course in general linguistics*. New York: McGraw-Hill.

Schwartz, T. (1972). *The responsive chord*. Garden City, NY: Anchor.

Schwartz, T. (1976). The inside of the outside. In R. Agranoff (Ed.), *The new style in election campaigns* (pp. 344-358). Boston: Holbrook.

Schwartz, T. (1985). *The 30 second president* [Videotape]. PBS Video. Alexandria, VA.

Searle, J. R. (1976). A classification of illocutionary acts. *Language in Society, 5*, 1-23.

Seymour-Ure, C. (1974). *The political impact of the mass media*. Beverly Hills, CA: Sage.

Shapiro, M. A., & Rieger, R. H. (1989, May). *Comparing positive and negative political advertising*. Paper presented at the meeting of the International Communication Association, San Francisco.

Shaw, D., & Bowers, T. (1973, August). *Learning from commercials: The influence of TV advertising on the voter political agenda*. Paper presented at the meeting of the Association for Education in Journalism, Ft. Collins, CO.

Shyles, L. C. (1983). Defining the issues of a presidential election from televised political spot advertisements. *Journal of Broadcasting, 27*, 333-343.

Shyles, L. C. (1986). The televised political spot advertisement: Its structure, content, and role in the political system. In L. L. Kaid, D. Nimmo, & K. R. Sanders (Eds.), *New perspectives on political advertising* (pp. 107-138). Carbondale: Southern Illinois University Press.

Singleton, L. (1989). *Global impact: The new telecommunication technologies*. New York: Harper & Row.

Smelser, N. (1963). *Theory of collective behavior*. New York: Free Press.

Smith, D. D. (1972). "Dark areas of ignorance" revisited: Current knowledge about Asian affairs. In D. Nimmo & D. Bonjean (Eds.), *Political attitudes and public opinion* (pp. 273-283). New York: McKay.

Smith, L. D., & Johnston, A. (in press). Burke's sociological criticism applied to political advertising: An anecdotal taxonomy of presidential commercials. In F. Biocca (Ed.), *Television and political advertising* (Vol. 2). Hillsdale, NJ: Lawrence Erlbaum Associates.

Smith, R. E., & Hunt, S. D. (1978). Attributional processes and effects in promotional situations, *Journal of Consumer Research, 5*, 149-158.

Smith, R. N. (1983). Federal election law, part III: Design for losers. *Campaigns & Elections, 3*, 19-35.

Smith, R. N. (1984). National committees: Party renewal through campaign assistance. *Campaigns & Elections, 5*, 12-19.

Sparks, G. G., & Fehlner, C. L. (1986). Faces in the news: Gender comparisons of magazine photographs. *Journal of Communication, 36*, 70-79.

Spero, R. (1980). *The duping of the American voter*. New York: Lippincott & Crowell.

Squier, R. (1987, May). Lecture at the School of Communication, University of Alabama, Tuscaloosa.

Starch, D. (1926). *Principles of advertising*. Chicago: Shaw.

Steele, R., Whitmore, J., Cumming, J., & Smith, V. (1976, November 22). The new pecking order. *Newsweek*, p. 26.

Steinberg, A. (1976). *The political campaign handbook*. Lexington, MA: Lexington.

Stengel, R. (1988a, February 22). Pilloried for pandering. *Time*, p. 22.

Stengel, R. (1988b, February 29). Accentuating the negative. *Time*, p. 46.

Sternthal, B., & Craig, S. (1973). Humor in advertising. *Journal of Marketing, 37*, 12-18.

Stewart, C. J. (1975). Voter perception of mudslinging in political communication. *Central States Speech Journal, 26*, 279-286.

Stone, J. (1981, October 10). Have calumny, will travel. *The Nation*, pp. 344-347.

Strand, P. J., Dozier, D. M., Hofstetter, C. R., & Ledingham, J. D. (1983). Campaign messages, media usage and types of voters. *Public Relations Review, 9*, 53-63.

Strong, D. S. (1972). Alabama: Transition and alienation. In W. C. Havard (Ed.), *The changing politics of the South* (pp. 427-471). Baton Rouge: Louisiana State University Press.

Strong, E. K. (1925). *The psychology of selling*. New York: McGraw-Hill.

Surlin, S. H., & Gordon, T. F. (1977). How values affect attitudes toward direct reference political advertising. *Journalism Quarterly, 54*, 89-98.

Swanson, D. L. (1976). Information utility: An alternative perspective in political communication. *Central States Speech Journal, 27*, 95-101.

Swinyard, W. R., & Coney, K. A. (1978). Promotional effects on a high versus low-involvement electorate. *Journal of Consumer Research, 5*, 41-48.

Tannenbaum, D. A., & Kerrick, J. (1954). Effects of newscasts' items leads upon listener interpretation. *Journalism Quarterly, 21*, 33-37.

Tannenbaum, P. H. (1967). The congruity principle revisited: Studies in the reduction, induction and generalization of attitude change. In L. Berkowitz (Ed.), *Advances in experimental social psychology* (Vol. 3, pp. 271-320). New York: Academic.

Tannenbaum, P. H., McCauley, J. R., Norris, E. L. (1966). Principle of congruity and reduction of persuasion. *Journal of Personality and Social Psychology, 2*, 233-238.

Tarrance, V. L., Jr. (1982). *Negative campaigns and negative votes: The 1980 elections*. Washington, DC: Free Congress Research & Education Foundation.

Taylor, P. (1986, October 5). Negative ads becoming powerful political force. *The Washington Post*, pp. A1, A6-A7.

Tiemens, R. K. (1970). Some relationships of camera angle to communicator credibility. *Journal of Broadcasting, 14*, 483-490.

Trent, J. S., & Friedenberg, R. V. (1983). *Political campaign communication: Principles and practices*. New York: Praeger.

Tucker, L. A., & Heller, D. J. (1987). Putting ethics into practice. *Campaigns & Elections, 7*, 42-46.

Ulanoff, S. M. (1975). *Comparative advertising: A historical perspective*. Cambridge, MA: Marketing Science Institute.

Ullmann, W. R., & Bodaken, E. M. (1975). Inducing resistance to persuasive attack: A test of two strategies of communication. *Western Speech Communication, 39*, 240-248.

Virginia State Board of Pharmacy v. Virginia Citizens Consumer Council, 425 U.S. 760 (1976).

Wade, S., & Schramm, W. (1969). The mass media as sources of public affairs, science and health knowledge. *Public Opinion Quarterly, 34*, 159-170.

Wadsworth, A. J., & Kaid, L. L. (1987, May). *Incumbent and challenger styles in presidential advertising*. Paper presented at the meeting of the International Communication Association, Montreal, Canada.

Wadsworth, A. J., Patterson, P., Kaid, L. L., Cullers, G., Malcomb, D., & Lamirand, L. (1987). "Masculine" vs "feminine" strategies in political ads: Implications for female candidates. *Journal of Applied Communication Research, 15*, 77-94.

Wagner, J. (1983). Media do make a difference: The differential impact of mass media in the 1976 presidential race. *American Journal of Political Science, 27*, 407-430.

Wakshlag, J. J., & Edison, N. G. (1979). Attraction, credibility, perceived similarity, and the image of public figures. *Communications Quarterly, 27*, 27-34.

Walker, E. E., Lindquist, J. H., Morey, R. D., & Walker, D. E. (1968). *Readings in American public opinion.* New York: American Book.

Walsh, K. T., & Emerson, S. (1986, October 20). It's dirty-tricks time again in politics. *U.S. News & World Report*, p. 26.

Wamsley, G., & Pride, R. (1972). Television network news: Rethinking the iceberg problem. *The Western Political Quarterly, 25*, 434-450.

Wanat, J. (1974). Political broadcast advertising and primary election voting. *Journal of Broadcasting, 18*, 413-422.

Warr, P., & Jackson, P. (1976). Three weighting criteria in impression formation. *European Journal of Social Psychology, 6*, 41-49.

Warshaw, P. R. (1978). Application of selective attention theory to television advertising displays. *Journal of Applied Psychology, 63*, 366-372.

Washburn, W. E. (1963). The great autumnal madness: Political symbolism in mid-nineteenth-century America. *Quarterly Journal of Speech, 49*, 417-431.

Washburn, W. E. (1972). Campaign banners. *American Heritage, 23*, 8-13.

Wayne, S. (1982a). Expectations of the presidency. In D. Graber (Ed.), *The president and the public* (pp. 17-38). Philadelphia: ISHI.

Wayne, S. (1982b). Great expectations: What people want from presidents. In T. Cronin (Ed.), *Rethinking the presidency* (pp. 185-199). Boston: Little, Brown.

Wayne, S. J. (1988). *The road to the White House: The politics of presidential elections.* New York: St. Martin's Press.

Weaver-Lariscy, R. A., & Tinkham, S. F. (1987). The influence of media expenditure and allocation strategies in congressional advertising campaigns. *Journal of Advertising, 16*, 13-21.

Weiss, W. (1966). *Effects of mass media of communication.* New York: Hunter College, Center for Research & Social Psychology.

Weiss, W. (1969). Effects of the mass media of communication. In G. Linzey & E. Aronson (Eds.), *Handbook of social psychology* (Vol. 5, pp. 77-195). Reading, MA: Addison-Wesley.

Why America doesn't vote. (1988). In *Elections '88* (pp. 139-147). Washington, DC: Congressional Quarterly.

Wilcox, D., Ault, P. H., & Agee, W. K. (1989). *Public relations: Strategies and tactics* (6th ed.). New York: Harper & Row.

Wilhite, A., & Theilmann, J. (1987). Labor PAC contributions and labor legislation: A simultaneous logic approach. *Public Choice, 53*, 267-276.

Wilke, W. H. (1934, June). An experimental comparison of the speech, radio and the printed page as propaganda devices. *Archives of Psychology*, No. 169.

Will, G. (1986, November 10). So much cash, so few ideas. *Newsweek*, p. 96.

Will, G. (1989, November 6). The pollution of politics. *Newsweek*, p. 92.

Wilson, P. O. (1987). Presidential advertising in 1988. *Election Politics, 4*, 17-21.

Wilson, R. D. (1976). An empirical evaluation of comparative advertising messages: Subjects' responses on perceptual dimensions. In B. B. Anderson (Ed.), *Advances in consumer research, 3*, 53-57.

Winsbro, J. (1987). Misrepresentation in political advertising: The role of legal sanctions. *Emory Law Journal, 36*, 853-916.

Witcover, J. (1977). *Marathon: The pursuit of the presidency, 1972-1976.* New York: Viking.

Wolff, H. A., Smith, C. E., & Murray, H. A. (1934). The psychology of humor: A study of responses to race-disparagement jokes. *Journal of Abnormal and Social Psychology, 28*, 341-365.

Wolff, M. (1989, October). Say it ain't so Joe! Is political radio dead? *Campaign & Elections*, 33-34.

Wolfinger, R. E., & Rosenstone, S. J. (1980). *Who votes?* New Haven, CT: Yale University Press.

Wolfson, L. W. (1972a, February 13). The media masters: Part one. *The Potomac Magazine, The Washington Post*, pp. 15-19, 34-37.

Wolfson, L. W. (1972b, February 20). The media masters: Part two. *The Potomac Magazine, The Washington Post*, pp. 13-15, 20-21, 24, 30-32.

Wolfson, L. W. (1972c, March 5). The media masters: Part three. *The Potomac Magazine, The Washington Post*, pp. 17-21, 38-39, 45-46.

Wood, G. S. (1978). The democratization of mind in the American Revolution. In R. H. Horwitz (Ed.), *The moral foundations of the American republic* (pp. 102-128). Charlottesville: The University Press of Virginia.

Wood, S. C. (1981, April). *Television: The technical mediator, a theoretical pancratia.* Paper presented at the meeting of the Eastern Communication Association, Pittsburgh.

Woods, J., & Walton, D. (1982). *Argument: The logic of fallacies.* Toronto: McGraw-Hill Ryerson.

Worchel, S., Andreoli, V. A., & Eason, J. (1974). Is the medium the message: A study of the effects of the media, communicator, and message characteristics on attitude change. *Journal of Applied Social Psychology, 5*, 157-172.

Wright, J. (1988, March). *PAC contributions, lobbying and representation.* Paper presented at the annual meeting of the Midwest Political Science Association.

Wurtzel, A. (1979). *Television production.* New York: McGraw-Hill.

Wyer, R. S. (1970). Information redundancy, inconsistency, and novelty and their role in impression formation. *Journal of Experimental Social Psychology, 6*, 111-127.

Zajonc, R. (1968). Attitudinal effects of mere exposure. *Journal of Personality and Social Psychology Monograph Supplement, 9*, 1-27.

Zajonc, R. A., & Rajecki, D. W. (1969). Exposure and effect: A field experiment. *Psychonomic Science, 17*, 216-217.

Zettl, H. (1973). *Sight-sound-motion: Applied media aesthetics.* Belmont, CA: Wadsworth.

Zettl, H. (1976). *Television production handbook* (3rd ed.). Belmont, CA: Wadsworth.

Zillmann, D. (1983). Disparagement humor. In P. E. McGhee & J. H. Goldstein (Eds.), *Handbook of humor research* (Vol. 1, pp. 85-107). New York: Springer-Verlag.

Zillmann, D., Bryant, J., & Cantor, J. R. (1974). Brutality of assault in political cartons affecting humor appreciation. *Journal of Research in Personality, 7*, 334-345.

Zillmann, D., & Cantor, J. (1972). Directionality of transitory dominance as a communication variable affecting humor appreciation. *Journal of Personality and Social Psychology, 24*, 191-198.

Zillmann, D., & Cantor, J. R. (1976). A disposition theory of humour and mirth. In A. J. Chapman & H. C. Foote (Eds.), *Humour and laughter: Theory, research and applications* (pp. 93-115). London: Wiley.

Author Index

Subject Index

U

Us against them ads, 107-
  anti-Washington, mentality, 118-120
  class warfare, 115-118
  Cowboys vs. the Yankees, 107-113

  Carter, Jimmy, 111-113
  Wallace, George, 44-45, 65, 109-111
us against foreigners, 113-115

For Product Safety Concerns and Information please contact our EU
representative GPSR@taylorandfrancis.com
Taylor & Francis Verlag GmbH, Kaufingerstraße 24, 80331 München, Germany